List of Illustrations

List of Drills and Timed Writings

Ninth Edition~Intensive Course

College Typewriting

D. D. Lessenberry
Professor of Business Education, Emeritus
University of Pittsburgh

S. J. Wanous
Professor of Education, Emeritus
University of California, L.A.

C. H. Duncan
Professor of Business Education
Eastern Michigan University

S. E. Warner
Head, Business Education
and Office Administration Department
University of Northern Iowa

Copyright © 1975
Philippine Copyright 1975
by South-Western Publishing Co.
Cincinnati, Ohio

ISBN: 0-538-20400-1
Library of Congress Catalog Card Number 74-79303
10 11 12 13 H 3 2 1 0
Printed in the United States of America

T40

Published by
SOUTH-WESTERN PUBLISHING CO.

CINCINNATI   WEST CHICAGO, ILL.   DALLAS   PELHAM MANOR, N.Y.
PALO ALTO, CALIF.   BRIGHTON, ENGLAND

CONTENTS

Division 1 Basic Typewritten Communications ... 1

LEVEL 1 BASIC TYPEWRITING SKILLS AND PROBLEMS

Division 2 Intermediate Typewritten Communications ... 97

LEVEL 2 BUSINESS LETTERS AND REPORTS

Division 2 **CONTINUED**

Division 3 Advanced Typewritten Communications   **205**

LEVEL 3 STAFF OFFICE PROJECTS

90-35899

PREFACE

COLLEGE TYPEWRITING, Intensive Course, 9th Edition, has been especially designed to help students and instructors meet their common goal—the achievement and refinement of a marketable skill in typewriting. This ninth edition is based on more than forty years of experience in organizing, researching, testing, and improving materials and methods of teaching typing to college students. It is thus a fundamentally sound teaching aid.

Organization

The organization of the textbook and accompanying materials reflects a responsiveness to changes in the teaching of typewriting. These materials are designed for any type of classroom environment—group, individualized, or a combination of the two approaches.

For the group approach, there is available a complete 150-lesson textbook, workbooks, tests, a teacher's manual, and (if desired) student self-check solutions.

For the individualized approach, three separate instructional packages are available. Each package includes one 50-lesson book (basic, intermediate, or advanced), lesson-by-lesson Self-Paced Learning Activity Guides, a teacher's manual describing individualized teaching techniques, and student self-check solutions.

Division 1 of COLLEGE TYPEWRITING, Intensive Course, stresses proper keyboard mastery and other aspects of machine operation. Through specially constructed drills and problems, students are led to acquire the sound techniques that are essential to the successful preparation, proofreading, and presentation of business papers.

Division 2 reviews and further develops the basic information presented in Division 1, and it presents the finer points of placement and style for letters and business reports. Emphasis is placed on the integration of communication skills, such as punctuation and capitalization. Composition and proofreading are stressed, as is statistical typing. Thus the first two divisions develop a basic understanding of the requirements underlying the typing of business papers.

Division 3 introduces the student to the world of the working typewriter. Through projects and sample papers representing work done in executive, accounting, professional, and government offices, students develop good judgment and taste, initiative, and the ability to plan their work and budget their time.

Special Features

In addition to the unique organization of the materials to meet both group and individualized approaches to the teaching of typing, there are special features in this 9th edition of COLLEGE TYPEWRITING, Intensive Course, which enhance the quality of this resource material.

1 The initial lessons in each division provide a checkup of basic skills and problem-solving competencies that help the instructor to determine the students' training needs before proceeding into the course.

2. Many opportunities are provided throughout the book to evaluate overall growth in skill, work habits, attitudes, production knowledge, proofreading ability, and other attributes of a successful typist.

3. Two proofreading procedures are explained: *comparing* and *verifying*. Desirable procedures are laid down; then drills, ranging from spotting typographical errors to catching errors in meaning, are provided to alert students to the kinds of errors they should look for in their work.

4. Triple-controlled copy is provided for building and for measuring basic typing skill. As a result, an easy-to-difficult approach to skill building and measurement has been used.

5. Early emphasis is placed on the most frequently used letters, words, and letter combinations to help students build stroking facility quickly.

6. Specially devised drills motivate the student to work toward progressively higher goals and to practice on progressively more difficult copy. In addition, individual practice exercises make it possible for the students to tailor practice to their own needs.

7. The problems in the book are a sample of those used in actual offices. They have been changed only to meet instructional requirements. Many full-size (or nearly so) illustrations give students accurate models from which to work and to use for comparison with their own solutions.

Acknowledgments

The authors express their sincere appreciation to the instructors, students, and business workers who contributed so generously to the content and organization of COLLEGE TYPEWRITING. Their recommendations and constructive criticisms have inspired the authors in preparing this Ninth Edition of the book.

Lessenberry • Wanous • Duncan • Warner

Division 1 | Basic Typewritten Communications

Introduction

The general teaching/learning goals of this division of the book are to enable you:

- To type the letter, figure, and most commonly used symbol keys by touch, using from the beginning the kind of stroking techniques and mental approach that will add to your problem-typing competence as you progress through the course

- To use those techniques that have been found to be most efficient in shifting for capitals, in tabulating, in returning the carriage, and in handling other operative parts of your typewriter

- To use the basic rules underlying the arrangement of copy on paper and, further, to apply skill and understanding to the production of a variety of letters and reports

- To type from printed, script, corrected, and revised copy and also to compose on the typewriter simple letters, reports, and abstracts

- To proofread your copy for typographical accuracy and to evaluate its acceptability as a finished piece of work

How well you meet these goals will depend largely upon you. No one learns anything without a desire to learn. This desire must be coupled with a willingness to work through a series of organized lessons and to engage in self-study and evaluation.

If you are ready, the lessons of Division 1 of this book can help you meet the foregoing goals. The keyboard charts, illustrations, printed statements, and specially designed drills that are included in this division will help you to acquire touch-typing skill and efficiency in using your typewriter. The technique cues accompanying each drill tell you how to type it. Study the illustrations and printed statements. Read the cues, and apply them as you type the drills. Evaluate your growth by analyzing your performance and by noting your progress on the specially constructed timed writings provided in the book.

After you have built basic skill to an acceptable level, you will start applying it to typing letters, reports, tables, and other commonly used forms. As each new application problem is introduced, it is illustrated. Complete directions for typing the illustrated problem are given, and ample opportunity to apply these directions is provided by additional unarranged problems. Study the illustrations and follow the directions as you type the problems. In this manner, you will build the foundation needed for solving arrangement problems as you will encounter them in an office—without full directions and without close supervision.

the letter style used. Letters longer than one page should use a second-page heading, which
includes the following information: (1) the first line of the address, (2) the page number, and (3) the date used in the dateline. This information may be blocked at the left
margin or spread horizontally on one line with the name at the left margin, the page
number centered, and the date ending flush with the right margin. The second-page
heading is started on Line 7 from the top. The body is continued a triple space below the
second-page heading.[2]

Complimentary close. The complimentary close is very much like the salutation. Its
use is controlled (1) by courtesy, (2) by the practice of business, and (3) by the relationship
of the writer to the reader.[3] The complimentary close is typed at the same horizontal position as the dateline. However, the AMS Simplified letter style does not use a complimentary close.[4]

Signature. The signature part of a business letter usually has three parts: (1) the
dictator's penwritten signature, (2) the dictator's typed name, and (3) the dictator's typed
title. The signature part is typed at the same horizontal point as the complimentary close.

Reference initials. The reference initials are typed a double space below the signature,
even with the left margin.

Supplementary Parts of a Business Letter

Mailing notation. All special mailing notations, such as AIRMAIL, SPECIAL DELIVERY,
or REGISTERED MAIL, should be typed in all capital letters midway between the dateline
and the first line of the address, even with the left margin.[5]

Attention line. The attention line is placed between the address and the salutation
and is typed a double space below the address, flush with the left margin.

Subject line. The subject line is typed a double space below the salutation. It may
be blocked at the left margin, typed at the paragraph point, or centered, with or without
the word "Subject."

Enclosure notation. The enclosure notation is typed a double space below the reference initials, flush with the left margin.

Carbon copy notation. The carbon copy notation is typed a double space below the
reference initials or enclosure notation, if used, even with the left margin.

Postscript. A postscript is the addition of one or more paragraphs to a letter after the
letter has been typed. It is typed a double space below the last part of the letter. It is
typed in the same form as a regular paragraph.

---

[2] Morris Philip Wolf and Robert R. Aurner, Effective Communication in Business (6th ed.; Cincinnati: South-Western Publishing Co., 1974), pp. 658-659. (40 words)

[3] Ibid., p. 660. (4 words)

[4] Neuner, loc. cit. (5 words)

[5] Wolf, op. cit., pp. 662-664. (7 words)

GETTING STARTED

Arrange your work area

1. Clear the desk of unneeded books and papers.

2. Have the front of the frame of the typewriter even with the front edge of the desk.

3. Place this textbook to the right of the typewriter on a bookholder, or put something under the top to raise it to a better position.

4. Place blank sheets of paper to the left of the machine, with the long side of the paper even with the front edge of the desk.

5. Start each class by observing the foregoing directions.

Know your typewriter

1. Find on *your* typewriter each of the parts identified on the typewriter illustrated below. When you are asked to find a machine part, look at the illustration, find the part there; then locate that part on the typewriter you are using.

2. The numbers that are assigned to the machine parts on the illustration are used also on the detailed diagrams on Reference Guide pages i-ii at the back of this book.

3. While typewriters are similar in design, the location of a part may vary among different makes. When this is the case, refer to the operating manual for your typewriter.

4. Operating manuals furnished by typewriter companies show illustrations with parts identified.

The numbers shown in boldface in the textbook are those assigned to the machine parts illustrated below and on the diagrams presented on pp. i-ii.

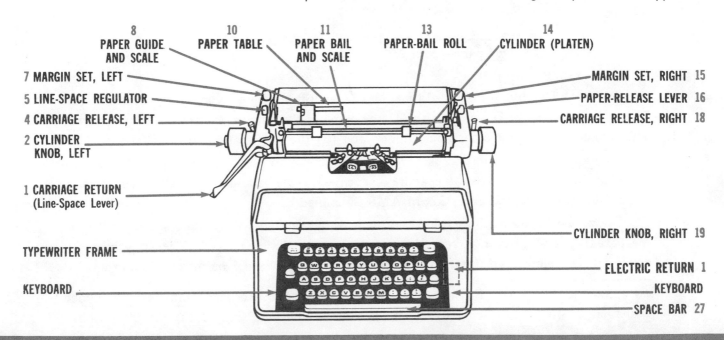

8 PAPER GUIDE AND SCALE
10 PAPER TABLE
11 PAPER BAIL AND SCALE
13 PAPER-BAIL ROLL
14 CYLINDER (PLATEN)

7 MARGIN SET, LEFT
5 LINE-SPACE REGULATOR
4 CARRIAGE RELEASE, LEFT
2 CYLINDER KNOB, LEFT
1 CARRIAGE RETURN (Line-Space Lever)
TYPEWRITER FRAME
KEYBOARD

MARGIN SET, RIGHT 15
PAPER-RELEASE LEVER 16
CARRIAGE RELEASE, RIGHT 18
CYLINDER KNOB, RIGHT 19
ELECTRIC RETURN 1
KEYBOARD
SPACE BAR 27

Type the following copy as an unbound manuscript. Top margin: 1½″ pica, 2″ elite; DS the paragraph copy; SS the body of the table; decide on the number of spaces between the columns; 5-space ¶ indentions; type footnotes on pages where references are made.

	Words
PARTS OF A BUSINESS LETTER	5

There are fourteen parts to a business letter. However, some are basic to almost all business letters, while some of the other parts are used only when there is a special need. In this report, the parts of a business letter are divided into two main categories: (1) basic parts of a business letter and (2) supplementary parts of a business letter. — 22, 40, 58, 76

Basic Parts of a Business Letter — 89

Letterhead or return address. Most business letters are typed on paper with a printed letterhead. However, if a personal business letter is typed on plain paper, a return address should be typed on the lines immediately above the dateline. — 111, 129, 143

Dateline. Every letter should be dated. The dateline may be typed even with the left margin or started at the center point of the paper. The length of the letter determines the line on which to type the date. The following placement table may be used as a general guide. — 161, 180, 197, 200

TS

PLACEMENT TABLE — 203

TS

Letter Length	Dateline on	Words
	DS	
Short--less than 100 words	Line 20	220
Average--101-300 words	Line 17-13	227
Long--301-350 words	Line 12	233
Two-page--over 350 words	Line 12	239

TS

Address. The address is typed four lines below the dateline, even with the left margin. The address should be complete with (1) the name of the person or business, (2) the street address and/or the post office box number, and (3) the city, state, and ZIP Code. — 259, 277, 294

Salutation. The salutation is a form of courtesy to the reader. The salutation is placed a double space below the address, even with the left margin. All letter formats use a salutation with the exception of AMS Simplified.[1] — 313, 330, 342

Body. The body of the letter is normally single-spaced with double spacing between the paragraphs. However, a very short letter may be double-spaced. The body begins a double space below the salutation. Paragraphs may be blocked or indented according to — 359, 377, 394

---

[1] John J. W. Neuner, B. Lewis Keeling, and Norman F. Kallaus, Administrative Office Management (6th ed.; Cincinnati: South-Western Publishing Co., 1972), p. 679. (42 words)

Insert paper

1. Adjust the **paper guide (8)** as directed on page iii, at the back of this book.

2. Pull the **paper bail (11)** forward—toward you—with your right hand.

3. Grasp the paper with your left hand, the thumb under the sheet, as shown below.

4. Drop the bottom edge of the paper behind the **cylinder (14)** and against the **paper guide (8)**. At the same time, bring the right hand to the right **cylinder knob (19)** and twirl the knob with a quick movement of the fingers and thumb.

5. Push the **paper bail (11)** back to hold the paper against the cylinder or platen; position **paper-bail rolls (13)** to divide paper into thirds.

Set margin stops

1. Some typewriters have hand-set margin stops; others have key-set margin stops. Note the illustration at the top of the next column. Determine whether your typewriter has hand-set or key-set margin stops.

Hand set   Key set

2. Set the **left margin stop (7)** 25 spaces to the left of the center of the paper.

3. Set the **right margin stop (15)** at the end of the scale. As you will type copy line for line in the first lessons, you do not need the right margin stop to indicate the line ending.

NOTE: To set margin stops on *your* typewriter, refer to Reference Guide pages iii-iv.

Adjust the line-space regulator

1. Set the **line-space regulator (5)** on "2" for double-spacing the lines you are to type in Lesson 1.

2. When directed to single-space, set the line-space regulator on "1." When directed to triple-space, set the regulator on "3."

Line-space regulator

Take correct typing position

Note the following features of good typing position:

1. Sit back in chair; body erect

2. Feet on floor, one slightly ahead of the other

3. Fingers curved and upright; wrists low

4. Forearms parallel to slant of keyboard; elbows in comfortable position at sides

5. Eyes on copy

Take the correct typing position as illustrated below.

EYES ON COPY

FINGERS CURVED; WRISTS LOW

ELBOWS NEAR THE BODY; FOREARMS PARALLEL TO SLANT OF KEYBOARD

SIT BACK IN CHAIR; BODY ERECT

TEXTBOOK AT RIGHT OF MACHINE, ELEVATED FOR EASY READING

TABLE FREE OF UNNEEDED BOOKS

FEET ON FLOOR, ONE JUST AHEAD OF THE OTHER

LESSON 150

150A Preparatory Practice [5] each line at least 3 times

Alphabet	Jud may give gifts to persons who can quickly open the new puzzle box.
Figure/symbol	Lyons & Rock (497 Doan Court) can't pay their $258.63 bill on June 10.
Long words	The experienced adjustment consultant gave us a conservative estimate.
Fluency	Burning the midnight oil doesn't help much if it is burned in the car.
	| 1 | 2 | 3 | 4 | 5 | 6 | 7 | 8 | 9 | 10 | 11 | 12 | 13 | 14 |

150B Growth Index [10] one 5′ control-level writing; record GWAM

All letters are used.

		GWAM 1′	GWAM 5′
¶ 1 1.5 SI 5.6 AWL 80% HFW	An employee in a business must be courteous. Especially when em-	13	3
	ployed in a service-type firm, you will discover that the manner in which	28	6
	the service is rendered is equally as important as the actual service	42	8
	itself. No act on the part of a customer or supplier can justify the	56	11
	breach of this basic rule of courtesy. The practice of being courteous	70	14
	is vitally important in our daily relations with those with whom we	84	17
	work within the company. We can expect to be treated courteously only	98	20
	if we are courteous to others. Perhaps we should always apply the Golden	113	23
	Rule: Do unto others as you would have them do unto you.	124	25
¶ 2 1.5 SI 5.6 AWL 80% HFW	Certain work must be completed each day within a limited time sched-	14	28
	ule in most business offices. In order to maximize the amount of com-	28	30
	pleted work, every employee must do a share in minimizing waste and	41	33
	avoiding unnecessary activities that may slow down or even stop the flow	56	36
	of work within the office. Like a chain, the efficiency of a business	70	39
	is only as good as its weakest element. That weak part must be replaced,	85	42
	upgraded, or bypassed in order for the work schedule to return to normal.	100	45
	If the person who is causing a problem does not change, the whole burden	114	48
	must be assumed by the remaining people in the office.	125	50
¶ 3 1.5 SI 5.6 AWL 80% HFW	An employee should be loyal to his employer. This is not to say	13	52
	that a person should not offer fair and constructive criticism about the	28	55
	policies of the firm; it does imply, however, that these comments should	42	58
	be made to the proper officials of the firm and not in public to those	56	61
	who may misinterpret the comments as disloyalty. A firm is evaluated	70	64
	quickly on the basis of the loyalty of its employees. It should be re-	85	67
	membered that there is a time and place for everything--the time for	98	70
	constructive comments is when they will be most helpful to management;	113	72
	the place for these comments is inside the firm.	122	74
1′ GWAM	| 1 | 2 | 3 | 4 | 5 | 6 | 7 | 8 | 9 | 10 | 11 | 12 | 13 | 14 |		
5′ GWAM	| 1 | 2 | 3 |		

LESSON 1

1A Finger Position For electric typewriters, turn **ON-OFF** switch to **ON** position.

Left hand

Right hand

1. With the help of the chart above, locate the left-hand guide or home keys on your typewriter: **A S D F.** Place the left-hand fingers on these keys.

2. Now locate the right-hand home keys: **J K L ;**. Place the right-hand fingers on these keys.

3. Take your fingers off the home keys. Replace them, saying the keys for each as you touch them: **ASDF JKL;**. (*Repeat.*)

4. To space after typing a letter or a word, operate the **space bar (27)** with a quick down-and-in motion of the right thumb.

5. Curve and hold the fingers lightly over the home keys. Hold the right thumb over the middle of the space bar. Keep your wrists low and relaxed.

6. Type the line below. Think and say each letter as you strike it.

```
ff jj dd kk ss ll a; sl dk fj a; sl dk fj a; fj fj
```

1B Carriage (Element Carrier) Return

To space the paper forward (upward) and return to the beginning of the line, use the **lever (1)** on a manual (nonelectric) typewriter or the **return key (1)** on an electric typewriter, as described and illustrated below.

Manual (Nonelectric). Move the left hand, fingers bracing one another, to the carriage return lever and move the lever inward to take up the slack; then return the carriage with a quick wrist-and-hand motion. Drop the hand to typing position without letting it follow the carriage across. Return the carriage. Operate the space bar several times and return again.

Electric. Reach the little finger of the right hand to the return key; tap the key and release it quickly. Return the fingers to home position.

On Selectric typewriters, the return key returns the element carrier (not a carriage) to the left margin.

Job 2: Table with One Braced Heading

Reading position; DS the report; 5 spaces between columns; draw the vertical rules with a ruler in ink

MARSHALL DISTRIBUTORS, INC.
Sales Records

Salesman	Total Sales		
	1972	1973	1974
Ralph P. Andrus	$38,400	$39,110	$48,870
Edward F. Cummings	21,300	37,310	29,860
Lewis M. DeWitt	40,200	41,300	43,970
Vernon J. Owens	42,100	39,100	48,700
Marion Snyder	38,300	39,240	48,880
Harold A. Stott	17,300	27,100	38,360
D. Jack Terry	50,000	51,010	56,550
Steven West	40,220	42,600	45,540
Greg R. Wilson	28,770	29,890	38,700

Source: Marshall Distributors, Inc., 19-- Annual Report.

Words: 6 8 30 33 41 44 54 63 71 78 85 92 100 107 113 121 131 143

Job 3: Interoffice Memorandum (WB p. 169)

TO: Gordon W. Hamilton, President — 6

FROM: Felix Leonardi — 9

DATE: June 25, 19-- — 12

SUBJECT: Presentation of Special Training — 18
Awards at Employees' Banquet — 24

(¶ 1) During the past six months, six of our — 32 employees have completed formal training — 40 programs at the University. Each of these — 49 employees took advantage of our educational — 57 release program. (¶ 2) The employees and — 64 their respective programs are as follows: — 73

Employee	Program	Words
Thomas Gorsch	Electronics Technology	79 / 87
Leon Hawkins	Machine Tooling	93
James Evans	Quality Assurance	99
Roger Hammond	Chemical Technology	105
James Karpel	Electronics Maintenance	113
Susan Borden	Plastic Molding	118

(¶ 3) Each person completing a course of — 125 study will receive a bronze plaque from us. — 134 These awards will be presented at the Em- — 142 ployees' Annual Awards Banquet at 8 p.m. on — 151 Thursday, July 10. (¶ 4) We would appre- — 158 ciate your making the official presentation of — 167 the awards to these employees. Would this — 176 time be convenient? — 180/185

1C Home-Key Stroking Practice

Type the lines as shown below. Think the letters as you type. Do not type line numbers or identifications.

Stroking Cue. Curve your fingers. Hold them lightly over the home keys. Strike and release a key quickly; then strike the next one the same way.

1 f j d k   ff jj ff jj fj fj fj dd kk dd kk dk dk dk fj dk fj   Return without looking up

2 s l a ;   ss ll ss ll sl sl sl aa ;; aa ;; a; a; a; sl a; sl

3 Home keys   dk fj dkfj a; sl a;sl dkfj a;sl a;sldk a;sldkfj a;   Think and say each letter

4 Home keys   all fall all fall ad lad ad lad as ask as ask fall

5 Space once   a lad; as a lad; a lad asks dad; ask all; all fall
   after ;

1D Location of H and E

1. Locate the new key on the keyboard chart, below.

2. Locate the new key on your typewriter keyboard.

3. Reach controlling finger to the new key a few times.

4. Type the location drill for that key as directed.

Type H with J finger

Type E with D finger

Touch **hj** lightly several times without moving the other fingers from their typing position. *Type Line 1, below, for tryout.*

Touch **ed** lightly several times, lifting the first finger slightly to free the d finger. *Type Line 2, below, for tryout.*

1E Location Drills for H and E   Type the lines as shown; then repeat them.

h   hj hj hj has hash lash dash hall halls shall shall

e   ed ed ed led fled led fled sale lake feel led sled

h e   he led a lad; he has a sled; he seeks a safe deal;

h e   she has; she has a desk; he has; he has had a desk

Space with a down-and-in motion

LESSON 149

149A Preparatory Practice [5] each line at least 3 times

Alphabet	My job is to help answer questions and advise K. Z. Cage on tax forms.
Figure/symbol	Lee Roe's note (plus $6\frac{1}{2}$% interest), due May 23, amounts to $84,091.75.
Drill an exa	I am exasperated by the exact number of examples that are exaggerated.
Fluency	The care they give their tools may indicate the quality of their work.
	| 1 | 2 | 3 | 4 | 5 | 6 | 7 | 8 | 9 | 10 | 11 | 12 | 13 | 14 |

149B Communication Aid: CAPITALIZATION AND PUNCTUATION [10]

Capitalize and punctuate as you type. Check your work with your instructor; then use the ¶ for 1′ writings. Determine your GWAM after each writing.

Full sheet; 70-space line; DS

1′ GWAM

over 250 years ago gottfried leibniz a clever german mathemati- 13
cian invented the way of writing numbers that we know as the binary 27
system. of little value at that time this system is highly useful 40
today in operating electronic computers. the binary system uses only 54
two numerals 1 and 0 compared to our decimal system which uses ten. 68

| 1 | 2 | 3 | 4 | 5 | 6 | 7 | 8 | 9 | 10 | 11 | 12 | 13 | 14 |

149C Production Measurement [35] 30′ writing; figure N-PRAM

Job 1: Accounting Report with Leaders

Substitute the actual year (19––) for "Year A" and last year for "Year B"; top margin, 2″; DS the report; use 3-space indentions

Words

PROVO SUPPLY CO., INC. 5
Statement of Retained Earnings 11
For the Year Ended June 30, Year A 17

	Year A	Year B	Words
Balance at beginning of period	$4,368,920	$3,786,284	35
Net income	1,265,630	985,634	47
Less:			49
Stock dividends	(124,710)	(98,265)	61
Cost of treasury stock retired . .		(10,650)	71
Cash dividends	(380,515)	(294,083)	88
Balance at end of period	$5,129,325	$4,368,920	109

1F Technique Practice: STROKING

Type the lines once; then repeat them. Type at an easy, controlled pace.

Stroking Cue. Snap the finger quickly toward the palm of the hand as you release the key.

Home keys	all lads fall; ask a lad; a fall fad; ask all lads
h e	he had a sled; he sells desks; a shelf held a safe
All keys	she sells jade; he held a lead; he has had a sale;
	sell all desks; see a hall safe; she has had jade;

1G Lesson Windup   Remove paper; center carriage; turn off electrics.

1. Raise or pull forward the **paper bail (11)**. Operate the **paper-release lever (16)** with your right hand.

2. Remove paper with left hand. Return paper-release lever to normal position with right thumb.

3. Depress the **right carriage release (18)**; hold the platen knob firmly. Center the carriage (approximately).

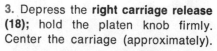

LESSON 2

2A Ready to Type   for each lesson in this section

1. Move front frame of typewriter even with edge of desk.
2. Adjust **paper guide (8)** and **paper bail (11)**.
3. Engage **paper release (16)**.
4. Set **line-space regulator (5)** on "1" for single spacing (SS).

5. Set **left margin stop (7)** about 25 spaces to left of center of paper; move **right margin stop (15)** to end of scale. *Note and use the numbers on the* **margin scale or paper-bail scale (11)** *for stop settings for this lesson and remaining lessons of this section.*

2B Preparatory Practice   Type the lines as shown.

Typing Position. Sit erect; feet on floor; wrists low; fingers curved. (See illustration on page 3.)

Stroking Cue. Strike the keys sharply; release them quickly.

1	Home keys	fj dk sl a; fd jk fds jkl fdsa jkl; fdsa jkl; fjdk
2		fj dk sl a; fd jk fds jkl fdsa jkl; fdsa jkl; fjdk
		DS (operate return twice)
3	h e	hj ed hj ed he she shed he held all hall shall has
4		hj ed hj ed he she shed he held all hall shall has
		DS (double-space)
5	All letters	he led; she fled; he held a desk; she has had jade
6	learned	he led; she fled; he held a desk; she has had jade
		TS (triple-space)

Job 2: Letter on Executive-Size Stationery (7¼″ x 10½″) (WB p. 163)
Block style; 1″ side margins; open punctuation

august 5, 19-- mr edgar a bigelow 1832 maryland parkway las vegas nv 89105 dear mr bigelow (¶ 1) This letter will confirm our verbal offer on August 4 of employment as a mechanical technician in our Production Engineering Department. (¶ 2) Your starting salary will be $190 a week. Please keep in mind that your starting rate is our evaluation of your present worth to us; but, even more important, it reflects our belief in you and your ability to grow and develop. (¶ 3) Our offer carries with it the usual stipulation that you must pass a company physical examina-tion. You can arrange for this at your convenience with Dr. William T. Jones, 435 Bell Drive, in Las Vegas. We have notified him that you will call for an appointment in the near future. (¶ 4) We shall pay all relocation expenses involved in moving your household goods and personal effects. (¶ 5) I can assure you that your future with us has very good potential. We are pleased that you have decided to accept our offer. If you have any questions, please call me collect. sincerely lowell r harris personnel director

Job 3: Informal Government Letter (WB p. 165)

Date: April 2, 19-- Reply to Attn of: SFBR Subject: FBI Participation in Program on May 14 and 15 To: Mr. Gregory R. Sandgren, Regional Administrator, Securities and Exchange Commission, 312 N. Spring Street, Los Angeles, CA 90012 (¶ 1) Thank you for your communication of March 10, which alerted us regarding the Securities Law Cooperative Enforcement Program scheduled for May 14 and 15 in San Francisco. (¶ 2) As you are no doubt aware, at the present time we cooperate completely with your agency. We deeply appreciate the cooperation which your office has always extended. On the basis of your information, I understand that we have been able to finalize three outstanding cases during this past year. (¶ 3) Just in case a copy of your letter did not go to Mr. Malcolm Eldridge, I am forwarding your letter to him. I am sure he will be able to represent our interest at your May Conference. DONALD P. KING, Special Agent in Charge cc: Mr. Malcolm Eldridge SFBR:DPKing:xx 4-2---

Job 4: Modified Block Letter; ¶s Indented; Mixed Punctuation (WB p. 167)

January 5, 19-- Roberts & Roberts 309 Radcliff Drive Billings, MT 59102 Gentlemen Subject: Accounting Operations Manual (¶ 1) According to your recommendations, our Accounting Department was moved to its new location in conjunction with the implementation of plans for centralizing the various functions of the Controller's Office. (¶ 2) Since this move is part of the second phase of the transition from manual to computerized accounting, it is essential that the enclosed Accounting Operations Manual be updated in accordance with the new accounting procedures that will go into effect the first of next month. (¶ 3) Will you please make the necessary changes and submit them to us so that we can have the new manual printed and distributed by February 1. Sincerely Hunter H. Holden, Controller xx Enclosure

2C Left Shift Key Type each line twice SS; DS after second typing of line.

To type a capital letter controlled by a finger of the right hand, depress the **left shift key (28)** with the **a** finger without twisting the elbow or moving the other fingers from typing position. Hold the shift key down until you have typed the capital. Release the shift key quickly and return the finger to typing position.

Ja Ja Ja Jake Jake Ha Ha Hall Hall La La Lake Lake

Jake led; Jeff fled; Hal fell; Les Hall; Jake Lake
                                                    DS

2D Technique Practice: STROKING

Type each line twice SS; then DS.

Stroking Cue. Avoid sidewise (slanting) strokes. Hold the hands directly over the keys. Type with quick, sharp strokes.

Incorrect finger alignment

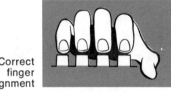
Correct finger alignment

1 All letters learned are
2 used

Return without looking up

1 Les leads; Jeff led all fall; Les has a safe lead;

2 Lee led; Hal fled; Jake had a sale; he sells jade;

3 Jeff Lake has a safe lease; Jake held a jade sale;

4 Hal leads all jade sales; Les Lee heads all sales;

5 Jess Leeds led all fall; he has held a shell sale;

6 Jeff Leeds seeks a safe deal; Jake has had a deed;

7 Les Kale had a hall desk; he has had a sales desk;

2E Pica or Elite Type

Does your typewriter have pica or elite type? The first line shown below is in pica type; the second, in elite type. Compare your type size with those shown below:

10 pica spaces to a horizontal inch
12 elite spaces to a horizontal inch (2.5 cm)

in.		1		2		3	
cm	1	2	3	4	5	6	7	8	

Note that pica type is larger than elite type. As a result, there are 10 pica spaces to an inch; 12 elite spaces.

The cylinder or carriage scale range is from 0 to 110 or more on elite machines; from 0 to 90 or more on pica machines. An 8½″ line has 102 elite or 85 pica spaces

2F Center Point of Paper

When paper is inserted with the left edge at 0 on the cylinder or carriage scale, the horizontal center point of 8½″ by 11″ paper will be 51 (or 50 for convenience) on elite machines; 42 on pica machines.

Tryout. Remove the paper from the machine. Place the left and right edges together. Make a slight crease at the exact center at the top.

Reinsert the paper with the center at 50 for elite type or at 42 for pica type (unless your instructor directs you to use another center point).

Move the paper guide against the left edge of the paper. For ease in centering your copy later, check to see that the paper guide is in this position at the beginning of each practice period.

LESSON 148

148A Preparatory Practice (5) each line at least 3 times

Alphabet	Zola and Peggy Mobray requested an extra week for their June vacation.
Figure/symbol	The final cost of labor on job #593 was $5,708.41 (62% of total cost).
Long words	We studied improvement of data processing through work simplification.
Fluency	It pays to let good manners show in both your letters and your speech.
	| 1 | 2 | 3 | 4 | 5 | 6 | 7 | 8 | 9 | 10 | 11 | 12 | 13 | 14 |

148B Control Building (10) two 3′ control-level writings; record GWAM of the better writing

All letters are used.

		GWAM 1′	GWAM 3′	
¶ 1 1.6 SI 5.8 AWL 75% HFW	Perhaps you did not realize that there are several basic principles	14	5	54
	of learning that are used to gain typewriting skill. Expert typists do	28	9	59
	not acquire their rapid and highly accurate scores simply by chance.	42	14	64
	They first must realize how necessary it is for them to take advantage	56	19	68
	of each of the common principles of learning if they are to perform with	71	24	73
	a maximum of efficiency.	76	25	75
¶ 2 1.6 SI 5.8 AWL 75% HFW	It is not unusual, for example, for a learning typist to reach a	13	30	79
	"plateau" in the quest for increased speed. To continue typing at the	27	34	84
	present rate is no problem, but it may appear impossible to climb to	41	39	89
	a higher level. When this happens, it seems imperative to dedicate	55	43	93
	some practice drills just to speed development, though a temporary accu-	69	48	98
	racy drop is incurred.	73	50	99
1′ GWAM	| 1 | 2 | 3 | 4 | 5 | 6 | 7 | 8 | 9 | 10 | 11 | 12 | 13 | 14 |			
3′ GWAM	| 1 | 2 | 3 | 4 | 5 |			

148C Production Measurement (35) 30′ writing; figure N-PRAM

Job 1: AMS Simplified Letter *(WB p. 161)*

	Words
june 16, 19-- mr ernest o walker jackson	9
electric corporation 1834 west capitol street	18
jackson ms 39209 PROJECT 6293--ORDER	26
CDT 2631 (¶ 1) we have received the instruc-	33
tion book for the low-voltage portion of this	42
substation and the drawings for the high-	50
voltage switch and transformer, but we have	59
not received the drawings for the low-voltage	69
equipment. (¶ 2) Without drawings of the	76
low-voltage section, we cannot review the in-	85
struction book to determine whether it is	93
adequate. As I glanced through the instruc-	102
tion book, I noted that there are no data for	111
an SCI relay or for an Agastat time-delay	119
relay. Such relays would be required for	128
motor-locked rotor protection unless John has	137
elected to use a different relaying system.	146
(¶ 3) I would appreciate your reminding John	154
that we have not as yet received drawings	162
and that we are very eager that they be deliv-	171
ered soon. guy a watts electrical engineer	180/199

LESSON 3

3A Ready to Type Review READY TO TYPE, page 6.

1. Align machine with edge of desk.
2. Adjust paper guide.
3. Insert paper; adjust paper bail.
4. Set machine on "1" for SS.
5. Set the left margin stop about 25 spaces to the left of the center of the paper; move the right margin stop to the end of the scale.
6. Observe posture points, page 3.

3B Preparatory Practice each line at least twice

Type Line 1 twice SS; then DS after the 2-line group. Type the remaining lines in the same way.

Stroking Cue. Keep the fingers deeply curved and your wrists low and steady. Type with quick, sharp strokes.

```
a; sl dk fj ed hj a;sl fjdk edhj Ja Ja Ka Ka La La
```

Return quickly without looking up

```
he held she shell all fall hall led lead sell fell
```

Space once after ;

```
Lee fell; Hal had all; Jess Hall held a fall sale;
```

3C Location of I and T

Type I with K finger

Type T with F finger

Reach the *k* finger up to **i**; lift the *j* finger slightly for improved stroking control. *Type Line 1, below, for tryout.*

Straighten the *f* finger slightly; reach to **t** without arching the wrist. *Type Line 2, below, for tryout.*

3D Location Drills for I and T

Type each line twice SS; *DS* after the second typing of each line.

Keep the fingers curved over the home keys. Make short, direct reaches to such keys as *e*, *t*, and *i*.

1 i   `ik ik ik if is his like dike file fill lid did hid`

Wrists and hands still

2 t   `tf tf tf let take tall tale the hat that last late`

3 i t   `ik tf ik tf fit sit; if it is; if he is; it is the`

4 Review   `Kate had a late file; if it is the; the last list;`

5 Review   `I had a list; Keith has left his list at the lake;`

Job 1: Leftbound Manuscript with Footnotes

Be sure to type the footnotes on the pages on which the footnote reference numbers appear.

Words

COMPONENTS OF THE COMPUTER SYSTEM — 7

(¶ 1) **A** computer system is made up of various pieces of equipment and devices which are known as hardware. The five components of a computer system are: (1) input, (2) processing, (3) storage, (4) control, and (5) output. Each component may consist of one individual unit, or it may be several pieces of equipment and/or devices. Each basic component of the computer system will be briefly explained in the following paragraphs. — 14, 23, 33, 42, 51, 59, 69, 77, 86, 94

Input Components — 101

(¶ 2) Input consists of two basic sources: (1) data to be processed and (2) instructions for processing the data. There are about seven forms of input used in a computer system. Usually one or more are used in each system. They include: (1) punched cards, (2) punched paper tape, (3) magnetic tape, (4) magnetic disks and drums, (5) optical scanners, (6) magnetic ink character readers, and (7) console typewriters and data terminals.[1] — 109, 118, 127, 136, 145, 154, 163, 171, 180, 188

Processing Component — 196

(¶ 3) The processing unit is sometimes referred to as the arithmetic unit. The processing of data results in the conversion of the input data into electrical impulses that use a binary code. The processing unit does only what the computer has been programmed to perform. — 203, 212, 221, 231, 239, 248, 250

Storage Component — 257

(¶ 4) This particular component is often referred to as the memory unit. The storage unit retains in coded binary form all input data and all processed data as instructed by the program. Data in the storage unit move back and forth between the storage unit and the processing unit as directed by the program. — 264, 272, 281, 290, 299, 307, 316, 318

Control Component — 325

(¶ 5) The control unit directs the processing operations and verifies that all program instructions have been performed properly. This component also stores the intermediate results of the operations and supplies the needed information in the arithmetic operations.[2] — 333, 341, 351, 359, 368, 377

Output Components — 384

(¶ 6) The end result of a computer program is some form of usable output data. The computer program indicates the type of output and its form. The major kinds of output devices are: (1) impact printers, (2) nonimpact printers, (3) cathode ray tube (CRT) terminals, (4) voice response units, and (5) computer output microfilm (COM) systems.[3] — 392, 401, 409, 418, 428, 436, 445, 452

[1] John J. W. Neuner, B. Lewis Keeling, and Norman F. Kallaus, Administrative Office Management (6th ed.; Cincinnati: South-Western Publishing Co., 1972), pp. 807-808.

[2] Ibid., p. 814.

[3] Ibid. (Words in footnotes: 52)

Job 2: Outline

Full sheet; center horizontally and vertically

Words

COMPUTER INPUT AND OUTPUT
COMPONENTS — 7

I. INPUT COMPONENTS — 12

    A. Punched Cards — 15
    B. Punched Paper Tape — 20
    C. Magnetic Tape — 23
    D. Magnetic Disks and Drums — 29
    E. Optical Scanners — 33
    F. Magnetic Ink Character Readers — 40
    G. Typewriters and Data Terminals — 47

II. OUTPUT COMPONENTS — 53

    A. Impact Printers — 57
    B. Nonimpact Printers — 62
    C. Cathode Ray Tube Terminals — 68
    D. Voice Response Units — 73
    E. Computer Output Microfilm Systems — 80

3E Location of C and . (Period)

Type C with D finger

Type . with L finger

Reach down to **c** with the *d* finger without twisting the elbow in or out or moving the hand down. *Type Line 1, below, for tryout.*

Extend the *l* finger down to type a . (period) without moving the hand downward or the elbow outward. *Type Line 2, below, for tryout.*

3F Location Drills for C and . each line twice SS; DS after second typing of each line

Spacing Rule. Space once after . (period) used at the end of an abbreviation; twice after . at the end of a sentence except when it is the last stroke in the line; then return the carriage without spacing.

c
```
cd cd cd dcd call sick check clad lacks jack stack
```

.
```
.l .l .l l.l adj. alt. La. Ill. Hal led all sales.
```
Return without spacing after .

c .
```
Jack called.  He lacks a check.  Lt. Leach has it.
```

c .
```
His chief has a late file.  Let Kit take the cash.
```

3G Technique Practice: STROKING each line once DS; repeat

Home-Row Stroking. Strike each key firmly; release it quickly, snapping the finger toward the palm of the hand.

Third-Row Stroking. Reach your finger to the third row (above home row) without arching the wrist or moving the hand forward.

First-Row Stroking. Make the reach to the first (bottom) row without moving the elbow in or out or changing the hand alignment.

All keyboard characters learned are used.

1 Home row
```
fj dk sl a; all fall; all lads fall; ask all lads;
```
Sharp strokes; quick release

2 h and e
```
she has jade; she leads all sales; she sells sleds
```

3 i and t (3d row)
```
it is; he hit it; he is still ill; take this list;
```
Finger reaches

4 c and . (1st row)
```
Jack called Lee.  His chief cashed all the checks.
```

5 All letters learned are used
```
I see that Jack has the file.  Keith has the list.
```
Still wrists and elbows

6 in Lines 5-8
```
I shall take this deed.  Jack Hale is at his desk.
```

7
```
Kit Hale has all the files.  He has the last list.
```

8
```
Lt. Leach said he cashed the checks that Kit left.
```

SECTION 27 Measurement: Basic and Production Skills

LESSONS 147-150

Section 27 provides basic and production skills measurement. Each lesson provides 30 minutes of timed production typing. You will be given approximately 5 minutes at the end of each period to figure your N-PRAM.

Drill Copy. SS; 70-space line

¶ Copy. DS; 70-space line; 5-space ¶s; full sheets

Production Measurement. Follow the directions given with the jobs. Make 1 cc of each letter; address appropriate envelopes.

Supplies Needed. Letterheads, interoffice memorandum, legal paper

LESSON 147

147A Preparatory Practice (5) each line at least 3 times

Alphabet	Extensive adjustment of the zoning law quickly boosted property taxes.
Figure/symbol	AT&T 5 1/2% bonds (due October 26, 1980) sold at 104 to 107 on July 3.
Long words	The recommendations are based exclusively on recent research evidence.
Fluency	We know it is always best to forgive and not to try to obtain revenge.

| 1 | 2 | 3 | 4 | 5 | 6 | 7 | 8 | 9 | 10 | 11 | 12 | 13 | 14 |

147B Speed/Control Building (10) four 1′ writings on the exploration level; then four 1′ writings on the control level

All letters are used.

1.7 SI
6.0 AWL
70% HFW

1′ GWAM

The adjustment letter is a vital part of a business. No one is per- 13
fect, so errors occur that need to be remedied. The seller and the buyer 28
must handle each end of the communication quickly and politely. It must 43
be recognized that a well-written adjustment letter fosters better busi- 57
ness relations. Customers can get speedier replies if they send clear, 71
positive letters explaining their problems. The person who composes a 86
reply to a complaint must have empathy if the letter is to answer any 100
criticism fairly, exactly, and without violating any of the basic prin- 114
ciples involved. Tact, honesty, and empathy are needed if a company's 128
reputation is to be retained or, hopefully, to be improved. 139

| 1 | 2 | 3 | 4 | 5 | 6 | 7 | 8 | 9 | 10 | 11 | 12 | 13 | 14 |

4A Ready to Type Review READY TO TYPE, page 6.

4B Preparatory Practice each line twice SS; DS after second typing of line

All strokes learned are used.

i t
```
ik ik tf tf dike fit that left lift jest tall tile
```
Eyes on copy

c .
```
cd cd .l .l sick lack lace call hack clad etc. La.
```

```
Jack called; he has a check.   Keith led this list.
```

4C Technique Practice: STROKING each line twice SS; DS after 2d typing of line

Strike each key with a sharp, quick movement of the fingers. The stroke should be downward toward the palm of the hand. Release the key quickly. Avoid pushing the key or raising the finger high over a key before striking it. Hold your fingers over the home keys. Raise them just enough to make quick, sharp strokes.

Striking the key

Releasing the key

All strokes learned are used.

1 Strike and release keys
```
the chief had the file; he leads the skills class;
```
Return quickly with eyes on copy

2 quickly
```
she had his aid; he held the jet; this is the list
```

3
```
it is; it is the; if it is; if it is the; if I had
```

4
```
I had the last list.   Jack called; he had a check.
```

5
```
Jack cashed the check.   Jeff had a safe cash deal.
```

6
```
Hal said Lt. Hale left the check file at his desk.
```

7
```
Jack Hill held the lead at the lake.   He liked it.
```

4D Right Shift Key each line twice SS; DS after second typing of line

To type a capital letter controlled by a finger of the left hand, depress the **right shift key (26)** with the ; finger. Hold the shift key down until you have struck and released the key for the capital; then release the shift key. Return the finger to typing position without pausing. *Type the lines below for tryout.*

```
Da Da Dale Dale Sl Sl Slade Slade Dale Slade Diele
```

```
Dale has the list.   Sid Fiske called.   Alf led it.
```

Job 1: Formal Government Letter (WB p. 155)

Window envelope; 1 cc

Words

May 5, 19-- mr samuel t bartholomew, jr | 9
pasadena better business bureau 1345 michi- | 17
gan avenue pasadena ca 91106 dear mr | 25
bartholomew (¶ 1) In order to improve the | 33
existing cooperation between State and Fed- | 41
eral Regulatory and Enforcement Agencies in | 50
the field of securities and fraud enforce- | 58
ment, as well as allied fields, the California | 67
Regional Office of the Commission and the | 76
Office of the California Securities Commis- | 84
sioner propose to sponsor jointly the third | 93
annual meeting in San Francisco, California, | 102
May 24 and 25, 19--. (¶ 2) In order to be as | 110
beneficial as possible to all concerned, we are | 120
seeking the attendance and participation of | 128
State Securities Commissioners, State Attor- | 137
neys General, Banking and Insurance Com- | 145
missioners, United States Attorneys, Postal | 154
Inspectors, Prosecuting Attorneys, represen- | 162
tatives of the Better Business Bureau, Federal | 172
Bureau of Investigation, San Francisco Stock | 181
Exchange, officials of the National Associa- | 189
tion of Securities Dealers, Inc., interested law | 199
enforcement officials and members of the aca- | 208
demic community, as well as their assistants | 217
and staff members. (¶ 3) The agenda is not | 224
firm as yet as to topics; accordingly, we solicit | 234
any comments which you might have concern- | 242
ing proposed topics for discussion. Please | 251
save the dates of May 24 and 25 and plan to | 260
attend this program. sincerely gregory r | 268
sandgren regional administrator (Office sym- | 275
bol: SESF; V. R. Jolley wrote the letter.) | 280

Job 2: Informal Government Letter (WB p. 157)

Window envelope; 3 cc's

Words

Date: May 5, 19-- Reply to Attn of: AFAW | 3
Subject: Shipment of Generators from Tren- | 10
ton Equipment Company To: Allan J. Fer- | 17
guson, Receiving Dock Foreman, Alexandria | 25
Dock (¶ 1) The shipment of generators that | 32
arrived at our shipping and receiving dock in | 42
Alexandria yesterday morning was complete | 50
according to the shipping memorandum dated | 59
April 30. As specified in our contract with the | 68
Trenton Equipment Company, one fourth of | 76
the requested number of generators have now | 85
been received. (¶ 2) Please confirm in writ- | 93
ing that three crates were broken open and | 101
their contents exposed. I hope that future | 110
shipments will be packaged in a manner cer- | 118
tain to protect them against such potential | 127
losses. (¶ 3) I understand that insufficient | 135
buffer material allowed the generators to slide | 145
against the sides of the crates causing the | 153
wooden slats to splinter. Perhaps if the gen- | 162
erators were nailed to a wooden track at the | 171
bottom of the crate, they would not shift. | 180
I have requested the Trenton Equipment | 188
Company to crate all future shipments in this | 197
fashion. Arnold R. Thompson, Chief, Fed- | 205
eral Supply Service cc: Alexandria Dock | 213
Superintendent, FSS Legal Officer AFAW: | 221
FGGowans:xx 5-5--- | 225

Job 3: Informal Government Letter (WB p. 159)

Window envelope; 1 cc

Words

Date: May 5, 19-- Reply to Attn of: AFAW | 3
AIRMAIL Subject: Modification of Contract | 10
RB-38764-W To: Morrison Stationery & | 17
Print Company Attention: Mr. R. John | 24
Hecht 123 North Jackson Street Topeka, | 32
KS 66603 (¶ 1) Please disregard Paragraph | 39
Four, Contract RB-38764-W, as it pertains to | 48
our most recent order placed with your com- | 57
pany. All other paragraphs should remain in | 66
effect, and delivery will be accepted in accor- | 75
dance therewith. (¶ 2) Due to recent changes | 83
in postal regulations, specifications as treated | 93
in Paragraph Four will no longer be required | 102
in filling our orders. (¶ 3) Please confirm | 110
this change. Arnold R. Thompson, Chief, | 118
Federal Supply Service AFAW:CRRobb:xx | 125
5-5--- | 127

4E Continuity Practice: PHRASES AND SENTENCES   each line once SS; then each line once DS

All strokes learned are used.

1   file this lease; cash the check; tell the late lad
2   if he; if he is; if she; if she is; if he had this
3   she had a safe lead; if it fits; I shall see that;
4   Dick held a jade sale at Dike Lake late last fall.
5   This is the field test that Sid Dahl let Cal take.
6   Jack asked Cliff if he had set the last test date.

Type without
pauses between
strokes

LESSON 5

5A Preparatory Practice   each line twice SS; DS after second typing of line

All letters learned are used in each line.

she called; if it is; Cliff sells jade; I like it.
Cal let Al Hall take the jade; he is at Lief Lake.
Dick Jacks said that he let Les Lee take the file.

Type slowly
but steadily

5B Location of O and R

Type O with L finger

Type R with F finger

Reach the *l* finger up to type **o** without moving the hand forward or the elbow outward. *Type Line 1, below, for tryout.*

Reach the *f* finger to **r** without moving the other fingers from home-key positions. *Type Line 2, below, for tryout.*

5C Location Drills for O and R   each line twice SS; DS after second typing of line

All letters learned are used.

1 o   ol ol ol old old fold cold to took so sold do dole
2 r   rf rf rf rid risk sir air hair chair here are lard
3 o r   or for ford fork rock frock jar car soar cord roll
4 Review   Ceil Ford had their old car. She had a hard ride.
5 Review   He had the food for the fair. Rod heard the talk.

LESSON 146

146A Preparatory Practice [5] each line at least 3 times

Alphabet	This Juarez plaza was extremely quiet and dark for an October evening.
Figure/symbol	In technical papers, you may use this form: 350′4″ x 217′9″ x 216′8″.
Long words	The copying processes shown were verifax, thermography, and photocopy.
Fluency	Though it is not an easy job, you can learn to type a word as a whole.
	| 1 | 2 | 3 | 4 | 5 | 6 | 7 | 8 | 9 | 10 | 11 | 12 | 13 | 14 |

146B Growth Index [10] one 5′ control-level writing; record GWAM

All letters are used.

		GWAM 1′	GWAM 5′	
¶ 1 1.5 SI 5.6 AWL 80% HFW	You can find simple, lasting joy in many walks of life; luckily, it	14	3	63
	is your disposition, not your position, that makes you a happy or an un-	28	6	65
	happy person. The people that long for social acceptance will endeavor	42	8	68
	to perfect the knack of holding a good conversation; but they will remem-	57	11	71
	ber, hopefully, to let it go once in a while.	66	13	73
¶ 2 1.5 SI 5.6 AWL 80% HFW	One who questions an opinion is canny; one who quarrels with plain	13	16	76
	facts is a fool; but anybody who recognizes the difference between cold	28	19	79
	facts and sheer opinion is likely to be perceptive. Many people are	42	22	81
	open-minded; they can usually see two points of view in a case--the	55	24	84
	wrong one and theirs. Hence, it is necessary to realize that often the	70	27	87
	broadest view comes from the narrowest mind.	78	29	89
¶ 3 1.5 SI 5.6 AWL 80% HFW	If you want efficiency and reliability, you will discover them if	13	32	91
	you find a busy person. We are apparently divided into two groups--one	28	34	94
	that succeeds and one that cannot be bothered. If you desire success,	42	37	97
	locate that busy group and join it. You will discover that the competi-	56	40	100
	tion is great, but you will find that you will be happier with the	70	43	103
	busy group.	72	43	103
¶ 4 1.5 SI 5.6 AWL 80% HFW	For every person who exhibits a tiny spark of genius, one can easily	14	46	105
	spot a dozen others who are experiencing serious ignition trouble. If	28	49	109
	you belong to the latter group, stop looking for easy solutions to your	42	52	112
	problems. Change your course of action and begin to search for the	56	55	114
	right solutions even if you find that you must work harder than you	70	57	117
	desire. Happiness is not a gift; it is earned through hard work.	83	60	120

1′ GWAM | 1 | 2 | 3 | 4 | 5 | 6 | 7 | 8 | 9 | 10 | 11 | 12 | 13 | 14 |

5′ GWAM | 1 | 2 | 3 |

5D Location of Z and N

Type Z with A finger

Type N with J finger

Reach the *a* finger down to type **z** without moving the hand down or the elbow in or out. *Type Line 1, below, for tryout.*

Move the *j* finger down to type **n** without moving the other fingers from their home keys. *Type Line 2, below, for tryout.*

5E Location Drills for Z and N each line twice SS; DS after second typing of each line

All letters learned are used.

1	z	aza za za za za haze jazz size zeal zoo doze froze
2	n	jnj nj nj nj nj an and then than can land hand not
3	z n	za nj za nj zone haze freeze fan ran rent kind den
4	Review	Fran Zier has land in this zone. The zoo is near.
5	Review	Zoe had lots of zeal and zest; this drill is done.

5F Spacing Summary Type the line twice.

1. Space once after a period at the end of an abbreviation. Do not space after internal periods.

2. Space twice after . at the end of a sentence; once after ; used as punctuation.

3. At the end of a line, make the return without spacing after the final stroke.

Dr. Zier sent it c.o.d. Zoe called; Jane can act.

5G Continuity Practice: PHRASES AND SENTENCES each line twice SS; then each line once DS

Continuity Cue. Type at a steady pace without pausing between strokes, words, or lines.

Stroking Cue. Type with your *fingers*, with minimum hand or arm motion. Use short, snappy strokes.

All strokes learned are used.

1	(From dictation)	to do; to do so; to do the; to do this; to do that
2		it is; it is the; it is here; it is there; it does
3		he can; he can take; he can seize it; in this zone
4	(From the book)	The hard freeze forced the school to close at ten.
5		Jake has size nine; he can send it to Scott c.o.d.
6		Liz needs the land in this zone. Roz left at one.

Short, quick strokes

Job 8: Informal Government Letter (WB p. 149)

No envelope needed

Type this informal letter in final form for duplication. The letter is from Mr. Thompson and is to be sent to: Purchasing Committee Members. Date the letter May 2, 19––. The subject is: Special Meeting for the Purchasing Committee.

(¶ 1) There will be a special meeting of the Purchasing Committee on Thursday at 2:30 p.m. The meeting will be held in the Conference Room. All department representatives are expected to attend. (¶ 2) The purposes of the meeting are: (¶ 3) a. To discuss the new FSS purchasing procedures that will become effective as of the new fiscal year. (¶ 4) b. To discuss the advantages and disadvantages of the proposed budget for the new fiscal year as it will affect FSS purchasing priorities. (¶ 5) c. To discuss and act on all urgent purchase requests. (¶ 6) d. To discuss other subjects pertinent to the Committee, as time permits. (¶ 7) All committee members are requested to be in attendance at this special meeting. Please acknowledge receipt of this letter by responding to my office by noon Wednesday.

Job 9: Informal Government Letter (WB p. 151)

Window envelope; 1 cc

The following letter was written by R. J. Christensen for Mr. Thompson's signature. Date the letter May 3, 19––. The subject is: U.S. Government Correspondence Procedures. Address the letter to Ms. Geraldine R. Swasey, 134 North Broadway, Lexington, KY 40507

(¶ 1) Thank you for your recent inquiry about standard procedures for typing Government letters. The style and form of this letter will illustrate for you the informal letter format generally used by U.S. Government offices. (¶ 2) The formal letter style is very similar to the block style used by most businesses. All parts of the letter, except numbered subparagraphs, begin flush with the left margin. (¶ 3) The formal letter stationery omits the printed captions in the upper-left margin. The following items should be noted when preparing a formal letter: (¶ 4) a. The dateline is typed on line 7 from the top. (¶ 5) b. The address is typed on line 14 so that a window envelope may be used. (¶ 6) c. A salutation and complimentary close may be used with mixed punctuation. (¶ 7) We are glad to send you the enclosed materials to illustrate further the procedures used in typing Government letters. If we can help you again, please let us know. Enclosure: United States Government Correspondence Manual, 1968

Job 10: Formal Government Letter (WB p. 153)

Window envelope; 2 cc's

The following letter was written by F. G. Gowans for Mr. Thompson's signature. Date the letter May 4, 19––. Subject: Arrival of Generators, Order X1549C Address: Trenton Equipment Company, 3950 Quakerbridge Road, Trenton, NJ 08619

(¶ 1) Your recent shipment of generators arrived at our Alexandria shipping and receiving dock this morning. Your order was complete as per your shipping memorandum dated April 30, 19––. According to our contract with you, one fourth of the generators ordered have now been received. According to our agreement, the remaining generators will be shipped at two-week intervals with the last of the order to be received not later than July 1, 19––. (¶ 2) We must inform you that three crates were broken open upon their arrival at our dock. Their contents were exposed; but, fortunately, there was no damage. We should like to encourage you to package the future shipments in such a manner as to ensure that the generators will be adequately protected against loss or damage. (¶ 3) Our examination of the crates revealed that insufficient buffer material allowed the generators to slide against the sides of the crates, causing the wooden slats to splinter. Nailing the generators to a wooden track at the bottom of these crates should prevent shifting, and we now request that all future shipments be crated in this fashion. cc: Alexandria Dock Superintendent

6A Ribbon Control Lever

At the beginning of each practice period, set the ribbon-control lever to type on the upper part of the ribbon.

The **ribbon-control lever (22)** can be set to type on the upper, middle, or lower part of the ribbon (or, if there are 4 adjustments on the typewriter, in

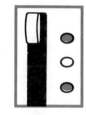

stencil position). If there are only 3 adjustments, the typing will be done on the upper or lower part of the ribbon (or in stencil position).

When the ribbon control is in stencil position, the ribbon is disengaged.

6B Preparatory Practice   each line twice SS; DS after second typing of line

All reaches learned   Roz called; Ed heard her.   Flo thinks Jan is fine.

o r   so sold to told or for rod road role rock door oar

z n   size zone haze not daze kind seize one fizz on zoo

Fluency (From dictation)   it is; if it is; to do; to do it; and to do; do so

6C Technique Practice: STROKING   each line twice SS; DS after second typing of line

Do not lean your hands over on the little fingers, or you will hit the keys with sidewise strokes.

Hold your hands directly over the home keys with fingers deeply curved. Strike the keys squarely.

 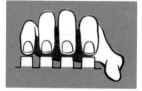

1 1st fingers   Jeff fir fine hen tin then join joint no nor north
2   He took tin to Jeff.   Join the force in the north.

Hold the hands directly over the home keys

3 2d fingers   kind dent cite rake deck rack crack die died dried
4   Ken had a soft drink; he dried an oar on the deck.

5 3d/4th fingers   sail loss hazed loaf load zeal hold salt jolt jail
6   Zoe can take the loaf; she had a jolt at the lake.

IF KEYS JAM

Key jamming is caused by striking a key before the preceding one is released or by a sluggish machine. To correct this fault, align fingers directly over the home keys and improve the timing of the strokes; or clean the typewriter.

To release jammed keys, proceed as directed at the right.

1. Use a special jammed-key release if your typewriter has this special key.

2. Depress the shift key; this sometimes works.

3. If the keys are still jammed, gently flick with your finger the stuck key nearest you; or push the keys slightly toward the platen to untangle them.

Job 6: Two-Page Formal Government Letter (WB pp. 143-145)

Window envelope; 2 cc's

April 30, 19-- mr william r ruben central maryland united fund 223 east 21st street baltimore md 21218 dear mr ruben (¶ 1) This is in reply to your letter to Lois Hafen, Federal Supply Service Combined United Fund Chairwoman, concerning the arrangements between the United Appeal of Central Maryland and the United Givers Fund of the National Capital Area involving Combined United Fund Campaign receipts from employees of the Federal Supply Service. (¶ 2) In establishing a Combined United Fund Campaign, the campaign area is ordinarily the same as the area of the local united fund which is involved in the campaign. However, the Fund-Raising Manual does not provide any hard-and-fast rules on this, and there are some variations depending on the local situation. The opportunity of giving where the employee works is fully recognized. For example, employees located in agencies in downtown Washington are covered by the United Givers Fund of the National Capital Area. (¶ 3) The situation in FSS, however, is different. Most employees do not reside in one area but are split between two separate united fund areas. This is also the case with other agencies where the Frederick County United Fund is involved. Because of the large number of employees residing outside the campaign area in which they work, a provision is made so that they may give to the fund representing the area in which they live. In an agency where 35-50 percent of the employees live in a united fund area other than the one in which the agency is located, it just doesn't appear desirable to try to force them to contribute to the fund covering the area in which the agency is located. To do so would simply impair the campaign. (¶ 4) In connection with FSS, I understand the practice prior to the Combined United Fund Campaign was to split receipts between the two funds. There does not seem to be any basis for changing it because of the Combined United Fund Campaign. In addiiton, it is my understanding that FSS officials representing the employees at the installation have asked to have the opportunity for the employees to pledge to the fund covering the area in which they live. Under such circumstances, it seems desirable to accede to the wishes of the employees if a successful campaign is to be conducted. (¶ 5) The problem you raise is one that can best be worked out by the local united funds involved along with officials of the particular agency in which you are raising funds. I was under the impression that you had agreed with the National Capital Area Givers Fund on the arrangement covering the proceeds from last fall's CUFC at Federal Supply Service. We would like to see any type of arrangement carried out that is agreeable to the local united funds. I see no basis for the FSS trying to make a decision in connection with the distribution of receipts. If FSS management and employees wish the opportunity to designate their contributions to the area in which they live, I would want this option to continue from a standpoint of a successful campaign in the agency. sincerely arnold r thompson chief, federal supply service cc: ms lois hafen mr robert j andersen mr philip c thorne (W. L. Proctor wrote the letter)

Job 7: Composing an Informal Letter (WB p. 147)

Mr. Thompson has asked that you prepare an informal letter to all employees of the Federal Supply Service announcing the upcoming Combined United Fund Campaign. The campaign begins on June 1. Ms. Lois Hafen is the agency chairwoman; she will be sending out a bulletin in the very near future. Mention that each employee should make every effort to contribute to this worthwhile effort. Each employee will be given the opportunity to select the particular fund that is representative of his home area. Date the letter May 1, 19--. This letter from Mr. Thompson will be duplicated; no envelopes.

6D Continuity Practice SENTENCE

Type each line 3 times SS. DS after the third typing of the line.

Continuity Cue. Type at a steady pace with fingers held directly over the keys.

All strokes learned are used.

1 He said that this is the size he sent to the fair.

No pauses between strokes

2 She can take the size she needs if it is in stock.

3 She had a zoo in this zone; she still has the zoo.

4 Fritz and Frank North do not like to ride at noon.

Type steadily

5 Jan lent a jar to Dan. Rod took the tire for Ann.

6 The staff thinks that Frank can find all the zinc.

7 Fern Thorne can take the late class at the school.

6E Sentence Guided Writing

1. Type each sentence twice without timing. Type at an easy, controlled pace. Avoid pausing after strokes and after words.

2. Type each sentence for 1 minute, trying to complete each sentence twice. (Your instructor may call the guide at the ½ minute to pace you.)

NOTE: Gross words a minute (*gwam*) are shown in Column 2 below.

All strokes learned are used.

		Words in Line*	GWAM 30" Guide
1	Jane can take her to the fair.	6	12
2	I think the first act is too short.	7	14
3	Dick trained for the race at Lake Dietz.	8	16
4	Rod can teach the class; he can do the drill.	9	18
5	Nan can ride the horse; she can find the old road.	10	20

| 1 | 2 | 3 | 4 | 5 | 6 | 7 | 8 | 9 | 10 |

* How typewritten words are counted

Five strokes are counted as 1 standard typewritten word. The figures in the first column at the right of the copy show the number of 5-stroke words in each of the lines. The scale below the copy shows the word-by-word count (5 strokes per word) for each line.

To determine number of words typed in 1 minute

(1) Note the figure at the end of each complete line you typed during the writing. (2) For a partial line, note (from the scale below the drill) the point at which you stopped typing. (3) Add these figures to determine the total words typed in 1 minute (*gwam*).

Job 5: Formal Government Letters *(WB pp. 135-141)*

Use the paragraphs below to type formal letters to the 4 addresses shown. Add an appropriate salutation and complimentary close for each letter. Use the letter style illustrated on page 284. Mr. Arnold R. Thompson, Chief, Federal Supply Service, will sign the letters. 1 cc of each letter; window envelopes.

Date all letters April 26, 19--

1 Your bid has been received, but it was not in compliance with our bidding regulations. Will you please review the bid requirements that were sent to you and make sure that you have complied with all specific items referred to under the section titled "Bid Requirements."

2. Perhaps you were using last year's bidding regulations. Please check and make certain that you are following the current regulations for the submission of bids.

3 If you need further clarification about any specific bid requirement, please contact us immediately. We have extended the bid closing date until May 31 in order to allow sufficient time for your bid to be adjusted.

Letter 1:

Mr. Harvey T. Winterton, President
Union Office Equipment Company
145 North Mill Street
Lexington, KY   40507

Letter 2:

Dr. Silvia J. Silver, President
Illinois Desk and Chair, Inc.
2599 South Faraday Street
Peoria, IL   61607

Letter 3:

Ms. Florence S. Kirkpatrick
Midwest Office Furniture Corporation
6319 Bradbury Avenue
Ft. Wayne, IN   46809

Letter 4: (See note below)

Mr. Conrad T. Hoggan, President
Kansas Furniture & Equipment Company
14688 East Bannister Road
Kansas City, MO   64139

NOTE: Add a final ¶ to Letter 4 stating that one of our Federal Supply Service officers, Miss Ruth Conders, will be in Kansas City on May 9 and will be available to confer with the company officials at their convenience. Arrangements can be made by contacting Mr. Thompson's office prior to May 7.

LESSON 7

7A Preparatory Practice each line 3 times SS; DS after third typing of line

All letters learned Karl took the case; Jan needs it to send to Fritz.

Shift keys Jack Steel and Ken Hale took the train to Red Oak.

Fluency **(From dictation)** and the; and if the; and if it did; and it did the

Sit in an erect position

7B Technique Practice: DOUBLE LETTERS each line twice SS; DS after second typing of line

Nonelectric. When typing double letters, do not allow full return of the key between strokes.

Electric. Allow time for the key to return to position before striking it again.

All letters learned are used.

soon took fool tool root cook door cool noon floor

fill till feel feet add jazz see class sheet steel

Al Steele took his class to the tool fair at noon.

Nell Coons can cross a street near the old school.

7C Location of U and W

Type U with J finger

FINGERS

Type W with S finger

Reach the *j* finger up to **u** without moving the other fingers from their home keys. *Type Line 1, below, for tryout.*

Reach the *s* finger up to **w** without moving the hand forward or arching the wrist. *Type Line 2, below, for tryout.*

7D Location Drills for U and W each line twice SS; DS after second typing of each line

All letters learned are used.

1	u	uj uj uj us use due cue hut hurt fun sun nut nurse
2	w	ws ws ws wit with worn sworn how show win won when
3	u w	four sure just turn thus with work wish want would
4	Review	We know June wants to show the house to us at two.
5	Review	Zeke will join the hunt for the first week or two.

Quiet hands and wrists

Job 2: Informal Government Letter (WB p. 129)

Window envelope; 2 cc's

Date: April 25, 19--

Reply to
Attn of: AFAW

Subject: Combined United Fund Campaign Supplies

To: Combined United Fund Campaign
1055 Taylor Avenue
Baltimore, MD   21204

(¶ 1) The Combined United Fund Campaign supplies have been packaged and are available for pickup. You may take delivery of these supplies at our Baltimore receiving dock located at 1503 Glen Keith Boulevard. (¶ 2) Included with the campaign supplies is the all new 16 mm, color, sound film to be used at the kickoff meetings. We were able to obtain ten copies of this film. Please do not forget to pick them up at the same time the other supplies are obtained. (¶ 3) These campaign supplies and films should be picked up before May 1 so that the installations will be able to schedule their kickoff meetings by the 10th of May. Our receiving dock is open daily, Monday through Friday, from 9:00 a.m. until 3:45 p.m. ARNOLD R. THOMPSON, Chief, Federal Supply Service cc: Baltimore Dock Superintendent AFAW:RL Black:xx 4-25---

Job 3: Formal Government Letter (WB p. 131)

Window envelope; 2 cc's

April 25, 19--   the reynold company, inc   2105 carver street   durham nc   27705   gentlemen (¶ 1) Because of the accumulated effect of several recent design changes, we request that you increase the height and width of the No. 24 container that we procure from your company. (¶ 2) The new specifications are as follows:

(Tabulate; 8 spaces between columns.)

	Present	Requested
Height	17.5"	19.0"
Width	12.0"	12.5"
Length	30.5"	30.5"

(¶ 3) Please acknowledge this change and confirm the earliest date that we shall be able to procure the new containers. sincerely arnold r thompson chief federal supply service   cc ms phyllis w warnick afaw:rlblack:xx 4-25---

Job 4: Informal Government Letter (WB p. 133)

No envelope; 1 cc

Date: April 26, 19--

Reply to
Attn of: AFAW

Subject: The 19-- Savings Bond Campaign

To: All Federal Supply Service Employees

(¶ 1) The 19-- Savings Bond Campaign is now underway throughout the Federal Government. (¶ 2) Savings bonds are a sound, safe investment. They are riskfree, lossproof, and theftproof; they can be quickly converted to cash to meet emergencies. There is no easier way to accumulate savings than through the Payroll Savings Plan. It is automatic and effortless. Many Americans have seen small savings bond allotments help finance a college education or a new home. Your keyman, who will be contacting you shortly, will explain all of the advantages of investing in bonds regularly through the Payroll Savings Plan. (¶ 3) Of course, when you buy savings bonds, you do more than invest in your own future; you invest in the future of our country, and you demonstrate your faith in America. (¶ 4) If you already buy bonds regularly and can increase your allotment, I recommend you do so. By buying bonds now, you will be helping yourself attain your personal goals; and you will be helping our country. arnold r thompson chief afaw:cranderson:xx 4-26---

7E Location of B and , (Comma)

Type B with F finger

Type , with K finger

Reach the *f* finger down to **b** without moving the hand from its typing position. *Type Line 1, below, for tryout.*

Reach the *k* finger down to , (comma). *Space once after a comma in a sentence. Type Line 2, below, for tryout.*

7F Location Drills for B and , each line twice SS; DS after second typing of each line

All strokes learned are used.

1	b	bf bf bf fbf bid fib fob bird bid bind bluff block
2	,	,k ,k ,k Kit, Ken, and Sue took a jet; I can, too.
3	b ,	to be, we can be, on the job, be sure, but it can,
4	Review	It will take us just two hours to cut these wires.
5	Review	Bud and Burt will count all the lots in this zone.

Center stroking in fingers

7G Continuity Practice: PHRASES AND SENTENCES each line twice SS; then each line once DS

Continuity Cue. You have now learned the locations of and reaches to 19 letter keys. Type them without pauses between strokes and words.

Stroking Cue. Keep the correct hand alignment with the keyboard. As you make the down reaches, do not twist the hands or elbows out of position.

All strokes learned are used.

1	with us, and with us, he will, he will do the work
2	if we knew; if we knew how; if we know how to show
3	if it will, if it will be, but this, but this will
4	Bill holds a job with the new branch of this bank.
5	Liz went to New Wells in June; Buzz will join her.

Quiet hands and elbows

| 1 | 2 | 3 | 4 | 5 | 6 | 7 | 8 | 9 | 10 |

7H Technique Practice: LETTER RESPONSE each line twice SS; DS after second typing of line

When typing one-hand words, type by *letter response* (think each letter); but pass from one letter to the next quickly. Speed up your typing by eliminating clumsy motions.

in as no at on are oil far kin set nil car ink add

was join face look dear kill wear hull trade farce

Job 1: Informal Government Letter (WB p. 127)

Type the letter shown below in pica type. At the end, use the current year in the *Identification of Office, Writer, and Typist* section. 1 cc; window envelope.

FEDERAL SUPPLY SERVICE

Washington, D.C. 20406

Date: April 25, 19--

Reply to
Attn of: AFAW   AIRMAIL

Subject: Format for the Informal Letter

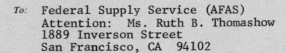

To: Federal Supply Service (AFAS)
Attention: Ms. Ruth B. Thomashow
1889 Inverson Street
San Francisco, CA 94102

This letter shows the format for preparing letters through-out the United States Government. This format will expedite the preparation of correspondence and save effort, time, and materials.

The following features of this format should please typists.

    a. All elements except the first line of lettered items are blocked along the left margin. This block style mini-mizes the use of the space bar, tabulator set key, and the tabulator bar.

    b. Salutations and complimentary closes are omitted in most letters. They may be included in formal letters to any individual on a personal or private matter (letters of con-dolence, notices of serious illness, where a warm and per-sonal feeling is paramount, etc.), or where protocol or tradition dictates. See the enclosed copy of a formal letter.

    c. The address is positioned for use in a window enve-lope, eliminating the need for typing an envelope.

ARNOLD R. THOMPSON
Chief, Federal Supply Service

2 Enclosures:
Copy of Formal Letter
United States Government Correspondence Manual, 1968

cc:
Official File--AFAW

AFAW:RLBlack:xx 4-25---   ◄──── Not shown on original copy

LESSON 8

8A Preparatory Practice each line twice SS; DS after second typing of line

1	All reaches learned	Tab, Al, and Jack worked for an hour; so did Zahl.
2	u w	use due jut hut hurt wit with sworn how show would
3	b ,	to bid, on the job, be here, this bill, to be safe
4	3d/4th fingers	zeal haze zone sale base loose lease saw slaw laws
5	Fluency (From dictation)	to be, to be the, if it be, to be sure, and is due

| 1 | 2 | 3 | 4 | 5 | 6 | 7 | 8 | 9 | 10 |

8B Technique Practice: STROKING each line twice

Curve your fingers, not your wrists.
Hold your wrists low and steady.

WRONG
Don't buckle
your wrists

RIGHT
Hold the
wrists low

Lines 1-2. Adjacent-key reach controls, such as *re*, *oi*, *tr*, and the like, need special attention. Make exact reaches to the keys, keeping your wrists low and steady.

Lines 3-4. Make direct reaches to such strokes as *ce*, *ec*, *br*, *un*, and the like, without returning the controlling finger to home position. Center the stroking action in your fingers.

1	Adjacent keys	are her soil coil has said short trade heads sales
2		Hare has a fine tire on sale; it has a safe tread.
3	Direct reaches	once force deck check herbs broke unit fun sun run
4		Brad checked the deck but once and found the dart.
5	Double letters	roof tell stuff foot took shrill shall cross class
6		Buzz will cross the trail at the foot of the hill.

8C Sentence Guided Writing

1. Type each sentence for 1', trying to complete each sentence twice as time is called.

2. Think and type as words the easy, 2-letter words such as *to*, *if*, and *he*.

	Words in Line	GWAM 30" Guide
Burt will work at the bank in June.	7	14
I can show the old house to June at two.	8	16
I know we own just four of these bronze sets.	9	18
A lad can be what he likes if he likes what he is.	10	20

1' GWAM | 1 | 2 | 3 | 4 | 5 | 6 | 7 | 8 | 9 | 10 |

typed on the seventh line from the top of the page, flush with the left margin. The body of the letter is resumed a double space below the page number.

Signature Element. The name of the signer of the letter is typed in all capital letters 4 lines below the last line of the body, flush with the left margin. The title of the signer is typed on the next line, flush with the name. If more than 1 line is needed for the signer's title, the succeeding lines are typed flush with the left margin. The entire signature element (name and title) should not exceed 4 lines.

Enclosures. The word "Enclosure" should be typed a double space below the signer's title. For more than 1 enclosure, the plural form should be used and the number of enclosures indicated, such as "5 Enclosures." If the enclosure(s) is not identified in the body of the letter, each enclosure should be listed on a separate line below the notation, flush with the left margin.

Material Sent Under Separate Cover. If material mentioned in the letter is to be sent under separate cover, the words "Separate cover:" should be typed flush with the left margin, 2 lines below the signer's title or the enclosure notation, if there is one. All material to be sent under separate cover should be listed, whether or not it is identified in the body of the letter. A copy of the letter should be sent with the material sent under separate cover.

```
Separate cover:
Form Letters Handbook
Plain Letters Pamphlet
```

Information Not Shown on the Original Copy. To exclude the information from the original copy, turn the cylinder knob toward you, rolling the carbon pack backwards. Insert a half sheet of fairly transparent paper in front of the original to cover the area where notations are to be typed; then turn the pack back to typing position. The notations can then be typed in the proper position.

Distribution of Copies. A carbon copy notation is shown only on the copy of the letter to be filed. It is typed a double space below the last line of the signer's title or the enclosure notation or separate cover listing, flush with the left margin. The names of the recipients are listed one below the other with office symbols when appropriate.

```
cc:
Official File - BRAR
Reading File - BRA
BRBD
```

Identification of Office, Writer, and Typist. The office symbol of the preparing office, the writer's initials and

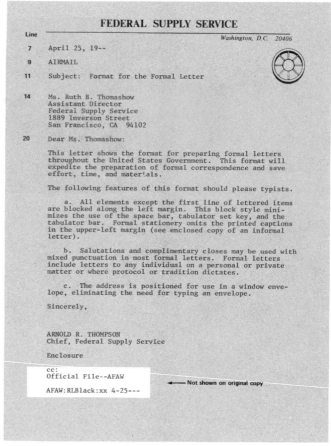

```
                    FEDERAL  SUPPLY  SERVICE
Line                                           Washington, D.C.  20406

 7    April 25, 19--

 9    AIRMAIL

11    Subject:  Format for the Formal Letter

14    Ms. Ruth B. Thomashow
      Assistant Director
      Federal Supply Service
      1889 Inverson Street
      San Francisco, CA  94102

20    Dear Ms. Thomashow:

      This letter shows the format for preparing formal letters
      throughout the United States Government.  This format will
      expedite the preparation of formal correspondence and save
      effort, time, and materials.

      The following features of this format should please typists.

           a.  All elements except the first line of lettered items
      are blocked along the left margin.  This block style mini-
      mizes the use of the space bar, tabulator set key, and the
      tabulator bar.  Formal stationery omits the printed captions
      in the upper-left margin (see enclosed copy of an informal
      letter).

           b.  Salutations and complimentary closes may be used with
      mixed punctuation in most formal letters.  Formal letters
      include letters to any individual on a personal or private
      matter or where protocol or tradition dictates.

           c.  The address is positioned for use in a window enve-
      lope, eliminating the need for typing an envelope.

      Sincerely,


      ARNOLD R. THOMPSON
      Chief, Federal Supply Service

      Enclosure

      cc:
      Official File--AFAW     ←— Not shown on original copy

      AFAW:RLBlack:xx 4-25---
```

Formal government letter; window envelope to be used

surname, the typist's initials, and the date are typed only on the file copies. In some cases the writer of the letter is not the same as the signer; therefore the name of the writer appears in the identification line. This line is typed flush with the left margin a double space below the last line used. Example:

```
FMSX:TNWilliams:bn 5-26-75
```

Formal Government Letters

Basic Style. The block style is used. Stationery without the captions "Date:," "Reply to Attn of:," "Subject:," and "To:" is used for formal letters. All other aspects are the same as those in the informal letter style. A salutation and complimentary close may be included with mixed punctuation.

Date. The dateline is typed on Line 7 at the left margin.

Address. The address is begun on Line 14 at the left margin.

8D Tabulator Control Type the drill twice.

To clear all tab stops

1. Move carriage to extreme left.

2. Depress **tab-clear key (31)** and hold it down as you pull the carriage all the way to the right.

To set tab stops

Move the carriage to the desired position; then depress the **tab-set key (23)**. Repeat this procedure for each stop needed.

Tabulating techniques

Nonelectric. Depress and hold the **tab bar (24)** [right index finger] or **key** [right fourth finger] until carriage has stopped.

Electric (and Some Nonelectric). Tap the **tab key (24)** [little finger] or **bar** [index finger] lightly; return finger to home-key position at once.

Clear all tabulator stops; set a tab stop 5 spaces, another 10 spaces, and still another 15 spaces to the right of the left margin.

Begin Line 1 of the drill at the left margin. Use the tab key or bar to type the remaining lines. Tab, release, and type quickly.

1 Margin		Liz sent cash to the bank; the bank wants a check.
2 Indent 5	_Tab once_ →	She will face the fact that a job takes work.
3 Indent 10	_Tab twice_ →	He took the old truck route to the fair.
4 Indent 15	_Tab three times_ →	Roz can be there for the fall show.

8E Continuity Practice: PARAGRAPH Type the paragraphs (¶s) as directed; determine GWAM.

1. Clear tab stops; then set a stop for a 5-space ¶ indention. Use DS.

2. Depress tab bar or key to indent the first line of each ¶.

3. Type the ¶s as shown; then type 1' writings on each of the ¶s.

All letters learned are used.

			Total Words 1' GWAM
¶ 1 1.0 SI 4.6 AWL 97% HFW	Tab →	All of us need to know how to talk and write	9
		well. We are sure to need these skills in school	19
		and in the world of work, too. Learn both now.	28
¶ 2 1.0 SI 4.6 AWL 97% HFW	Tab →	To these skills, we can add the need to know	37
		how to count. All jobs of the size we shall want	47
		should teach us to think as we use skills, too.	57

1' GWAM | 1 | 2 | 3 | 4 | 5 | 6 | 7 | 8 | 9 | 10 |

Copy Difficulty. The ease or difficulty of copy to be typed is influenced greatly by 3 factors: (1) Syllable intensity (SI) or average number of syllables per word; (2) stroke intensity or average word length (AWL); (3) incidence of high-frequency words (HFW) or the percent of words used from among the 1,254 most-used words. In this section of lessons, the ¶s are *very easy*.

How to Determine GWAM. The ¶s are marked with the 4-word count shown in figures and with an in-between count of 2 words shown by a dot to aid you in determining your 1' **gwam**. If ¶ 1 is typed and a part or all of ¶ 2 in the 1' writing, use the *cumulative* total word count given in the column at the right, plus the count for the incomplete line shown below the second ¶.

You are now employed as a typist in the General Services Administration, Washington, D.C. Government style and format are somewhat different from those used in most business offices. Study carefully the Production Typing Information section so that you will be able to do the jobs in this section properly.

Production Typing Information: GOVERNMENT CORRESPONDENCE

Informal Government Letters

Basic Style. The block style memorandum form is used with letterhead stationery. The captions "Date:," "Reply to Attn of:," "Subject:," and "To:" are printed in the left margin. Main paragraphs are typed flush with the left margin. Subparagraphs (either numbered or lettered) have the first line indented 4 spaces. Informal letters are single-spaced with double spacing between paragraphs. A letter of 1 paragraph or less than 10 lines, however, is double-spaced.

Special-Size Stationery. Agencies of the United States Government use 8″ x 10½″ stationery.

Margins. The left margin is set 2 spaces to the right of the printed captions "Date:," "Reply to Attn of:," "Subject:," and "To:" near the top of the form. The right margin should be 1 inch, and the bottom margin should be not less than 1 inch.

Sender's Reference. The official symbol should be typed flush with the left margin in line with the "Reply to Attn of:" caption. It should be typed a double space (2 typing lines) below the date. An office that does not have a symbol should type the abbreviated name of the office.

Special Mailing Instructions. Instructions for special mailing, such as AIRMAIL, SPECIAL DELIVERY, CERTIFIED, or REGISTERED, are typed on the same line as the sender's reference, starting at the center of the page. These instructions are placed on the face of the letter only when special mailing is required and the typist does not prepare the envelope. If the reference element extends to or beyond the center of the page, the special mailing instructions are begun 3 spaces to the right of it.

Subject. The first letter of each word is capitalized, except for articles, prepositions, and conjunctions. If more than 1 line is required for the subject, each succeeding line is begun flush with the first line.

Address. The address is typed at the left margin in line with the "To:" caption. The address is single-spaced in block style. When a window envelope is to be used, no line of the address may be longer than 4 inches. If a line must be divided, the second line is indented 2 spaces from the left margin. An address should not exceed 5 lines.

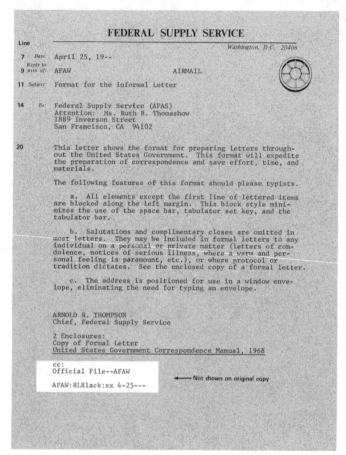

Informal government letter; window
envelope to be used

Attention Line. The attention line, if used, is placed as the second line of the address. The word "Attention" is followed by a colon and the name of the person intended.

Body. The body of a letter is started at least 2 lines below the "To:" section. When a window envelope is to be used, the body of the letter should be started at least 6 lines below the "To:" caption—about Line 20. If a paragraph is broken into subparagraphs, the subparagraphs may be numbered or lettered. The first line of a subparagraph should be indented 4 spaces; the second and succeeding lines are typed flush with the left margin.

Succeeding Pages. The second and succeeding pages of a letter are typed on plain paper. The page number is

LESSON 9

9A Preparatory Practice   each line 3 times SS; DS after third typing of each line

All letters learned   Jack worked with Burt, Saul, and Fred; so did Roz.

Direct reaches   Lance found the wrecked cab and checked the tires.

Fluency   (From dictation)   if he, if he is, if he is to do, if he is to do it

Make direct reaches for ce, ec, un, tr

Think words

9B Technique Practice: WORD RESPONSE   each line twice SS; DS after second typing of each line

it fit he the then do so us for aid laid with such

an and land hand he she end lend own down of or an

(From dictation)   do so│for us│with the│and the│and then│it did land

Read word groups

9C Location of Y and X

Type Y with J finger

Type X with S finger

Reach the *j* finger up to type **y** without arching the wrist or moving fingers from home keys. *Type Line 1, below, for tryout.*

Reach the *s* finger down to type **x** without moving the hand downward. Reach with the finger. *Type Line 2, below, for tryout.*

9D Location Drill for Y and X   each line twice SS; DS after second typing of each line

1 y   yj yj yj jay jay lay lay fly day say way sway yard

2 x   xs xs xs six fix fox next fixed lax sixth box jinx

3 y x   yes dry cry boy hay flax flex they next lynx ax by

4 Review   Clay Blyth can take the next tax case to Rex Knox.

5 Review   Rex says that he can fix the next box for Al Byrd.

LESSONS 142-145

Lessons 142, 144

Use the following daily lesson plan for Lessons 142 and 144. Retain all jobs until you have completed Lesson 145.

Preparatory Practice (5′). Type 142A, below, as directed.

Production Typing (45′). Type the jobs on pages 285-289. Follow the directions for each job; where specific directions are not given, use your own good judgment. Proofread carefully; correct all errors.

Lessons 143, 145

Use the following daily lesson plan for Lessons 143 and 145. Retain all jobs until you have completed Lesson 145.

Preparatory Practice (5′). Type 142B, below, as directed.

Technique Mastery (5′). Type 142C, below, as directed.

Production Typing (40′). Continue typing the jobs on pages 285-289. Follow the same general directions given for Lessons 142 and 144.

142A Preparatory Practice (5) each line at least 3 times

Alphabet	Judge Zerb will not acquit the expert; the key witness may have proof.
Figure/symbol	Boone & Strong paid invoice #9863 totaling $470.52, less 15% discount.
Double letters	I feel that good manners are essential to success in business affairs.
Fluency	It is the right and the duty of all citizens to vote in the elections.

| 1 | 2 | 3 | 4 | 5 | 6 | 7 | 8 | 9 | 10 | 11 | 12 | 13 | 14 |

142B Preparatory Practice (5) each line at least 3 times

Alphabet	Jim made several dozen quaint wicker baskets with wax fruit for Peggy.
Figure/symbol	The total of the 732 checks was $4,608.51 (or 49% of the May payroll).
Shift keys	Wilbur Pollard and Roy Granville went to the Memorial Day Speed Races.
Fluency	Seat yourself when you type so the arms slope down from hand to elbow.

| 1 | 2 | 3 | 4 | 5 | 6 | 7 | 8 | 9 | 10 | 11 | 12 | 13 | 14 |

142C Technique Mastery (5) each line at least twice without error

Drill on pol	The policy of the police was never to discuss politicians or politics.
Long reaches	My brother showed nerve in interrupting with his unnecessary opinions.
Stroke response	Executives prepared for retirement psychologically and sociologically.
Word recognition	It is not hard to do good work if you will make up your mind to do it.
Combination response	A microfilm camera will now film both sides of records simultaneously.

| 1 | 2 | 3 | 4 | 5 | 6 | 7 | 8 | 9 | 10 | 11 | 12 | 13 | 14 |

9E Location of V and P

Type V with F finger

Type P with ; finger

Reach the *f* finger down to type **v**. Hold the elbow in position and the hand in alignment. *Type Line 1, below, for tryout.*

Straighten the ; finger slightly and move up to type **p**. Avoid twisting the elbow out. *Type Line 2, below, for tryout.*

9F Location Drills for V and P   each line twice SS; DS after second typing of each line

1	v	vf vf vf vie view save salve sieve live loves have
2	p	p; p; p; pad paid pen spend spent paid prize plans
3	v p	vote van solve prove place drive drove prize stove
4	Review	Steve Prince will vote for the peace plan at five.
5	Review	A vote for Pat Vance is a vote for a low tax rate.

9G Continuity Practice: SENTENCE

Type each line 3 times SS; DS after the third typing of a line. Compute *gwam*.

Type at a smooth and steady pace. Hold the hands and arms quiet—almost motionless.

1	y	Syl Clay can pay Faye Kyle for the new style play.	Type
2	x	Knox can sell a box of flax seed to Rex next week.	without
3	v	Dave Volk served on the leave board for five days.	pauses
4	p	Pete has the pep, push, and poise for the top job.	
5	v p	Van pays in cash and saves; it proves a fine plan.	

| 1 | 2 | 3 | 4 | 5 | 6 | 7 | 8 | 9 | 10 |

9H Continuity Practice: PARAGRAPH

Type twice for practice; then type one or more 1' writings. Compute your *gwam*.

Sit erect. Keep your eyes on the copy as you type. Type at a steady, even pace.

All letters learned are used.

1.0 SI
4.6 AWL
95% HFW

If you plan to sell land lots, take the next
trip in space, write jazz, or wash cars, find the
bunch that thinks as it works. You do not need a
seer to know that those who think will have a job.

141D Communication Aid: CAPITALIZATION AND PUNCTUATION ⑮

Capitalize and punctuate each sentence as you type it. Check your work with your instructor; then retype the sentences. Do not number the sentences.

1   please send the invoice to mr raymond e jones 1357 brooklyn avenue

2   "the shipment from japan said bill will arrive tuesday afternoon"

3   six hundred seventy seven organizations purchased the new irs booklet

4   i conduct 5 10 and 15 day tours of the beautiful hawaiian islands

5   the airplane was hijacked to a small arab country on the persian gulf

6   the group will meet at the hilton hotel on monday may 2 at 1:30 pm

7   an up to date calendar is available from either ms king or mr brown

8   jamaica is located in the caribbean sea kingston is the capital city

| 1 | 2 | 3 | 4 | 5 | 6 | 7 | 8 | 9 | 10 | 11 | 12 | 13 | 14 |

141E Speed Building ⑩ one 5' writing; record GWAM

All letters are used.

	GWAM 1'	5'

¶ 1
1.6 SI
5.8 AWL
75% HFW

World population has been growing at quite a phenomenal rate during   14 | 3 | 52
the twentieth century. At the beginning of this century, the world popu-   28 | 6 | 55
lation was estimated to be only one and a half billion. Experts have   42 | 8 | 58
predicted that the population on the earth will increase five times dur-   57 | 11 | 61
ing this century; by the year two thousand, there will be about seven   71 | 14 | 64
and a half billion people living on the earth.   80 | 16 | 66

¶ 2
1.6 SI
5.8 AWL
75% HFW

The world population is increasing at a rapid two percent per year.   14 | 19 | 68
Latin America is growing faster than any other area in the world with a   28 | 22 | 71
growth rate of nearly three percent annually. At this rate, the popula-   43 | 24 | 74
tion will double in twenty-five years. Although many countries in the   57 | 27 | 77
industrial parts of the world have stabilized their populations, the   71 | 30 | 80
large majority of the countries of the world have a high growth rate.   84 | 33 | 83

¶ 3
1.6 SI
5.8 AWL
75% HFW

Africa has an estimated population of four hundred million. The   13 | 35 | 85
area's annual growth rate is about three percent, which will result in a   28 | 38 | 88
doubling of the population in about thirty years. At present the death   42 | 41 | 91
rate is about fifty per thousand, which is also the world's highest. If   57 | 44 | 94
improved medical programs in Africa lower this current high rate, the   71 | 47 | 97
growth of this area could increase a lot more than is now predicted.   84 | 50 | 99

1' GWAM | 1 | 2 | 3 | 4 | 5 | 6 | 7 | 8 | 9 | 10 | 11 | 12 | 13 | 14 |
5' GWAM | 1 | 2 | 3 |

10A Preparatory Practice   each line twice SS; DS after second typing of each line

All letters learned are used.

1	Review	Joyce Vaux won a prize for her work on the drives.
2	y x	by say yet year you your box boxed six sixth fixed
3	v p	five live serve save view pad prize plan pen spend
4	One hand	base you face pull fear join traced look bear hill
5	Fluency (From dictation)	he did, he did the, he did the work, if he did the

| 1 | 2 | 3 | 4 | 5 | 6 | 7 | 8 | 9 | 10 |

10B Technique Practice: SHIFT KEY AND SHIFT LOCK   each line twice SS; DS after second typing of each line

Shift Keys. Hold the shift key down until you have struck the key for the capital; then release the shift key and return the finger to typing position without pausing.

Shift Lock. Depress the **shift lock (29)** and leave it down until you have typed the combination to be capitalized. To release the lock, operate the shift key.

1	Right shift	Scott Zier saw Vance Boone at the Trent Book Fair.
2		Charles Vale said he wrote to the Red Star Cab Co.
3	Left shift	Hale Jones asked Lance Poole to join her in Hayes.
4		John Hertz will paint the boats at June Lake soon.
5	Both shifts	Josh Wertz will see Lyle Branch in Oak Creek Park.
6		The Frank Bentz Co. will fix the desk for Jo Holt.
7	Shift lock	He saw each of the new shows on NBC, ABC, and CBS.
8		He joined the NEA and CBEA. He works for the IRS.

10C Sentence Guided Writing

Type each sentence for 1', trying to complete each one twice as time is called. (The ½' guides may be called to pace you.)

Technique Cue. All the words are typed with alternate (balanced) hands. Try to read, think, and type the words by *word response*.

	Words in Line	GWAM 30" Guide
She is to do the work for the town.	7	14
They paid for the field of corn with us.	8	16
Fiske paid for the work they did by the lake.	9	18
I own the land, but he paid for the work they did.	10	20

1' GWAM | 1 | 2 | 3 | 4 | 5 | 6 | 7 | 8 | 9 | 10 |

SECTION 26 Typing in a Government Office

LESSONS 141-146

Section 26 is designed to provide you with experience in typing jobs that you would normally be expected to do in various government offices.

Drill Copy. SS; 70-space line

¶ Copy. DS; 70-space line; 5-space ¶s; full sheets.

Production Typing. Follow the directions for each job.

Supplies Needed. Letterheads or paper cut to 8″ x 10½″; full sheets

LESSON 141

141A Preparatory Practice [5] each line at least 3 times

Alphabet Quivering and almost frozen, the six boys crawled over a jutting peak.

Figure/symbol Invoice #1624 (June 3) totaled $9,057, less discounts of $8\frac{1}{2}\%$ and $14\frac{1}{4}\%$.

Direct reaches My Uncle Bert graded the verses and sent only the best one to Harvard.

Fluency The quantity of work we do may depend on how soon we get around to it.

| 1 | 2 | 3 | 4 | 5 | 6 | 7 | 8 | 9 | 10 | 11 | 12 | 13 | 14 |

141B Skill-Comparison Typing [10] two 1′ writings on each line of 141A; compare GWAM

141C Action Typing [10] Type twice; as you type, follow the directions in the ¶s.

Words

When you have typed this paragraph, center (in all captials) the 13
following headings, "guesstimating" their position as closely as pos- 26
sible. Triple-space after each heading. 35

portable typewriter 39
unabridged dictionary 43
executive pedestal conference desk 50
electronic calculator 55
executive swivel chair 59

Now use the backspace-centering method to center each heading below 73
its first typing; compare the first typing with the second. 85
(The last word count includes the second typing of the headings.) 109

10D Technique Practice: STROKING   Type the drill once as shown.

Lines 1-2. Reach directly to such strokes as *ce*, *br*, *un*, and the like, without returning the controlling finger to home position.

Lines 3-4. Type adjacent keys such as *re*, *poi*, and the like, by training your eyes to see quickly the correct letter sequences. Make each reach precisely.

1	Direct	why lace once branch debt hunt lunch brisk aft nut	
2	reaches	Herb Brill can hunt for the checks; he is in debt.	
3	Adjacent keys	has poor suit buy oil cards talk point three treat	
4		start here; few buy silk; we were there; fast dash	
5	Double letters	pool jazz roll off pass need Anne feel loss jarred	Distinct
6		Anne stopped off at school on her way to the pool.	strokes
7	3d/4th fingers	coax laws craze wax please loop size pop ooze ease	Quiet arms
8		see a sloop of war; please wax the car; pass a law	and wrists

10E Continuity Practice: PARAGRAPH

1. Type the ¶ twice for practice. Note any words that cause stroking difficulty.

2. Type the difficult words 2 or 3 times; then type one or more 1' writings on the ¶.

All letters learned are used.

1.0 SI
4.4 AWL
95% HFW

       First, use your head on a job; then try your
hand at it. You will find that the sense of this
line pays off in the end. Size up each job; know
what you have to do next to do it with skill.

10F Individual Practice

1. Type each line once. Place a check mark before the lines that seemed difficult.

2. Type 2 or more times each line that you checked as difficult.

1	b	Burt, not Bob, will buy the new bonds at the bank.
2	z	Liz Zahl will join Zoe at the new zoo in our zone.
3	x	Tex Cox waxed that next box for Jinx and Rex Knox.
4	p	Pat Parks can help pay for part of the prize plan.
5	y	Kaye said you should stay with Faye for five days.
6	n	Ken Knolls has done the dance; now Sven can do it.

| 1 | 2 | 3 | 4 | 5 | 6 | 7 | 8 | 9 | 10 |

Job 1: Medical History Report

	Words
MEDICAL HISTORY	3

Name. Ralph N. Holden Age. 25 Sex. M 13
Date. 8/25/19-- 17

Address. 510 Brady Street, Topeka, KS 66607 27

Entrance complaint. Pain in lower back. 39

Present illness. Patient fell from a ladder 51
about 10 days ago. Other than minor discom- 59
fort at the time of the accident, he felt that 69
he had not seriously injured himself. He has 78
had no subsequent injuries. Patient has been 87
developing severe pain down his left leg, espe- 96
cially after standing or sitting in one position 106
for a prolonged period of time. 113

Past history. Usual childhood illnesses. Left 125
wrist broken at age 12. Thrown from a horse 134
with no apparent injury at age 19. 141

Systems Review 147
  Gastrointestinal. Good appetite. Weight 159
  unchanged for 5 years. No appendix; re- 167
  moved at age 15. 170

  E.N.T. Tonsils and adenoids intact; do 179
  not cause any unusual obstruction. Has 187
  chronic sinusitis. 191

  Cardiovascular. Negative. 200

  Locomotor. No cogent history. 208

Family history. Youngest of 5 children, all 220
living and well; parents well. 226

Social history. Patient is married. Two chil- 238
dren. High school science teacher. He does 247
not use tobacco or alcoholic beverages. 255

Job 2: Legal Document with Endorsement

	Words
POWER OF ATTORNEY	4

(¶ 1) KNOW ALL MEN BY THESE PRESENTS, 10
that I, SUSAN T. WILSON, of the City of Provo, 19

County of Utah, State of Utah, do make, con- 28
stitute and appoint RONALD R. TEW, of the 36
City of American Fork, County of Utah, State 45
of Utah, as my lawful and legal attorney, to 54
act for me and in my name, place and stead, 63
for all matters relating to my business trans- 72
actions for the period of time January 1, 19--, 82
through and including July 31, 19--; and I 90
hereby ratify and confirm all transactions that 100
my said agent or attorney may do lawfully in 109
connection with my business transactions dur- 118
ing the above-stated period of time. (¶ 2) 125
IN WITNESS WHEREOF, I have hereby signed 134
and sealed this Power of Attorney on this the 143
22d day of December, 19--. 148

——————————————— 154
Susan T. Wilson 157

NOTE: Type an acknowledgment similar to the one in Job 1, page 270. Use December 22, 19--, as the date of the acknowledgment. The attorney is Carlton Z. Featherstone, 415 N. University Avenue, Provo, UT 84601. (Words: 93)

Job 3: Memorandum (WB p. 123)

	Words

TO: Dr. Andrew R. Garland FROM: Lucille T. 7
Black DATE: Current SUBJECT: Deadline 13
for Research Proposal Submission (¶ 1) We 20
have just received a notice from Dr. Archibald 29
W. Franklin, Chairman of the Board, stating 38
that all research proposals must be submitted 47
to the screening committee on or before 55
December 31. (¶ 2) Please acknowledge the 63
receipt of this notification. Also send a tenta- 72
tive list of the proposed research projects that 82
your division will submit. If possible, also 91
include an estimate of the total funding that 100
will be required. I shall expect to receive this 110
information within two weeks from today. 119/123

LESSON 11

11A   Preparatory Practice   each line 3 times SS; DS after third typing of each line

All letters learned   Bev Lentz picked this jazz show for our next year.

One hand   waste junk rest hulk treat you vase pill beat hunk

Fluency (From dictation)   to do, to do the, if the, if he did, if he did the

| 1 | 2 | 3 | 4 | 5 | 6 | 7 | 8 | 9 | 10 |

11B   Continuity Practice: SENTENCE   each line twice SS; DS after second typing of each line

He can do the drill in an hour or so, I feel sure.

Ned felt that the size of the vote would help Rod.

The tone of this fine harp has kept it at the top.

Rex Dix and Herb Cox saw a new show at the school.

| 1 | 2 | 3 | 4 | 5 | 6 | 7 | 8 | 9 | 10 |

Keep on typing; do not pause

11C   Location of Q and M

Type Q with A finger

Type M with J finger

Reach the *a* finger up to type **q** without swinging the elbow out or arching the wrist. *Type Line 1, below, for tryout.*

Reach the *j* finger down to type **m**. Do not move the hand down; just your finger. *Type Line 2, below, for tryout.*

11D   Location Drill for Q and M   each line twice SS; DS after second typing of each line

1 **q**   qa qa qa quit quite quote quaint quell queen quick

2 **m**   mj mj mj mat mist jam firm form harm come sum drum

3 **q m**   quiz quack quest qualm much must meet arm ham most

4 **Review**   Mr. Queen read the quaint myth on the blue mosque.

5 **Review**   Mark Quinn may make a quick trip to an old square.

LESSON 140

140A Preparatory Practice [5] each line at least 3 times

Alphabet Ben Marvin requested exactly a dozen jackets for the long winter trip.

Figure/symbol All $12,000 4½% bonds (Series 3E) were sold for a profit of $5,568.79.

Balanced hand The gowns worn by the girls lent an air of enchantment to the evening.

Fluency They will not get very far until they have learned to make time count.

| 1 | 2 | 3 | 4 | 5 | 6 | 7 | 8 | 9 | 10 | 11 | 12 | 13 | 14 |

140B Growth Index [10] one 5′ control-level writing; record GWAM

All letters are used.

GWAM 1′ 5′

¶ 1 1.5 SI 5.6 AWL 80% HFW

A typing job can be found in the professional office for the good 13 3
typist. In order to succeed, the person must be able to type all the 27 5
work in a very efficient manner. This means typing rapidly with a very 42 8
high degree of accuracy. Also, the typist must be able to "think" and 56 11
make the decisions required in the routine day-to-day work assignments. 70 14
Some of the offices that hire good typists are legal, medical, and 84 17
scientific offices. 88 18

¶ 2 1.5 SI 5.6 AWL 80% HFW

A typist in a legal office must be able to type all forms of reports 14 20
and documents. A person doing the typing must know how to arrange the 28 23
material so that it will be acceptable in our courts of law. Legal for- 42 26
mat is not the same as regular manuscript typing format; therefore, a 56 29
person must know this special format and type all legal documents using 71 32
this format. Although erasures are not wanted on any legal manuscript, 85 35
corrections can be made; an individual should learn how to make these 99 37
corrections in a manner that would be acceptable in the courts of law. 113 40

¶ 3 1.5 SI 5.6 AWL 80% HFW

A medical typist will find the work very challenging and demanding. 14 43
The words a physician uses in his reports and letters may not be common, 28 46
everyday terms to the neophyte typist. Therefore, the typist must be 42 49
very alert and check the spelling of any word that is not familiar. The 57 52
basic formats used in a medical office are the same as those used in any 72 54
business office. However, as in any office, a typist may be required 86 57
to learn specific formats for both letters and reports that are used 100 60
only in that one particular office. 107 61

¶ 4 1.5 SI 5.6 AWL 80% HFW

A person who gets a job as a typist in a scientific organization 13 64
may find that he must learn, in addition to new terms, new formats for 27 67
reports and must become proficient in the use of scientific symbols. 41 70
Most offices have typewriters that are equipped with special keys for 55 73
the most commonly used scientific symbols; but at times a person may 69 75
be required to insert something in ink. A typist in this kind of 82 78
office must be able to accept and to meet these challenges without 96 81
too much extra frustration. 101 82

1′ GWAM | 1 | 2 | 3 | 4 | 5 | 6 | 7 | 8 | 9 | 10 | 11 | 12 | 13 | 14 |
5′ GWAM | 1 | 2 | 3 |

11E   Location of G and ? (Question)

Type G with F finger

Type ? with ; finger

Reach f finger to type **g** without moving the other fingers from their home keys. *Type Line 1, below, for tryout.*

Shift to type **?**. *Space twice after ? at the end of a sentence. Type Line 2, below, for tryout.*

11F   Location Drills for G and ?   each line twice SS; DS after second typing of each line

1	g	gf gf gf go got fog fig rug dug flag right lug bug
2	?	;?; ?; ?; Is he? Is he next? Did Jo eat in town?
3	g ?	Is Peg right? May Doug and I go? May I see Trig?
4	Review	Does Marg have the right books for the new course?
5	Review	Can George take a group of young boys to the camp?

Do not space after ? at end of line

11G   Continuity Practice: PARAGRAPH

Type each ¶ for practice; then type a 2' writing on each one. Compute *gwam* (page 18).

Stroking Cue. Hold your hands directly over the keys with fingers curved. Strike the keys squarely.

All letters are used.

		2' GWAM
¶1	Of all the words that have been used to tell	4
1.0 SI	you how to type, none are so prized as those that	9
4.4 AWL	point out the need of a clear, fixed view. Learn	14
95% HFW	to know how to do what must be done each day.	19
¶2	As you type, work for quick, firm strokes of	23
1.0 SI	all the keys. Do not press them, for that is the	28
4.6 AWL	wrong way to do this job. Do not move your hands	33
95% HFW	up and down or from side to side as you type.	38

2' GWAM | 1 | 2 | 3 | 4 | 5 |

second curve could probably best fit the data from heat fluxes of 1000 to 2000 Btu/Hr/Ft^2. This curve would probably be represented by a straight line with a low slope that lies between .1 and .2 $\times$ 10^{-4}(Ft^2–°F–Hr/Btu/Hr).

TS

Heat Flux
DS

(¶ 10) The main thing that can be gathered from these data and these correlations is that the heat flux has the greatest effect on fouling rate of any single item. Certainly there are numerous other items that must have an effect; however, we do not understand enough about the fouling system to make an exact correlation. These empirical equations do appear to contain the data and represent it reasonably well.

TS

Unknown Factors
DS

(¶ 11) An effect such as solid particle size needs to be considered as a factor, but this is one of several unknown factors at this time. The particle growth from one cooler mixer circuit to the other has to be considered also, but this is unknown too. With time and experience, better correlations will be possible as more data and information are gathered about our system. (¶ 12) The % solids in the reactor system appear to have a significant effect on the fouling rate also. We could certainly say that our fouling can be reduced by increasing the % solids.

---

[1] One run is considered that period of time when the reactor coolers are cleaned until they are fouled and have to be cleaned again.

Job 10: Table for Technical Report

1. Use the same information at the top of this page that you used for the report in Job 9. Type the report title 1″ from the top.
2. Remove your paper from the typewriter and reinsert it sideways with the typed heading to the right.

3. Type the following table. Use exact vertical placement; center horizontally between the left edge of the paper and the ruling beneath the page heading at the right. Leave 3 spaces between the columns; DS the body.

TABLE OF DEVIATION AND CORRELATON INFORMATION

Item	Reactor Cooler			
	1	2	3	4
K$_1$ $\times$ 10^8	.0015	.0012	.0007	.0006
K$_2$ $\times$ 10^8	$-$ 766.6201	$-$ 945.7964	$-$ 418.1755	$-$ 586.1715
K$_3$ $\times$ 10^8	9,835.2	14,459.09	4,570.36	6,462.05
dR/d θ Deviation $\times$ 10^4	.1969	.2216	.0874	.1340
Correlation Coefficient	.8597	.8741	.9302	.3242

Job 11: Title Page for a Technical Report

Prepare a title page for the technical report prepared in Jobs 9 and 10. Arrange the following information appropriately on the title page: title of the report; the report number; date of the report (November 15, 19___); name and address of the company. Staple together, ½″ from the left edge, the report (Job 9), the table (Job 10), and the title page (Job 11).

LESSON 12

12A   Preparatory Practice   each line twice SS; DS after second typing of each line

Alphabet	Roz Groves just now packed my box with five quail.
q m	quite quilt qualm squirm milk mock much most smoke
Fluency (From dictation)	to do, to do the work, to go with, to go with them
Easy	He can do the job, but he should go with them now.

| 1 | 2 | 3 | 4 | 5 | 6 | 7 | 8 | 9 | 10 |

12B   Backspacer

Use the **backspace key (30)** to fill in an omitted letter or to position the carriage.

Electric. Reach with the little finger (right or left depending upon key location); tap and release the key quickly.

Nonelectric. Reach with the appropriate finger; depress the key firmly; release it quickly.

Tryout Drill. Type the first incomplete word as shown in black; backspace and type in the missing letter (shown in color).

Type the remaining words in the same way.

a d mo t b nd thou ht bl nk dr nk cou d f re do e
  n   s   o   g   a   i   l   n

12C   Technique Checkup: STROKING   each line twice SS; DS after second typing of each line

1	1st finger	Gregg Grout may yet try to get a toy gun for them.	Direct strokes
2	2d finger	Dick Dike said he did check the ice on Kech Creek.	Direct strokes
3	3d/4th fingers	Quartz and zinc were prized in this part of Spain.	Finger action
4	1st row	The men may get the bomb from the box in the cave.	Quiet elbows
5	Home row	Hal Hall held a sale. Alf shall add a half glass.	Light key contact
6	3d row	Trent wrote to Troy Trapp. He did not quote Ruth.	Wrists low
7	Double letters	Will Buzz and Gregg take some books to the troops?	Distinct strokes
8	One hand	as we saw, we look on, my grade, you were, see him	Letter response
9	Balanced hand	If they wish, he may make the forms for the disks.	Word response
10	Left shift	Kate Long and Pat Hunt will join them in New York.	Wrists low and quiet
11	Right shift	Fred, Don, Van, and Rod will go to Green Bay soon.	

| 1 | 2 | 3 | 4 | 5 | 6 | 7 | 8 | 9 | 10 |

Correlation Tests

DS

(¶ 5) The fouling rate data collected from the current hydroclone runs and the data of the previous January runs of the four reactor coolers have been correlated to fit the following equations:

(Type each equation on one line; insert the large parentheses in ink. The symbol θ is made by typing the zero (0) and then backspacing and typing a hyphen (-).)

(TS and indent 5 spaces.)

Reactor Coolers 1 – 3:

(TS and indent 10 spaces.)

$$dR/d\,\theta = K_1(Q/A)^2 + K_2(\% \text{ Solids in } \#3 \text{ Reactor}) + K_3$$

Reactor Cooler 4:

(Insert the large parentheses in ink.)

$$dR/d\,\theta = K_1(Q/A)^2 + K_2\left(\frac{Q_4}{Q_1 + Q_2 + Q_3 + Q_4} + 100\right) + K_3$$

(If a definition of one of the following symbols requires more than one line, DS and indent 25 spaces.)

Where:

(DS and indent 10 spaces.)

$dR/d\,\theta$ = Rate of change in fouling resistance in $\left(\dfrac{Ft^2\text{–}°F\text{–}Hr}{Btu}\right)/Hr$

(TS and indent 10 spaces.)

Q/A = Heat flux in individual reactor with units of $Btu/(Hr\text{-}Ft^2)$

Q_{1-4} = Heat transfer rate in Reactor Coolers 1 through 4 in Btu/Hr

Discussion of Correlation Tests

(¶ 6) Heat flux is the greatest single factor affecting the fouling rate with % solids acting as a modifying term. The % solids in the No. 3 Reactor were used to correlate Reactors 1 and 2 since this reactor had more analyses of solids than Reactors 1 and 2, and also because the % solids in Reactors 1 and 2 are directly related to the % solids in Reactor 3. The cooler for Reactor 4 is not generally affected by the solids in Reactor 3, and the best correlation for Reactor 4 was found to be with the heat flux combined with the percentage of the total heat release in Reactor Cooler 4; i.e.,

(Insert Σ with ink in the following equation.)

$Q_4/\Sigma(Q_1 - Q_4) \times 100$. (¶ 7) The correlation coefficients indicate reasonable correlation for Coolers 1 through 3. The deviation indicates the greatest deviation for Coolers 1 and 2.

(Leave 10 spaces between columns; DS body.)

TS

SUMMARY OF DEVIATION AND CORRELATION

TS

Reactor Cooler	$dR/d\,\theta$ Deviation $\times 10^4$	Correlation Coefficient
1	.1969	.8597
2	.2216	.8741
3	.0874	.9302
4	.1340	.3242

(¶ 8) The correlation coefficient for Reactor 4 is quite low and certainly cannot be considered very useful. Generally, the fouling rate on the No. 4 Cooler has been much lower than the fouling rates on Coolers 1 through 3. This is due to the solids' size in No. 4 being small and thereby having a much greater surface area than the solids that are in the Reactors 1 through 3.

TS

Conclusion

TS

(¶ 9) The fouling rates with flux for Coolers 1 through 3 show the fouling rate curves to be from 1000 to 4000 $Btu/(Hr\text{-}Ft^2)$. With this correlation, the fouling rate becomes a negative number at the lower heat fluxes; this is certainly not possible and will not occur. This is due to the form of equation used to represent the greatest mass of data. A

12D Skill Checkup: STROKING

1. Type each sentence as a 1' writing, typing it as many times as you can until time is called.

2. Type Sentences 1, 3, and 5 for 1' each. Compare the *gwam* for the writings.

Stroking Cue. Think and type the easy words as words. Slow down for such words as *are*, *saw*, and *crossed*.

		Words in Line	1' GWAM
1	Is there a job for all of us to do?	7	14
2	Shoes of this size are too hard to find.	8	16
3	John saw the car just as it crossed the line.	9	18
4	If he is to do this work for us, he can do it now.	10	20
5	All of them know they must put first things first.	10	20
6	He knows they can do the work well on the new job.	10	20
7	In fact, a man with push can pass a man with pull.	10	20

1' GWAM | 1 | 2 | 3 | 4 | 5 | 6 | 7 | 8 | 9 | 10 |

12E Typing Checkup: CONTINUITY

1. Type each ¶ once for practice. Type each troublesome word 2 or 3 times.

2. Type a 1' writing on each ¶. Compute *gwam*.

3. Type a 2' writing on each ¶. Compute 2' *gwam* and compare it with 1' *gwam*.

4. Finally, type a 2' writing on both ¶s.

NOTE: Use the first-column *gwam* and the scale to determine the rate for 2' on single ¶s. Use the second 2' column and the scale to determine your 2' rate on both ¶s.

All letters are used.

		2' GWAM	
¶ 1 1.0 SI 4.8 AWL 95% HFW	You will learn to type what you now write by	4	4
	hand. This is one of the prized end goals of the	9	9
	course. This change will not be quick, but it is	14	14
	sure to come. Just give it time, trust, and help.	19	19
¶ 2 1.0 SI 4.6 AWL 95% HFW	The hope is that you can type as fast as you	4	24
	can think. This goal may not be reached, but you	9	29
	should type at least three times the rate you can	14	34
	write by hand. This is a sound claim, not a hoax.	19	39

2' GWAM | 1 | 2 | 3 | 4 | 5 |

As a typist for Temporaries, Inc., you are to report to Louisiana Reactors Research Corporation, 5805 Attaway Street, Shreveport, LA 71108. Your assignment will be to type a technical report.

Job 9: Technical Report

Use leftbound manuscript style.

1. The first page of the report that you will type is shown below in pica type in correct form. Type it as it appears (or as nearly so as possible); then type the remainder of the material in similar form.

2. On all subsequent pages, type the information that appears at the top of the first page. This includes a page number, the report number, and the title underlined as shown. Type each page number on the fourth line from the top. Type the report title 2" from the top of the first page and 1" from the top of subsequent pages. TS after the title.

3. The footnote for this report appears at the end of the problem. Type it on the page on which its reference figure appears.

Page 1
Report No. RC-386

UNIT REACTOR HEAT EXCHANGER FOULING RATE CORRELATION TESTS

Summary

The fouling rates of the reactor coolers can be reduced significantly by adequate control of the heat flux. The statistical analysis of the data collected for this report is inconclusive beyond the high correlation between the heat flux and the fouling rates.

Other items undoubtedly have an effect on the fouling rates; i.e., solid particle size, particle growth from one cooler mixer circuit to another, and the % solids in the reactor system. As soon as more empirical data concerning the fouling system can be generated, better correlations will be possible.

Introduction

This statistical evaluation of the fouling rates of the reactor coolers was undertaken to determine whether the significant factor relating to the fouling of the reactor coolers was due to heat flux.

Procedures

Since the hydroclone solids recycle system was started up on June 15, reactor heat exchanger operation has been at

First page of a technical report

Page 1 | Report No. RC-386

UNIT REACTOR HEAT EXCHANGER FOULING RATE CORRELATION TESTS
TS

Summary
TS

(¶ 1) The fouling rates of the reactor coolers can be reduced significantly by adequate control of the heat flux. The statistical analysis of the data collected for this report is inconclusive beyond the high correlation between the heat flux and the fouling rates. (¶ 2) Other items undoubtedly have an effect on the fouling rates; i.e., solid particle size, particle growth from one cooler mixer circuit to another, and the % solids in the reactor system. As soon as more empirical data concerning the fouling system can be generated, better correlations will be possible.
TS

Introduction
TS

(¶ 3) This statistical evaluation of the fouling rates of the reactor coolers was undertaken to determine whether the significant factor relating to the fouling of the reactor coolers was due to heat flux.
TS

Procedures
TS

(¶ 4) Since the hydroclone solids recycle system was started up on June 15, reactor heat exchanger operation has been at much higher heat fluxes for sustained periods of time than before. Data have been collected from hydroclone Runs 1 through 3 and a portion of Run 4.[1]
TS

Machine Adjustments. 60-space line, with left margin 30 spaces to left of center and right stop at end of scale. SS sentences and drill lines, with DS between groups of repeated lines.
DS ¶ copy. Set a tab stop for 5-space ¶ indention.

Time Schedule. A time schedule for this and following lessons will be a guide for your minimum practice. The minutes for each part is shown within a circle. Vary the schedule if you need more practice on one part, less on another. Retype selected lines as time permits.

LESSON 13

13A Preparatory Practice ⑧ each line 3 times

Alphabet	Having just made six quick points, we simply froze the ball.
x and p	Dixon put six stamps on that box for the next postal pickup.
Fluency	He may pay the firm the usual price for the eight new forms.

```
|   1   |   2   |   3   |   4   |   5   |   6   |   7   |   8   |   9   |   10   |   11   |   12   |
```

13B Technique Practice: SHIFT KEYS ⑧ each line twice; see Shift Lock, in 10B, page 21

Keep the hands in home-key position as you reach the little fingers to the shift keys. Hold the shift key down until you have struck the key for the capital; then release the shift key and return the finger to typing position.

1	Left shift	Otto, Nate, Lyle, and I will go to Yellowstone Park in June.
2		Pat and Mary Young will meet Kate and Nancy Moore in Hawaii.
3	Right shift	Fred left for France, but Wes Quinn went to Spain with Eric.
4		Rodney Zahl won the Grant Ford award at the games in Quebec.
5	Both shifts	Ralph has gone to New York. Marv and Vince will go to Iowa.
6		Kirk Spitz will talk to the West Side Youth Club in January.

```
|   1   |   2   |   3   |   4   |   5   |   6   |   7   |   8   |   9   |   10   |   11   |   12   |
```

13C Technique Practice: RESPONSE PATTERNS ⑭ each line 3 times; Lines 1, 5, and 6 from dictation

Word Response. Some short, frequently used words (like **to**, **and**, **the**, and **work**) are so easy to type they can be typed as words instead of letter by letter. *Think and type the word.*

Letter Response. Many words (like **only**, **state**, **exceed**, and **extra**) are not so easy to type even though they are often used. Such words are typed letter by letter. *Think the letter; type it.*

Combination Response. Most copy is composed of both word and letter sequences that require variable speed: high speed for easy words, lower speed for hard ones *Learn to recognize the difference.*

1	Word	if he is|to go with|she did the work|he may show|to show the
2	response	Dixie may go to the firm to pay for the forms that Kent got.
3	Letter	only states jolly daze plump verve join extra upon great him
4	response	You exceeded the stated rate; only the street guard saw you.
5	Combination	to do my|and the date|it is only|and they care|if he saw the
6		and the joy|for she was|it is you|he did look|to see them go

```
|   1   |   2   |   3   |   4   |   5   |   6   |   7   |   8   |   9   |   10   |   11   |   12   |
```

Type the medical history on plain paper. (See the illustration below.) SS the copy under each heading; DS between sections of the report; block the ¶s.

MEDICAL HISTORY

Name. George M. Fulbright   Age. 51 Sex. M   Date.   8/1/19--

Address. 875 Snow Street, Shreveport, LA 71101

Entrance complaint. Patient admitted for hypertensive workup due to headaches.

Present illness. The patient states that he has had headaches over the right frontal area, oftentimes worse toward the end of

MEDICAL HISTORY

Name. George M. Fulbright Age. 51 Sex. M Date. 8/1/19--

Address. 875 Snow Street, Shreveport, LA 71101

Entrance complaint. Patient admitted for hypertensive workup due to headaches.

Present illness. The patient states that he has had headaches over the right frontal area, oftentimes worse toward the end of the day, but tolerable. The past several months the patient has also had an increased work load and has developed some substernal chest discomfort radiating to the jaw and lasting 3 to 4 minutes; this discomfort occurred in January and May of this year.

Past history. Dengue fever and amebic dysentery during World War II. The patient had his gallbladder removed in 1962; a tonsillectomy and adenoidectomy at age 14.

Systems Review

(Indent ¶s 5 spaces from both margins.)

General. No fever, chills, or weight loss.

Head, eyes, ears, nose, and throat. See present illness. No visual disturbance, tinnitus, hearing loss, hoarseness, epistaxis, or dysphagia.

Neck. No symptoms of thyroid over/under activity, and no history of goiter.

Skin. No rashes or other problems.

Cardiorespiratory. See present illness.

Gastrointestinal. No food intolerance, nausea, vomiting, diarrhea, or abdominal pain.

Genitourinary. There is no hematuria, dysuria, frequency or history of renal stones.

Back. No particular complaints.

Extremities. No arthritic complaints.

Neurologic. No numbness or tingling and no weakness or paralysis.

Family history. The patient's father died at age 90; his mother died at age 65 of pneumonia.

Social history. The patient does not smoke or use alcohol. He averages 4 cups of coffee per day. He sleeps 6 to 7 hours at night.

13D Paragraph Guided Writing ⑳ timed writings as directed

¶ 1. Type two 1' writings on ¶1. Determine *gwam* for the better writing. Use this as the base rate for setting a new goal as directed at the right.

New Goal. Add 4 *gwam* to your base rate. Note the 1' and ½' goals in your copy. Type three 1' writings at the new goal rate. Your instructor will call the ½' guides to pace you.

¶s 1-2. Type a 2' writing without the guides. Begin with ¶ 1 and type as much of ¶ 2 as you can. Determine *gwam*. Disregard errors temporarily.

All letters are used.

		2' GWAM
¶ 1 1.2 SI 5.0 AWL 94% HFW	As you size up the job of typing at a practical speed, keep in mind the thought that a gain results from the right mix of the mind and the hand. Your mind must always remain alert.	5 | 5 11 | 11 17 | 17 18 | 18
¶ 2 1.2 SI 5.0 AWL 96% HFW	Good form is needed also; there is no question on this point. The hands should be held just over the keys. Every stroke must have quality. It must be quick, but it must be firm and sure. Your mind will tell you how to type.	5 | 24 11 | 30 17 | 35 23 | 40

2' GWAM | 1 | 2 | 3 | 4 | 5 | 6 |

LESSON 14

14A Preparatory Practice ⑧ each line 3 times

Alphabet   Milford J. Zorn will give a trophy to the six quickest boys.

3d/4th fingers   The producer is quite puzzled by my apparent lack of talent.

Fluency   Did the clerks study the bids for the work on the city dock?

| 1 | 2 | 3 | 4 | 5 | 6 | 7 | 8 | 9 | 10 | 11 | 12 |

14B Technique Practice: SPACE-BAR CONTROL ⑩ each line at least twice

Operate the space bar with a short, quick, down-and-in thumb stroke in rhythm with typing the letters. Do not pause before or after making the space-bar stroke.

Left-hand ending   the be is its quit send and for year off thing via new basic

Right-hand ending   can when by any they to do will all with each you them thank

Combination endings   The camera is so small that you can slip it into your purse.

Combination endings   I think you can expect the prices to drop if she is elected.

| 1 | 2 | 3 | 4 | 5 | 6 | 7 | 8 | 9 | 10 | 11 | 12 |

In the remaining part of this section, you will be a typist employed by Temporaries, Inc., 499 Albany Road, Shreveport, LA 71105. Your first assignment as a temporary typist is with the Shreveport Medical Clinic, 159 Louisiana Street, Shreveport, LA 71101.

Dr. Andrew T. Mansfield is the director of the clinic and is responsible for all administrative operations, including the office and medical records. The jobs you will type are typical of those you might do in any medical office.

Job 6: Form Letter on Executive-Size Stationery (7¼″ x 10½″) (WB pp. 113-121)

Type the following letter in modified block style with indented ¶s. Type 5 originals, using the addresses at the right below. Use 1″ side margins.

August 1, 19-- (*Letter address*) Dear Dr. _____
SUBJECT: Tenth Annual Neurosurgery Seminar (¶ 1) The Shreveport Neurosurgery Association will hold its Annual Neurosurgery Seminar on Sunday, August 11, 19--, in Room 357 of the Shreveport Plaza Center, 1509 Logan Street. (¶ 2) The seminar will begin with a luncheon at 1:00 p.m. Immediately after the luncheon, Dr. J. LaVell Campbell, one of the nation's leading neurosurgeons, will conduct a three-hour seminar session. We hope to adjourn at 5:30 p.m. (¶ 3) Will you please respond to Dr. William S. Cronk, 159 Louisiana Street, Suite 32, Shreveport, LA 71101, before August 10. Sincerely Andrew T. Mansfield, M.D. SNA President (Words in body: 104)

Dr. Lois W. McMillian
Shreveport Clinic
4402 South Lakeshore Drive
Shreveport, LA 71109

Dr. Franklin S. Petersen
2250 Lee Street
Shreveport, LA 71104

Dr. Carols C. Mangum
133 Madison Park Blvd.
Shreveport, LA 71104

Dr. Russell R. Fernwood
Fernwood Clinic
1505 Southern Avenue
Shreveport, LA 71101

Dr. Andrea S. Thorne
Medical Plaza
Suite 209
8400 Roosevelt Drive
Shreveport, LA 71109

Job 7: Radiology Report

If no form is available, type the radiology report on plain paper. DS between sections of the report; SS the copy under each paragraph heading; block the ¶s. See page 274 for general style.

RADIOLOGY REPORT
Name George M. Fulbright X-Ray No. 387B-867
Address 875 Snow Street, Shreveport LA 71101
Age 51 Sex M In Patient XX Out Patient
Attending Physician Andrew T. Mansfield, M.D.
Date 8/2/19--

Radiologic Consultation

(*Indent ¶s 5 spaces from both margins.*)

(¶ 1) Brain and renal scan. Because the patient was having both brain and renal scan, it was elected to use Technetium 99 DPTA.

He was injected with 5.6 millicuries, and films were taken of the neck vasculature. This proved to be normal in all respects. (¶ 2) Static study of the brain through four views demonstrated equal concentration of the isotope through the entire area. No areas of increase or decrease concentration were detected. (¶ 3) Four hours later the patient was returned to the department where a scan of both kidneys was done. The scan showed normal-appearing kidneys, without evidence of hot or cold spots, and a normal contour. (¶ 4) Impression. The brain scan, both dynamic and static studies, is within normal limits. The renal scan is within normal limits.

14C Technique Practice: STROKING ⑭ each line at least twice

1	Direct	fund any group fourth accept number broil young grinder thus
2	reaches	Irv Munce must bring records of any debts to Herbert Breece.

3	Adjacent	toil mask trap condemn wreck bulk pole wears sad buys cavern
4	keys	Was there a wreck where the fast New Hope traffic builds up?

5	Double	book dinner little abbey occur possible account apply effort
6	letters	Will Buzz and Lee carry the supplies across the street soon?

7	Awkward	exact copy; was pleased; excess debt; extra point; next size
8	reaches	I am pleased to get extra copies of opposing points of view.

| 1 | 2 | 3 | 4 | 5 | 6 | 7 | 8 | 9 | 10 | 11 | 12 |

14D Paragraph Guided Writing ⑱

1. Type 1' writings on each ¶ below as directed in 13D, page 28.

2. Type a 2' writing, beginning with ¶1 and typing as much of ¶2 as you can.

All letters are used.

		2' GWAM
¶1 1.2 SI 4.8 AWL 94% HFW	The major aim of this book is to help you learn how to	6
	type. Its second aim is to help you improve how you write,	12
	for you will not always be able merely to copy all the work	18
	you need to prepare. You will have to compose, also.	23
¶2 1.2 SI 4.8 AWL 94% HFW	As you practice to learn how to type, try to develop a	29
	writing skill, too. The next time you are asked to compose	35
	a paper for class, size up the job and set about writing it	42
	on the machine. It may be quite slow at first, but keep on.	47

2' GWAM | 1 | 2 | 3 | 4 | 5 | 6 |

LESSON 15

15A Preparatory Practice ⑧ each line 3 times

Alphabet	One judge was baffled as five boys quickly mixed the prizes.
Shift lock	We hope to read TO RACE THE WIND and TIME OUT FOR HAPPINESS.
Fluency	Major cities are rich with problems but poor with solutions.

| 1 | 2 | 3 | 4 | 5 | 6 | 7 | 8 | 9 | 10 | 11 | 12 |

FIRST CODICIL TO WILL OF
GEORGE LEROY KING

(¶ 1) KNOW ALL MEN BY THESE PRESENTS, that I, GEORGE LEROY KING, of the City of Dayton, State of Ohio, being of sound and disposing mind and memory, do hereby make, publish and declare this to be my Codicil to my Last Will and Testament of July 29, 19––, as follows: (¶ 2) The Second Item of my Last Will and Testament is hereby changed, and I give and bequeath to SHERMAN G. KING the sum of Twenty-five Thousand Dollars ($25,000), this being in lieu of, and not in addition to, the provision of the Second Item of my Last Will and Testament of July 29, 19––. (¶ 3) In all other respects, with the exception of the effect of this Codicil upon the Second Item of my Last Will and Testament, applying to the residue of my estate, I wish to expressly ratify my Last Will and Testament of July 29, 19––. (¶ 4) In testimony whereof, I, GEORGE LEROY KING, have hereunto subscribed my name at the City of Dayton, Ohio, to this Codicil, and I do declare this to be my Codicil to my Last Will and Testament under my seal at Dayton this the 4th day of April, 19––.

_____
George LeRoy King

(¶ 5) The foregoing Codicil was by GEORGE LEROY KING signed, sealed, published and declared to be his Codicil to his Last Will and Testament; and we, at the same time, and at his request and in his presence and in the presence of one another, have subscribed our names as attesting witnesses to said Codicil. (¶ 6) Dated at the City of Dayton, Ohio, this the 4th day of April, 19––.

_____ residing at _____

_____ residing at _____

_____ residing at _____

POWER OF ATTORNEY

(¶ 1) I, JOHN HAROLD NELSON, of 271 Timberline Drive, City of Dayton, County of Montgomery, State of Ohio, hereby constitute, make, and appoint my wife, SANDRA RUTH NELSON, of the above address, City of Dayton, County of Montgomery, State of Ohio, my true and lawful attorney in fact, for me, on my behalf, and in my name, place, and stead to take possession of, manage, encumber, exchange, lease, or sell any and all real property now held by me separately, severally, or jointly, with full power to sell and convey such property, or any interest therein, without reservation of any right therein; and such rights, powers, and authority shall remain in full force and effect until December 31, 19––. (¶ 2) Dated July 28, 19––.

_____
John Harold Nelson

STATE OF OHIO   )
                  : ss.
County of Montgomery)

(¶ 3) Before me, a Notary Public in and for the County and State aforesaid, personally appeared the above-named person and acknowledged the signing of the foregoing instrument to be his voluntary act and deed for the uses and purposes therein stated. (¶ 4) In testimony whereof, I have hereunto subscribed my name at Dayton, Ohio, this 29th day of July, 19––.

_____
Notary Public

My commission expires on June 30, 19––.

15B Technique Practice: TABULATOR ⑦

Clear all tabulator stops; set a tab stop 5 spaces, another 10 spaces, and still another 15 spaces to the right of the left margin.

Begin the first line of the drill at the left margin. Use the tab key or bar to type the remaining lines. Tab, release, and type quickly.

Margin   Typing beats writing with a pen, so learn how to type right.

Indent 5 ——*Tab once*——→ No typewriter is made that can do your writing for you.

Indent 10 ——*Tab twice*——→ We all must learn to say just what we want to say.

Indent 15 ——*Tab three times*——→ Typing skill is a highly prized writing tool.

15C Technique Practice: STROKING ⑩ each line twice; Line 1 from dictation

1 Fluency   it is | if it is | to do the | and did it | if they go | if they do go

2 Long words practice condition choice luxury visit country respect happy

3 un   sun sunk bun bunt burn runs lung hunt rung trunk young under

4 One hand   As we agreed, John erected extra seats. Jim saw only a few.

5 Balanced
  hand   Did the girls do the work? The men may find the right firm.

6 Combination He based his case on the data he got from the tax statement.

15D Paragraph Guided Writing ⑱

1. Type 1' writings on each ¶ below as directed in 13D, page 28.

2. Type a 3' writing, beginning with ¶1 and typing as much of ¶2 as you can.

All letters are used.

	3' GWAM

¶1
1.2 SI
5.0 AWL
96% HFW

      Believe it or not, some things in life are still free,   4 | 35

the respect of close friends, the luxury of a day or two in 8 | 39

the quiet country, or the practice of free choice. Perhaps 12 | 43

you now know how much value these things do add to a life. 16 | 47

¶2
1.2 SI
5.0 AWL
96% HFW

      You can also extend a helping hand or a kind word to a 19 | 50

fellow who needs it, enjoy a clear breeze, or visit with an 23 | 54

old friend. These things, and many more, cost nothing. As 27 | 58

you may know, a happy condition comes from a state of mind. 31 | 62

3' GWAM | 1 | 2 | 3 | 4 |

Job 2: Will *(WB pp. 103–105)*

The tenth paragraph may be either single- or double-spaced for acceptable paging.

LAST WILL AND TESTAMENT OF GEORGE LEROY KING

(¶ 1) I, GEORGE LEROY KING, a married man, residing in the City of Dayton, State of Ohio, do make, publish and declare this instrument to be my Last Will and Testament, hereby revoking and canceling all former Wills and Codicils by me at any time made. (¶ 2) FIRST: I direct that all of my just debts, including the expenses of my last illness and funeral, shall be paid out of my estate by my executrix hereinafter named. (¶ 3) SECOND: I give and bequeath my complete coin collection and the sum of Ten Thousand Dollars ($10,000) to my son, SHERMAN G. KING, if living at the time of my death, otherwise to his wife and children equally. (¶ 4) THIRD: I give and bequeath my professional library and the sum of Ten Thousand Dollars ($10,000) to my daughter, GEORGIA M. WRIGHT, if living at the time of my death, otherwise to her husband and children equally. (¶ 5) FOURTH: All articles of household furniture and furnishings, books, pictures, silverware, my automobiles, all of my clothing and jewelry, not otherwise disposed of, all similar articles of household use and wearing apparel, which I may own at the time of my death, and the residue of my estate, I give and bequeath to my wife, BERNICE H. KING, as her absolute property. (¶ 6) FIFTH: I give and devise my real estate situated in the City of Dayton, State of Ohio, which is known as my home,

to my wife, her heirs and assigns forever. (¶ 7) SIXTH: I direct my executrix to pay all estate and inheritance taxes, and succession duties assessed by the United States, any state thereof, or any foreign government, against my estate predicated upon my death as the taxable event. (¶ 8) SEVENTH: I hereby nominate, constitute, and appoint BERNICE H. KING, as executrix of my Last Will and Testament. (¶ 9) IN WITNESS WHEREOF, I have hereunto subscribed my hand and seal to this my Last Will and Testament, at the City of Dayton, State of Ohio, this 29th day of July, 19--.

_____
George LeRoy King

(¶ 10) We, the undersigned, do hereby certify that GEORGE LEROY KING, the above-named testator, on the day and year above written, signed the foregoing instrument in our presence, and published and declared the same to be his Last Will and Testament, and we, at the same time, at his request, in his presence, and in the presence of one another, have hereunto set our hands as subscribing witnesses; and we further certify that at such time he was of sound and disposing mind and memory.

_____ residing at _____

_____ residing at _____

_____ residing at _____

Job 3: Legal Backs

Prepare a legal back for each of the first two jobs in this section. Since the legal cap in the workbook that you are using is 8½″ x 11″, fold the paper in thirds and type the endorsement on the middle third.

15E Individual Practice ⑦

1. Type each line once. Place a check mark before each line that seemed difficult.

2. Type 2 or more times each line that you checked as difficult.

1 p x   mix pack toxic group fixed price wrap place coax plate sixth

2 q m   quit most acquit room quick game liquid warm qualm may quake

3 z y   lazy graze fry seize yet freeze lonely azure your zone money

4 n t   count ton nothing string thing went sent lent slant not lint

5 b u   but buy bunch number lumber jumble rumble rubber built blunt

6 v ?   Can Vince vote? Can Merv go? Did Dave move? Did Vi drive?

LESSON 16

16A Preparatory Practice ⑧ each line 3 times

Alphabet   Pride in his work quickly gave Jim Fitz his next big chance.

q and m   Mark Quinn is not quite sure he can take my next major quiz.

Fluency   A light touch is the right touch to use to build good skill.
           | 1 | 2 | 3 | 4 | 5 | 6 | 7 | 8 | 9 | 10 | 11 | 12 |

16B Skill Checkup: STROKING ⑫

Type a 1′ writing on each sentence, typing it as many times as you can until time is called. Determine *gwam*.

Stroking Cue. Keep your eyes on the copy. Make low, quick reach-strokes. Keep the hands and arms quiet.

		Words in Line
1	Can men differ, yet have the same goals?	8
2	Many young people are looking for new ideals.	9
3	Some are trying to put these ideals into practice.	10
4	The rules under which men have lived are being changed.	11
5	In sum, this whole problem is being attacked on many fronts.	12
6	We must expand our horizons and work for progressive change.	12
7	Any change for the sake of joining the crowd is unjustified.	12

| 1 | 2 | 3 | 4 | 5 | 6 | 7 | 8 | 9 | 10 | 11 | 12 |

Production Typing Information: PREPARING A BACK FOR THE ENDORSEMENT

1. Fold down the top 1″. This fold will later be the binding for the legal document.

2. Bring the bottom edge of the sheet even with the creased top edge and crease neatly.

3. Bring the folded bottom edge to the top and crease.

The legal back has now been folded into 4 equal parts, not counting the 1″ binding fold.

4. Type the endorsement on the back of the sheet, confined within the second fold from the top. Place the sheet in the typewriter with the top 2 folds exposed and the 1″ binding fold at the left.

In the first part of this section you will be a typist for an attorney—Roland W. Pond, 323 Dearborn Avenue, Dayton, OH 45417. The jobs you will type are typical of those you might do in any attorney's office.

The workbook provides 8½″ x 11″ legal cap rather than 13″ or 14″ paper; a second sheet is provided for long jobs. Use plain paper for all legal backs. On plain paper prepare 1 cc of each legal document.

Job 1: Warranty Deed *(WB p. 101)*

WARRANTY DEED

(¶ 1) RALPH G. RICHARDS, being married, of 352 Ace Place, City of Dayton, County of Montgomery, State of Ohio, for valuable consideration paid, grants, with general warranty covenants, to HAROLD P. COUNTS, whose tax-mailing address is 605 Ivy Court, City of Akron, County of Summit, State of Ohio, the following described real property in the County of Montgomery, State of Ohio: *(Indent 10 spaces from both margins; SS.)*

Lot 392 of Tract 3845, as per map recorded in Book 1077, at pages 231-235 of Maps, in the records of the County Recorder of said County.

(¶ 2) PRIOR instrument reference: Volume 34, page 186, June 1, 1965. THELMA ANDERSEN RICHARDS, the wife of the grantor, releases all rights of dower therein. (¶ 3) WITNESS my hand this 23d day of July, 19--.

TS

_____ (L.S.)
Ralph G. Richards
DS

STATE OF OHIO)
: SS.
County of Montgomery)

(¶ 4) Before me, a Notary Public in and for the County and State aforesaid, personally appeared the above-named person and acknowledged the signing of the foregoing instrument to be his voluntary act and deed for the uses and purposes therein mentioned. (¶ 5) In testimony whereof,

I have hereunto subscribed my name at Dayton, Ohio, this 26th day of July, 19--.

TS

Notary Public
DS

My commission expires on June 30, 19--.

Approximate 2″ top margin	
Heading centered between ruled lines	WARRANTY DEED
10 space ¶ indention; DS except quoted copy and land descriptions; all typing within marginal rules; names in body of instrument in all caps	CAROLYN ANNE WILSON, being single, of 2509 Rembrandt Boulevard, City of Dayton, County of Montgomery, State of Ohio, for valuable consideration paid, grants, with general warranty covenants, to SUSAN LYNNE COX, whose tax-mailing address is 1703 Coventry Road, City of Dayton, County of Montgomery, State of Ohio, the following described real property in the County of Montgomery, State of Ohio:
Land description	Lot 188 of Tract 3192, as per map recorded in Book 965, at pages 56-57 of Maps, in the records of the County Recorder of said County.
	PRIOR instrument reference: Volume 32, page 99.
	WITNESS my hand this 7th day of May, 19--.
	_____ (L.S.) Carolyn Anne Wilson
Acknowledgment SS	STATE OF OHIO) : ss. County of Montgomery)
	Before me, a Notary Public in and for the County and State aforesaid, personally appeared the above-named person and acknowledged the signing of the foregoing instrument to be her voluntary act and deed for the uses and purposes therein mentioned.
	In testimony whereof, I have hereunto subscribed my name at Dayton, Ohio, this 26th day of July, 19--.
	_____ Notary Public
	My commission expires on June 30, 19--.
One-page instrument does not need a page number	

Warranty deed

16C Proofreading [5] Type the ¶ once, making needed corrections as you type.

There are two ways to proofread: (1) by comparing and (2) by verifying.

Comparing. A typist checks his own work by a careful reading of his copy and by checking it against the original when spelling of words or meaning is uncertain or when figures or proper names are encountered.

Verifying (Recommended for Statistical Copy, Stencils, and Spirit Masters). One person reads from the original while another (preferably not the typist) reads the new copy. Tricky words are spelled; punctuation marks are indicated.

Common errors are circled in the sample shown at the right.

How wellyou write mean just how deft ly you
put words together say what your want to say. It
does now mean ho well you can use a epn. If you
you learn to type well. you can imprve the clarity
as will as if the manner of you writing.

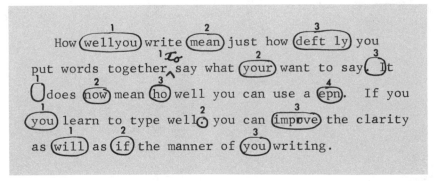

Line 1. (1) No space, (2) missing letter, (3) faulty spacing
Line 2. (1) Omitted word, (2) added letter, (3) incorrect spacing
Line 3. (1) Uneven left margin, (2) misstroke, (3) omitted letter, (4) transposition
Line 4. (1) Added word, (2) period for comma, (3) strikeover
Line 5. (1) Changed word, (2) added word, (3) changed word

16D Growth Index [18] three 3′ writings

Type three 3′ writings; determine *gwam* and number of errors on each one.

Proofread the first two writings by comparing. Proofread the third writing by *verifying*.

All letters are used.

		3′ GWAM	
¶ 1 1.2 SI 5.0 AWL 96% HFW	When you write something, read it. Ask yourself these	4	35
	questions. Does this have life, does it move, does it take	8	39
	you along with it? Or is it a haze of sorry old words that	12	43
	really fail to evoke any drive in you? Does it turn you on?	16	47
¶ 2 1.2 SI 5.0 AWL 96% HFW	Remember this when writing. Just talk to a reader the	19	51
	way you would if you could visit with him in your own home.	23	55
	Try it; then see if your style is not more natural. Do not	27	59
	expect to hold your reader if your style is cold and stale.	31	63

3′ GWAM | 1 | 2 | 3 | 4 |

16E Individual Practice [7] Type as directed for 15E, page 31.

1 p x Mexico package relax piece wrapped placed hoax mixture parts
2 q m quiet must acquaint rumor quickly request germ quorum mosque
3 z y hazards graze fly siezed hazy lonely zone youth mainly dizzy
4 n t fountain tin notice being dent grant country untold not tent
5 b u bushel shrubs rubbish hub build burn bundle tube jumped burr
6 v ? Vince Vogt gave verbal orders? Have David and Ervin shaved?

Production Typing Information: LEGAL DOCUMENTS

Paper. Printed forms are available for many legal instruments. If not, use legal paper (8½″ x 13″ or 14″) with ruled left and right margins.

Titles on Legal Forms. Center the title in all capital letters between the marginal rulings.

Margins and Spacing. On legal paper, type within the ruled lines; leave a space or two between the lines and the typing. On plain paper, set the margin stops for a 1½″ left margin and a ½″ right margin. Indent paragraphs 10 spaces; double-space the copy except land descriptions and quoted matter, which should be single-spaced and indented 10 spaces from both margins.

On each page, leave a top margin of about 2″ (12 blank lines); on a full page, a bottom margin of about 1″.

Page Numbers. The first page is usually not numbered, except on a will. Numbers of subsequent pages are centered between the margins 3 blank lines from the bottom of the page. Type a hyphen before and another after the page number.

Signature Lines. The maker or makers of an instrument sign at the right of the page. Witnesses, if any, sign at the left. Signature lines are about 3″ long, and 2 or 3 spaces are left between them.

At least 2 lines of typing must appear on the page that contains the signature of the maker and those of the witnesses.

Erasing. Anything as important as numbers, names, or sums of money should not be erased unless (1) all parties concerned initial each erasure or (2) the double writing of numbers in both figures and words provides positive identification of the correct amount (in this case probably no legal question would be raised if one digit or letter were erased).

Proofreading. The verifying method should be used to proofread all legal documents.

Copies. Photocopies are used in lieu of carbon copies in many law offices; therefore, the preparation of carbon copies may be reduced or eliminated when typing some legal documents.

Latin Abbreviations. When the instrument is "under seal," the signature to the instrument is followed by "L.S.," which refers to the Latin phrase *locus sigilli*. The abbreviation "ss." is used for the Latin word *scilicet*, which means "to wit."

Legal Backs and Endorsements. A legal document may be bound in a cover (a *legal back*) that is somewhat heavier and larger than the sheets on which the document is typed. On it is sometimes typed information (the *endorsement*) giving the name of the paper and the names of the parties thereto. You will prepare legal backs for some problems in this section.

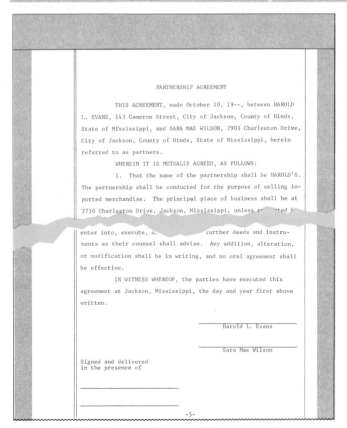

Partial pages of partnership agreement

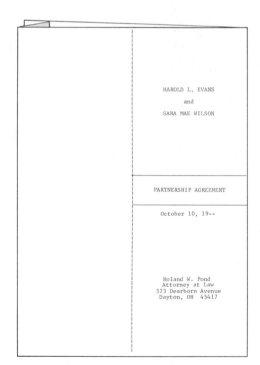

Endorsement on legal back

Machine Adjustments. *Use a 60-space line.* Set the left margin stop at center — 30. Move the right margin stop to the extreme right. SS sentence drills, with DS between repeated lines. DS and indent paragraphs 5 spaces.

In this section you will type figures and some new punctuation marks. You will also build your basic skills to higher levels. The paragraph copy is rated *easy*.

LESSON 17

17A Preparatory Practice (8) each line twice; in Line 3, do not type the dividers

Alphabet	Did Evelyn Wellington quiz Peter Jackson about his tax form?
br	brows bright brush broil braid brave brace broom break brisk
Combination resp.	with you|for him|did look|and regard|if it sets|to read well
Fluency	When Rod paid the girls, did he make them sign the new form?

| 1 | 2 | 3 | 4 | 5 | 6 | 7 | 8 | 9 | 10 | 11 | 12 |

17B Location of 5, 8, and 1 (3)

 Type 5 with F finger

Type 8 with K finger

1. Locate the new key on the keyboard chart.
2. Find the key on your typewriter keyboard.
3. Study the reach illustration for the new key.
4. Type the drill below for that key.

If your typewriter has a special key for figure 1, reach up to it with the left fourth (little) finger. If your typewriter does not have a special key for figure 1, use the small letter l to type 1.

Reach Technique. Move the controlling finger (not the hand) up to type figures in the top row.

17C Location Drills for 5, 8, and 1 (12) Lines 1, 2, and either 3 or 4 twice for tryout; then each line twice

1	5	f f5f 5f 5f 5f 55 555 55 floors, 555 feet, 5 gallons, 5 rods
2	8	k k3k 8k 8k 8k 88 888 88 knots, 888 kits, 8 inches, 88 and 8
3	Figure 1	a a1a a1 a1 a1 11 111 11 aides, 111 attacks, 1 and 11 quarts
4	Letter l as 1	l ll .l l. .ll l.l. My ll men worked from May l to June ll.
5	Review	Is it Channel 5, 8, or 11? Was the score 5 to 8, or 8 to 5?
6	Review	Three of the 158 men are absent; the other 155 arrived at 5.

| 1 | 2 | 3 | 4 | 5 | 6 | 7 | 8 | 9 | 10 | 11 | 12 |

LESSONS 134-139

Lessons 134, 136, 138

Use the following daily lesson plan for Lessons 134, 136, and 138. Retain all jobs until you have completed Lesson 139.

Preparatory Practice (5′). Type 134A, below, as directed.

Production Typing (45′). Type the jobs on pages 269-277. Follow the directions for each job; where specific directions are not given, use your own good judgment. Proofread carefully; correct all errors.

Lessons 135, 137, 139

Use the following daily lesson plan for Lessons 135, 137, and 139. Retain all jobs until you have completed Lesson 139.

Preparatory Practice (5′). Type 134B, below, as directed.

Technique Mastery (5′). Type 134C, below, as directed.

Production Typing (40′). Continue typing the jobs on pages 269-277. Follow the same general directions given for Lessons 134, 136, and 138.

134A Preparatory Practice (5) each line at least 3 times

Alphabet	Elizabeth just accepted the quick excuse which Ivy made for Genevieve.
Figure/symbol	Please pay bill #485012 for $1,671.98, but first add $3\frac{1}{2}\%$ to the total.
Left hand	After the wet December weather, Eve's crabgrass grew excessively fast.
Fluency	We should take pride in our work if we have sincerely done our utmost.
	| 1 | 2 | 3 | 4 | 5 | 6 | 7 | 8 | 9 | 10 | 11 | 12 | 13 | 14 |

134B Preparatory Practice (5) each line at least 3 times

Alphabet	The public was amazed to view the keen dexterity of the quick juggler.
Figure/symbol	Is the new rate on our #8964 note for $5,300 (dated May 12) to be $7\frac{1}{4}\%$?
Double letters	A bookkeeper will tell the association to settle all accounts in full.
Fluency	The firm must show signs of vigor if it is to make a profit this year.
	| 1 | 2 | 3 | 4 | 5 | 6 | 7 | 8 | 9 | 10 | 11 | 12 | 13 | 14 |

134C Technique Mastery (5) each line at least twice without error

Direct reaches	I am unable to make any progress on the service contract for my truck.
One hand	In Kim's opinion, the wages in our trade are in excess of the average.
3d, 4th fingers	We saw at least six fellows who were watching our opening performance.
Long words	Please offer your suggestions concerning bibliographic materials used.
Balanced hand	This is the work the chairman told them to do, and they can do it now.
	| 1 | 2 | 3 | 4 | 5 | 6 | 7 | 8 | 9 | 10 | 11 | 12 | 13 | 14 |

17D **Technique Practice:** STROKING (10) each line twice

Technique Cue. Reach with your fingers. Reach to the top row without moving your hand, twisting your elbow, or arching your wrist.

Words

1   Tour 851 to the Orient is set to depart on August 15, 8 a.m.   12

2   *Don arrived on Flight 881; he leaves on Flight 151 at 5 p.m.*   12

3   Send Model 1851 in pecan finish.   I am returning Model 5588.   12

4   *They paid that bill with check No. 88551, dated November 18.*   12

5   The assignment covers pages 8 through 15 and 88 through 151.   12

6   *These 18 men picked 855 crates of tomatoes in just 15 hours.*   12

17E **Speed/Control Building** (17) one 1' writing on each ¶ for speed; repeat for control
one 3' writing on all ¶s for speed; repeat for control

Exploration (Speed) Level of Practice. Use the *exploration level* when the purpose of practice is to reach out into new speed areas.

Control Level of Practice. When the purpose of practice is to type with ease and control, drop down in rate and type on the *control level*.

All letters are used.

		3' GWAM
¶ 1 1.3 SI 5.2 AWL 90% HFW	Without question this is an age of numbers. Ask someone his age, and you receive a number. A number also marks a tax return, a class card, or a highway route.	4 | 44 8 | 48 11 | 51
¶ 2 1.3 SI 5.2 AWL 90% HFW	It is thus important that you master the top row on your machine. Whether you work as a typist or just type your own papers, you will prize highly your skill in typing numbers. Begin to build it now.	14 | 54 19 | 59 23 | 63 24 | 64
¶ 3 1.3 SI 5.2 AWL 90% HFW	Numbers are assigned to a good many other things, such as your home address, the time of day, or ZIP Code. When you go to a food store, a number will determine your turn at the counter. We may one day exchange numbers for personal names.	28 | 68 32 | 72 36 | 76 40 | 80

3' GWAM | 1 | 2 | 3 | 4 |

133D Statistical Timed Writing ⑩ two 3' writings; record GWAM of the better writing

All letters and figures are used.

		GWAM	
		1'	3'

¶ 1
1.6 SI
5.8 AWL
75% HFW

In 1973, the total revenue of the clinic was $2,486,000; this was an — 14 | 5 | 50
increase of nearly 35% over the previous year's revenue of $1,845,000. — 28 | 9 | 55
Quite a substantial percentage of this tremendous increase was due to — 42 | 14 | 59
the expansion of the clinic and to the hiring of several more doctors. — 56 | 19 | 64
The actual increase in revenue per physician was just 12%. — 68 | 23 | 68

¶ 2
1.6 SI
5.8 AWL
75% HFW

The 1974 financial picture of the clinic showed that a sizable in- — 13 | 27 | 72
crease in revenues was the direct result of taking 2,576 new patients. — 28 | 32 | 77
Income for 1974 was $3,060,000 (a 23% increase over 1973 income), al- — 41 | 36 | 82
though the capacity of the physicians and building was calculated to — 55 | 41 | 86
have only an 82% use factor at the close of the 1974 fiscal year. — 68 | 45 | 91

1' GWAM | 1 | 2 | 3 | 4 | 5 | 6 | 7 | 8 | 9 | 10 | 11 | 12 | 13 | 14 |
3' GWAM | 1 | 2 | 3 | 4 | 5 |

133E Speed Building ⑮ two 5' writings; record GWAM of the better writing

All letters are used.

		GWAM	
		1'	5'

¶ 1
1.6 SI
5.8 AWL
75% HFW

Seventy years ago, we were living in a horse-and-buggy era; the — 13 | 3 | 48
conveniences of modern society were undeveloped. People who recall — 26 | 5 | 51
those bygone days of uncertain, hazardous safaris over muddy roads may — 40 | 8 | 54
question whether they were really alive at all. It is likely safe to — 54 | 11 | 56
believe that few are hankering to trade their present situation for a — 68 | 14 | 59
return to the good old days. — 74 | 15 | 60

¶ 2
1.6 SI
5.8 AWL
75% HFW

Today, we are able to travel on our superhighways in luxury and ease — 14 | 18 | 63
or jet through the air at supersonic speeds. We can use fewer hours to — 28 | 20 | 66
cross the continent than it formerly took for a shopping tour. Our — 42 | 23 | 69
accomplishments in travel, as well as in any of a dozen other areas we — 56 | 26 | 72
might mention, have become possible largely through increasing require- — 70 | 29 | 74
ments of the consumers. — 75 | 30 | 75

¶ 3
1.6 SI
5.8 AWL
75% HFW

At one time, manufacturers produced goods with hardly any attempt — 13 | 32 | 78
to find out what the public really wanted to buy. This rather foolish — 27 | 35 | 81
procedure is surely no longer the case. A producer in today's economy — 42 | 38 | 84
who scorns the needs and desires of the consumer does so at great risk. — 56 | 41 | 87
To be successful in a highly competitive market, a producer must serve — 70 | 44 | 89
the whims and caprices of the potential buyer. — 79 | 46 | 91

1' GWAM | 1 | 2 | 3 | 4 | 5 | 6 | 7 | 8 | 9 | 10 | 11 | 12 | 13 | 14 |
5' GWAM | 1 | 2 | 3 |

LESSON 18

18A Preparatory Practice ⑧ each line twice

Alphabet	Wilbur Jamieson packed the very large box of quartz mineral.
1 5 8	The numbers of the lockers in question are 15, 58, and 1581.
Combination resp.	on the|with my|this date|for you|go to him|and they saw only
Fluency	Would he like to know how the men who work for us save time?

| 1 | 2 | 3 | 4 | 5 | 6 | 7 | 8 | 9 | 10 | 11 | 12 |

18B Location of 2, 0, and : (Colon) ③

Type 2 with S finger

Type 0 with ; finger

Colon. Type the : (colon) by shifting the ;. Do not space before or after the colon to separate hours and minutes in stating time; space twice after the colon in other uses.

18C Location Drills for 2, 0, and : ⑫ Lines 1, 2, and 3 once for tryout; then each line twice

1	2	s s2s 2s 2s 2s 22 222 22 sets, 222 shots, 22 stops 222 sacks
2	0	; ;0; 0; 0; 0; 00 000 10 poles, 50 lines, 80 loads, 505 oars
3	:	; ;:; :; :; :; 8:01 1:15 5:10 Call at 5:15; arrive at 8:10.
4	Review	Get there by 8:00 or 8:05; the opera begins at 8:15 or 8:20.
5	Review	One of these models will be in stock: 28, 202, 505, or 805.

18D Technique Practice: STROKING ⑩ each line twice

Words

1		Whether you are 20 or 50, each workday there begins at 8:15.	12
2		*Her flight, No. 258, lands at 10 p.m. on Thursday, March 15.*	12
3		You ordered No. 508, but you may wish to change to No. 2015.	12
4	Space twice after colon	*I suggest you try one of these models: 2001, 5002, or 8112.*	12
5		If you arrive by 8:15 a.m., we can set the meeting for 8:20.	12

| 1 | 2 | 3 | 4 | 5 | 6 | 7 | 8 | 9 | 10 | 11 | 12 |

SECTION 25 Typing in a Professional Office

LESSONS 133-140

Section 25 provides experience in typing jobs normally done in legal, medical, and scientific offices.

Drill Copy. SS; 70-space line

¶ Copy. DS; 70-space line; 5-space ¶s; full sheets

Production Typing. Follow the directions given for each job.

Supplies Needed. Full sheets; carbon paper; second sheets; envelopes, and legal-size ruled paper

LESSON 133

133A Preparatory Practice [5] each line at least 3 times

Alphabet	Jack and Mary did not question Vickie Wolfe about her puzzling excuse.
Figure/symbol	On January 9, 32% (480) selected Plan 25; 68% (1020) selected Plan 17.
Long reaches	My uncle undoubtedly hunted for hundreds of unknown uniforms annually.
Fluency	If our work is worth doing, it is worth doing as well as we can do it.
	| 1 | 2 | 3 | 4 | 5 | 6 | 7 | 8 | 9 | 10 | 11 | 12 | 13 | 14 |

133B Skill-Comparison Typing [10] two 1′ writings on each sentence in 133A; record GWAM of the better writing

133C Paragraph Guided Writing [10] the superior dots and figures show the 2′ count

1. Type a 2′ writing on the *control level* to establish your base rate.
2. Choose a rate 4 to 8 words above this base rate.
3. Type three 2′ writings, trying to reach the higher rate on each writing while maintaining the *control level*. The half minutes will be called.

1.7 SI
6.0 AWL
70% HFW

1′ GWAM

Would you enjoy being a legal secretary for a lawyer? Would you 13
like managing the work and assuming responsibilities that such a job 27
demands, where basic prerequisites are the ability to type and take dic- 41
tation accurately? Because of the nature of the business transacted in 56
most legal firms, a person must use extra caution in examining all work. 70
It must be accurate––absolutely accurate––to the last period. The duties 85
of such a secretarial job differ, depending on the size of the firm and 100
the varieties of legal affairs handled. Without exception, though, such 114
work is fascinating and challenging to one who enjoys dealing with the 128
unusual, participating behind the scenes for a lawyer who goes to court. 143

| 1 | 2 | 3 | 4 | 5 | 6 | 7 | 8 | 9 | 10 | 11 | 12 | 13 | 14 |

18E Skill-Transfer Typing ⑰

Type two 1' writings on each ¶. Compare *gwam* on the two ¶s. Type two more 1' writings on the ¶ with the lower *gwam*.

Finally, type two 3' writings on both ¶s. Determine *gwam*. Compare your better 3' *gwam* with the best 1' *gwam* on each of the two ¶s.

All letters are used.

		1'	3'	
			GWAM	
¶ 1	We are told that people in business fall into three	10	3	38
1.3 SI	large classes. In the first class is the worker who has to	22	7	42
5.2 AWL	be told in detail everything to be done. This person is a	34	11	46
90% HFW	heavy burden to the company. Basic skills and a mind that	46	15	50
	thinks for itself are lacking.	52	17	52
¶ 2	The worker in the next class is little better. He does	11	21	56
1.3 SI	just what is required, then quits and fiddles. This person	23	25	60
5.2 AWL	has some ability, but he lacks a sincere interest in what he	35	29	64
90% HFW	is doing. An interested man can size up a job, decide what	47	33	68
	must be done, and do it.	52	35	69

1' GWAM | 1 | 2 | 3 | 4 | 5 | 6 | 7 | 8 | 9 | 10 | 11 | 12 |
3' GWAM | 1 | 2 | 3 | 4 |

LESSON 19

19A Preparatory Practice ⑧ each line twice

Alphabet	Mary very quickly mixed a big jar of soap for the new prize.
0 :	On June 10, Flight 20 left at 2:20 with 10 men and 20 women.
Combination response	and the case|for they saw|to do my|if they join|it is on the

| 1 | 2 | 3 | 4 | 5 | 6 | 7 | 8 | 9 | 10 | 11 | 12 |

19B Technique Practice: STROKING ⑩ each line twice

1	Direct	bright muscle verb exceed serve debt gravy hurry brush nurse
2	reaches	Grace Hunter made delectable braised celery and great gravy.

3	Adjacent	report enter mast sulk people respond balk column opens true
4	keys	We said that poised talk has triumphed over violent actions.

5	Double	account appears sudden merry common sunny eggs supply buffet
6	letters	Ann Hobbs will collect puzzles, books, buttons, and glasses.

7	Figures	Read: Unit 5, 8 pages; Unit 8, 20 pages; Unit 10, 12 pages.
8		What is the sum of 5 and 55 and 585 and 188 and 881 and 558?

Job 1: Leftbound Manuscript with Carbon Copy

Words

AUTOMATION IN THE OFFICE   5

Alice Winterton   8

(¶ 1) Automation in the office attempts to   16
eliminate the handling and writing of records   25
countless times in order to get needed infor-   34
mation or to make reports available. Automa-   42
tion cuts down or eliminates manual duplica-   51
tion. Procedures for doing this vary from   60
system to system. (¶ 2) "Automatic" office   67
systems are never wholly automatic. They   76
depend upon humans. Someone must gather   84
data, prepare them for use in a form the ma-   93
chinery can handle, and interpret the results.   102
Without intelligent directions, even the most   111
sophisticated equipment loses its utility. (¶ 3)   120
Codes and input media. Some equipment––   132
the Optical Character Reader, for example––   141
can "read" printed information. Usually, how-   150
ever, special codes are used. Such codes are   159
made a part of a medium upon which the   167
machine feeds. Examples of such media are   176
punched cards and tape, mark-sensed cards,   184
magnetic tape, and magnetic ink characters.   193
(¶ 4) Punched cards and tape. Machines can   205
interpret and process data that have been   214
punched as holes in cards and tape. The   222
punched card is so widely used for this pur-   230
pose that it is often referred to as the "work-   240
horse of automation." Once data have been   248

punched into cards, the machines can sort,   257
classify, calculate, and print the data. Paper   266
tape is a continuous medium, whereas punched   275
cards are of fixed length. The tapes are usu-   284
ally produced simultaneously with the comple-   293
tion of a document on a typewriter, billing   302
machine, calculator, or other piece of equip-   311
ment. (¶ 5) Mark-sensed cards. Some ma-   321
chines can read and process data marked on   330
cards with a pencil. This method makes it   338
possible to record data on cards in the plant   347
or field, thus eliminating the rewriting of these   357
records in the office. (¶ 6) Magnetic tape.   368
Information recorded on tapes similar to those   377
used in ordinary tape recorders can be read   385
and processed by certain electronic data pro-   394
cessing equipment. (¶ 7) Magnetic ink char-   405
acters. Some of the machines that can process   416
printed data require that information be   424
printed in distinctive style in magnetic ink.   433
Such a procedure is often used by banks for   442
handling checks and deposits. (¶ 8) Data   449
processing by automation begins with the in-   458
formation in plain language; it ends in a   466
report or business paper in plain language.   475
Between these two steps, however, the data   484
must often be converted to some code that   492
can be understood by data processing equip-   500
ment used.   502

Job 2: Purchase Order (WB p. 99)

1 cc; follow the form on page 262.

Words

To: Wilmington Electronics, Inc., 1745 Limestone Road, Wilmington, DE   13
19804; **Order No.:** 94326; **Date:** August 17, 19––; **Terms:** 2/10, n/30; **Ship**   21
Via: Interstate Transport Co.   26

Quantity	Catalog No.	Description	Price	Total	
13 doz.	04–025	Relays FBV153B91/101	19.86	258.18	36
9 doz.	04–046	Mica condensers 10000PF1KV	6.13	55.17	47
8	01–001	Main motors, Model 345	39.82	318.56	56
11 doz.	06–019	Condensers Q-AK-1	5.33	58.63	65
5 doz.	07–004	Tension rotary switches	8.49	42.45	75
7 doz.	14–010	Sermistors B2B	3.21	22.47	83
14 doz.	13–108	Variable condenser rubber bushes	.73	10.22	96
					97
				765.68	

19C Location of 3, 6, and / (Diagonal) ③

Type 3 with D finger

Type 6 with J finger

Diagonal. Move the right fourth (little) finger down to ? (question) and without shifting, type /.

Space once between a whole number and a fraction typed with the diagonal: 3 1/3.

19D Location Drills for 3, 6, and / (Diagonal) ⑫ Lines 1, 2, and 3 once for tryout; then each line twice

1 3   d d3d 3d 3d 3d 33 333 33 disks, 333 dams, 33 steps, 33 and 3

2 6   j j6j 6j 6j 6j 66 666 66 jars, 6 jobs, 66 helpers, 666 years

3 /   ; ;/; /; /; /; 1/8 or 1/5 Type this copy: 2 1/2 6 1/6 1/6.

4 Review Read pages 33, 66, and 363. Give Al 10, 20, 30, or 50 feet.

5 Review Take No. 62 for 5 1/3 miles; then follow No. 6 for 12 miles.

19E Sentence Guided Writing ⑰

1. Type Line 1 as a 1' writing, with the call of the line ending each 15, 20, or 30". Then, try to type Line 2 at the same rate. Repeat 1' writings on the figure line as time permits.

2. Type each of the other pairs of lines in this way.

	All letters and all figures learned are used.	G W A M 30" 20" 15"
1	Did Rex see Van and Max at the new pool?	16 24 32
2	We have these sizes: 8, 10, 11, and 12.	16 24 32
3	John Quick may meet the mayor of Troy in May.	18 27 36
4	Ship 26 feet of No. 58 and 18 feet of No. 60.	18 27 36
5	You can live in luxury at the Mayflower in Dayton.	20 30 40
6	I can see you before 10:15 a.m. or after 2:20 p.m.	20 30 40
7	He may dine at any restaurant and simply sign the bill.	22 33 44
8	Please send us 16 5/8 feet of No. 3820 canvas covering.	22 33 44
9	To learn more about this unique car, visit your dealer soon.	24 36 48
10	The car has a V8 engine, disc brakes, and 15 optional items.	24 36 48

| 1 | 2 | 3 | 4 | 5 | 6 | 7 | 8 | 9 | 10 | 11 | 12 |

LESSON 132

132A Preparatory Practice (5) each line at least 3 times

Alphabet	Jackson Poulson led the expedition down the foggy river to Mozambique.
Figure/symbol	Ordered 1 gross of #2 pencils @ 39¢/dozen; total was $4.68 (up 5.07%).
Hyphen	Submit an up-to-date account of your father-in-law's May transactions.
Fluency	Be big enough to admit that you are wrong whenever you make a mistake.

| 1 | 2 | 3 | 4 | 5 | 6 | 7 | 8 | 9 | 10 | 11 | 12 | 13 | 14 |

132B Growth Index (15) two 5' control-level writings; record GWAM of the better writing

All letters are used.

	GWAM 1'	5'

¶ 1
1.5 SI
5.6 AWL
80% HFW

You can safely consider that bad stroking habits are generally the
cause of failure to achieve high typing speeds and are the basic reasons
for plateaus; but you can find material especially designed to help
develop quick, sharp stroking. Use a part of the drill period each day
to work on these special drill exercises. You may not notice an immediate change, but it will come if you work for it.

13	3	68
28	6	71
42	8	74
56	11	77
70	14	80
80	16	82

¶ 2
1.5 SI
5.6 AWL
80% HFW

Among other specific ideas to keep before you is the advice that all
drills must be practiced with a definite goal in mind. Unless you know
what you are trying to attain, you can't hope to achieve any particular
degree of success. Pounding away day after day at the keyboard in the
hope that practice makes perfect is useless. Your drills should be done
with very specific objectives in mind.

14	19	84
28	22	87
43	25	90
57	27	93
71	30	96
79	32	97

¶ 3
1.5 SI
5.6 AWL
80% HFW

The requirement of having goals is not just limited to your working
for higher speed. You arrive safely and faster at any point if you use
a good road map. An individual who aspires to a higher job will work
more diligently toward that end. Sound learning principles--knowing the
why, where, and how of your activities--might be applied to a great many
areas of your everyday, personal life style.

14	35	100
28	37	103
42	40	106
57	43	109
71	46	112
80	48	113

¶ 4
1.5 SI
5.6 AWL
80% HFW

Not much is accomplished in the world simply by an accident. Any
major achievement is realized by following a good plan of attack. Many
people have a limited amount of luck "going for them," but relying too
heavily on luck is just foolish. If your typewriting skill needs to be
improved, learn what you need to practice. Use any aids available to
you; but, above all, take the responsibility for your own growth--and
take pride in it, too.

13	50	116
28	53	119
42	56	122
56	59	125
70	62	127
84	65	130
89	66	131

1' GWAM | 1 | 2 | 3 | 4 | 5 | 6 | 7 | 8 | 9 | 10 | 11 | 12 | 13 | 14 |
5' GWAM | 1 | 2 | 3 |

LESSON 20

20A Preparatory Practice (8) each line twice

Alphabet	Max Quigley hopes Dick Webster can leave for Zurich in July.
Figures	Type the figures that follow: 58, 20, 16, 33, 20, 616, 310.
Fractions	Now type these fractions: 1/3, 5/6, 2/5, 3/8, 1/6, and 5/8.
Fluency	There is little doubt in his mind that he can make the trip.

| 1 | 2 | 3 | 4 | 5 | 6 | 7 | 8 | 9 | 10 | 11 | 12 |

20B Technique Practice: RESPONSE PATTERNS (7) each line twice; Lines 1, 3, and 5 from dictation

1 Word
2 response

1 the right form|they may go|it is due|to work at|for that man
2 It is the duty of men to work; their wish, to make a profit.

3 Letter
4 response

3 only you|after my|you saw|my tax case|refer to our|were ever
4 As you are aware, my estate tax case was, in fact, deferred.

5 Combination
6

5 if they look|when the facts|if they imply|they also serve to
6 He treated the data with care; he stated my case with vigor.

| 1 | 2 | 3 | 4 | 5 | 6 | 7 | 8 | 9 | 10 | 11 | 12 |

20C Technique Practice: TAB MECHANISM AND FIGURES (10) Type the drill twice, DS.

Procedure for setting tab stops

Clear all tab stops. (See page 18, if necessary.) For Column 1, set the left margin stop for a 60-space line. For Column 2, set a tab stop 8 spaces from the left margin. For Column 3, set a tab stop 8 spaces from the first tab stop.

Set stops for remaining columns in a similar manner. When the left margin stop and all tab stops have been set, operate the tab mechanism for a full line without typing.

Technique emphasis

Nonelectric. Depress and hold down the tab bar or key until the carriage stops. Move quickly back to home position and type the next item.

Electric. Flick the tab key or bar lightly. Return the controlling finger to its home position at once.

Eyes on copy during return

Reach with the fingers							
to	it	do	if	go	so	the	did
15	85	55	88	15	51	185	558
as	no	be	on	we	in	you	pat
55	88	15	18	51	81	888	555
be	of	an	me	by	as	row	now
88	55	11	85	58	18	151	881

KEY |2| 6 |2| 6 |2| 6 |2| 6 |2| 6 |2| 6 |3| 6 |3|

Job 10: Interoffice Memorandum (WB p. 97)

TO: Joseph Bailey, President

FROM: Carl R. Wright

DATE: August 16, 19––

SUBJECT: In-Plant ADP Course for Office Workers

(¶ 1) Upon receipt of your memorandum of July 31, our department began a study to determine the need for and the feasibility of offering an in-plant training course in automated data processing for our office employees. (¶ 2) Harold Anders and Alice Winterton assisted me in surveying the staff as to their wishes about such a course. Many of them were in favor of participating in an ADP class (as you said you thought they would be) and indicated they would be willing to remain after work if necessary if the class time did not extend beyond six o'clock. (¶ 3) Accordingly, beginning September 9 and running until December 10, the three of us will hold a two-hour lecture-and-discussion meeting every Wednesday afternoon from four until six in the staff training lounge. In a sense, the firm is "giving" an hour of working time; and the employee will match it with an hour of his own time. (¶ 4) We shall prepare a detailed course outline and send a copy of it to you at least one week before the first training session. We shall be happy to welcome you at this session if you care to attend it. Perhaps you would like to take this opportunity to open the course with a few words of encouragement.

Job 11: Summary of Expenses

Petty Cash Disbursement

No. _383_ Date _8/1_ Code _153_

Pay from petty cash $ _11.00_

To _A. & B. Delivery Co._

For _C. O. D. charge_

Disbursed by _____

Petty cash voucher

The illustration above shows a petty cash voucher that was completed when money from the petty cash fund was disbursed. For unit record data processing, the voucher would be considered a *source document*; and the data from a number of such vouchers would be punched directly into cards. A tabulator would automatically update the amounts in the proper accounts according to code numbers and, in addition, print a summary of all disbursements similar to the one at the right.

On a full sheet with double spacing, type the summary in duplicate as shown at the right.

PETTY CASH DISBURSEMENTS FOR

THE MONTH OF AUGUST

Code 153	Voucher 383	$11.00
387	384	8.35
465	385	1.50
198	386	15.00
508	387	3.99
735	388	2.25
248	389	5.00
601	390	1.95
337	391	8.37
404	392	3.33
511	393	10.00
624	394	5.50
239	395	1.67
497	396	8.48
		$86.39

Job 12: Notice

Using the interoffice memorandum you completed for Job 10 as your source document, type an announcement for the office bulletin board that gives the details about the training course in automated data processing. Use a full sheet; make the notice brief, attractive, and informative.

20D Location of 4 and 9 ③

Type 4 with F finger

Type 9 with L finger

Technique Cue. Reach to the top row of keys without moving the hand to the figure row and without twisting the elbow outward or arching the wrist. Try to hold the other fingers over their home keys.

20E Location Drills for 4 and 9 ⑩ Lines 1 and 2 once for tryout; then each line twice

4	f f4f 4f 4f 4f 44 444 44 feet, 4 fields, 444 files, 44 firms
9	l l9l 9l 9l 9l 99 999 99 lines, 9 leads, 99 oars, 99 leaders
Review	The clerk checked Items 14, 19, and 94 on pages 194 and 249.
Review	On June 19 we sent Check 4991 to 4926 Lynn Street, Portland.

20F Skill-Transfer Typing ⑫

Type two 1′ writings on each ¶. Compare *gwam* on the two ¶s. Type two more 1′ writings on the ¶ with the lower *gwam*.

Finally, type one 3′ writing on both ¶s. Determine *gwam*. Compare your 3′ *gwam* with the best 1′ *gwam* on each of the two ¶s.

All letters are used.

		GWAM		
		1′	3′	
¶ 1 1.3 SI 5.2 AWL 90% HFW Straight copy	You guessed it. In the third class are the individuals	11	4	40
	who do the job assigned to them. They do not require close	23	8	44
	attention. You know they will do good work. They have a	35	12	48
	sincere interest in their jobs and will try to find new and	47	16	52
	better ways of doing them.	52	17	54
¶ 2 1.3 SI 5.2 AWL 90% HFW Statistical	Neither the age of a person, nor his size, nor the exact	11	21	57
	number of years he attended school has much to do with job	23	25	61
	commitment. People under 25 or 30 with no more than 12 or	35	29	65
	13 years in school are often more resourceful than are those	47	33	69
	over 50 or 60 with 15 or 16 years of education.	57	36	72

1′ GWAM | 1 | 2 | 3 | 4 | 5 | 6 | 7 | 8 | 9 | 10 | 11 | 12 |
3′ GWAM | 1 | 2 | 3 | 4 |

Job 8: Request for Quotation (WB p. 93)

Type in duplicate the following request for quotation as illustrated below.

To: Western Electronics Mfg. Co., 833 North Michigan Avenue, Pasadena, CA 91104

Date Issued: August 9, 19--

Date Required: August 15, 19--

Quantity	Description
18 doz.	Diodes S2A20
6	VU meters V3 wide scale
4 doz.	Push-button switches VE-42
20 doz.	3P E jacks
8 doz.	Block condensers PQ40.450V
10 doz.	Rotary switches Y-4-13-3
15 doz.	VR 30K ohm A18 bias adjusters

Request for Quotation - - This is not an order.

J.B.WHOLESALE DISTRIBUTORS, INC.,

Telephone
404—552—8179

1099 Gwinnet Street
Augusta, Georgia 30901

To: Universal Electronics, Inc.
1325 Oakwood Avenue, NE
Cedar Rapids, IA 52402

Date Issued: August 9, 19--   Date Required: August 19, 19--

Quantity	Description
25 doz.	Transistors 2SB75

Request for quotation

J.B.WHOLESALE DISTRIBUTORS, INC., 1099 Gwinnet Street, Augusta, GA 30901

(404) 552-8179

Purchase Order

Order No. 94324

Date August 14, 19--

Terms 1/10, n/30

Shipped Via REA Express

To   Universal Electronics, Inc.
1325 Oakwood Avenue, NE
Cedar Rapids, IA 52402

Quantity	Cat. No.	Description	Price	Total
12 doz.	X-4783	Vacuum tubes 12AD7	4.39	52.68
10 doz.	X-9835	Fixed resistors 1/4W L 10M ohm	2.59	25.90
10 doz.	X-9837	Fixed resistors 1/4W P 1M ohm	2.79	27.90
10 doz.	X-9843	Fixed resistors 1/2W P 250K ohm	3.13	31.30
5 doz.	X-0687	Relays FBV153 91/101	12.67	63.35
20 doz.	X-0052	Fuses 3A	.33	6.60
1 doz.	X-8635	20mH peaking coils	15.83	15.83
				223.56

BY_____
PURCHASING AGENT

Purchase order

Job 9: Purchase Order

(WB p. 95)

Type a purchase order in duplicate for the items listed in Job 8. Order the quantities indicated; include the prices.

To: Western Electronics Mfg. Co. 833 North Michigan Avenue Pasadena, CA 91104

Order No.: 94325

Date: August 15, 19--

Terms: 2/10, n/30

Ship Via: P.I.E. Express

Quantity	Cat. No.	Description	Price	Total
18 doz.	D-3746	Diodes S2A20	8.95	161.10
6	M-0021	VU meters V3 wide scale	5.25	31.50
4 doz.	S-87421	Push-button switches VE-42	4.43	17.72
20 doz.	J-2673	3P E jacks	3.78	75.60
8 doz.	C-40450	Block condensers PQ40.450V	12.66	101.28
10 doz.	S-4133	Rotary switches Y-4-13-3	10.09	100.90
15 doz.	A-8674	VR 30K ohm A18 bias adjusters	9.55	143.25
				631.35

LESSON 21

21A Preparatory Practice [8] each line twice

Alphabet	James quickly helped fix a latch to be given to Ezra Wilson.
4 9	The 44 men had 99 days in which to make 494 No. 1499 wagons.
Figure review	What is the sum of 5 and 30 and 26 and 84 and 93 and 95 1/8?
Fluency	There are more ways than one to do a job; use the right one.
	| 1 | 2 | 3 | 4 | 5 | 6 | 7 | 8 | 9 | 10 | 11 | 12 |

21B Typing from Dictation [5] once with the book open, once with it closed

the them lend land for form go got he held their light sight

it is the | to do the | go with them | and wish to | and do the work

and lend | the form | they held | to go with | for them | with the bid

Do not type the dividers

21C Location of 7 and - (Hyphen) and -- (Dash) [3]

Type 7 with J finger

Type - with ; finger

Dash. Type the dash with two hyphens without spacing before or after, as in: His speed--50 mph--was not excessive.

21D Location Drills for 7 and - [12] Lines 1, 2, and 3 once for tryout; then each line twice

1	7	j j7j 7j 7j 7j 7 77 777 77 jars, 77 jets, 777 units, 7 for 7
2	-	; ;-; -; -; -; co-op, up-to-date book, first-class newspaper
3	--	; -- ; -- Use a 6-inch line--60 pica spaces--for your paper.
4	Review	His speed--50 mph--was not excessive; he made 476 3/8 miles.
5	Review	FOR SALE: 8-room, 3-bath house--4/5 acre at 290 Pine Drive.
		| 1 | 2 | 3 | 4 | 5 | 6 | 7 | 8 | 9 | 10 | 11 | 12 |

Preliminary Information

For the remaining jobs in this section, you will be the typist for the J. B. Wholesale Distributors, Inc., 1099 Gwinnet Street, Augusta, GA 30901. Directions are given for each job.

The following jobs provide further examples of work that might be handled with data processing equipment. Some forms might be typed on a typewriter-calculator, a tape-punching typewriter, or a keypunch; others might be produced by equipment such as a tabulator or a printer. As you complete the jobs, therefore, keep in mind that such work exemplifies the terms *data* (as input) or *information* (as output) as a part of a data processing system and that probably hundreds of such forms could be prepared with data processing equipment while you are typing one.

Production Typing Information: BUSINESS FORMS

Business forms such as purchase requisitions, purchase orders, and invoices can be typed quickly and efficiently if the following procedures are observed by the typist.

1. Set tab stops for the name and address section, for the items in the Description column, and for the items in the section giving the general information about the form (order number, date, terms, method of shipment).

2. SS the items in the body of the form when there are 4 or more lines. DS the items in the body of the form when there are 3 or fewer lines.

3. If an item in the body of the form requires more than 1 line, indent the second and succeeding lines 3 spaces.

4. Begin the items in the Description column about 2 spaces to the right of the ruled line. Center the items in the other columns by judgment rather than by calculation.

5. Underline the last figure in the Total column; then DS before typing the total amount.

6. Type *across* the form rather than vertically.

Job 7: Purchase Requisition (WB p. 91)

Type in duplicate the purchase requisition as illustrated below.

Deliver To: Harold J. Thomas

Location: Room 312

Job No.: 8117

Requisition No.: 6903

Date: August 9, 19--

Date Required: August 25, 19--

Quantity	Description
18 doz.	Diodes S2A20
6	VU meters V3 wide scale
4 doz.	Push-button switches VE-42
20 doz.	3P E jacks
8 doz.	Block condensers PQ40.450V
10 doz.	Rotary switches Y-4-13-3
15 doz.	VR 30K ohm A18 bias adjusters

Purchase Requisition

J.B.WHOLESALE DISTRIBUTORS, INC., 1099 Gwinnet Street, Augusta, GA 30901
(404) 552-8179

Deliver To Harold J. Thomas   Requisition No. 6902

Location Room 312   Date August 8, 19--

Job No. 8116   Date Required August 20, 19--

Quantity	Description
25 doz.	Transistors 2SB75

purchasing agent

Purchase requisition

21E Growth Index ⑩

Type two 3′ writings on these ¶s. Proofread by comparing. Circle errors. Determine *gwam*. Compare results on the two writings.

Proofreading Cue. Read for meaning, catching changed, omitted, or repeated words in your copy. Check tricky words such as *finesse* with the book for spelling.

All letters are used.

		3′ GWAM
¶ 1	Just how well can you speak and write? Is it almost	4 | 40
1.3 SI	impossible for you to put your own ideas into words that	7 | 44
5.2 AWL 90% HFW	others can understand? If so, you can learn how to use them	11 | 48
	with finesse and ease. The odds are in your favor; your	15 | 52
	chances are excellent.	17 | 54
¶ 2	Some people believe that it is essential to use complex	20 | 57
1.3 SI	terms to impress others; but it is the correct choice of word,	25 | 61
5.2 AWL 90% HFW	not the size of the word, that is important. Be as concise as	29 | 66
	possible in your quest to enhance your writing. Use as many	33 | 70
	words as you need--but only that many--to state your points.	37 | 74

3′ GWAM | 1 | 2 | 3 | 4 |

21F Individual Practice ⑫

1. Type each line once. Place a check mark before each line that seemed difficult.

2. Type 2 or more times each line you checked as difficult.

1	1 6 :	By 11:16 a.m., he reread these pages: 16, 66, 116, and 166.
2	2 7	She ordered 27 pens, 72 notebooks, 227 maps, and 772 rulers.
3	3 8 –	Buy 3- and 8-yard lengths--not those that are 33 or 88 feet.
4	4 9	They can also use Items 44, 49, 494, 949, and 994 very soon.
5	5 0	In just 5 years, we made 50 changes in Models 5005 and 5055.
6	Fractions	The rods come in these sizes: 14 3/8 inches and 6 1/5 feet.
7	Shift lock	The editors will review THE ODESSA FILE and OPERATION RHINO.

| 1 | 2 | 3 | 4 | 5 | 6 | 7 | 8 | 9 | 10 | 11 | 12 |

Sideways on a full sheet; top margin, ½"; line length: 89 spaces total, including 4 spaces between columns; SS the body of the table; type line for line as in the copy; indent 3 spaces the second line of a 2-line item in the last column.

EDUCATIONAL REQUIREMENTS FOR COMPUTER OCCUPATIONS

	High School	Technical	College	Special Study
Applications Engineer	. . . . .	. . . . .	Required	Math and Computers
Auxiliary Equipment Operator	Required	Desirable	. . . . .	. . . .
Coding Clerk	Required	. . . . .	. . . . .	. . . .
Computer Operator	Required	One year	Desirable	Data Processing
Control Clerk	Required	. . . . .	. . . . .	Experience
Data Coder Operator	Required	. . . . .	. . . . .	Typewriting
Data Examination Clerk	Required	. . . . .	. . . . .	
Data Typist	Preferred	. . . . .	. . . . .	Typewriting
Electronics Mechanic	Required	Two years	. . . . .	Electronics
Engineering Analyst I	. . . . .	. . . . .	Required	Phys. Sci. and Math
High-Speed Printer Operator	Preferred	Desirable	. . . . .	. . . .
Keypunch Operator	Preferred	. . . . .	. . . . .	Typewriting
Manager, EDP	Required	Two years	Desirable	Business or Engineering
Operations Research Analyst	. . . . .	. . . . .	Required	Statistics and Comp. Sci.
Peripheral Equipment Operator	Required	Desirable	. . . . .	. . . .
Programmer, Business	Required	1-2 years	Desirable	Business
Programmer, Chief, Business	. . . . .	Required	Desirable	Experience
Programmer, Detail	Required	Desirable	. . . . .	Programming
Programmer, Engineering	. . . . .	. . . . .	Required	Mathematics
Project Director, Business	. . . . .	. . . . .	Required	Mathematics and Comp. Sci.
Scheduler	Required	. . . . .	. . . . .	Experience
Small Computer Operator	Required	Required	Desirable	. . . .
Supervisor, Computer	Required	Desirable	. . . . .	Electronic Data Processing
Systems Analyst, Business	. . . . .	. . . . .	Required	Adv. Math and Experience
Systems Engineer, EDP	. . . . .	. . . . .	Required	Engineering
Tape Librarian	Required	. . . . .	. . . . .	Business

Adapted from U.S. Department of Labor, Occupations in Electronic Computing Systems, 1972.

SECTION 4 The Basic Symbol Keys

LESSONS 22-26

In this section you will learn to type symbols. You will also improve figure control and build higher basic skill. Some of the copy will be presented in rough draft.

Machine Adjustments. Use a 60-space line (set the left margin stop at center — 30; move the right margin stop to the extreme right). SS sentence drills with DS between repeated lines. DS and indent paragraphs 5 spaces.

Lessons 22 and 23. The symbols presented in these lessons are located on the same keys for nonelectric and electric typewriters. The same fingers control the keys.

LESSON 22

22A Preparatory Practice (7) each line twice

Alphabet	Jenny Quarry packed the zinnias in twelve large, firm boxes.
Figures	The box is 6 5/8 by 9 1/2 feet and weighs 375 to 400 pounds.
Tricky spelling	occur excels forty tempt oblige using yield siege relic rely
Fluency	It is great to have talent; it is tragic not to use it well.

| 1 | 2 | 3 | 4 | 5 | 6 | 7 | 8 | 9 | 10 | 11 | 12 |

22B Location of $, &, ( ) [Left and Right Parentheses] (5)

$ (Dollars). The **$** is the shift of **4**. Type it with the *f* finger: f4f f$f

& (Ampersand or "And"). The **&** is the shift of **7**. Type it with the *j* finger: j7j j&j

([Left Parenthesis]. The **(** is the shift of **9**. Type it with the *l* finger: l9l l(l

) [Right Parenthesis]. The **)** is the shift of **0**. Type it with the *;* finger: ;0; ;);

22C Location Drills for $, &, (, and) (15) Lines 1, 3, and 5 once for tryout; then each line twice

1 $ f4f f$f $f $f for $488, from $427 to $832, a balance of $144
2 We received checks for $488 and $744 from them on August 14.

3 & j7j j&j &j &j Brown & Nelson, H. B. Jones & Son, Bye & Colts
4 D. K. Jones & Company sold the plant to Boswell & Carpenter.

5 ( ) l9l l(l (l (l ;0; ;););); due in 90 (ninety) days (May 15)
6 Most of the companies (129 to be exact) have tried the plan.

| 1 | 2 | 3 | 4 | 5 | 6 | 7 | 8 | 9 | 10 | 11 | 12 |

ELECTRONIC DATA PROCESSING

Russell T. Andreasen

(¶ 1) In 1945, few businessmen would have risked their reputations for clear thinking by predicting the appearance in offices of electronic data processing. Today, many of those same men could not make the decisions they do without the aid of a computer system. In fact, electronic data processing has become so commonplace that anyone who works in an office must know how the system works if he is to understand his job. (¶ 2) Stripped of its glamour and mystery, the computer system includes the following three basic steps: (*SS and indent 5 spaces from the left margin.*)

1. The input or source data are written into the system.
2. The data are processed within the system.
3. The end result or output is written out.[1]

(¶ 3) Input and output media. Data processing machines do not generally read regular print. Input data, therefore, can be recorded in cards and paper tape as punched holes; on magnetic tape, disks, or drums as magnetized spots; on documents as characters printed in magnetic ink or printed in certain type fonts.[2] The processed data coming from the computer are printed on paper or recorded in cards, in paper tape, or on magnetic tape. Special units can convert recorded data from one medium to another automatically. (¶ 4) Data entering the system are stored, sorted, and analyzed.

Calculations are performed. These functions are performed by three major units of the computer; namely, the storage, control, and processing (arithmetic) units. (¶ 5) The storage feature is the unique characteristic of electronic computers. Two types of information are stored in the computer: (1) the data to be processed and (2) the detailed instructions needed to process them, commonly referred to as the program. (¶ 6) Control unit. When processing starts, each instruction in a program that has been stored in the computer enters the control unit where it is interpreted and carried out.[3] It is obvious that the program must be carefully worked out in detail if chaos is to be avoided, as the computer works with lightning speed. (¶ 7) Processing unit. Computations are made in the processing unit of the computer. Any problem for which a program can be devised can be solved; but to obtain the correct answer, the steps in the program must be carefully and logically set down.

---

[1] S. J. Wanous, E. E. Wanous, and A. E. Hughes, Introduction to Automated Data Processing (Cincinnati: South-Western Publishing Co., 1968), p. 97.

[2] John J. W. Neuner, B. Lewis Keeling, and Norman F. Kallaus, Administrative Office Management (6th ed.; Cincinnati: South-Western Publishing Co., 1972), pp. 807-808.

[3] Ibid., p. 814.

22D **Proofreading:** IDENTIFYING ERRORS (5) **Type each line once, making needed corrections as you type.**

1	Spacing, punctuation	How canwe become true, happy; viv acious, genuine, and free?
2	Misstrokes	Not by chance, not bu magic, not byy just hopinf and waiting.
3	Omissions	We get thes things meetin joyful, genuine, free people
4	Strikeovers, transpositions	You cah leatn ot distinguish between hte true and hte phony.
5	Word substitution	Best of all, he will learn it become an honest humane being.
6	Review	You can then life in har mony with yourslf and your friends.

22E **Skill-Transfer Typing** (14)

1. Type a 3′ writing beginning with ¶ 1 and typing until time is called. Proofread by comparing. Circle errors. Determine *gwam*.

2. Type two 1′ writings on each ¶.

3. Repeat Step 1. Compare results.

Difficulty controls for "mixed" copy (words and figures) are determined for the words only. Punctuation marks and symbols used with words, such as quotation marks and parentheses, are considered to be a part of the word with which they are typed. See ¶ 2.

All letters are used.

		3′ GWAM	
¶ 1	You need to have a special goal for each writing. If	4	38
1.3 SI, 5.2 AWL, 90% HFW, Straight copy	the immediate aim is to improve your speed, move quickly	7	42
	from word to word. If control is a problem, drop back in	11	46
	speed to type with greater ease. Adjust the rate to the	15	49
	purpose of the practice.	17	51
¶ 2	How many GWAM can you type today: 18, 20, 22, 24, or	20	55
1.3 SI, 5.2 AWL, 90% HFW, Statistical	more? You may be able to add some words to your rate by	24	58
	stressing the right kind of typing habits. Do not freeze	28	62
	as you type. Instead, space very quickly and begin the next	32	66
	word at once. Type without pausing.	34	69

3′ GWAM | 1 | 2 | 3 | 4 |

22F **Control Building:** RATE CONTROL (4) **four ½′ writings**

1. Type ¶ 1 in 22E, above. This time, type at a specific, predetermined rate: 20, 30, or 40 words a minute (*wam*). Select your rate.
2. With light pencil marks, mark your ¼′ and ½′ goals, based on your selected rate.
3. Your instructor will call the ¼ and ½ minutes. Control your rate so that you will be typing your goal word just as the signals are given.

BASIC COMPONENTS OF A DIGITAL COMPUTER SYSTEM

I. INPUT

    A. Card Readers
    B. Paper Tape Readers
    C. Magnetic Tape Units
    D. Magnetic Disk Units
    E. Optical Scanning devices
    F. CRT devices
    G. Console Typewriters
    H. Others

II. STORAGE

    A. Primary (Memory)
    B. Secondary (Files)
    C. Off-Line

III. PROCESSING (ARITHMETIC/LOGICAL UNIT)

IV. CONTROL (CPU CONTROL UNIT)

V. OUTPUT

    A. Card Punches
    B. Paper Tape Punches
    C. High-Speed Printers
    D. Magnetic Tape Units
    E. Magnetic Disk Units
    F. CRT devices
    G. Console Typewriters
    H. Others

LESSON 23

23A Preparatory Practice (7) each line twice

Alphabet   Willis Garvey put a dozen quarts of jam in the box for Jack.

$ &   Bond & Rossi gave us checks for $50.12, $489.75, and $20.63.

( )   The Zorn & Son check (dated June 15) was sent to 315 Oak St.

Fluency   One of these new problems can be solved at our next meeting.
　　　　| 1 | 2 | 3 | 4 | 5 | 6 | 7 | 8 | 9 | 10 | 11 | 12 |

23B Location of #, %, ½, ¼ (5) (same location on all typewriters)

 # (Number or Pounds). The # is the shift of **3**. Type it with the *d* finger: d3d d#d

NOTE: Before a figure, # stands for *number*; after a figure, it stands for *pounds*. See Line 2 of 23C below.

% (Percent). The % is the shift of **5**. Type it with the *f* finger: f5f f%f

½ (Fraction Key). Type ½ (at the right of the letter *p*) with the *;* finger. No shift: ;½; ;½;

¼ (Fraction Key). The shift of ½ is ¼. Type it with the *;* finger: ;½; ;¼;

23C Location Drills for #, %, ½, ¼ (15) Lines 1, 3, and 5 once for tryout; then each line twice

1 **#**   d3d d#d #d #d deed #389, lot #372 for lot No. 372, #921, #33
2   Ship order #365 for 33# of Compound #72 as soon as possible.

3 **%**   f5f f%f %f %f at a 5% rate, 55% are used, the city tax of 6%
4   Will the 6% rate be changed to 7% or possibly to 8% by June?

5 **½ ¼**   ;½; ½; ½; 23½, 57½, 31½ and 4½, ;¼; ¼; ¼; 12¼ and 7¼ and 13¼
6   Type fractions in the same way: 1/2 and 2/3--not ½ and 2/3.

7 **Review**   His 7½% note (for $300) was paid on April 29 by check #4658.
　　　　| 1 | 2 | 3 | 4 | 5 | 6 | 7 | 8 | 9 | 10 | 11 | 12 |

23D Individual Practice (10) Use 21F, page 41.

1. Type each line once. Place a check mark before any line on which you made more than 1 error.

2. Type 2 or more times each line you checked. Type slowly; think of the individual strokes.

Job 3: List of Data Processing Terms

Full sheets; title: GLOSSARY OF DATA PROCESSING TERMS; top margin pica, 1½″; top margin elite, 2″; 1″ side margins; SS each item; indent second and succeeding lines of each item 5 spaces; TS between items; arrange the items in alphabetic order.

DATA FIELD: A column or group of columns on a card which has been designated to receive information of a given kind.

MICR (Magnetic Ink Character Recognition): A system used to sort and process numeric data that have been recorded in special magnetic ink characters on checks and other papers.

EXTERNAL STORAGE: A storage device that can be removed and held separate from the computer system, or replaced in the computer system, which can store information in a form readable by the computer.

WORD: A set of characters that occupies one storage location and is treated as a unit.

ACCESS TIME: The time required for a storage unit to deliver a requested unit of information to the central processor or to an output device.

RANDOM-ACCESS: Access to storage under conditions which the next location from which data are to be obtained is in no way dependent on the location of the previously obtained data.

BATCH PROCESSING: A technique by which items to be processed must be coded and collected into groups prior to processing.

PROGRAMMING LANGUAGE: A defined set of characters that are used to form symbols, words, etc., and the rules for combining these into meaningful communications.

SOFTWARE: The changeable internal program or routines that are professionally prepared to simplify programming and computer operations.

CORE STORAGE: A form of high-speed storage that utilizes magnetic cores.

NANOSECOND: A billionth of a second.

MICROSECOND: A millionth part of a second.

PICOSECOND: A trillionth of a second.

MILLISECOND: A thousandth of a second.

ALPHAMERIC: Information containing both alphabetical and numerical data.

FLOWCHART: A diagram which represents a sequence of activities or operations.

ON-LINE: A description of a system and peripheral equipment which is under the control of a central processing unit.

MNEMONIC CODE: A technique of coding which assists the human memory.

HARDWARE: All devices or components of a computer system such as cabinets, tubes, transistors, wires, motors, etc.

CRT (Cathode Ray Tube): A vacuum tube on which information may be presented on a screen by means of a multigrid modulated beam of electrons.

ELECTRONIC DATA PROCESSING (EDP): The processing of data through the use of electronic equipment.

HOLLERITH CARD: A card with 80 columns and 12 rows in which coded information may be recorded in the form of rectangular holes.

CPU (Central Processing Unit): The central processor of a computer system containing the main storage, arithmetic unit, and special register groups.

23E Skill-Transfer Typing ⑬

1. Type three 1' writings on each ¶. Compare the *gwams* for the best writing on each ¶.

2. Type a 3' writing. Proofread by verifying. Circle errors. Determine *gwam*.

All letters are used.

	GWAM 1'	GWAM 3'

¶ 1
1.3 SI
5.2 AWL
90% HFW

Some of us worry so much about our writing style that we | 11 | 4 | 39

fail to get the job under way. Remember this about style: | 23 | 8 | 43

Once you have a message to convey, your words will seem to | 35 | 12 | 47

flow in a simple, direct way. Style results from knowing the | 48 | 16 | 51

idea that you want to express. | 54 | 18 | 53

¶ 2
1.3 SI
5.2 AWL
90% HFW

Organize your ideas; write. If you know what to write, | 11 | 22 | 57

you will not have to worry about style. You will have it. | 23 | 26 | 61

Put fresh ideas into your work. If you do not have anything | 35 | 30 | 65

novel to say, you are not ready. In writing, it is quality, | 48 | 34 | 69

not volume, that counts. | 52 | 35 | 71

1' GWAM | 1 | 2 | 3 | 4 | 5 | 6 | 7 | 8 | 9 | 10 | 11 | 12 |
3' GWAM | | 1 | | 2 | | 3 | | 4 |

LESSON 24

24A Preparatory Practice ⑦ each line twice

Alphabet	Doug Zola expects to fly to Quebec to visit with Jack Monti.
# %	Ship 233# of your #316A bulbs. Bill me at retail, less 15%.
½ ¼	His 6½% and 7¼% notes (for $950 and $300) are due next week.
Fluency	The work is done, and they will leave by the end of the day.

| 1 | 2 | 3 | 4 | 5 | 6 | 7 | 8 | 9 | 10 | 11 | 12 |

24B Control Building: RATE REDUCTION ⑩

Type two 3' writings on 23E, above. Type at a rate that is 4 to 8 words lower than the rate you made on the 3' writing in Lesson 22. Circle errors. Compare the number of errors on writings in the two lessons.

Lessons 24 and 25. The symbols and special characters in these lessons are located on different keys on non-electric and electric typewriters. Learn key locations and controlling fingers for your typewriter.

In the first half of this section you will be a typist in the Training Division of Hawaii Data Processing Services, Inc., 2536 Kamehameha Highway, Honolulu, HI 96819. The jobs you will type are typical of those you might do in similar data processing offices. Type each job on a separate sheet with 1 cc. Use the current date on all the memorandums.

Job 1: Interoffice Memorandum *(WB p. 89)*

TO: Jerry R. Swan FROM: Russell T. Andreasen

DATE: Current SUBJECT: Statistical Programs to Be Reviewed with New Trainees

(¶ 1) Attached is a list of the statistical programs that all new trainees should know and be able to use correctly. These programs can provide quick results in video or printed form for a variety of problems. Information on other new programs will be sent to you sometime next week. (¶ 2) All trainees should be given a thorough orientation of the program storage facility. The new hours for the Program Storage Center will be from 8 a.m. to 9 p.m. seven days a week. (¶ 3) If you would like to have someone assist you during the initial presentation of these statistical programs, please get in touch with Dr. J. Harvey Williams, Ext. 3216. I have already talked with Dr. Williams, and he will be ready to assist you whenever you need him. (¶ 4) I would suggest that you contact Karen Thurman and arrange a complete demonstration of (1) all the statistical programs, (2) the use of the teletype, and (3) the use of our time-sharing programs. Attachment

Job 2: List of Statistical Programs

Full sheet; 2″ top margin; 60-space line; SS each program but DS between programs; 2 columns; heading of first column: Program Number; heading of second column: Program

STATISTICAL PROGRAMS

1 Computation of the sum, sum of squares, the mean, variance, and standard deviation(s) of a set of numbers.

2 Computation of the mean, variance, and standard deviation for data grouped in classes.

3 Computation of r, the linear correlation coefficient.

4 Computation of the sums necessary for correlation of regression.

5 Least squares regression. Gives estimates of the slope and intercept for the line $y = a + bx$.

6 Gives a chi-square value for a 2 x 2 contingency table. (The value is corrected for continuity.)

7 Gives a chi-square value for a 2 x 2 or 2 x 3 contingency table.

8 Calculation of probabilities from a binomial distribution.

9 Evaluation of probabilities from a normal distribution.

10 One-sample t-test. Tests a hypothesis, assuming the population variance is not known.

11 Two-sample t-test. Tests a hypothesis, assuming the population variance is the same for both groups and unknown.

12 Paired t-test. Tests a hypothesis, but in this case the data are paired.

24C Location of ', ", ! [5] (located on different keys for nonelectric and electric)

Nonelectric—top row only

Electric—top three rows only

Spacing Rule. Space twice after an exclamation point at the end of a sentence.

' (Apostrophe) Nonelectric. The ' is the shift of **8**. Type it with the *k* finger: k8k k'k

' (Apostrophe) Electric. The ' is at the right of the semicolon key. Type it with the *;* finger. No shift: ;'; ;';

" (Quotation) Nonelectric. The " is the shift of *2*. Type it with the *s* finger: s2s s"s

" (Quotation) Electric. The " is the shift of '. Type it with the *;* finger: ;'; ;";

! (Exclamation Point) Made. Type ' and backspace; then type a period. (!).

! (Exclamation Point) Special Key. If your machine has a key for ! (usually the shift of the special figure 1), type it with the *a* finger: Try! Don't stop!

24D Location Drills for ', ", ! [15] Line 1 or 2, Line 3 or 4, and Lines 5 and 6 once for tryout; then same lines twice

1 ' (Nonelectric) k8k k'k 'k 'k It's here. I'm ready. It can't be 4 o'clock.
2 ' (Electric) ;'; ;'; '; '; It's here. I'm ready. It can't be 4 o'clock.

3 " (Nonelectric) s2s s"s "s "s He typed "its" for "it's" and "see" for "sea."
4 " (Electric) ;"; ;"; "; "; He typed "its" for "it's" and "see" for "sea."

5 ! Jump! Don't stop! Great! Type faster! Type with control!

6 Review The principal said, "It's right! Stand by your principles!"

| 1 | 2 | 3 | 4 | 5 | 6 | 7 | 8 | 9 | 10 | 11 | 12 |

24E Sentence Guided Writing [13]

1. Type a 1′ writing on each sentence. Determine *gwam*. Compare rates on each pair of sentences.

2. Type additional 1′ writings on the figure and symbol sentences with the greatest differences in rates.

		Words in Line
1	Please send this order to our plant in Boise.	9
2	See the first 29 pages of our 1974-75 report.	9
3	The papayas were shipped air express from Florida.	10
4	I paid the 7½% note by check #93--on the date due.	10
5	The price does not cover shipping charges or insurance.	11
6	We hold Reed & Long's note for $3,000 (dated March 12).	11
7	I look forward to hearing from you soon about the paintings.	12
8	When it's on time, Flight 568 leaves Des Moines at 6:15 a.m.	12

| 1 | 2 | 3 | 4 | 5 | 6 | 7 | 8 | 9 | 10 | 11 | 12 |

LESSONS 127-131

Lessons 127, 129, 131

Use the following daily lesson plan for Lessons 127, 129, and 131. Retain all jobs until you have completed Lesson 131.

Preparatory Practice (5′). Type 127A, below, as directed.

Production Typing (45′). Type the jobs on pages 256-263. Follow the directions for each job; where specific directions are not given, use your own good judgment. Proofread carefully; correct all errors.

Lessons 128, 130

Use the following daily lesson plan for Lessons 128 and 130. Retain all jobs until you have completed Lesson 131.

Preparatory Practice (5′). Type 127B, below, as directed.

Technique Mastery (5′). Type 127C, below, as directed.

Production Typing (40′). Continue typing the jobs on pages 256-263. Follow the same general directions given for Lessons 127, 129, and 131.

127A Preparatory Practice [5] each line at least 3 times

Alphabet A good zone trap will quickly exhibit the defensive judgment of a boy.

Figure/symbol Susan hoped to purchase 19 dozen @ 57¢ per dozen ($10.83) plus 4% tax.

Double letters If you succeed in applying a wood filler, call him tomorrow afternoon.

Fluency When you are trying to start something exciting, learn what is needed.

| 1 | 2 | 3 | 4 | 5 | 6 | 7 | 8 | 9 | 10 | 11 | 12 | 13 | 14 |

127B Preparatory Practice [5] each line at least 3 times

Alphabet Experts were able to judge quickly the size and volume of the beehive.

Figure/symbol I shipped 1,395# of supplies and was billed $2.46/cwt. ($34.32 total).

Long reaches It was undoubtedly unnecessary for my brother to bring me the uniform.

Fluency A good typist has the ability to type rapidly at a high control level.

| 1 | 2 | 3 | 4 | 5 | 6 | 7 | 8 | 9 | 10 | 11 | 12 | 13 | 14 |

127C Technique Mastery [5] each line at least twice without error

Left hand The best rewards at a drag race are for the fast cars and eager crews.

Right hand In my opinion, no nylon from our nonunion mills was used in my kimono.

Bottom row Zebras can be made to run very quickly when frightened by loud noises.

Third row You tried to wire your sister yesterday; perhaps you should try today.

Balanced hand The man and the girls work for the auditor of the firm, Mr. Al Patman.

| 1 | 2 | 3 | 4 | 5 | 6 | 7 | 8 | 9 | 10 | 11 | 12 | 13 | 14 |

LESSON 25

25A Preparatory Practice ⑦ each line twice

Alphabet	Fire hazards of the job were quickly explained by Mr. Novig.
' !	That's the way to do this job! It's simple if you know how!
"	"This," the man said, "is the right way to make a decision."
Fluency	He can always see those antique chairs at our downtown shop.

| 1 | 2 | 3 | 4 | 5 | 6 | 7 | 8 | 9 | 10 | 11 | 12 |

25B Location of *, ¢, @, and Underline ⑦ (located on different keys for nonelectric and electric)

Nonelectric—top three rows only

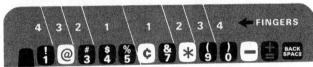

Electric—top row only

Spacing Rules. (1) Space before and after typing @, which is used in typing bills. **(2)** Do not space between ¢ and the figure preceding it. **(3)** Do not space between a figure and #, $, %, /.

To Underline. Backspace (or move carriage by hand) to the first letter of the word; then type the underline once for each letter in the word.

* (Asterisk) Nonelectric. The * is the shift of -. Type it with the ; finger: ;-; ;*;

* (Asterisk) Electric. The * is the shift of 8. Type it with the *k* finger: k8k k*k

¢ (Cent or Cents) Nonelectric. The ¢ is at the right of the ;. Type it with the ; finger. No shift: ;¢; ;¢;

¢ (Cent or Cents) Electric. The ¢ is the shift of 6. Type it with the *j* finger: j6j j¢j

@ (At) Nonelectric. The @ is the shift of ¢. Type it with the ; finger: ;¢; ;@; ;¢; ;@;

@ (At) Electric. The @ is the shift of 2. Type it with the *s* finger: s2s s@s

_ (Underline) Nonelectric. The _ is the shift of 6. Type it with the *j* finger: j6j j_j

_ (Underline) Electric. The _ is the shift of the hyphen. Type it with the ; finger: ;-; ;_;

25C Location Drills for *, ¢, @, Underline ⑮ appropriate line of each pair once for tryout; then same lines twice

1	*	(Nonelectric)	;-; ;*; *; *; My first * refers to page 129, ** to page 307.
2	*	(Electric)	k8k k*k *k *k My first * refers to page 129, ** to page 307.
3	¢	(Nonelectric)	;¢; ;¢; ¢; ¢; The prices Jones quoted are 57¢, 79¢, and 94¢.
4	¢	(Electric)	j6j j¢j ¢j ¢j The prices Jones quoted are 57¢, 79¢, and 94¢.
5	@	(Nonelectric)	;¢; ;@; @; @; Ship 56 lbs. @ 7¢ a lb. and 16 lbs. @ 9¢ a lb.
6	@	(Electric)	s2s s@s @s @s Ship 56 lbs. @ 7¢ a lb. and 16 lbs. @ 9¢ a lb.
7	_	(Nonelectric)	j6j j_j _j _j Use a <u>quick</u> stroke. Please <u>think</u> as you type.
8	_	(Electric)	;-; ;_; _; _; Use a <u>quick</u> stroke. Please <u>think</u> as you type.

| 1 | 2 | 3 | 4 | 5 | 6 | 7 | 8 | 9 | 10 | 11 | 12 |

126D Typing Figures ⑩ 70-space line; SS

Type two 3' writings, starting with the number 11 and alternating consecutive numbers with the word *and* as shown below. If you reach 100 before time is called, begin again with 11.

Scoring. From the last number (or total number if you started to repeat) in your writing, deduct 1 for each error. Try to improve your score on the second writing.

11 and 12 and 13 and 14 and 15 and 16 and 17 and 18 and 19 and 20 and

21 and 22 and 23 and 24 and 25 and 26 and 27 and 28 and 29 and 30 and

126E Statistical Timed Writing ⑳ three 5' writings; record GWAM of the best writing

All letters are used.

		GWAM
		1' / 5'

¶ 1
1.6 SI
5.8 AWL
75% HFW

The United States is a country composed of 50 separate states; 49 are located on the North American continent and one is the Hawaiian Island group. The total area of the United States is 3,615,122 square miles, including 78,267 square miles of inland water area; but that does not include the 60,306 square miles of area occupied by that part of the Great Lakes which is included within our boundaries.

¶ 2
1.6 SI
5.8 AWL
75% HFW

Education in the United States for the year 1971-72 is summarized as: The number of pupils enrolled in the primary grades was 36.7 million, and the number of primary teachers was 1,308,000; the number of students enrolled in the secondary grades and the vocational area was 15.2 million, and the number of teachers in these areas was 1,051,000; and in the higher education area, which includes all post-secondary levels, the number of students enrolled was 8.4 million, and the number of teachers on the staff was 617,000.

¶ 3
1.6 SI
5.8 AWL
75% HFW

The large volume of foreign trade by the United States can best be illustrated by using 1971 data. Our total imports were $45,602,000,000, and our total exports were $43,555,000,000 (excluding our military aid). Most of our imports (57%) came from: Canada, 28%; Japan, 16%; West Germany, 8%; and the United Kingdom, 5%. Also, most of our exports (43%) were shipped to the same areas. Machinery was our major export and was about 27% of the total exports shipped by the United States. There is a need to balance our export and import areas.

GWAM column (1' / 5'):
13 / 3 / 61
27 / 5 / 64
41 / 8 / 67
56 / 11 / 70
71 / 14 / 73
81 / 16 / 75
13 / 19 / 78
27 / 22 / 80
41 / 24 / 83
55 / 27 / 86
69 / 30 / 89
82 / 33 / 92
97 / 36 / 94
104 / 37 / 96
13 / 40 / 99
28 / 43 / 101
43 / 46 / 104
56 / 48 / 107
70 / 51 / 110
84 / 54 / 113
98 / 57 / 115
109 / 59 / 118

1' GWAM | 1 | 2 | 3 | 4 | 5 | 6 | 7 | 8 | 9 | 10 | 11 | 12 | 13 | 14 |
5' GWAM | 1 | 2 | 3 |

25D Skill-Transfer Typing ⑬ each line twice

1. Type two 1' writings on each ¶. Compare your *gwams* on the better writing on each ¶.

2. Type a 3' writing on all ¶s. Proofread by verifying. Circle errors. Determine *gwam*.

All letters are used.

		GWAM 1'	3'
¶ 1 1.3 SI 5.2 AWL 90% HFW Straight copy	Just one year ago today you opened an account with us,	11	4
	so this is a suitable time to express our thanks for your	23	8
	friendship and business. Serving you, Mr. Smith, has been a	35	12
	pleasure. All of us here hope that you will always find a	47	16
	helping hand in our store.	52	17
¶ 2 1.3 SI 5.2 AWL 90% HFW Figures	You can hear almost anything you want to hear about the	11	21
	dazzling speed of new copiers. Claims range from 30 to 75 or	24	25
	more copies a minute. The new 824 makes 65 good, clean copies	36	29
	a minute; and it works for days without a stop.	46	32
¶ 3 1.3 SI 5.2 AWL 90% HFW Figure/ symbol	We are pleased to reserve one double room for July 26 to	11	36
	30. If you plan to arrive after 4 o'clock, please forward a	24	40
	deposit of $18.50 to hold the room. We look forward to serving	36	45
	you and hope you will enjoy your Quebec visit.	46	48

1' GWAM | 1 | 2 | 3 | 4 | 5 | 6 | 7 | 8 | 9 | 10 | 11 | 12 |
3' GWAM | 1 | 2 | 3 | 4 |

25E Typing from Corrected Copy ⑧ Study the correction symbols; then type each drill line twice.

Errors are often circled in copy that is to be retyped. The typist must know what corrections to make. Sometimes correction symbols are used. Those at the right are quite common.

Symbol	Meaning
Cap ≡	Capitalize
∧ ⟋	Insert
⟋	Delete (take out)
⌐__	Move to left

Symbol	Meaning
#	Add horizontal space
lc /	Lowercase letters
◡	Close up space
∾	Transpose

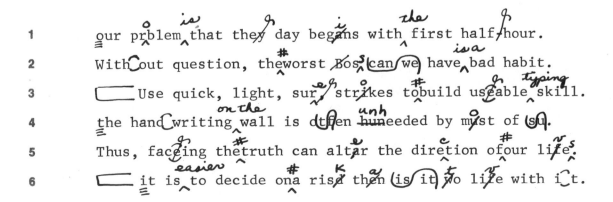

1   our problem that they day begans with first half hour.
2   Without question, the worst Bos can we have bad habit.
3   Use quick, light, sur strikes to build useable skill.
4   the hand writing wall is often unneeded by most of us.
5   Thus, facing the truth can altar the direction of our life.
6   it is to decide on a risk then is it to life with it.

SECTION 24 Typing in a Technical Office

LESSONS 126-132

Section 24 provides opportunity to type problems normally encountered in a technical office.

¶ **Copy.** DS; 70-space line; 5-space ¶ indentions; full sheets

Production Typing. Directions about paper size, line length and spacing, ¶ indentions, carbons, and other instructions are given with each problem if needed; for no directions, you make a decision. Correct errors.

Supplies Needed. Intreoffice memorandum forms; special business forms (purchase requisitions, requests for quotations, purchase orders); carbon paper

LESSON 126

126A Preparatory Practice [5] each line at least 3 times

Alphabet	Jacques Kelly wrote a very exciting play about Zeus, god of mythology.
Figure/symbol	The large jewelry boxes--$9\frac{1}{2}''$ x $14\frac{1}{2}''$ x $27\frac{1}{4}''$--sell for $36.58, less 10%.
Shift keys	Ask James if he has seen Tom, Keven, Frank, Phillip, Weldon, or Harry.
Fluency	The box is just the right size; it is not too big nor is it too small.
	| 1 | 2 | 3 | 4 | 5 | 6 | 7 | 8 | 9 | 10 | 11 | 12 | 13 | 14 |

126B Skill-Comparison Typing [5] each line of 126A for a 1′ writing; compare GWAM

126C Control Building [10] each line 3 times without error

1	Adjacent fingers	As we discovered, the money was not deposited to our account in Ghana.
2	One hand	Address my letters in care of Bret Edwards or John Baxter in Honolulu.
3	Double letters	His business success occurred suddenly when it hardly seemed possible.
4	Long reaches	My brother may bring the unbroken bronze statue to the British Museum.
5	Shift keys	Sue called New York in an effort to locate Vickie, Karen, and Georgia.
6	Long words	Management has preferred the qualitative to the quantitative approach.
7	Stroke response	Administration representatives defended the transportation facilities.
8	Word response	It was my job to put the new files on his desk at the end of each day.
9	Combination	Miniaturization may be a possible solution to this perplexing problem.
10	3d, 4th fingers	Phil and Zack quipped as piqued Paula quickened her pace on the piano.
		| 1 | 2 | 3 | 4 | 5 | 6 | 7 | 8 | 9 | 10 | 11 | 12 | 13 | 14 |

26A Preparatory Practice ⑦ each line twice

Alphabet   We have six men doing quick flying jumps on the trapeze bar.

* ¢   Use the * (asterisk) for your footnote. Send 57¢ in stamps.

@ _   Send only 189 qts. @ 46¢ a qt. Read the book Jungle Cowboy.

Fluency   These cash benefits are yours to use for every kind of bill.

| 1 | 2 | 3 | 4 | 5 | 6 | 7 | 8 | 9 | 10 | 11 | 12 |

26B Location of = (equals) and + (plus) symbols ③

Nonelectric—top two rows only

Electric—top row only

Some typewriters have = and + symbols at the right end of either the top row or the third row. The + is the shift of =. Type with the ; finger: ;=; ;+;

If your typewriter does not have this key, make the symbols.

    Plus: + (diagonal; backspace; hyphen)

    Equals: = (hyphen; backspace; roll platen forward slightly; hold it in position; type hyphen; return to line position)

A space precedes and follows each of the symbols.

26C Location Drills for = and + ⑩ each line twice

1   **= +**   The answer: 827 + 64 = 891. My solution: 522 + 104 = 626.

2   **Review**   Beverly bought 16 7/8 yards @ $3.92 and 5 2/3 yards @ $4.00.

3   **Review**   Space after @, but not between the figure and ¢, %, #, or $.

4   **Review**   "Truth," a man once said, "doesn't hurt unless it ought to."

5   **Review**   O'Neil & Bond's $750 note (due 4/29) was paid by check #625.

6   **Review**   Ford & Rhode's $739.25 check (check #194) is dated March 16.

26D Typing from Corrected Copy ⑥ Type once, making needed corrections as you type.

	Words
If ~~this~~ these advantage makes sense, ~~to you,~~ any should not try you	11
the Journal for a few weks on a regluar bases? Your ~~may~~ I can	22
start right now. just select as many weeks as you like for	34
just ~~83~~ 80 cents a Week for a minmum of 15 weeks. we pay the	46
postage to you home or office.	53

Words

Current date

Mr. Marvin T. Strong
733 Carpenter Lane
Philadelphia, PA 19191

Subject: Account Past Due—$195

We have written to you each month for the past four months requesting that you settle your outstanding account with us.

There has been no activity in your account since your last payment on *May 15.*

Will you please send us your check to clear your account. If we do not hear from you within 10 days, your account will be given to our attorney for collection.

Sincerely   RUSSO MANUFACTURING COMPANY   Steven C. Wimmer   Credit Manager

In each letter to you, we have asked that you send us your check for $195 or let us know when you would be able to make a payment on your account. We are still waiting to receive either your check or a letter of explanation.

According to our records, your account activity from April 12 through May 15 was as follows:

Date	Purchase	Payment	Balance
April 12	$1,000		$1,000
April 20		$ 300	700
April 30		100	600
May 10		200	400
May 15		205	195

3
7
11
16
26
35
48
95
106
159
171
183
192
203
206/219

26E Growth Index ⑭

1. Type a 3′ writing. Proofread by comparing. Circle errors. Determine *gwam*.
2. Type two 1′ writings on each ¶, typing once for speed and once for control.

3. Type a second 3′ writing on the *control level*. Proofread by comparing. Circle errors. Determine *gwam*. Compare your rate and number of errors with those on the first writing.

All letters are used.

		3′ GWAM
¶1 1.3 SI 5.2 AWL 90% HFW	Novelty in everything is prized, perhaps too much, as	4 | 42
	an end in itself. There is a quest for a "sense of self" in	8 | 46
	the way we think and act. We don't like the feeling of being	12 | 50
	put together by a production line. We demand things that fit	16 | 54
	our personal wishes.	17 | 55
¶2 1.3 SI 5.2 AWL 90% HFW	Take the case of cars, for example. They are made by	21 | 59
	factory methods to keep costs down. We can get them, however,	25 | 63
	with variety in color, size, body style, and number and kind	29 | 67
	of extras. They meet our own personal taste. The job a man	33 | 71
	has must meet the same test. It must give him a chance to	37 | 75
	express himself.	38 | 76

3′ GWAM │   1   │   2   │   3   │   4   │

26F Individual Practice ⑩

1. Type each line once. Place a check mark before any line that seemed difficult.

2. Type 2 or more times each line you checked as difficult.

1	Lesson 22	Was Hale & Gordon's check (or was it Mr. Hale's) for $2,500?
2	$ & ( )	Kahn & Bail, Inc., gave checks of $350 and $275 to the club.
3	Lesson 23	The 10% discount on bill #1592 for cassettes comes to $7.25.
4	# % ½ ¼	Please send us 15 dozen envelopes which are 9½ by 4¼ inches.
5	Lesson 24	O'Hanlon doesn't know the difference between "to" and "two."
6	' ! "	Ken's father said, "Might won't make right!" He's so right!
7	Lesson 25	The * refers to item #17. Send 72 tubes of glue @ 79¢ each.
8	* ¢ @ _	The Master Spy and Decision at Sea are on your reading list.

| 1 | 2 | 3 | 4 | 5 | 6 | 7 | 8 | 9 | 10 | 11 | 12 |

125C Production Measurement ㉚ 25′ typing; figure N-PRAM

Job 1: Schedule of Accounts Receivable

Center vertically and horizontally; DS; leave 6 spaces between columns

RUSSO MANUFACTURING COMPANY

Schedule of Accounts Receivable

July 31, 19--

Accounts	Amount Due	Original Amount	Age (Months)
Fred L. Alexander	$ 799	$1,799	2
James Q. Bigelow	1,350	1,350	1
Dwight J. Cruze	50	550	4
Harold R. Evenson	2,500	5,000	3
Andrew C. Forsyth	250	250	1
Garth M. Grimmett	935	2,935	2
Kenneth J. Jacobs	300	300	4
Levi S. Klein	645	995	2
Maurice K. Linley	3,500	3,500	1
Frank S. Nichols	250	500	2
Gregory R. Pope	1,200	1,200	6
Marvin T. Strong	195	1,000	4
Vernon W. Zimmer	400	400	1
Total	$12,374		

Words
6
12
15
38
42
48
60
68
75
80
87
93
99
105
110
117
122
129
135
141
146
157

Job 2: Capital Statement

Full sheet; DS; reading position; 65-space line; all dates current year

RUSSO MANUFACTURING COMPANY

Capital Statement

For the Year Ended July 31, 19--

Capital, August 1, 19--		$306,900
Net income for the year	$78,392	
Add capital stock sold	50,000	
Increase in capital		128,392
Capital, July 31, 19--		$435,292

Words
6
9
16
27
37
50
60
76

SECTION 5 Memorandums; Announcements; Centered Reports

LESSONS 27-32

Goals. In this section you will learn the basic rules of centering copy and of applying these rules in typing announcements, memorandums, and short reports. You will also learn some guides for dividing words and sentence parts at the ends of lines. In addition, you will continue to improve your typing skills.

Machine Adjustments. 70-space line, with left margin stop set 35 spaces left of center of page. Set right margin stop at end of scale unless otherwise directed. SS sentence drills; DS and indent ¶s 5 spaces; space problem copy as directed. Special Supplies Needed: 5″ by 3″ and 6″ by 4″ cards.

LESSON 27

27A Preparatory Practice (8) each line 3 times SS; DS between three-line groups

Alphabet	Did Blair expect to solve the jigsaw puzzle more quickly than Francis?
Figure	Bob moved 720 cardboard boxes, 395 of which went to Rooms 146 and 188.
Figure/symbol	Our check for $1,275, dated February 18, was sent to O'Donnell & Sons.
Fluency	You may thus enjoy trying to do the tasks that others find hard to do.

| 1 | 2 | 3 | 4 | 5 | 6 | 7 | 8 | 9 | 10 | 11 | 12 | 13 | 14 |

27B Technique Practice: RESPONSE PATTERNS (5) each line at least 3 times

Letter response	We were regarded as the team to beat after winning only three debates.
Word response	A sure way to raise his speed is to study the way he strikes the keys.
Combination	Thank you for taking the time to write us about the error on the form.
	We were pleased to learn that you received the shipment in good order.

| 1 | 2 | 3 | 4 | 5 | 6 | 7 | 8 | 9 | 10 | 11 | 12 | 13 | 14 |

27C Problem Typing: SIMPLE MEMORANDUM FORM (8) half sheets; 60-space line

Problem 1: Memorandum Specifications

Current date 1″ (7th line space) from the top; leave 3 blank lines below the date. Proofread by comparing; circle errors.

NOTE: Three words (15 strokes are counted for the date)

Operate return 4 times (3 blank line spaces)

Words 3

SUBJECT: Simple Memorandum Form 10

DS

This is a simple half-sheet memorandum form. In this form 21
the date is always typed one inch (six blank line spaces) 33
from the top. The subject line is typed on the fourth line 45
space below the date. 49

The memorandum is typed in block style. Note that all lines 61
begin flush with the left margin with a double space (one 73
blank line space) between paragraphs. This style is commonly 85
used for memorandums. 90

LESSON 125

125A Preparatory Practice [5] each line at least 3 times

Alphabet	Jack Squires won the rich prize by driving many extra hours last fall.
Figure/symbol	I need 670 feet of 5/8 plywood and 291 feet of 3/4 plywood by tonight.
Shift keys	Mr. Roger P. Calvin lives on West Newton Street, Salt Lake City, Utah.
Fluency	A quick, light, firm stroke of each key will make you a better typist.
	1 | 2 | 3 | 4 | 5 | 6 | 7 | 8 | 9 | 10 | 11 | 12 | 13 | 14

125B Growth Index [15] two 5′ control-level writings; record GWAM of the better writing

All letters are used.

		GWAM 1′	5′	
¶ 1 1.5 SI 5.6 AWL 80% HFW	Management ability has led to better jobs and increased pay for	13	3	70
	many who began as skilled clerical workers. Most of us view a manager	27	5	73
	as someone who directs the work of others, but there is much more to it	41	8	76
	than just that. Managers handle materials, methods, machines, and money	56	11	79
	as well as people. A manager is one who is eager to accept responsi-	70	14	81
	bility, to find solutions to the varied problems that arise each day,	84	17	84
	and to take action quickly. A manager must be able to plan, organize,	98	20	87
	and control; these three jobs are known as the functions of a manager.	112	22	90
¶ 2 1.5 SI 5.6 AWL 80% HFW	Planning is the creative part of a manager's job. It involves a	13	25	93
	determination of what is to be done, how and where it is to be done, and	28	28	95
	who will be responsible. The initial step in planning is to determine	42	31	98
	the goals or objectives. The fundamental objective or goal of any busi-	56	34	101
	ness organization is to realize a profit by providing goods or services	71	37	104
	to its customers. To achieve this objective, specific goals must be set.	86	40	107
	These goals not only provide a basis for actions to be taken, but they	100	42	110
	also serve to measure the amount of progress that has been achieved.	113	45	113
¶ 3 1.5 SI 5.6 AWL 80% HFW	Controlling is the activity which is designed to make sure that a	13	48	115
	job is being done as it was planned and organized. In very simple terms,	28	51	118
	it consists of assuring that each person does the right thing, at the	42	54	121
	right time, at the right place, and with the right materials. If not,	56	56	124
	corrective action must begin. Personal supervision is the most exact	70	59	127
	method of control, but reports of all kinds play an important role.	84	62	129
	Regardless of the means used, the aim of control is to help the manager	98	65	132
	achieve the goals of the company in the most effective way feasible.	112	68	135
1′ GWAM	1 | 2 | 3 | 4 | 5 | 6 | 7 | 8 | 9 | 10 | 11 | 12 | 13 | 14			
5′ GWAM	1 | 2 | 3			

Problem 2: Memorandum on Basic Centering Information

Type with 1″ top margin; leave 3 blank lines below the date; DS before and after paragraphs.

Proofread by comparing. Compare figures with those in original copy. Circle errors.

Words

Current date — 3

SUBJECT: Center Point — 8

Most typing paper is 8½ inches wide and 11 inches long with 66 lines to the page. A half sheet 8½ by 5½ inches has 33 lines. There are thus 6 vertical lines to an inch. — 20 / 32 / 43

A line has 102 elite or 85 pica spaces. The exact center of the paper is at 51 for elite or 42½ for pica type. Unless otherwise directed, use 50 for the elite center (instead of 51) and 42 for the pica center (instead of 42½). — 55 / 67 / 79 / 89

Problem 3: Memorandum on Proofreading Figures

Use the directions given for Problem 2, above.

Words

Current date — 3

SUBJECT: Proofreading Figures — 9

An undetected error in figures can be embarrassing, if not costly, to a writer. Generally, $150.20 can make as much sense in a letter as can $15.20. As a result, a typist should take great care in checking the accuracy of figures. — 21 / 33 / 44 / 56

Compare all figures in your copy with those in the original. If your copy contains numerous figures, consider proofreading by the verifying method. In this method, one person reads from the original while the typist checks the new copy. — 68 / 80 / 92 / 103

27D Individual Practice ⑩

1. Type each line once. Place a check mark before any line that seemed difficult.

2. Type 2 or more times each line you checked as difficult.

1	3d row	We try to treat the young workers as we treat the top men of our firm.
2	Double letters	Will Gregg attempt to sell his three accounting books to Heddy Brooks?
3	One hand	As Frederick Webster swears, they were regarded as brave but defeated.
4	3d/4th fingers	As was pointed out by six of the seniors, the quiz questions are easy.
5	Adjacent keys	We truly hope you were pleased with the glass dishes I sent as a gift.
6	Hyphen	Bob thinks we have an up-to-the-minute plan for our out-of-town sales.
7	Direct reaches	After my brother wrecked my car, Brolen charged for emergency service.
8	Long words	Automatic typewriters are highly effective with repetitive procedures.
9	Shift key	The Laser Bulletin, published in Dayton, Ohio, will be issued in July.

| 1 | 2 | 3 | 4 | 5 | 6 | 7 | 8 | 9 | 10 | 11 | 12 | 13 | 14 |

124D Production Measurement ㉚ 25' typing; figure N-PRAM

Job 1: Letter (WB p. 73)
Modified block style; indented ¶s; mixed punctuation

	Words
mr oscar thompson county recreation director	12
st. george ut 84770 dear mr thompson (¶ 1)	21
My attention has been called to the manner in	30
which you handled the report of the Environ-	38
mental Protection Agency with respect to the	47
proposed recreational development project	56
along the Virgin River. (¶ 2) We also would	64
like to see this development occur and want	72
to compliment you on your explanation of the	81
action to be taken. As you know, this sort	90
of environmental question can be grossly	98
misunderstood if the issues are not thoroughly	108
and objectively analyzed. (¶ 3) If your travel	116
brings you to Salt Lake City, I would appre-	125
ciate the opportunity of meeting and visiting	134
with you. (¶ 4) Congratulations on your re-	142
cent promotion. sincerely utah recreation	150
association b j evans executive director	159/173

Job 2: Memorandum (WB p. 75)

	Words
TO: richard r andrews general manager	7
FROM: helen z fitzgerald	11
DATE: Current	14
SUBJECT: departmental job openings for june	21
(¶ 1) Each department has submitted its per-	29
sonnel requests for the month of June. We	37
expect to hire a total of 17 new employees.	46
The following list summarizes the number of	55
new employees by department: (*List.*) Account-	62
ing Department––2; General Office Depart-	70
ment––3; Shipping and Receiving Depart-	78
ment––1; Purchasing Department––2; Sales	85
Department––4; Advertising Department––2;	93
Manufacturing Department A––2; Manufac-	101
turing Department B––1 (¶ 2) All the per-	108
sonnel requests are for replacements. As re-	117
quested, all departments are continuing to	125
operate at last month's personnel levels.	134/141

Job 3: Table with Braced Heading
Full sheet; DS body; reading position; horizontal and vertical rulings

	Words
Main heading: LOCAL CHORAL GROUPS IN	5
THE GREATER SALT LAKE AREA	10
Braced heading over Columns 2, 3, and 4: Membership	31
Column 1 heading: Group	
Column 2 heading: Females	
Column 3 heading: Males	
Column 4 heading: Totals	46

Group	Females	Males	Totals	Words
The Swingers	35	35	70	60
The Sundowners	5	20	25	65
Sweet Sounds	50	20	70	70
The Melodies	10	10	20	74
The Soft Sounds	15	10	25	88

LESSON 28

28A Preparatory Practice ⑧ each line 3 times SS; DS between three-line groups

Alphabet	Jack may provide a few extra quiz questions or problems for the girls.
Figure	The 1974 edition of this book has 5 parts, 23 chapters, and 680 pages.
Figure/symbol	Our order dated June 17 reads: Ship 148 bags of 25# ea. @ 39¢ per lb.
Fluency	No problem that we tackle is ever so big as the problem that we evade.

| 1 | 2 | 3 | 4 | 5 | 6 | 7 | 8 | 9 | 10 | 11 | 12 | 13 | 14 |

28B Skill-Transfer Typing ⑩ 60-space line

1. Type each sentence three times. Try to type each line at the rate of the first one.

2. If time permits, repeat the sentence on which you make the most errors.

Words

1	Fluency	When you look, try to see; when you hear, try to understand.	12
2	Figure	If the flight is to leave at 7:45, we must check in by 7:10.	12
3	Symbol	Don't space between ¢, %, or # and the figure typed with it.	12
4	Script	*A letterhead should tell people that your product is unique.*	12
5	Corrected copy	it is my such easier todo work right than that to do it over.	12
6	Error Recognition	It is will to push hard or speed an drop back four control.	12

28C Horizontal Centering ⑨ 8½″ by 5½″ half sheet; DS; begin on Line 11 from the top

1. Check placement of paper guide. Turn to Reference Guide page iii for directions. Insert paper with the short edge at the left (at **0** on the paper guide scale).
2. Move both margin stops to the ends of the scale. Clear all tabulator stops. Move the carriage to the center point; set a tab stop here to use for each line.
3. From the center point, backspace once for each 2 spaces in the line to be centered. Disregard a leftover stroke.
4. Begin to type where you complete the backspacing.

Words

DR. ROBERT DUNHAM	4
TS	
Announces the Location of His	10
DENTAL OFFICES	13
in the Franklin Medical Center	19
3200 Santa Monica Boulevard	24

SECTION 23 Measurement: Basic and Production Skills

LESSONS 124-125

Section 23 provides basic and production skills measurement. Each lesson gives 20 minutes of production typing. If you finish all jobs before time is called, begin the first job again. You will have about 5 minutes at the end of the period to figure your N-PRAM.

Drill Copy. SS; 70-space line

¶ Copy. DS; 70-space line; 5-space ¶ indentions; full sheets

Production Measurement. Unless otherwise directed, use the following styles and procedures.

Letters. Use modified block style with indented ¶s and open punctuation; the current date; your reference initials. Type 1 cc; address an envelope.

Tables. Follow directions for each problem; no cc's.

Manuscript. Follow the binding form indicated; no cc.

LESSON 124

124A Preparatory Practice (5) each line at least 3 times

Alphabet	The men glazed calyxes of blue flowers on pink antique jars and vases.
Figure/symbol	Order #917524 from Robb & Frank for 3,800 pens was filled on August 6.
Adjacent reaches	Drew returned the funds without reading the directions in the booklet.
Fluency	Send the names of those who are entitled to the stock dividend checks.

| 1 | 2 | 3 | 4 | 5 | 6 | 7 | 8 | 9 | 10 | 11 | 12 | 13 | 14 |

124B Skill-Comparison Typing (5) Use material in 124A, above; 1′ writing on each line, compare GWAM.

124C Guided Writing (10)

Type a 1′ control-level writing to establish your base rate. Type three 2′ writings, trying to hit the exact letter of your base rate each time. Regulate your rate by a signal given at half-minute intervals.

All letters are used.

1.5 SI
5.6 AWL
80% HFW

	GWAM 1′	2′	
Africa is often referred to as the Dark Continent, a place of mys-	13	7	61
tery and intrigue where the weary traveler must always be on guard for	27	14	68
the dangers that might quickly come upon him. We do realize that there	42	21	75
are still many wild and dangerous parts of Africa, but so are there in	56	28	83
almost every large city in our own country. A country is feared just by	70	35	90
those who are inexperienced and uninformed; for the individual who knows	85	43	97
and understands Africa, it is a beautiful and most friendly continent--	99	50	104
indeed, for the most part, a completely safe place.	109	55	109

1′ GWAM | 1 | 2 | 3 | 4 | 5 | 6 | 7 | 8 | 9 | 10 | 11 | 12 | 13 | 14 |
2′ GWAM | 1 | 2 | 3 | 4 | 5 | 6 | 7 |

28D Problem Typing: CENTERED ANNOUNCEMENTS ⓴ each problem on a half sheet, short edge at the left

Problem 1: Unarranged Copy

DS; begin on Line 8; center each line

	Words
CORRECT TYPING POSITION	5
TS	
Eyes on Copy; Copy at Right of Typewriter	13
Body Erect; Sit Back in Chair	19
Feet on Floor, One Ahead of the Other	27
Forearms Parallel to Slant of Keyboard	35
Fingers Curved over Second Row of Keys	42
Wrists Down, Not Arched	47
Front Frame of Machine Even with Desk Edge	56
Table Free of Unneeded Books	62

Problem 2: Corrected Copy

DS; begin on Line 10; center each line

	Words
ALMOND SON'S ← TS	2
IS	3
Proud to ~~Announce~~ Present	6
Felix de Vega Couture Collection	13
Exciting, Beautiful Fashions , Exotic	20
Wednesday (27 September), 19--	26
Sunset Boulevard at Hampton court	33

28E Evaluate Your Work ③

1. Examine your finished copy. Compare your solution lines to those above and below them. Do the numbers of extended or indented strokes at the ends of lines appear to be equal?
2. Is the spacing between lines correct?

NOTE: For an exact check of your spacing, use a regular ruler. A special stroke and line-space ruler can be obtained from the publisher of this textbook. With this ruler, you can measure the number of strokes and the number of typewritten lines.

LESSON 29

29A Preparatory Practice ⑧ each line 3 times SS; DS between three-line groups

Alphabet	Owens thinks freezing prices at July fixed levels may be questionable.
Figure	On January 29 they ordered 186 books, 370 pens, and 45 reams of paper.
From dictation	if they, if they go, if they go to do, it is, it is the, it is the job
Fluency	If they do this job when they should, they may stay at the large lake.

| 1 | 2 | 3 | 4 | 5 | 6 | 7 | 8 | 9 | 10 | 11 | 12 | 13 | 14 |

29B Control Building: ERRORLESS TYPING ⑦ each line twice without error or 3 times with not more than 1 error to a line

One hand	I was not at union headquarters when a new wage contract was defeated.
Shift keys	Send Fields & Marshall ten copies of the new book by Niels and Atwood.
Long words	Analysis of the experimental data provides an estimate of probability.
Fluency	A man should want work enough to do and strength enough to do it well.

Job 2: Model Memorandum for Duplication *(WB p. 69)*

		Words
TO:	All Branch Offices	4
FROM:	Michelle England	7
DATE:	June 10, 19––	10
SUBJECT:	Branch Offices Supplies List	16

(¶ 1) Attached is the latest revised Branch 23
Offices Forms Supplies List (Section 1) with 32
the form titles listed alphabetically. Your in- 42
dividual Branch Office Lists (Section 2) are 51
also included. (¶ 2) The "Standard Pkg. 57
Quantity" column indicates the number of 65
sheets or sets that make up one pad, or the 74
number of sheets, cards, or sets contained 83
within a package or box. This column is for 92
information only to help determine quantity 101
to order. (¶ 3) The "Unit of Issue" column 108
gives the unit to be used in ordering; i.e., 117
sheets, cards, sets, pads, etc. The minimum 126
quantity that the stockroom will issue is also 135
shown in this column; however, multiples of 144
the quantity may be ordered. Where no mini- 153
mum quantities are shown, your usage should 162
determine the quantity to be ordered. (We 170
recommend that a four to six months' supply 179
be stocked in order to obtain the most eco- 187
nomical quantity.) (¶ 4) Please allow us rea- 195
sonable time to process your orders. If you 204
are caught short from time to time, we shall 213
do our best to expedite such orders. We sug- 222
gest a periodic inventory of your forms to 231
minimize the possibility of a depleted supply. 240
As a guide, we suggest that items be reordered 250
on Form FP-99834-A and sent to Joan Framp- 258
ton approximately three weeks before ex- 266
pected depletion. (¶ 5) If you have any ques- 273
tions regarding the attached list, please do not 283
hesitate to contact me. attachment 291/295

Job 3: Letter *(WB p. 71)*

Words

june 10, 19–– mr ralph q bird 135 warrenton 9
avenue hartford ct 06105 dear mr bird (¶ 1) 18
We have reviewed your recent correspondence 27
and application with our management, and we 35
are interested in learning more about you. 44
(¶ 2) We should like you to visit our Pennsyl- 52
vania operation whenever your schedule per- 60
mits. This trip will be at our expense, and 69
you will be reimbursed while in Warren for 78
your round-trip expenses. Please make your 87
travel arrangements and then call Miss Lois 95
Roundy at 723-8900, Ext. 213, collect so we 104
shall know when to expect you. We shall be 113
happy to make overnight reservations for you 122
at the Avalon Inn, 9519 East Market Street; 131
and we should like to begin your interview at 140
8:30 the following morning. (¶ 3) Thank you 148
for your interest in our company. I look for- 157
ward to meeting you soon. sincerely yours 165
russell g wellington personnel director 174/186

Job 4: Reminders on Plain Paper

Margins: 2″ top and side
Heading: REMINDERS FOR JUNE
SS; DS between items

Words

1. June 10 is your daughter's birthday. 2. 13
June 13-15 is your National Guard bivouac. 21
3. June 16 you have a speaking engagement 30
at the Lions Club at 8:30 p.m. 4. June 20 is 39
your wedding anniversary. 5. June 21 you 48
have a dental appointment with Dr. Cloward 56
at 9:00 a.m. 6. June 25 is the Company's An- 65
nual Summer Picnic at the Rotary Park, 73
1:00 – 8:30 p.m. 7. June 26 is the Board of 82
Directors meeting at 2:00 p.m. in the Execu- 91
tive Conference Room. 8. June 30 is your 99
appointment with the Mayor and City Council 108
at 1:30 p.m. in the Mayor's office. 115

29C Typing Outside the Margins ② 60-space line

left margin: center — 30
right margin: center + 30

1. Depress the **margin release** or **margin bypass (25)**, and backspace 5 spaces into the left margin.
2. Type the sentence below. When the carriage locks, depress the margin release or margin bypass and complete the typing.
3. Repeat 1 and 2.

The chief rule of teamwork: Be considerate of others in little things.

29D Vertical Centering: MATHEMATICAL METHOD ⑩ 8½″ by 5½″ half sheet

1. Count the lines and blank line spaces in the copy.
2. Subtract lines needed from 66 for a full sheet or from 33 for a half sheet.
3. Divide by 2 to get top and bottom margins. If a fraction results, disregard it in computing the top margin.

4. To leave the correct *blank* space, space down from the top edge of the paper 1 more than the number of lines in the top margin.
Alternate Procedure. Before inserting the paper, use your stroke and line-space ruler to mark with a do the starting line.

> **Reading position**
>
> For *reading position*, which is above the exact vertical center, subtract 2 from the exact top margin.

DS; center each line horizontally; center entire report vertically

	Words
VERTICAL CENTERING TS	4
Count the lines to be centered.	10
Count 2 for the triple space after heading.	19
Count 1 for each blank line space in double-spaced lines.	31
Subtract total lines from 66 (full sheet) or 33 (half sheet).	44
Divide the result by 2 for top margin.	52
If a fraction results, disregard it.	59
Space down that number plus 1.	65

29E Problem Typing: CENTERED ANNOUNCEMENTS ⑳

Problem 1: Exact Center

On a half sheet, type the announcement at the right, DS. Center the lines horizontally and the entire announcement vertically.

Problem 2: Reading Position

On a full sheet, type the announcement at the right, DS. Center the lines horizontally and the entire announcement in *reading position* vertically.

	Words
THE VINCENT BARNES ART GALLERY TS	6
cordially invites you to attend a	13
reception and preview showing	19
of the new Lynwood Village store	26
Thursday, August tenth, five to seven	33
930 Lynwood Boulevard	38

29F Evaluate Your Work ③ Use your stroke and line-space ruler.

1. Proofread by comparing; circle errors.
2. For Problem 1, are there an equal number of line spaces in the top and bottom margins?
3. For Problem 2, are there 4 fewer line spaces in the top margin than in the bottom?

4. Compare your solution lines to those above and below them. Do the numbers of extended or indented strokes at the ends of lines appear to be equal?
5. Is the spacing between the lines correct?

¶ 4
1.5 SI
5.6 AWL
80% HFW

Although the size of the office may determine the actual kinds of jobs that an individual will be given as an executive typist, the manner in which you attack and solve a task will to a very large degree determine how successful you will be as an executive typist. Whether you consider a job large or small, simple or complex, should not affect the way you complete the assignment. Your employer wants typists who will be willing to accept the routine tasks as well as the more complex and challenging problems. No task should be considered unworthy of your complete attention; you will undoubtedly be evaluated on the basis of your daily performance on the simple tasks just as much as on the performance on the more difficult jobs. Treat each assignment as though it were the most important job in the world. Remember the age-old adage: A job worthy of doing is worth doing well.

	1'	5'
	13	82
	28	85
	42	88
	57	91
	71	94
	85	96
	100	99
	115	102
	129	105
	143	108
	157	111
	171	113
	178	115

1' GWAM | 1 | 2 | 3 | 4 | 5 | 6 | 7 | 8 | 9 | 10 | 11 | 12 | 13 | 14 |
5' GWAM | 1 | 2 | 3 |

123C Production Measurement ㉚ 25' writing; figure N-PRAM

Job 1: Letter on Executive-Size Stationery (WB p. 67)

Modified block; ¶s indented; mixed punctuation; date: June 10, 19––; address letter to: Ms. Lucille T. Ellertson, President, Ellertson, Inc., 7150 West Euclid Avenue, Milwaukee, WI 53219; closing lines: Sincerely yours, Sandra V. Rushmore, Vice President; 1 cc

Words

Thank you for your letter of June 5. It will be a pleasure for Warren Associates to survey the organizational structure and management practices of your company.

During the week of June 21, I am planning a trip to Pittsburgh, St. Louis, and Chicago. I can fly to Milwaukee on June 25 for our initial conference if this date is convenient for you.

For our initial meeting, will you please have available a copy of your latest organization chart, copies of job descriptions, and any procedures manuals you may have published.

I am looking forward to meeting you and hope that we may meet on June 25.

36
45
54
59
68
78
87
97
106
115
124
132
139
158/177

LESSON 30

30A Preparatory Practice (8) each line 3 times SS; DS between three-line groups

Alphabet	Packard Bigelow may yet fly to Verz Cruz to inquire about his next job.
Figure	Flight 372 will leave at 10:46 a.m. and arrive in Buffalo at 9:58 p.m.
Figure/symbol	Bob's policy #818429 for $49,500 has been renewed for another 3 years.
Fluency	Money spent for knowledge pays high interest. We must learn to think.

| 1 | 2 | 3 | 4 | 5 | 6 | 7 | 8 | 9 | 10 | 11 | 12 | 13 | 14 |

30B Speed/Control Building (7)

1. Type the paragraph once on the EXPLORATION LEVEL; then twice on the CONTROL LEVEL.

2. Proofread; circle errors. Compare the **number of errors** on the three writings.

1.4 SI
5.4 AWL
85% HFW

Here is our new growth plan: We do well that which we know well. We also make room for ideas that permit us to use our expertise. Such thinking has brought about our emerging as one of the largest makers of photographic equipment in the world, creating dozens of jobs and products that serve the public in many ways.

30C Special Characters (25) each line at least twice

NOTE: If your keyboard provides one of the following characters, use it. If not, type the character as described below.

'	Minutes or feet	Apostrophe	—	Minus	Hyphen (leave space before and after)
"	Seconds, inches, or ditto	Quotation mark	×	Times or by	Lowercase x (leave space before and after)
°	Degree	Roll platen forward ½ space; lowercase o; return platen	÷	Divided by	Hyphen; backspace; colon
+	Plus	Diagonal; backspace; hyphen	=	Equals	Hyphen; backspace; roll platen forward; hyphen; return platen

The 2' speed range, typed with the 15" call of the guide, is 30 to 46.
A rug 15'6" x 18'9" will be just right for a room that is 20'6" x 25'.
His problem is 27 × 89 — 364 ÷ 2. What is the sum of 157 + 509 — 263?
Type: 15 × 90 — 62 + 136 ÷ 2 = 712 and 7 × 284 — 965 + 301 ÷ 2 = 662.
If 32 × 564 — 897 + 109 equals 17,260, what would 57 + 590 — 63 equal?
The boiling point of water is 212° F. and the freezing point is 32° F.

| 1 | 2 | 3 | 4 | 5 | 6 | 7 | 8 | 9 | 10 | 11 | 12 | 13 | 14 |

LESSON 123

123A Preparatory Practice [5] each line at least 3 times

Alphabet	The moving experts quickly adjusted ten gauges before the water froze.
Figure/symbol	Flight #796 leaving here at 12:30 is scheduled to reach Paris at 4:58.
Drill on min	The minister was mindful that the minor spent a minimum of one minute.
Fluency	To type in the right way, one must get rid of the jerks in his typing.

| 1 | 2 | 3 | 4 | 5 | 6 | 7 | 8 | 9 | 10 | 11 | 12 | 13 | 14 |

123B Growth Index [15] two 5′ control-level writings; record GWAM of the better writing

All letters are used.

GWAM 1′ 5′

¶ 1
1.5 SI
5.6 AWL
80% HFW

Typists in a large executive office may be required to do a variety 13 3
of tasks and activities. In addition to the routine letters, reports, 28 6
and memos, a typist should expect to do many things other than just typ- 42 8
ing. Most of the positions for a typist in these offices require that a 57 11
good deal of initiative be brought with the worker. Many employers still 72 14
feel that a vast part of the daily tasks must be completed without spe- 86 17
cific directions from the boss. Should you prefer not to have a variety 100 20
of assignments, then you should avoid any executive typing job that may 115 23
be offered to you. 118 24

¶ 2
1.5 SI
5.6 AWL
80% HFW

Some of the types of activities that a typist will have to do in- 13 26
clude such things as making a list of the boss's appointments; this could 28 29
be done in either pen or in type. Speeches and outlines must be proof- 42 32
read and typed; this can be a very interesting part of being a good execu- 57 35
tive typist. Any paper, either to be used solely within the firm or to 71 38
be sent outside the firm, must have all words spelled properly and must 86 41
have no grammatical errors. A good typist will make all of these correc- 100 44
tions and will not change the meaning of the material. The typist will 115 47
also be responsible for the typing of summaries, press releases, itiner- 129 49
aries, and reminders. 133 50

¶ 3
1.5 SI
5.6 AWL
80% HFW

A person typing in an executive office must know how to make copies 14 53
using the various multiple-copy processes. The person typing the job 28 56
must know which process to select: carbon, direct-copy, spirit, sten- 42 59
cil, or offset. A typist should know that the carbon copy process is 56 61
for one to four copies; the direct-copy process is used for one to ten 70 64
copies; the spirit process is used for ten to one hundred copies; and 84 67
the stencil and offset processes are used when more than one hundred 98 70
copies are needed. Of course, there are other considerations that a 111 73
person must use in helping to decide which of the multiple-copy processes 126 76
should be used for any given job; one very important aspect is the qual- 141 78
ity required of the copy. 146 79

(Timed writing continued on next page.)

1′ GWAM | 1 | 2 | 3 | 4 | 5 | 6 | 7 | 8 | 9 | 10 | 11 | 12 | 13 | 14 |
5′ GWAM | 1 | 2 | 3 |

30D Centering Data on Special-Size Paper ⑧

To find the horizontal center of special-size paper or cards

1. Insert the paper or card into the machine; add the numbers at the left and right edges of the paper to obtain the number of strokes available on a line.

2. Divide this sum by 2. The result is the horizontal center point for that paper.

3. Follow the steps for horizontal centering on page 53.

Practice Problem

1. Insert a half sheet with the long edge at the left (5½″ by 8½″). For a 3½″ top margin, start on Line 22.
2. Center each line horizontally; DS the lines.
3. Type the information requested at the right.

The name of your college (all caps)

The street address

The city and state address

Your name

Today's date

30E Evaluate Your Work ③ Use your stroke and line-space ruler.

1. Examine your finished copy. Are top and bottom margins approximately equal?
2. Compare your solution lines to those above and below them. Do the numbers of extended or indented lines appear to be equal?
3. Is the spacing between lines correct?
4. If you are not satisfied with your solution, retype the problem as time permits.

30F Centering a Heading on a Horizontal Line ③

With the underline key, type a 3-inch line on your paper. (30 pica or 36 elite strokes). Use the procedure in 30D to determine the center point; then center on the line the heading at the right.

Centered Heading

30G Problem Typing: CENTERING ON SPECIAL-SIZE PAPER OR CARDS ⑮

Problem 1: Data on 5″ x 3″ Card (WB p. 11)

NOTE: Laboratory (workbook) materials are available for use with this textbook. The workbook page on which a specific form or stationery item appears is given in the textbook with the appropriate problem. Cards for Problems 1 and 2 are on workbook page 11 (WB p. 11). Students without workbooks should use paper cut to 5″ by 3″ and 6″ by 4″.

1. Insert 5″ by 3″ card with short edge at the left.

2. Start on Line 5; DS.

3. Center each line horizontally.

4. Evaluate your solution. Use your stroke and line-space ruler to check your work.

Card holders

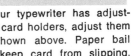

If your typewriter has adjustable card holders, adjust them as shown above. Paper bail will keep card from slipping.

Words

CENTERING DATA ON SPECIAL-SIZE PAPER   7

TS

Insert the card or paper into the machine.   16

Add the scale numbers at both edges.   24

Divide the sum by 2.   28

The result is the horizontal center.   38

Problem 2: Data on 6- by 4-Inch Card

1. Type Problem 1 on a 6″ by 4″ card (or paper) with the short edge at the left. Start on Line 8; DS. Center each line horizontally.

2. Evaluate your solution, using your stroke and line-space ruler.
3. Proofread by comparing.

Job 13: Model of Dinner Program

With the paper sideways, type a model copy for stencil duplication of the program for the annual employees dinner in the style illustrated. Use the asterisk to type the design.

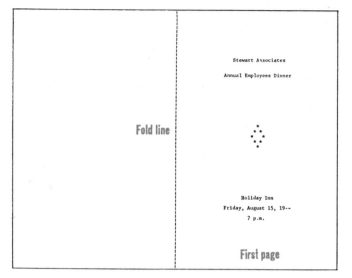

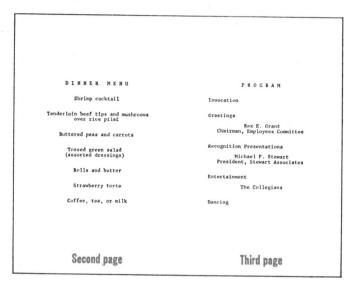

First Page	Second Page	Third Page
BLACKSTONE CORPORATION	D I N N E R M E N U	P R O G R A M
Annual Employees Dinner	Shrimp/crab cocktail	Invocation
✲	Prime rib with mushrooms	Greetings
✲ ✲	Baked potato with sour	Stanley R. Fox
✲ ✲	cream dressing	Chairman, Employees Association
✲ ✲	Tossed green salad	Blackstone Service Awards
✲	(choice of dressing)	Frederick R. Blackstone
	Rolls and butter	Chairman of the Board
Thunderbird Jantzen Beach Hotel	Cherry cheesecake	Blackstone Corporation
Friday, April 24, 19--	Coffee, tea, or milk	Entertainment
7:30 p.m.		The Portland Ambassadors
		Dancing
		Irwin Bond Orchestra

Job 14: Composing a Memorandum Announcement   (WB p. 65)

Compose a memorandum announcing the Annual Employees Dinner. Include the location (hotel address is 1401 North Hayden Island Drive), time, the dinner entree, and the highlights of the evening's program. This memo is from Mr. Speicher and is to all Blackstone employees and guests. Date memo April 20, 19--.

LESSON 31

31A Preparatory Practice [8] each line 3 times SS; DS between three-line groups

Alphabet	When quizzed, Julia Volberg stated she expected no more work for July.
Figure	Our latest inventory includes 958 rings, 3,064 pins, and 172 brooches.
Rule for figures	Type invoice numbers in figures: Invoice #5172 is dated September 30.
Fluency	They sent us these ornaments from an ancient temple in a foreign land.
	| 1 | 2 | 3 | 4 | 5 | 6 | 7 | 8 | 9 | 10 | 11 | 12 | 13 | 14 |

31B Speed/Control Building [5]

1. Type the paragraph once on the EXPLORATION LEVEL; then twice on the CONTROL LEVEL.

2. Proofread; circle errors. Compare the number of errors on the three writings.

All letters are used.

1.5 SI
5.6 AWL
80% HFW

In composing a letter, you may find it hard to recognize that the result need not sound like a corporation. A corporate business does consist of actual people; a message or request to one of them should extend warmth--should project the image that the message is from a living person, not a vague, impersonal name on a letterhead.

| 1 | 2 | 3 | 4 | 5 | 6 | 7 | 8 | 9 | 10 | 11 | 12 | 13 | 14 |

31C Setting the Right Margin Stop [5]

1. Set the margin stops for an exact 60-space line (left: center − 30 | right: center + 30).

2. Type the sentence below; stop on the stroke on which the typewriter bell rings. Instead of typing the remainder of the sentence, type the figures 123 etc. until the carriage locks. The last figure typed is the number of spaces on your typewriter between the bell and the carriage lock.

3. When you are not to type copy line for line, set the right-hand stop for the bell to ring 3 spaces before the desired line ending.

Thus: Subtract 3 from the last figure typed in Step 2. Add the difference to the figure at which the right-hand margin stop would be set for an exact line length.

4. Usually 3 to 7 spaces must be added to the right-hand stop setting, depending upon your typewriter.

REMEMBER YOUR ADJUSTMENT FIGURE.

Example. If your bell rings 9 spaces before the desired line ending, add 6 to the point at which a stop would be set for exact line length.

To get a bell cue, add your adjustment figure to the exact-margin figure.

31D Technique Practice: BELL CUE [7] Type the ¶ in 31B 3 times as directed below.

First Typing. 60-space line *plus* your adjustment figure; DS; 5-space ¶ indention. Be guided by the bell to return. If the bell rings and the carriage locks, depress the margin release key; complete the word.

Second Typing. 50-space line with adjustment figure added. Be guided by the bell to return.

Third Typing. 40-space line with adjustment figure added.

Evaluation. Using your stroke and line-space ruler, see if the left and right margins are approximately equal.

Type the following report of the Expansion Committee as an unbound manuscript; 1½″ top margin; 1″ side margins; SS; 1 cc

EXPANSION COMMITTEE PRELIMINARY REPORT *of the*

Feasibility of ~~locating~~ *Constructing New* a fabrication Plant in eugene *TS*

I. Labor *DS*

lc EUGENE is a major producing and shipping point for lumber and plywood *lc* in Western Oregon. It is *also* the home of major businesses consisting primarily of *light* industry and agricultural *processing* plants. Eugene has a population of 78,389 (1970 census) and is a part of an SMSA, comprising a ~~population of~~ 213,358. There should be *very little* difficulty *in* obtaining a sufficient work force for a new *lc* plant; *however,* Substantial training will be required. *TS*

(standard metropolitan statistical area)

II. POWER AND FUEL *) Center* *DS*

Eugene is located in an *area* ~~area~~ in which power and fuel costs are "average." Electricity and other public utilities are *municipally* ~~city~~ owned and *operated* ~~runned.~~ Chances are *excellent* ~~good~~ that a special *utility* rate will be granted by the city of Eugene as an inducement to *build* ~~locate~~ our plant there.

IV ~~III.~~ TAXES

At ~~present,~~ *the present time* tax concessions are being made to *new* industries if they will *locate* ~~build~~ in Eugene. The amount of *the tax* concession is *strictly* depend *ent* ~~upnt~~ upon the negotia- *lc* tions; *but* In some instances, the city and county have granted tax reductions up to 25 *%* ~~percents~~ for the first *four* ~~two~~ years. *The tax situation is much more favorable than in many other cities.*

III ~~IV.~~ Water

Because of Eugene's close proximity to various reservoirs and rivers, the water supply is abundant and relatively *inexpensive.* ~~cheap;~~ *This is also one of the major advantages of locating our new fabrication plant in Eugene.*

V. TRANSPORTATION

Eugene is situated favorably with regard to transportation facilities. *Because* ~~Since~~ this is a lumbering center, a *major* railrad *division point* is located in Eugene. Most of our products require shipping via railroad; *therefore,* Eugene is an ideal site. Air and motor freight services are *also* available. ~~in Eugene also.~~

Problem 1: Report on Word Division

1. Center the main heading horizontally. After typing the first line, reset the left margin stop 4 spaces to the right.

2. To type the numbers for the remaining ¶s, depress the margin release and backspace 4 spaces into the left margin.

3. Proofread by comparing; circle errors; use your stroke and linespace ruler to check top and side margins.

Full sheet; 60-space line; center report vertically in reading position; SS; DS between items.

	Words
GUIDES FOR WORD DIVISION	5

2 spaces ⟶ ↓ *Reset margin*

1. You may divide words at the ends of lines to keep the — 17
   right margin as even as possible. Excessive division — 27
   should, however, be avoided. — 33

Use margin release; then backspace 4 spaces ⟶ 2. Divide words between syllables only, as fore-noon and — 46
   bom-bard. When in doubt, use the dictionary to help — 58
   solve word-division problems. — 64

3. Do not divide words of only one syllable, such as friend, — 78
   thought, or trained. Do not separate a syllable without — 92
   a vowel; as, didn't. — 97

4. Do not divide a word of five or fewer letters, such as — 109
   also, duty, or going. — 116

5. Do not separate a one-letter syllable at the beginning — 127
   of a word; as, enough. — 133

6. Do not separate a one- or two-letter syllable at the end — 145
   of a word; as, ready, largely, higher. — 156

7. You may usually divide a word between double consonants; — 169
   as, cor-rect, mil-lion, mes-sage. — 180

8. When adding a syllable to a word that ends in double — 191
   letters, divide after the double letters of the root — 202
   word; as, express, express-ing. — 212

9. When the final consonant is doubled in adding a suffix, — 224
   divide between the doubled letters; as, begin, begin-ning. — 238

Problem 2: Word Division

Half sheet inserted short edge at left; DS; 70-space line; 10 spaces between columns; center the problem vertically

Type the hyphen to show preferred word divisions in typewritten work, as in Line 1. If necessary, refer to Problem 1 or to a dictionary.

WORD DIVISION
TS

Tabulate from column to column	steady	will-ing	blan-ket	quickly
	input	enumerate	luggage	preferred
	afraid	rustproof	cutting	safety
	billed	newsroom	messenger	spirally
	alerted	rectify	skillful	changeable

KEY | 7 | 10 | 9 | 10 | 9 | 10 | 10 |

guarantee the shipment of this equipment by September 1, 19––. (¶ 21) If you have any questions regarding this quotation, please telephone me at our main office in Portland, (503) 463-2980, or contact our sales representative for your area:

(Center the longest line below.)

Richards & Richards, Inc.
3815 DeLeon Street
Houston, TX   77017

Attention Mr. Dean A. Richards

Phone: (713) 649-6328

(¶ 22) We thank you for this opportunity of quoting on your requirements and hope that we may receive your order. sincerely yours BLACKSTONE CORPORATION harold f speicher executive vice president   enclosures 5   cc mr dean a richards

Job 10: Vacation Schedule

Margins: 2″ top, 1½″ sides; DS; use leaders

VACATION SCHEDULE FOR EXECUTIVE OFFICE

June 1, 19–– – August 31, 19––

Period	Employee
June 1 – June 7	Ruth Anne Greenfield
June 8 – June 21	Anne R. Williams
June 8 – June 14	Katherine R. Jones
June 15 – June 21	David R. Winters
June 22 – June 28	Karen P. Sloan
June 29 – July 12	Frank N. Heaps
July 6 – July 19	Andrea C. Oliver
July 13 – August 2	Harold F. Speicher
July 20 – July 26	Sylvia T. Anderson
July 27 – August 2	Ruth C. Carter
August 3– August 16	Carol Sue Francis
August 10 – August 16	Henry V. Silverton
August 17 – August 30	Steven W. Fox
August 24 – August 30	John R. Alexander

Job 11: Letters on Executive-Size Stationery
(7½ x 10¼) *(WB pp. 53–63)*

Type the following letter to each member of the board of directors listed below. Mr. Speicher prefers that an original copy be sent to each member of the board. Make a carbon copy of only the first letter and list the other addressees on the back of that carbon copy.

April 17, 19–– *(Use appropriate salutation.)*   (¶ 1) The Blackstone Corporation's Board of Directors will hold its next meeting in the Executive Conference Room on Tuesday, April 28, 19––, at 3:30 p.m. (¶ 2) The major item of business at this meeting will be the Expansion Committee's report concerning the feasibility of constructing a new fabrication plant in Eugene, Oregon. A preliminary report of the committee is enclosed for your review. A copy of the complete agenda will be mailed to you by April 24. sincerely yours   frederick r blackstone chairman of the board *(Words in body: 92)*

Board Members:

Mrs. Susan T. Brookfield
104 Babler Avenue, SE
Portland, OR   97222

Mr. Richard L. Sutherland
337 Golf Court Road, NE
Portland, OR   97211

Dr. Rosanna F. Wilkinson
Suite 203A
Portland Medical Plaza
3900 Grand Street, SE
Portland, OR   97214

Mr. Carl T. Blackstone
1509 Licyntra Lane, SE
Portland, OR   97222

Ms. Carolina K. Wiggins
Andrew Arms Apartments, Suite 609
10450 Lincoln Avenue
Portland, OR   97222

Dr. A. Kenneth Lancaster
15099 Knott Street, NE
Portland, OR   97230

LESSON 32

32A Preparatory Practice ⑧ each line 3 times SS; DS between three-line groups

Alphabet   Hugh Wilcox printed five dozen banquet tickets for my meeting in June.

Figure   We are sending 2,795 of the 4,680 sets now and the balance on June 13.

Rule for figures Type weights in figures: The largest box weighs 207 pounds 13 ounces.

Fluency   Keep the right margins of the papers you type just as even as you can.

| 1 | 2 | 3 | 4 | 5 | 6 | 7 | 8 | 9 | 10 | 11 | 12 | 13 | 14 |

32B Technique Practice: RESPONSE PATTERNS ⑥ each line at least 3 times

Letter response   We are aware that the union monopoly case is exaggerated by the staff.

Word response   They can handle their profit problem if they do their work with vigor.

Combination   He may find the basic elements of the problem too subtle to determine.

                  A wise neighbor said that most of us have potential that we never tap.

| 1 | 2 | 3 | 4 | 5 | 6 | 7 | 8 | 9 | 10 | 11 | 12 | 13 | 14 |

32C Growth Index ⑪ one 3' and one 5' writing; determine GWAM; proofread; circle errors

All letters are used.

		GWAM	
	2'	3'	5'

¶ 1
1.5 SI
5.6 AWL
80% HFW

	2'	3'	5'
What is word processing? It is a new term that identifies the	6	4	3
effort currently being made to enable an executive to turn his or her	13	9	5
ideas into letters and reports at top speed, with utmost accuracy, with	20	14	8
the least work, and at the lowest cost. The equipment that plays the	27	18	11
most vital part in this process is the automatic typewriter. Many com-	38	23	14
petent experts report that the frequency of the use of writing papers	41	28	17
by this new process will multiply by more than four times in just the	48	32	19
next few years.	50	33	20

¶ 2
1.5 SI
5.6 AWL
80% HFW

	2'	3'	5'
Automatic typewriters have long been used to produce form letters.	7	38	23
Because the letters are typed instead of printed, they have a personal-	14	43	26
ized look about them. Another way in which these typewriters are used	21	47	28
is to record on tape the copy that is typed on paper. The writer edits	26	52	31
the copy, and the typist changes it by locating the places to be changed	35	57	34
and inserting the new copy. The final copy, which is then produced from	43	62	37
the tape at a rapid rate, is correct.	46	64	39

2' GWAM | 1 | 2 | 3 | 4 | 5 | 6 | 7 |
3' GWAM | 1 | 2 | 3 | 4 | 5 |
5' GWAM | 1 | 2 | 3 |

Job 9: Three-Page Letter *(WB p. 51)*

april 17, 19—— walker manufacturing company 2699 pocohontas street baton rouge la 70805 attention mr craig r snelgrove purchasing department gentlemen subject Quotation on R-2798C Vapor System (¶ 1) We refer to our telephone conversation of today in which we discussed the subject system. This quotation is to consolidate the alternates you have elected to take. (¶ 2) The principal elements in our vapor system are the fired heater, the flash tank, the circulating pump, and the controls. The flash tank and the pump are shipped separately for piping and wiring in the field by someone other than Blackstone. The heater and controls may be shipped separately for piping and wiring by others, or burner controls and piping may be shop-assembled as explained in the following paragraphs.

DS
FIRED HEATER
DS

(¶ 3) We offer a vertical circular unit with an all-welded carbon steel coil. The heater coil is of serpentine design with welded return bends at both ends of the straight tubes. A typical heater of this size is shown on the enclosed Drawing A. (¶ 4) The heater is shipped shop-assembled except for stack, ladders, and burner. We quote an optional 360° platform at the top of the radiant section, and this is installed after erection. (¶ 5) The heater shell and structure are mechanically cleaned to remove loose scale and rust; then external surfaces are given one coat of red oxide primer. The stack and breeching are lightly sandblasted and given one coat of heat-resistant paint. (¶ 6) The heater is equipped with a natural draft burner. This burner is furnished with modulating controls.

DS
FLASH TANK
DS

(¶ 7) The flash tank is a 2,700-gallon size and is equipped with safety valve, reflex-level gauge, and low-level cutout.

DS
CIRCULATING PUMPS
DS

(¶ 8) The two circulating pumps are Type Z545 with a Type 9 single inside unbalanced seal. Coolant is required for the mechanical seal gland and for the bearing housing. (¶ 9) We include one "seal guard" system, which provides a flushing stream of cooled and filtered Dowtherm over the mechanical seal. The seal guard is Model C250X. (¶ 10) If you install a spare circulating pump, one seal guard system should be sufficient, with valves to permit switching from one pump to the other.

DS
CONTROLS
DS

(¶ 11) Our basic price provides for controls shipped separately for piping and wiring in the field by someone other than Blackstone, except for the items contained in the instrument panel. Our basic price includes a control panel for outdoor installation. Wiring between the panel and controls is to be done by someone other than Blackstone. (¶ 12) As required by FIA, our price includes a Dowtherm low-flow cutout. The D/P transmitter and manifold are supplied by us but installed by someone else. (¶ 13) Our price includes two dial thermometers with thermowells and two pressure gauges with valves and siphons. However, these are shipped separately for installation in your connecting piping. One gauge is to be installed in the flash tank. (¶ 14) Controls and safety interlocks are designed to meet FIA requirements.

DS
PRICE AND DELIVERY
DS

(¶ 15) The controls included in our price are marked on the enclosed system specification sheet. The prices below are all f.o.b. shipping point(s) and will be held firm for acceptance within 30 days. The heater itself would be shipped from Los Angeles, California, with an estimated weight of 58,000 pounds. *(Indent one-line ¶s 16 and 17 five spaces from each margin.)* (¶ 16) Basic price of one R-2798C Vapor System . . . . $153,698 (¶ 17) Extra for a 360° platform . . . . 1,850 (¶ 18) The space requirements are per attached drawings of heater, flash tank and pump, and control panel. An outline set of drawings for your approval can be mailed within three weeks after receipt of your written order. (¶ 19) Wiring diagrams are submitted to you first for approval and then are submitted to FIA. (¶ 20) Your firm order would have to be received by April 30, 19——, in order for us to

(Continued on page 242)

Problem 1: Short Half Page Report

Half sheet; 65-space line; DS; exact vertical center; SS and indent numbered ¶s 5 spaces. Align second and following lines of the numbered ¶s as shown.

(This style is "left indention with blocked lines.")

Evaluation. Use your stroke and line-space ruler to check top, bottom, and side margins.

Words

DIVIDING WORDS AND SENTENCE PARTS
TS

7

In addition to the guides included on page 59, here are some   19

guides that you should keep in mind: 26

1. Divide hyphened compounds only at the point of the hyphen.   39
   DS

2. Avoid dividing abbreviations, numbers, and proper names.   51
   When necessary, separate a surname from the initials or   63
   given name.   66

3. Separate the parts of a date, if necessary, between the   78
   day of the month and the year.   85

4. Do not divide the last word on a page.   93

Problem 2: Report on Full Sheet

Type the report on a full sheet in reading position; 60-space line; DS; TS after the heading; indent the 3 items 5 spaces.

Words

WRITING NATURALLY

4

Most letters are too wordy. Writing long, involved letters   16
is the letter writer's greatest sin. These three principles   28
can help you cut out useless words: 35

Prefer familiar words to the farfetched.   44

Prefer concrete words to the abstract.   52

Prefer short words to the long.   58

Words that add nothing but weight to your letter should be   70
tossed out. Words are bridges between people. Build this   82
bridge with short, simple words—the kind of words you use   94
when you speak to people.   99

Problem 3: Announcement on Half Sheet Inserted Sidewise

Words

1. Insert a half sheet with the long edge at the left.

2. Center each line horizontally; DS the lines.

3. Type the data at the right.

Mr. Robert M. Ferrell   5
Cordially Invites You   10
to a Preview of the New Voss/Lyons   17
Jamaica Boulevard at Estes   21
April Eighth, 10 a.m. to 6 p.m.   28

2″ top margin; 1″ side margins; indent individual reports 7 spaces from left margin; insert leaders between columns

Blackstone Corporation
Agenda for Meeting of the Board of Directors ⟩DS
April 28, 19--
TS

1. Call to Order _ _ _ _ _ _ _ _ _ _ _ Frederick R. Blackstone
2. Reading of Minutes _ _ _ _ _ _ _ Craig T. Washington DS
   ^and approval
                                                                    DS
3. (Officers' Reports of)
      President's Report _ _ _ _ _ _ Sharon J. Blackstone ⟩SS
      Executive Vice President _ _ Harold F. Speicher
      Vice President _ _ _ _ _ _ _ Karl V. Garcia
      Controller _ _ _ _ _ _ _ _ _ Michael J. Andrus
                                                                    DS
4. Reports of Production Committees
      Steam Generators _ _ _ _ _ _ John T. Peterson ⟩SS
      Air Conditioning _ _ _ _ _ _ Hans V. Shultz
                                                                    DS
5. Report of Expansion Committee
      Present Plant Capacity _ _ _ _ _ Paula A. Jones ⟩SS
      Ten-Year Production Forecast _ _ Kent C. Farmer
      Feasibility of Eugene, Oregon _ _ Janice Armstrong
6. Declaration of Dividend _ _ _ _ _ Sharon J. Blackstone DS
                                                                    DS
7. Other New Business
                                                                    DS
8. Adjournment

Goal. When you have completed the lessons of this section, you should be able to type modified block style business letters with open or mixed punctuation and position them attractively on the page.

Machine Adjustments. 70-space line; SS sentence drills: DS and indent ¶s 5 spaces; space problem copy as directed. For problems and ¶ copy, use an adjusted right margin (see page 58).

LESSON 33

33A Preparatory Practice ⑦ each line 3 times SS; DS between three-line groups

Alphabet	The king and queen brought dozens of expensive jewels from the colony.
Figure/symbol	Does the 10% discount on Bender & Hunt's invoice #4697 come to $23.58?
Rule for numbers	Type policy numbers without commas: My policy #5923748 is for $6,500.
Fluency	How well did the eight boys do the problems you assigned for homework?

| 1 | 2 | 3 | 4 | 5 | 6 | 7 | 8 | 9 | 10 | 11 | 12 | 13 | 14 |

33B Technique Practice: STROKING ⑩ each line at least 3 times

1	Direct reaches	Mike Goldfarb hunted from jungle to desert for the special king cobra.
2	Double letters	Will Bill sell his sleek-looking car to Miss Nell Pool of Mississippi?
3	One hand	A fast steed's jump at the races deserves to be rewarded with a treat.
4	1st row	Max and Vern Bench expect to be in breezy Vera Cruz, Mexico, next May.
5	3d/4th fingers	Zealous players seldom overlook opportunities to win a valuable prize.

33C Aligning and Typing over Words ⑩

On your typewriter, locate the **variable line spacer (3)** and the **aligning scale (33).**

1. Type the line below, but do not make the return.

Use the aligning scale to align your copy.

2. Move the carriage (or carrier) so that a word with the letter *I* is above the scale. Note that a colored line points to the vertical part of the letter.

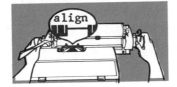

3. Study the relative position of the top, horizontal lines of the scale to the bottom of the descenders of letters like q, y, p, g, and j. Get a visual picture of this relationship to be able to adjust the paper correctly and type over a word with exactness.

4. Remove the paper; reinsert it. To adjust the line so that the bottoms of the letters align correctly with the aligning scale, do this:

- To raise or lower the line of writing, operate the **variable line spacer (3).**
- To center a letter *I* over one of the colored vertical lines, operate the **paper release (16)** to move the paper left or right.

5. Check the accuracy of your alignment by setting the **ribbon control (21)** for stencil position and typing over one of the letters. Make any necessary adjustments. *Return the ribbon control to inking position.*

6. Type over any words in the sentence that contain the letter *I*. Make any further adjustments necessary.

7. Repeat the entire drill. (You will use this procedure frequently to make corrections in your typewritten work.)

To: Harold F. Speicher, Executive Vice President
From: Andrea C. Oliver
Date: April 16, 19--
Subject: Recommendation on a WATS Band 6

As we discussed this morning, I have been watching your (AI/2HX) telephone calls to determine if/when a full-time WATS line would be to your advantage. Up to this point, you have not reached the cost of a full-time WATS Band 6, which is $1,885 a month, plus 10-11 percent tax.

Your calls for this fiscal year work out as follows:

WATS Charges	Toll Calls	Subtotal	Credit Card	Total
$1,310.76	$320.68	$1,631.44	$167.11	$1,464.33
1,116.80	294.56	1,411.36	20.91	1,390.45
1,369.46	406.41	1,775.87	127.76	1,648.11
1,525.13	509.07	2,034.20	347.55	1,686.65
1,720.43	391.12	2,111.55	230.90	1,880.65
1,353.31	201.31	1,554.62	82.96	1,471.66
1,673.46	222.05	1,895.51	150.68	1,744.83

These charges include all taxes. As you can see, I have deducted the amount of your credit card calls to give you the figure which could be made on WATS Band 6. Obviously, the credit card calls could not be made on the WATS Band 6, as these are made when your men are traveling.

If you have any questions, please give me a call.

cc Mrs. Anne R. Williams

33D Speed/Control Building (13)

1. Type two 5' writings on these ¶s. Type the first writing for *speed*; the second for *control*. Compare the *gwam* and number of errors on the two writings.

2. Proofread by comparing. Check with the original such commonly misspelled words as *across*, *usable*, and *likely*.

All letters are used.

	5' GWAM
¶ 1 Words are the tools with which we communicate with others—vocally	3 | 34
1.4 SI as well as in writing—and like other tools, words must be chosen wisely	6 | 37
5.4 AWL **85% HFW** and used with care. In general, prefer a short, simple word to a long	8 | 40
one; but do not hesitate to use whatever word will convey your meaning.	11 | 43
¶ 2 Be quick to realize that a large vocabulary is vital to successful	14 | 46
1.4 SI writing. The more extensive your store of usable words and word mean-	17 | 49
5.4 AWL **85% HFW** ings, the more precise your message is likely to be. On the topic of	20 | 51
words, be sure you have the right ones at hand.	22 | 53
¶ 3 You must try hard to build a good vocabulary. You must read exten-	24 | 56
1.4 SI sively, look up the meanings of unfamiliar words, and actively use those	27 | 59
5.4 AWL **85% HFW** words. In this way you can learn to produce quickly the exact word to	30 | 62
get just the effect you seek in your writing.	32 | 64

5' GWAM | 1 | 2 | 3 |

33E Individual Practice (11)
each line 2 times; retype any lines on which you made more than 2 errors in the 2 writings

1	One hand	Bart Kimmon was aggravated after only a few union cases were referred.
2	Balanced hand	Bud and eight girls may bicycle to the lake for a trip to Duck Island.
3	Combination	The staff at the car lot wanted him to make a trade after ten minutes.
4	Combination	They may award the contract to a downtown auditor at the minimum rate.
5	Adjacent keys	Three guides were in a column as we went over the trails after a lion.
6	Double letters	Bill and Ann will soon see the bookkeeping committee from Mississippi.
7	Figure/symbol	Approximately 10% of the #237 machines were priced incorrectly at $89.
8	Direct reaches	Myrtle took to a rummage sale the junk Fred left at the service plaza.
9	1st row	Anna Mae McVay became excited when Calvin Bixmont raced over the line.
10	3d row	Is it true that you were the ones who raised the issue of party lines?

| 1 | 2 | 3 | 4 | 5 | 6 | 7 | 8 | 9 | 10 | 11 | 12 | 13 | 14 |

Job 4: Letter on Executive-Size Stationery (WB p. 43)

april 14, 19-- mr fred r stevens data systems incorporated 4533 lincoln street SE portland or 97215 dear mr stevens (¶ 1) Thank you for your letter of April 12 to Mr. Speicher. As time does not permit Mr. Speicher to observe your presentation, I shall be most happy to see you. (¶ 2) Accordingly, I shall look forward to your presentation on Thursday, April 23, at 9:00 a.m. at the Hillrise Hotel. sincerely mrs anne r williams administrative assistant to executive vice president cc Mr. H. F. Speicher (Words in body: 54)

Job 5: Memorandum (WB p. 45)

TO: Michael J. Andrus, Controller

FROM: Anne R. Williams

DATE: April 15, 19--

SUBJECT: Branch Offices and Sales Representatives

(¶ 1) Attached for your reference is a revised listing of our branch offices and sales representatives delineating the territory covered by each office. In a separate package I am sending 150 copies for you to distribute to our branch offices and sales representatives. (¶ 2) Please note that effective May 16, 19--, Mr. H. W. Bales is moving our Chicago sales office. The mailing address will remain the same (P.O. Box 325, La Grange, IL 60525). The new street address is 10 Buttonwood Court, Indian Head Park, IL 60525. Also beginning May 16, the new office telephone numbers to be used for the Chicago sales office are:

(312) 246-8515 and -8516

(¶ 3) Mr. Bales requests that the 246-8515 number be used for WATS line calls made by our operators. His new residence phone number will be (312) 246-6381. Attachment

Job 6: Memorandum (WB p. 47)

TO: Anne R. Williams, Executive Department

FROM: Andrea C. Oliver

DATE: April 15, 19--

SUBJECT: Replacement of Typewriters

(¶ 1) In connection with the replacement of the typewriters which have been giving us problems, I recommend that we purchase the following reconditioned IBM typewriters from the Roberts Typewriter Company:

For the Purchasing Department:

(Indent the items 5 spaces from the left.)

2 13" carriage, fabric ribbon, pica type style	$ 798.00

For the Accounting Department:

2 20" carriage, carbon ribbon, elite type style	888.00

For the Executive Department:

2 17" carriage, executive model, Mid-Century type style; vertical spacing, 5 to one inch; horizontal spacing, 1/36	1,070.00
1 11" writing line, Selectric, 12 pitch, Courier 12 (Code 067-12 pitch)	425.00
	$3,181.00
Less 5% discount	159.05
	$3,021.95
Less: equipment sold previously	320.00
equipment to be traded in	935.00
Total cost of 7 reconditioned machines	$1,766.95

(¶ 2) If purchased new, the above equipment would cost us, less trade-in allowance, $3,680. (¶ 3) We are also allowed a 2/10 discount. Tax is paid after trade-in and the discount. cc Mr. F. N. Heaps

34A Preparatory Practice ⑦ each line 3 times SS; DS between three-line groups

Alphabet	Dwight Mystronio lives in a quiet area six blocks from the Jasper zoo.
Figure	David Parker moved from 479 East 135th Street to 228 West 60th Street.
Figure/symbol	Was his 4-year lease (May 23 expiration) renewed May 10 at a 5% boost?
Fluency	Will five of these men work with the foreman for the next eight weeks?

| 1 | 2 | 3 | 4 | 5 | 6 | 7 | 8 | 9 | 10 | 11 | 12 | 13 | 14 |

34B Technique Practice: RESPONSE PATTERNS ⑥ each line at least 3 times

Letter response	We erected a farm house and garage on the best acreage in Union, Ohio.
Word response	To throw their pots, they dug one-eighth ton of clay from Jay's field.
Combination	Our visual display at the civic arts center show was observed by many.
	We send large packages overseas by surface; small items go by airmail.

| 1 | 2 | 3 | 4 | 5 | 6 | 7 | 8 | 9 | 10 | 11 | 12 | 13 | 14 |

34C Problem Typing: PERSONAL/BUSINESS LETTERS IN MODIFIED BLOCK STYLE ㉘

Problem 1: Style Letter 1, Page 65 (WB p. 13)

On a full sheet type the letter illustrating the modified block style with block paragraphs and open punctuation shown on page 65. Use a 60-space line; follow the spacing directions given on the letter.

Vertical spacing directions are standard for all letter styles—with this exception: The number of blank line spaces in the top margin varies with the lengths of the bodies of the letters.

Become familiar with the terms used to identify the various parts of the letter.

Problem 2: Letter with Changes

Starting the return address on Line 18, retype Style Letter 1, this time omitting the second ¶.

34D Addressing Small Envelopes (No. 6¾, 6½″ x 3⅝″) ⑥ (WB p. 15)

Study the illustration at the right; then address an envelope for the letter typed in Problem 1.

> **1. Return Address.** Type the writer's name and address in block style, SS, in the upper left corner of the envelope. Start 3 spaces from the left edge on Line 2.
> **2. Envelope Address.** Begin about 2″ (on Line 11 or 12) from the top and 2½″ from the left edge. Use block style and single spacing. The last line must always be the city, state name or abbreviation, and ZIP Code.

NOTE: Small envelopes are commonly used for half-size stationery or 1-page letters on regular stationery.

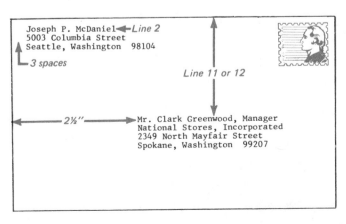

Job 3: Two-Page Memorandum (WB p. 41)

Second-page headings for memorandums are the same as second-page headings for letters. Use either the block (vertical) or the horizontal (one-line) form for this 2-page memorandum.

TO: Sharon Z. Blackstone, President FROM: Harold F. Speicher DATE: April 14, 19— SUBJECT: Validity Dates for Andersen Company Quotations (¶ 1) The current high level of interest in air conditioning installations has resulted in our receiving a large number of inquiries from the Andersen Company about our new refrigerated air conditioning units. Processing of these inquiries and providing the Andersen Company with competitive prices and realistic delivery schedules are creating problems which I feel should be reviewed with you in order to avoid any misunderstandings. (¶ 2) As a typical example, I have a current inquiry from them requesting a firm price and delivery information on five air conditioning units to be delivered at the end of October, 19—. In attempting to comply with their request, we must evaluate the following factors: *(Type the number of each enumerated item at the left margin. Begin each succeeding line under the first word of the item.)* (¶ 3) 1. Material Escalation. Quoting firm prices for a validity period of seven months is extremely difficult in the present unsettled material market. Our suppliers will not give us price protection; therefore, we are forced to use our best judgment in evaluating material prices which will be in effect at some extended future date. This is becoming increasingly difficult because there appears to be no predictable pattern to the material cost increases we have experienced over the past several months. (¶ 4) 2. Material Quantity Discounts. Under normal conditions, purchasing materials for several air conditioning units rather than for a single unit would result in appreciable quantity discounts. This condition is not true at the present time. We must now depend on past relationships with our suppliers to influence them to provide us with a favorable position in their production schedules, and these suppliers are not presently receptive to negotiating discounts for large orders. (¶ 5) 3. Labor Efficiency. There is some labor efficiency realized when manufacturing several air conditioning units; however, the efficiency improvement on our new air conditioning units is not so pronounced as might be expected. Our shop has gone through the learning curve with the large number of units manufactured in past years, and we cannot improve significantly on our established procedures. The units do not lend themselves to cost reduction techniques, such as multiple drillings of tube sheets, etc. We do apply a quantity factor on our labor hours when we are quoting prices for multiple air conditioning units. (¶ 6) 4. Labor Escalation. We have hourly shop-rate adjustments twice a year; therefore, when we quote prices for air conditioning units on multiple orders, the manufacture of each air conditioning unit may fall into a different labor-rate period. Obviously, we cannot simultaneously manufacture five of these large air conditioning units. Our pricing for each air conditioning unit must, therefore, reflect the hourly rate which will be in effect at the time a particular air conditioning unit is being manufactured. (¶ 7) 5. Shop Space Availability. It is not possible for us to guarantee shop space availability at some extended future date. The sharp increase in demand in recent months for air conditioning units, steam generators, and our other processing equipment is placing a severe burden on our present manufacturing capacity. In addition, the relatively long lead time we require in all our products from the date of an order until we can convert it into the manufacturing process makes it extremely difficult for us to reserve shop space for work which may or may not materialize. Should a particular job not develop, we could find it impossible to fill the resultant production gap. (¶ 8) We must try to remain the prime supplier of air conditioning units to the Andersen Company. Do you have any suggestions as to how we should handle this Andersen Company problem?

	Words in Parts	Total Words

*Tabulate to center to type
return address and date*

Return address   Line 17   3981 Montecello Avenue   5   5
San Jose, California 95125   10   10
Dateline   December 12, 19--   14   14
Operate return 4 times   2 spaces

Letter address   Mrs. Vincent Meyerson   18   18
9402 Mohican Drive   22   22
San Jose, California 95123   28   28
DS

Salutation   Dear Mrs. Meyerson   4   31
DS

**Body
of
letter**
Because I think that you may be interested in learning about   16   44
a new project in our community, I should like to introduce   28   55
you to Hand Art Notes. The response to these notes has been   40   68
encouraging.   42   70

A group of students, of which I am a member, design and silk-   82
screen handmade all-purpose note cards. They are unusual and   95
attractive, and we can design them to convey your individual   107
message.   108

Hand Art Notes can be used for all occasions: party invita-   12   120
tions, thank-you notes, holiday cards, birthdays, and other   24   132
types of special events. I think you may enjoy looking at   36   144
some of the unique sample notes we have prepared. If you   47   156
will call me at 396-9456, I can arrange to come to your home   60   168
any evening convenient to you.   66   174
DS

Complimentary close   Sincerely yours *Operate return 4 times*   69   177

Geraldine Phillips

Typed name   Miss Geraldine Phillips   73   181

*Tabulate to center to type
complimentary close and
writer's name*

Open punctuation omits marks of punctuation after the salutation and
complimentary close. These two elements would not be abbreviated.

Style Letter 1: PERSONAL/BUSINESS LETTER IN MODIFIED BLOCK STYLE, OPEN PUNCTUATION

You are employed in the office of Harold F. Speicher, Executive Vice President of the Blackstone Corporation, 12145 Ridgecrest Road, SE, Portland, OR 97266. All letters typed in this section should be modified block with indented ¶s and mixed punctuation. Strive for neat, attractive copy.

Job 1: Two-Page Letter (WB p. 37)

april 13, 19–– mr john stans, vice president chamberlain company 2609 ming road bakersfield ca 93304 dear mr stans (¶ 1) Thank you for your telephone call of April 12 concerning a visit to Portland to discuss representing our company in Asia for our Thermoflood steam generators. As I informed you, an immediate meeting seemed to be premature because we had not had an opportunity to evaluate your proposal. (¶ 2) You have suggested that we contribute $1,000 a month to your company to help to defray expenses while you attempt to develop the Asian market. The monthly contributions made by us would be credited against commissions due you on any future sales of our equipment which you might generate. I believe that this correctly represents your basic proposal. (¶ 3) We have analyzed your proposal and have concluded that we cannot justify our participation for the following reasons: (*Type the numbered paragraphs in the indented ¶ style used in the letter.*) (¶ 4) 1. Thermoflood generators are effective only in specialized applications requiring relatively thick oil sands of high permeability and viscous crude oil. We do not know whether such conditions exist in the Asian oil fields and thus have no assurance that there is even a potential market for Thermoflood steam generators. (¶ 5) 2. Even if a steamflooding market develops in Asia, we believe that such a market for U.S. imports would be of short duration because of the size and weight of our generators. Ocean freight costs and transportation time would dictate manufacture of the equipment in the Far East. (¶ 6) 3. Burners and controls comprise a significant part of steam generators and require a high spare parts inventory. In addition, steam generators require fairly sophisticated water treatment, burner and control adjustment, etc. We have real concern over the potential operating problems which might develop with such units in Asia and also the possible demands on our limited personnel for servicing. (¶ 7) Our production has reached a point where we would be unable to produce additional steam generators without increasing our plant. To invest in additional capital improvements without assurance that we could increase our sales would not be a financially sound move for us. (¶ 8) We thank you for offering us the opportunity of participating in the marketing effort you plan on initiating in Asia. However, we do not believe such participation would be in our best interests. sincerely yours harold f speicher executive vice president (copy to mr m o frank)

Job 2: Letter on Executive-Size Stationery (WB p. 39)

Production Typing Information:

BLIND CARBON COPY NOTATION

If it is desirable to send a copy of a letter to someone without disclosing that fact to the addressee of the letter, a notation is omitted from the original copy. This notation, called a *blind carbon copy notation*, is typed at the left margin a double space below the last typed line. Insert a heavy piece of paper between the ribbon and the original (first) sheet; type the notation (for example: *bcc Mr. John Brown*) on the inserted piece of paper. The notation will appear on the carbon copy but not on the original copy.

april 13, 19–– portland business machines 4369 beech street, NE, portland or 97213 gentlemen (¶ 1) Enclosed is our check for $2,651.25 to cover the maintenance contract on the enclosed list. You will note we have deleted three machines: Serial Nos. 00926897, 00516963, and 00098897. (¶ 2) We would like to add Friden calculator, Serial No. 727897, to your maintenance agreement. Please send us a maintenance contract for this machine, prorated to expire with the rest of the calculators. (¶ 3) If you have any questions about the enclosed list, please give me a call. sincerely andrea c oliver executive office manager enclosures bcc accounts payable department (Words in body: 92)

34E Folding and Inserting Letters: SMALL ENVELOPES ③

Folding a letter for a small envelope

Step. 1. With the letter face up on the desk, fold from the bottom up to ½″ from the top.

Step 2. Fold the right 1/3 to the left.

Step 3. Folding from left to right, fold the left 1/3 to about ½″ of the last crease to allow for ease of unfolding.

Step 4. Insert last-creased edge first.

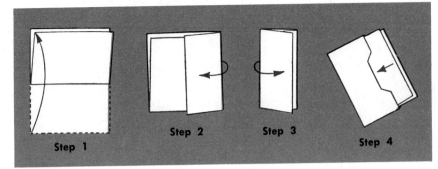

Step 1   Step 2   Step 3   Step 4

LESSON 35

35A Preparatory Practice ⑦ each line 3 times SS; DS between three-line groups

Alphabet	Our unexpected freezing weather may have killed John Quinley's shrubs.
Figure	Walford reported on the following rooms: 6, 10, 25, 37, 129, and 148.
Figure/symbol	Miller & Southeby (local grocers) sold 1,256# of bananas @ 24¢ per lb.
Fluency	Of the major elements, I think the first is by far the most important.

| 1 | 2 | 3 | 4 | 5 | 6 | 7 | 8 | 9 | 10 | 11 | 12 | 13 | 14 |

35B Skill-Transfer Typing ⑩ 65-space line; each line 3 times with not more than 1 error per line; for Line 5, type correct words for those that are circled

Words

1	Straight copy	Can a new van move the six heavy zinc boxes to their local plant?	13
2	Statistical	My order #73649 totals $528.90 and must be shipped by January 14.	13
3	Script	*The two artists worked steadily on in spite of the stifling heat.*	13
4	Corrected copy	Ed expected the ^last^ quiz ⌊be to⌋ very dificult for the ~~twelve~~ *nine* boys.	13
5	Proofreading	They shall ⊙by⊙ most ⊙please⊙ to ⊙recieve⊙ ⊙you⊙ comments on the ⊙giude⊙.	13

35C Problem Typing: BUSINESS LETTERS IN MODIFIED BLOCK STYLE ㉚ *(WB p. 17)*

1. Study Style Letter 2, page 67. Note the placement of the date and closing lines. Read the brief explanations of mixed and open punctuation.
2. 60-space line; modified block with block ¶s; mixed punctuation; date on Line 15.

3. Set a tab stop at horizontal center to indent for typing the dateline and closing lines.
4. After typing the letter, proofread by comparing. Check names, addresses, and tricky words. Make pencil corrections; then retype the letter.

35D Evaluate Your Work ③

Compare your final copy with the model on page 67. With your stroke and line-space ruler, check the vertical placement of the letter parts.

LESSONS 118-122

Lessons 118, 120, 122

Use the following daily lesson plan for Lessons 118, 120, and 122. Retain all jobs until you have completed Lesson 122.

Preparatory Practice (5′). Type 118A, below, as directed.

Production Typing (45′). Type the jobs on pages 236-244. Follow the directions for each job; where specific directions are not given, use your own good judgment. Proofread carefully; correct all errors.

Lessons 119, 121

Use the following daily lesson plan for Lessons 119 and 121. Retain all jobs until you have completed Lesson 122.

Preparatory Practice (5′). Type 118B, below, as directed.

Technique Mastery (5′). Type 118C, below, as directed.

Production Typing (40′). Continue typing the jobs on pages 236-244. Follow the same general directions for Lessons 118, 120, and 122.

118A Preparatory Practice (5) each line at least 3 times

Alphabet	With a fixed goal in mind, quickly size up a job before making a move.
Figure/symbol	Ruth said, "In our 1975 class of 863 seniors, 204 won various awards."
Long words	The morning speaker outlined the characteristics of digital computers.
Fluency	The past is of use to us only as it can make fuller the life of today.
	| 1 | 2 | 3 | 4 | 5 | 6 | 7 | 8 | 9 | 10 | 11 | 12 | 13 | 14 |

118B Preparatory Practice (5) each line at least 3 times

Alphabet	Jack will ship by express the quantity of goods that we have itemized.
Figure/symbol	T & M will send #7069*Q tacks in these sizes: 1/4, 3/8, 1/2, and 3/5.
Long reaches	Many executives may attend the evening exercises in Myron-Bryson Hall.
Fluency	The man who makes his mind work for him is sure to go far in his work.
	| 1 | 2 | 3 | 4 | 5 | 6 | 7 | 8 | 9 | 10 | 11 | 12 | 13 | 14 |

118C Technique Mastery (5) each line at least twice without error

Stroke response	Can he discriminate between fact and principle, evidence and argument?
Word response	Keep your book at the right side so you can see it well when you type.
Combination	If you will work diligently, you are bound to improve your efficiency.
Rhythm	The giant flakes did not melt, so they kept their usual size and form.
Direct reaches	Many of the mementos my brother collected were brought to Grady Thumb.
	| 1 | 2 | 3 | 4 | 5 | 6 | 7 | 8 | 9 | 10 | 11 | 12 | 13 | 14 |

Communications Design Associates

801 JACKSON STREET, WEST   CABLE: COMDA
CHICAGO, ILLINOIS   60607   TELEPHONE: (312) 342-9753

		Words in Parts	5' GWAM
		4	1

Date and closing lines at center point

Dateline   Line 15 → February 17, 19--

Operate return 4 times

Letter address
Miss Elizabeth M. Bradford   9   2
Cascade Engineering Company   15   3
218 Jefferson Street, West   20   4
Springfield, IL   62702   **DS**   25   5

Salutation
Dear Miss Bradford: **DS**   28   6

Body of letter
This letter is typed in modified block style with block   11   8
paragraphs and mixed punctuation, a style widely used in   23   10
business. The style has a number of distinctive features.   34   13

The spacing between parts of the letter is standard. The   12   15
spacing between the top edge of the letterhead and the date   24   17
is variable. Short letters require leaving more line spaces   36   19
than do long ones.   39   20

The date, the complimentary close, and the name and official   12   23
title of the writer are begun at the horizontal center of the   25   25
paper. With mixed punctuation, a colon follows the saluta-   36   28
tion and a comma follows the complimentary close. Notation   48   30
lines are typed at the left margin, a double space below the   61   33
last of the closing lines.   66   34

I am pleased to enclose a booklet describing a number of   11   36
letter styles and special letter features.   **DS**   20   38

Complimentary close
Sincerely yours,   23   38

Operate return 4 times

Space for handwritten signature

Charles Harley Chambers

Typed name
Charles Harley Chambers   28   39
Official title
Public Service Director   **DS**   33   40

Reference initials
mew   34   40

Enclosure notation
Enclosure   35   41

Carbon copy notation
cc Mr. Alvin Meyer, Jr.   40   42

Style Letter 2: MODIFIED BLOCK STYLE, BLOCK PARAGRAPHS, MIXED PUNCTUATION

Mixed Punctuation. With *mixed punctuation*, as illustrated above, a colon follows the salutation and a comma follows the complimentary close.

Open Punctuation. With *open punctuation*, no punctuation follows the salutation and complimentary close.

117C Speed Building ⑮ two 1' exploration-level writings on each ¶; record GWAM of the better writing; one 5' exploration-level writing

All letters are used.

		1'	5'	
				GWAM

¶ 1
1.6 SI
5.8 AWL
75% HFW

Perhaps the most evident impact of the trend to automation involves a vital need for better education. Qualified workers must be found, and our education system must make them available. Moreover, a time may be imminent when more insight about automation will be needed by almost everyone; and it will then be the duty of the schools to provide it.

¶ 2
1.6 SI
5.8 AWL
75% HFW

Education for living in an automated age should mean more for us than merely taking some technological courses. A liberal education to comprehend the broad implications of automation is essential. It is not enough just to know how the computer runs; we should appreciate, also, the effects it might have on man and on the world in which he lives.

¶ 3
1.6 SI
5.8 AWL
75% HFW

Education is studying about people; it is a study of their globe, history, societies, and relationships. Yet, education must do more than just inspect these few areas; it must teach a person to use his or her brain for creative purposes and not for just storing memorized facts. It should educate a person to live in an increasingly complex world.

GWAM column ¶1: 14 3 45 / 28 6 48 / 43 9 50 / 56 11 53 / 70 14 56
¶2: 13 17 58 / 27 19 61 / 42 22 64 / 56 25 67 / 70 28 70
¶3: 13 31 72 / 28 33 75 / 42 36 78 / 57 39 81 / 70 42 84

1' GWAM | 1 | 2 | 3 | 4 | 5 | 6 | 7 | 8 | 9 | 10 | 11 | 12 | 13 | 14 |
5' GWAM | 1 | 2 | 3 |

117D Control Building ⑳ two 1' control-level writings on each ¶; record GWAM of the better writing; two 5' control-level writings; record GWAM of the better writing

All letters are used.

¶ 1
1.6 SI
5.8 AWL
75% HFW

Educated people have learned that they can discover important details through the simple act of listening. The secret, however, as is well known, is to listen with discretion. Our usual ability to hear forces us to tune in thousands of noises, while our keen listening ability lets us select only what is vital from what is minutiae. Often our only contribution is a question; and if our listening spot is an important television program, we don't have to make any comment at all.

¶ 2
1.6 SI
5.8 AWL
75% HFW

The classroom is still useful even if we may have completed a formal part of our education. Higher degrees are possible and desirable. For the person who does not wish to enter a degree program yet needs to obtain some additional, perhaps specialized, education, classes are often offered. Adult classes in a locality, for example, have been known to run from interior design to judo, from art to philately. Some of these classes are fun, for learning can be fun as well as useful.

GWAM column ¶1: 13 3 41 / 27 5 44 / 41 8 47 / 55 11 50 / 70 14 53 / 84 17 56 / 97 19 58
¶2: 13 22 61 / 28 25 64 / 42 28 67 / 56 31 69 / 69 33 72 / 84 36 75 / 97 39 78

1' GWAM | 1 | 2 | 3 | 4 | 5 | 6 | 7 | 8 | 9 | 10 | 11 | 12 | 13 | 14 |
5' GWAM | 1 | 2 | 3 |

LESSON 36

36A Preparatory Practice ⑦ each line 3 times SS; DS between three-line groups

Alphabet	Tex queried Kipp and Vince about your jewel boxes for the zircon gems.
Figure/symbol	He ordered 48 boxes of #573 @ $2.69, less 10%, from O'Brien & Company.
Rule for figures	In even amounts of money, omit decimal and ciphers: I sent $85 today.
Fluency	He will be named as chairman for the next meeting of your study group.

| 1 | 2 | 3 | 4 | 5 | 6 | 7 | 8 | 9 | 10 | 11 | 12 | 13 | 14 |

36B Growth Index ⑫ one 3' and one 5' writing; determine GWAM; proofread and circle errors

All letters are used.

	GWAM		
	1'	3'	5'

¶ 1
1.5 SI
5.6 AWL
80% HFW

A noted philosopher said that the mind is a very unusual invention. `14 | 5 | 3`
It starts working the instant we are born and never stops until we get up `29 | 10 | 6`
to speak in public. Generally, nobody questions that practice makes per- `43 | 14 | 9`
fect--nor that we can learn and apply codes on which to base that prac- `57 | 19 | 11`
tice according to our needs. `63 | 21 | 13`

¶ 2
1.5 SI
5.6 AWL
80% HFW

While we can memorize rules, the essence of making an excellent `13 | 25 | 15`
talk may still elude us. The truth is, the kind of eloquence that will `27 | 30 | 18`
excite the imagination of listeners may be impossible to acquire. We `41 | 35 | 21`
can learn many things by rules, but a feeling for what will really move `56 | 40 | 24`
people is apparently an inborn trait. `63 | 42 | 25`

¶ 3
1.5 SI
5.6 AWL
80% HFW

A talk about nothing--however eloquent--can become rather tiresome. `14 | 47 | 28`
The speaker must believe in his subject. He must know it very well. The `29 | 52 | 31`
listeners can spot a phony a mile away. A good speech is a short one. `43 | 56 | 34`
Some say that a person who hops to his feet, skips over the introduction, `58 | 61 | 37`
and makes a concluding statement will always get the heartiest applause. `72 | 66 | 40`

1' GWAM	1	2	3	4	5	6	7	8	9	10	11	12	13	14
3' GWAM		1		2		3		4		5	
5' GWAM		1		2		3	

36C Erasing and Correcting Errors ⑥

Type the sentences exactly as shown below, DS. Study the guides for erasing that are given at the right; then erase and correct each error in the 4 sentences.

Eraes lightly, usnig a hard eraser.

Don't dampen eth eraser.

Retype the wrod lightlh.

An eraser sheild prevents smudgee.

Guides for Erasing

1. Use a plastic shield and a hard eraser.

2. Roll the paper forward if the error is on the upper two thirds of the page. Roll the paper backward if the error is on the lower third.

3. Move the carriage (carrier) to the left or right as far as possible to keep dirt out of the mechanism.

4. Use a plastic eraser shield to protect the writing that is not to be erased. Erase lightly—don't scrub the error. Brush any eraser particles away from the page.

5. Return the paper to writing position and type.

SECTION 22 Typing in an Executive Office

LESSONS 117-123

Section 22 provides you with some experience in typing jobs normally done in an executive office situation.

Drill Copy. SS; 70-space line

¶ Copy. DS; 70-space line; 5-space ¶ indentions; full sheets

Production Typing. For incomplete directions, use your judgment. Correct errors; make cc's as directed.

Supplies Needed. Executive-size letterheads; regular letterheads and plain paper; appropriate envelopes

LESSON 117

117A Preparatory Practice (5) each line at least 3 times

Alphabet	Excited voices kept buzzing as qualified members of the jury withdrew.
Figure/symbol	Mark's term policy #803268 (for $149,750) will expire on September 14.
Shift keys	Violet Spring flew to France on Tuesday and later will go to Portugal.
Fluency	It is said that men who succeed are able to learn from their failures.

| 1 | 2 | 3 | 4 | 5 | 6 | 7 | 8 | 9 | 10 | 11 | 12 | 13 | 14 |

117B Communication Aid: WORD CHOICE (10)

Read the sentences at the right; then, from the words at the left, select the correct one to insert at the point of the blank space. Supply the correct word and capitalize and punctuate each sentence as you type it. After checking your work with your instructor, retype the sentences.

1	you, your	we regret ______ having to ask us for mr browns address a second time
2	principal, principle	the ______ reason we believe for retaining any position is skill
3	capital, capitol	if assets are overstated ______ figures i think are also affected
4	affects, effects	my fundamental act was simple however the ______ were most complex
5	advice, advise	the councils ______ favors the development of a simple novel answer
6	access, excess	the president of the company has ______ to all confidential documents
7	accept, except	do not ______ packages between 915 am and 530 pm on february 25
8	formally, formerly	mr lawrence tilton who was ______ an office manager is efficient
9	ascent, assent	it is required that all parties ______ to the dissolution she said
10	altar, alter	when working with legal material one must be careful not to ______ it

36D Problem Typing: BUSINESS LETTERS IN MODIFIED BLOCK STYLE, BLOCK ¶s ㉕ 3 letterheads

Problem 1 (WB p. 19)

60-space line; date on Line 16; standard spacing of letter parts (as shown on p. 67); mixed punctuation; erase and correct errors.

NOTE: Vertical lines indicate line endings. ¶ indicates new paragraph; xx indicates your initials.

	Words
Current date	3

Ms. Beverly N. Montez | Supervisor, Office Services | V. V. Hil- | 15
lotte & Company, Inc. | 14339 Maryland Avenue, NE | St. Peters- | 27
burg, FL 33703 | Dear Ms. Montez: (¶ 1) A personal title, such as | 39
Mr., Mrs., Miss, or (if a woman's | marital status is unknown) Ms., | 52
should precede the names of | individuals in letter addresses. Such | 65
professional titles | as Dr., Professor, and Reverend may be used | 78
instead of the | personal titles. (¶ 2) In letter closings, a personal or | 92
professional title never | precedes a man's name in the signature; | 105
however, a considerate | woman writer indicates an appropriate title, | 118
either typed |without parentheses in the signature line or written with | 132
parentheses preceding her handwritten signature. | Sincerely yours, | 146
Mrs. Eva St. Clair | Associate Editor | xx | 154

Problem 2 (WB p. 21)

60-space line; date on Line 15; standard spacing of letter parts (as shown on p. 67); mixed punctuation; erase and correct errors.

	Words

October 27, 19-- |Ms. Gladys F. Woodman, Dean |Lakeview College | 12
of Business | 943 North Burbank Avenue | Milwaukee, WI 53224 | 24
Dear Ms. Woodman: (¶ 1) We are pleased to send you today a com- | 36
plimentary copy of our | communications layout guide: | 46

DS and center

STYLED TO THE READER'S TASTE | 52

DS

(¶ 2) This little booklet has become a popular item on the shelves | 64
of many college bookstores. (¶ 3) After you have used the guide as a | 78
reference for a few days, | you will probably want each of your stu- | 90
dents to have one. It | is available at $1.50 a copy from Mr. George | 103
Peters, Reference | Books, Inc., 1285 Ramayne Avenue, Racine, Wis- | 116
consin 53402. (¶ 4) Thank you for your interest in our communica- | 128
tion practices. | We shall be pleased to receive any comments and | 141
suggestions |you may have for the improvement of our layout guide. | 155
Sincerely yours, | John D. Marvin | Sales Manager | xx | Enclosure | 167

Problem 3 (WB p. 23)

60-space line; date on Line 18; standard spacing of letter parts (as shown on p. 67); mixed punctuation; erase and correct errors.

	Words
Current date	3

Mrs. Anne Longworth | Vogel-Sanderson Company | 7302 Shertz | 14
Street | Peoria, IL 61611 | Dear Mrs. Longworth: (¶ 1) The U.S. | 26
Postal Service encourages the use of the two-letter |ZIP abbreviation | 39
(without periods or spaces) for state names. | These abbreviations, | 53
however, may be used only with ZIP Codes. (¶ 2) If the ZIP abbrevia- | 65
tion is not known, the standard abbreviation | may be used; or the | 78
state name may be spelled in full. |Good arrangement of address data | 92
is the deciding factor. (¶ 3) A report of state names and their ZIP | 105
abbreviations is en- |closed for your reference. |Sincerely yours, |Charles | 119
Harley Chambers | Public Service Director | xx | Enclosure | 130

Words

ACME RENTALS, INC.   4

Balance Sheet   6

December 31, 19--   10

Assets   13

lc Current Assets: 16
    Cash . . . . $ 40,000   27
    Accounts recievable $42,000   37
       Less allowance for doubting accounts . $ 1,000   41,999   49
    lc Office Supplies   1,200   61

lc Total current Assets 72,200   71

    Long-lived assets: 75
    Land . . . . $ 10,000   85
    Buildings $45,000   96
       Less depreciaton 1,250   34,750   109
    lc Office Equipment . . . . $ 4,700   119
       Less depreciaton 726   3,794   133

       Total long-lived assets 57,724   144

       Total assets $129,924   154

Liabilities and Capital)Center   164

lc Current Liabilities: 168
    Accounts payable $25,399   179
    Notes payable 342   190
    Taxes payable 2,492   202
       Total current liability . . . . $ 28,232   212

    Long-term liabilities: 216
    lc Mortgage Payable 30,999   227

    Capital: 229
    Capital stock $69,399   239
    lc Retained Earnings 2,395   251

lc Total Capital 71,963   263

lc Total liabilities and Capital $129,924   278

37A Preparatory Practice ⑦ each line 3 times SS; DS between three-line groups

Alphabet   Next week qualified judges will have to analyze our club performances.

Figure/symbol   Kauffman's invoice #3278 for $461.50 (less 2%) was paid on November 9.

Rule for figures   Type exact ages in figures: June is 18 years 4 months and 9 days old.

Fluency   It is now thought that the men in business who read more achieve more.
                   | 1 | 2 | 3 | 4 | 5 | 6 | 7 | 8 | 9 | 10 | 11 | 12 | 13 | 14 |

37B Technique Practice: RESPONSE PATTERNS ⑦ each line at least 3 times

Letter response   Did you regard my opinion of the minimum reserve rates as regrettable?
Word response   Six or eight of their men lent a hand with the work of the city audit.
Combination   Their union steward may draft a formal statement to the next chairman.
                   A man must learn to control himself before he tries to control others.
                   | 1 | 2 | 3 | 4 | 5 | 6 | 7 | 8 | 9 | 10 | 11 | 12 | 13 | 14 |

37C Addressing a Large Envelope (9½″ x 4¼″) and Folding a Letter ⑥

Large (No. 10) envelopes are used for letters of 2 or more pages or letters with enclosures. In practice, large envelopes are frequently used for full-size 1-page letters as well.

Type state names in full; use the standard abbreviation; or, with a ZIP Code, the special 2-letter abbreviation (without periods or spaces). See Reference Guide p. viii.

SS all addresses, regardless of number of lines. Study the illustration, and observe the placement and spacing notations. Type an envelope from the illustration.

Type addressee notations (*Hold for Arrival, Personal, Please Forward,* and the like) a triple space below the return address and 3 spaces from the left edge of the envelope. Underline or use all capitals.

Type mailing notations in all capitals, (AIRMAIL, SPECIAL DELIVERY, REGISTERED, and the like) at least 3 line spaces above the envelope address and below the stamp position.

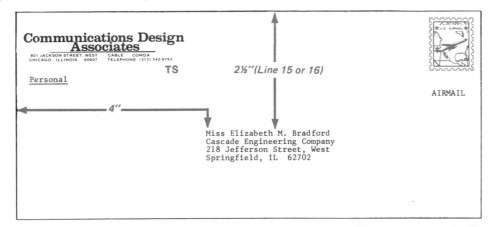

Communications Design
Associates
801 JACKSON STREET, WEST   CABLE   COMDA
CHICAGO, ILLINOIS 60607   TELEPHONE (312) 342-9753
                                  TS

Personal

2½″(Line 15 or 16)

AIRMAIL

←———— 4″ ————→

Miss Elizabeth M. Bradford
Cascade Engineering Company
218 Jefferson Street, West
Springfield, IL 62702

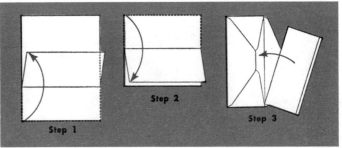

Folding a letter for a large envelope

Step 1. With the letter face up on the desk, fold slightly less than 1/3 of the sheet up toward the top.

Step 2. Fold down the top of the letter to within ½″ of the bottom fold.

Step 3. Insert the letter into the envelope with the last-creased edge toward the bottom.

Step 1   Step 2   Step 3

116C Production Measurement (30) 25′ writing; figure N-PRAM

Job 1: Letter with Tabulation (WB p. 35)

Because of the lines required by
the table, use 1″ side margins.

	Words

Current date mr eric r burns, controller acme | 10
rentals inc 209 east red bridge road kansas | 19
city mo 64114 dear mr burns subject: depre- | 29
ciation methods (¶ 1) In reply to your tele- | 36
phone call yesterday, I have briefly sum- | 44
marized the generally accepted depreciation | 53
methods by the use of an illustration. Let us | 62
assume that an asset has a cost of $10,000 and | 72
a useful life of 5 years with a salvage value | 81
of $500. The following table compares the | 89
amount of depreciation for the first year: | 98

(Tabulate and indent 5 spaces from side margins.)

Straight-line . . . . $1,900 | 109
Declining-balance . . . . 4,507 | 120
Double-declining-balance . . . . . 4,000 | 131
Sum-of-the-years-digits. . . . . . 3,167 | 142

(¶ 2) The last three methods are known as | 149
accelerated methods of depreciation. The | 158
amount of depreciation is considerably higher | 167
during the first years of an asset's life; how- | 176
ever, in the latter years, the amount of depre- | 185
ciation is very small. (¶ 3) The schedule for | 194
the depreciation for the five years covering | 203
the life of the equipment according to the | 211
straight-line and the declining-balance | 220
methods is attached. (¶ 4) I shall be at | 228
your office next Thursday as we planned, and | 237
I shall present a recommendation at that time. | 246
sincerely smith, smith and andersen suzanne | 255
r smith partner certified public accountant | 264
attachment (Words in body: 214) | 266/285

Job 2: Table with Braced Headings

*Leave 5 spaces between columns; DS body;
extend rulings 4 spaces into the margins*

DEPRECIATION COMPARISON

Year	Method		Words
	Straight-line	Declining-balance	5
			26
			27
			36
			43
			54
1	$1,900	$4,507	58
2	1,900	2,533	61
3	1,900	1,900	64
4	1,900	1,267	67
5	1,900	633	70
			80

37D Speed/Control Building [5]

1. Type the paragraph once on the EXPLORATION LEVEL; then twice on the CONTROL LEVEL.

2. Proofread; circle errors. Compare the number of errors on the three writings.

All letters are used.

1.4 SI
5.4 AWL
85% HFW

Paragraph	GWAM 1′	GWAM 2′	
The size of a business may not indicate the number of its owners.	13	7	37
A large company may be owned solely or by several partners on an equal	28	14	44
basis. On the other hand, a small corporation may belong to a relatively	42	21	52
large number of stockholders whose rights extend just as far as the num-	57	28	59
ber of shares they own.	61	31	61

1′ GWAM | 1 | 2 | 3 | 4 | 5 | 6 | 7 | 8 | 9 | 10 | 11 | 12 | 13 | 14 |
2′ GWAM | 1 | 2 | 3 | 4 | 5 | 6 | 7 |

37E Problem Typing: BUSINESS LETTERS IN MODIFIED BLOCK STYLE, BLOCK ¶s [25]

Problem 1 (WB p. 25)

Letterhead, large envelope; 60-space line; date on Line 12; open punctuation; address an envelope; correct or circle errors.

Words

February 19, 19-- | Mr. Harold F. Janowski | 8
Manager, Actron Corporation | 6530 North 16
Lincoln Avenue | Chicago, IL 60645 | Dear 24
Mr. Janowski (¶ 1) Thank you for telephon- 31
ing this morning to discuss the possi- | bility of 40
our providing some temporary office help dur- 49
ing | the months of April and May. We shall 57
be glad to work with | you in any way that 66
will be beneficial. (¶ 2) We can furnish on 73
short notice any typists, stenographers, | and 82
bookkeepers required. All operators are ex- 91
perienced. | They are capable of using stan- 99
dard equipment. If you need | operators for 108
specialized equipment, we shall make every | 116
effort to provide them. (¶ 3) The enclosed 124
brochure describes our functions and outlines | 133
briefly our methods of operation. The table 142
of pay rates for | various job classifications 151
will give you a good idea of the | cost of the 160
work you want to have done. (¶ 4) Mr. Albert 167
Valdez, one of our work-relations coordi- 175
nators, | will call you early next week to 183
arrange an appointment to | consider your job 192
requirements in detail. You will find him | 201
helpful in matching the worker to the job. | 209
Sincerely yours | John D. Marvin | Sales 217
Manager | xx | Enclosure 221/240

Problem 2 (WB p. 27)

Letterhead, large envelope; 60-space line; date on Line 15; open punctuation; address an envelope; correct or circle errors.

Words

Current date | Mr. William Poole-Wilson | 8
Office Manager | Universal Industries, Inc. | 16
42 Asbury Avenue | Farmingdale, NJ 07727 | 24
Dear Mr. Poole-Wilson | (¶ 1) The Whitney 31
plain paper copier can take any size origi- 39
nal up | to 14 by 18 inches and reduce it 48
to 8½ by 11 inches. Your | computer print- 56
outs or magazine spreads are easier to han- 65
dle, | easier to carry, and easier to file. 73
(¶ 2) You get your first copy in 3.5 seconds. 81
That's faster than | any other plain paper 90
copier. You have three copies in your | 97
hand before most others give you one. (¶ 3) 105
You can get high-quality plain paper copies, 114
halftones, and | fine lines. You can even 123
copy from bound volumes or three- | dimen- 130
sional objects. See the Whitney plain paper 139
copier, | and let us show you how reduction 148
capability can help make | your copying more 156
convenient. If you want to see what's new | 165
in copying, it's time to call us. | Yours 173
very truly | Oscar B. Bailey | Sales Manager | 181
xx 182/203

LESSON 116

116A Preparatory Practice (5) each line at least 3 times

Alphabet	By refining techniques, Jane will realize excellent skill development.
Figure/symbol	Use two dollar signs in such expressions: $169 to $350; $270 or $480.
Long reaches	Five hunters told my uncle they were cold and hungry much of the time.
Fluency	Let your goal be to get ahead of yourself, not to get ahead of others.
	| 1 | 2 | 3 | 4 | 5 | 6 | 7 | 8 | 9 | 10 | 11 | 12 | 13 | 14 |

116B Growth Index (15) two 5′ control-level writings; record GWAM of the better writing

All letters are used.

		GWAM 1′	5′	
¶ 1	A typist for an accountant will be expected to be a very skilled	13	3	69
1.5 SI 5.6 AWL 80% HFW	worker, who will be typing a lot of numbers and symbols. Some jobs will	28	6	72
	be almost entirely quantitative; this means that when a person is typing	42	8	75
	numbers, it is very important that there be no errors allowed to remain	57	11	78
	uncorrected. An improper digit or symbol can't be detected like a mis-	71	14	80
	spelled word.	73	15	81
¶ 2	The preparation of charts and tables will naturally be a significant	14	17	84
1.5 SI 5.6 AWL 80% HFW	part of the work-load arrangement if you become a typist for an accoun-	28	20	86
	tant. Since so much of accounting work involves numbers, it stands to	42	23	89
	reason that some parts of longer reports can be presented best in graphic	57	26	92
	or tabulated form, such as a chart or table. It is not unusual for longer	72	29	95
	reports to have as many as a dozen effective displays.	83	31	97
¶ 3	A typist in an accounting office will type many letters and memo-	13	34	100
1.5 SI 5.6 AWL 80% HFW	randums. When a change in procedure is to be effected, a memo is typed	27	37	103
	and sent to all concerned. The typist will need to know the exact number	42	40	106
	of copies to make before starting to type to ensure that all people	56	42	109
	affected will be sure to receive the notice of change. Most internal	70	45	111
	communication between the accounting office and other areas is by memo.	84	48	114
¶ 4	Just as in any other typing job, the typist in an accounting office	14	50	117
1.5 SI 5.6 AWL 80% HFW	must be good at the job of proofreading. Accounting reports and records	28	54	120
	are perhaps equal to legal papers in regard to accuracy of content. Many	43	57	123
	typists team up with a second person in the office for the purpose of	57	59	126
	"calling." Calling is a term used to refer to the proofreading process;	72	62	129
	one person calls aloud the typed page while the other person checks the	86	65	131
	text with the source page.	91	66	132
1′ GWAM	| 1 | 2 | 3 | 4 | 5 | 6 | 7 | 8 | 9 | 10 | 11 | 12 | 13 | 14 |			
5′ GWAM	| 1 | 2 | 3 |			

LESSON 38

38A Preparatory Practice [7] each line 3 times SS; DS between three-line groups

Alphabet	J. V. Packard may excel in law, but Hal Ford is quite good in zoology.
Figure	Please turn to page 350 and answer Questions 2, 4, 6, 7, 8, 9, and 17.
Figure/symbol	Order #678 for 24 chairs (@ $10.35 each) was shipped to you on May 19.
Fluency	Think the words as you type, but let your fingers do the work for you.
	| 1 | 2 | 3 | 4 | 5 | 6 | 7 | 8 | 9 | 10 | 11 | 12 | 13 | 14 |

38B Speed/Control Building [5]

1. Type the paragraph once on the EXPLORATION LEVEL; then twice on the CONTROL LEVEL.

2. Proofread; circle errors. Compare the number of errors on the three writings.

1.4 SI
5.4 AWL
85% HFW

Under our economic system the customer can choose from many products and services what he wants to buy. The producer can set the price of the product; but if it is too high, the customer will not buy it. So, in effect, he controls the price that a business can charge for its product. The business that does not win customers, fails.

38C Assembling, Inserting, and Erasing a Carbon Pack [10] 60-space line; DS; 5-space ¶ indention

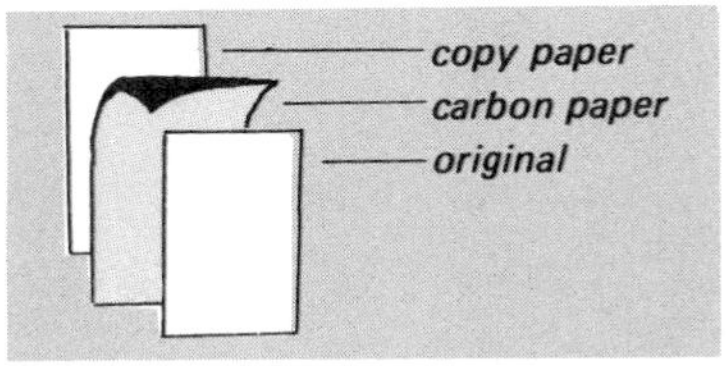

1. Read ¶ 1 at the right and assemble a carbon pack as directed.

2. Read ¶ 2; then insert the pack as directed.

3. Starting on Line 17, type the copy at the right. Proofread; erase and correct errors.

ASSEMBLING, INSERTING, AND ERASING A CARBON PACK

TS

Place on the desk the sheet on which the carbon (file) copy is to be made; then place a sheet of carbon paper, carbon side down, on the paper. Finally, place the sheet for the original on top of the carbon paper.

Pick up the papers and tap the bottom edges lightly on the desk. Insert the pack with the carbon side toward you as you insert the papers. Roll in the pack until the feed rolls have gripped the papers; then operate the paper release lever to prevent possible wrinkles.

To erase errors, pull the original sheet forward and place a small card in front of the carbon sheet. Erase the error on the original with a hard (typewriter) eraser; remove the card. With a soft (pencil) eraser, erase the error on the file copy.

Dates: Substitute the current year for "This year" and the preceding year for "Last year" throughout the report. Center vertically; use 1" side margins and 3-space indentions; DS the report except the indented items.

WORLD INTERNATIONAL CORPORATION

19–– Financial Highlights

	Amounts in U.S. Dollars	
	This year	*Last year*
Net sales	$7,898,762	$7,081,298
Income before Federal and other taxes	616,103	439,040
Net income after taxes	339,647	276,171

Return on sales:

Before taxes: *This year*; 7.8% ; *Last year,* 6.2%
After taxes: *This year*; 4.3% ; *Last year,* 3.9%

Earnings per share of common stock:

This year, $4.22; *Last year,* $3.56

Dividends:

On 6% preferred stock	30,000	30,000

Per share of preferred stock:
This year, $1.50; *Last year,* $1.50

On common stock	156,975	128,040

Per share of common stock:
This year, $1.95; *Last year,* $1.65

Income reinvested in business	152,672	118,131

Book value per share of common stock:

This year, $39.66; *Last year,* $39.18

Number of shares of stock outstanding:

Common stock, $50 par: *This year,* 80,500; *Last year,* 77,600
6% preferred stock, $25 par: *This year,* 20,000; *Last year,* 20,000

38D Problem Typing: BUSINESS LETTERS IN MODIFIED BLOCK STYLE, BLOCK ¶s ㉘

Problem 1 (WB p. 29)

Letterhead; 2 sheets of carbon paper; 2 sheets of copy paper; 1 large envelope; 60-space line; open punctuation; date on Line 17; address an envelope. Indent the listed items 5 spaces from the left margin, SS with DS above and below the list; correct errors

	Words
February 21, 19-- | Miss Vivian Hartshorn |	8
3129 Kaskaskia Street | Springfield, IL 62702 |	17
Dear Miss Hartshorn (¶ 1) Mrs. Lee has	23
asked me to send you the following payroll	32
record | forms to be completed before you	40
report for work on March 15: | 1. Employee's	49
Withholding Exemption Certificate | 2. Health	58
insurance application | 3. Personal data card	67
(¶ 2) We certainly are pleased that you have	75
decided to join our | company when you move	84
to Chicago next month. We shall do what-	92
ever we can to make your adjustment to new	100
surroundings smooth | and pleasant. Please	109
let us know how we can help. | Cordially	116
yours | Miss Beverly Newburg | Secretary to	124
Mrs. Lee | Enclosures | cc Mrs. Alma Reed	132
Lee	133/146

Problem 2 (WB p. 31)

Letterhead; carbon paper; 1 copy sheet; large envelope; 60-space line; mixed punctuation; date on Line 18; address an envelope; correct errors

	Words
February 23, 19-- | Christ Chialtas Com-	8
pany | 7720 Jefferson Street | Nashville, TN	16
37208 | Gentlemen (¶ 1) This letter will con-	23
firm our telephone conversation yesterday |	32
morning. We shall appreciate your sending	40
us information on | any electronic calculators	49
you have available for sale. (¶ 2) We are	56
particularly interested in printing calculators,	66
recon- | ditioned or in "as is" condition. They	75
should, however, be | operable. (¶ 3) Let us	83
hear from you soon about the machines you	91
now have in | stock. Keep us in mind when	100
additional printing or nonprint- | ing elec-	108
tronic calculators, copying machines, or edit-	117
ing type- | writers become available. We rent	126
such machines to offices | that we service and	135
have a heavy demand for them. | Sincerely	143
yours | Allan Wunsch | Purchasing Depart-	150
ment | xx	152/165

Problem 3 (WB p. 33)

Letterhead, carbon paper, copy sheet, large envelope; date on Line 17; 60-space line; mixed punctuation; address an envelope; correct errors

	Words
November 16, 19-- | Dr. R. D. Redford, Chair-	8
man | Business Department | Jourdan Com-	15
munity College | Chicago, IL 60620 | Dear Dr.	24
Redford: | (¶ 1) We are processing the em-	31
ployment application of Anne Morris, | who	39
lists you as one of her references. We should	48
like to | have your personal assessment of her.	58
(¶ 2) The job requires someone who is compe-	65
tent in shorthand, type- | writing, filing, Eng-	74
lish, and mathematics. As dictation must | be	83
taken from several people, we need someone	92
who can adapt | to different situations. She	101
must be able to work under | a great deal of	109
pressure at times. (¶ 3) In your opinion, would	118
Miss Morris be able to handle this | job? We	127
shall appreciate your giving us this informa-	135
tion | either on the enclosed form or by letter.	145
| Sincerely yours, | Mrs. Alma Reed Lee | Per-	153
sonnel Officer | xx | Enclosure	158/177

Production Typing Information: BRACED HEADINGS

A braced heading is a heading that applies to 2 or more column headings. Proceed as follows: (1) Leave the necessary vertical space for the columnar and braced headings. (2) Type the first line of the table, leaving 2 or 3 spaces following the last leader and 2 or more spaces between columnar entries. (3) To center each columnar heading, turn the cylinder back (down) twice and center the heading over the column. (4) To center the braced heading, turn the cylinder back (down) twice and center the heading over the columns. Draw the vertical rules (if used) with a ruler in ink.

Job 8: Table with Horizontal and Vertical Rulings and Braced Heading

Full sheet inserted sideways; center vertically and horizontally; DS; 5 spaces between columns; draw the vertical rules with a ruler in ink

SMITH, SMITH AND ANDERSEN
DS

Employee Earnings in Department B
DS

Week Ending August 29, 19--
DS

| Employee | Employee Number | Gross Earnings | Deductions SS | | | Net Pay SS |
			F.I.T.	F.I.C.A.	Other	
Philip Williams	3682	$ 204.78	$ 32.00	$11.98	--	$160.80
Samuel Jones	2621	198.25	17.40	11.60	$10.00	159.25
Gary Grant	5628	252.88	37.00	14.79	50.00	151.09
Swen Gilbert	1823	215.29	31.20	12.59	5.00	166.50
Tnomas Sweet	2871	281.25	44.20	16.45	20.00	200.60
Helen Higley	3309	210.90	25.40	12.34	14.00	159.16
Totals		$1,363.35	$187.20	$79.75	$99.00	$997.40

LESSON 39

39A Preparatory Practice ⑦ each line 3 times SS; DS between three-line groups

Alphabet   The objective of the tax quiz was clarified by checking samples of it.
Figure/symbol   Interest accumulated in 1974 to $280.56 when the rate increased by 3%.
Rule for figures   Type invoice numbers in figures: Invoice #9705 is dated September 26.
Fluency   The chairman said a large bequest had been made to the endowment fund.

| 1 | 2 | 3 | 4 | 5 | 6 | 7 | 8 | 9 | 10 | 11 | 12 | 13 | 14 |

39B Skill-Transfer Typing ⑦ 60-space line

1. Type each sentence three times. Try to type each line at the rate of the first one.

2. If time permits, repeat the sentence on which you make the most errors.

Words

Straight copy   All the girls in this firm work with speed but without rush.   12

Figure/symbol   Order #836 comes to $197.50 and is to be shipped by June 24.   12

Script   *Harley will handle the problem of forms for your firm today.*   12

Corrected copy the new chairman will not your to sign that amendment.   12

39C Speed/Control Checkup ⑧ 70-space line

Type a 5' writing on both ¶s. Determine *gwam* and number of errors. Proofread by comparing.

All letters are used.

		GWAM	
	1'	2'	5'

¶ 1
1.5 SI
5.6 AWL
80% HFW

If there is any one secret of doing a difficult job well, it is the
ability to concentrate. The efficient person does first things first and
does them one at a time. This is not so simple as it first appears, in
that the busy worker has the most demands upon his time and thus faces
a more difficult problem in priorities. To put tasks in the order of
their importance requires skill and experience, and to concentrate solely
on one job takes patience and a disciplined mind. People with these
particular qualities know how to avoid the unnecessary jobs and the useless efforts and how to apply their time to the really important things.

14	7	3
28	14	6
43	21	9
57	27	11
71	35	14
86	42	17
100	50	20
114	57	23
129	65	26

¶ 2
1.5 SI
5.6 AWL
80% HFW

The typical person hurries. Nothing to which he gives attention
gets enough time. Capable people do not race. They set an easy pace,
but they continue working steadily. Also, the typical person tries to
do a dozen tasks at once. As a result, he does not have adequate time
for any of the activities on his agenda. If one of his duties must be
slighted, his entire program collapses. More often than not, crises--
not people--make decisions. Generally this tactic does not pay, as not
enough time is spent on each element in a decision. The able person
avoids this trap by doing first things first, one at a time.

13	6	28
27	13	31
41	20	34
56	28	37
70	35	40
84	42	43
98	49	45
112	52	48
124	62	51

1' GWAM | 1 | 2 | 3 | 4 | 5 | 6 | 7 | 8 | 9 | 10 | 11 | 12 | 13 | 14 |
2' GWAM | 1 | 2 | 3 | 4 | 5 | 6 | 7 |
5' GWAM | 1 | 2 | 3 |

Job 5: Arranging Copies

Collate in order of completion the copies of the schedules, statements, and letters into three groups—original, first carbon copy, and second carbon copy. Fasten each group of papers at the left into a folder or a binder.

Job 6: Typing Labels (WB p. 31)

Production Typing Information: TYPING LABELS

Insert a sheet of paper until the top edge is ½″ above the ribbon. Place the label back of the top edge of the paper and against the cylinder. Roll the cylinder toward you until the label is in position for typing the first line; type the information.

Prepare on 5″ x 3″ cards labels to be attached to the folders. On each label type the information given at the right.

```
PETERSEN TEMPORARIES, INC.

ANNUAL FINANCIAL REPORT

June 30, 19--



Prepared by
Smith, Smith and Andersen
Certified Public Accountants
```

Job 7: Letter with Table and Enclosure (WB p. 33)

August 25, 19-- Ms. Ramah Castleton, Treasurer, World International Corporation 4309 East Linwood Blvd., Kansas City, MO 64128 Dear Ms. Castleton (¶1) Our staff has compiled a statement of last year's financial highlights of your firm in response to your request of August 10. We have used those figures that we feel would be most meaningful and interesting to your stockholders. The enclosed table can probably be inserted directly into your annual report. (¶2) In addition to the financial highlights enclosed, the employment data given below may be useful if space permits. The first column of figures is for last year; the second, for year before last. (Tabulate) Number of Employees 125, 121   Total Payroll $1,062,500, $980,100 (¶3) If you need additional information for your report, we shall be happy to provide it. Sincerely Thomas S. Smith, Senior Partner Enclosure

(Words in body: 128)

39D Problem Typing Review (28)

These problems omit punctuation in the opening and closing lines. Punctuate. Correct or circle errors, as directed.

Materials Needed. 2 letterheads, 1 plain and 3 copy sheets, 2 carbon sheets; 1 small and 2 large envelopes

Problem 1: Business Letter (WB p. 35)

Modified block style, block ¶s, mixed punctuation; 60-space line; date on Line 17; 1 cc; address large envelope

	Words
Current date │ Raymond Laboratories Co │ 1673	9
Como Avenue │ St Paul MN 55108 │ Gentle-	17
men (¶ 1) Anyone can run the Lusk Dupli-	24
cator and turn out clear, sharp │ prints fast--	33
for a fraction of a cent a copy! Sure, it's │	42
easy to punch the "On" button of a photo-	50
copier; but it is the │ slow, high-cost way to	59
make copies. (¶ 2) With a Lusk Duplicator	66
you can quickly and very inexpensively │ print	75
all the copies you want, when you want	83
them--in color │ if you wish. You can use	91
almost any paper or card stock and │ get up	99
to 140 copies a minute. Use the Lusk Dupli-	108
cator for │ price lists, bulletins, catalog pages,	118
and routine forms-- │ and use your regular	126
office staff. (¶ 3) Lusk Duplicators come in	134
many models to fit all needs. Send │ the en-	142
closed coupon for complete information. │	150
Yours very truly │ Alva M Hilgers │ Sales Pro-	159
motion │ xx │ Enclosure	163/175

Problem 2: Business Letter (WB p. 37)

Modified block style, block ¶s, open punctuation; date on Line 14; 2 cc's; address large envelope

	Words
Current date │ Ms Charlotte Mueller │ Office	8
Manager │ Columbia Corporation │ 1539 Au-	16
waiolimu Street │ Honolulu HI 96813 │ Dear	24
Ms Mueller (¶ 1) What can an editing type-	31
writer do? (¶ 2) --It can turn out perfect	38
copy very quickly no matter how many │ re-	46
writes, changes, deletions, and additions you	55
have made. (¶ 3) --It corrects a typo simply	63
by backspacing to the point where │ the typo	71
was made and typing in the correction. (¶ 4)	79
--It finds coded paragraphs, sentences, and	88
pages and types │ them in the order you spec-	97
ify. (¶ 5) --It permits the storage of complex	105
format information so that │ edited material is	114
typed out in the required style. (¶ 6) Does	121
the editing typewriter sound like something	130
your office │ can use? Write or telephone us	139
for more information. │ Yours very truly │	147
John D Marvin │ Sales Manager │ xx │ cc Mr	155
Bruce Hofstra	157/176

Problem 3: Personal/Business Letter

Plain sheet modified block style, block ¶s, mixed punctuation; 60-space line; return address on Line 15; address small envelope

	Words
3069 Theresa Avenue │ Lincoln, Nebraska	8
68504 │ February 15, 19-- │ (*Operate return*	13
times.) Mr. Thomas Rodriguez │ Golden Holi-	19
day Tours │ 1750 Sewell Street │ Lincoln,	27
Nebraska 68509 │ Dear Mr. Rodriguez (¶ 1)	34
Let me tell you again how pleased we were	42
with our tour of │ the South Pacific, Tour	50
1022. It was a fantastic experience. (¶ 2)	57
Helping to make it so was your efficient tour	67
director, Mr. │ Leland Hopkins. He was a	75
superb guide, well organized, clear │ in expla-	83
nations, and pleasant. He got us through cus-	92
toms and │ immigration quickly and painlessly.	101
(¶ 3) We saw all the features advertised for	109
the tour--and then │ some. We had preferen-	117
tial seating at most of the special │ events.	126
There were very few commercial stops. All	135
these │ things we liked about the tour and	143
Mr. Hopkins. (¶ 4) Soon we plan to take a	151
trip to South America. If you have a │ tour	159
of interesting places there, I should appreciate	169
your │ sending me information on it. (*Tab to*	176
center.) Yours sincerely (*Operate return 4 times; tab*	179
to center) Harold Thiel	181

Job 3: Schedule of Land Holdings

Leave 3 spaces between columns; use 5-space indentions; place the footnote below the last line of the table in standard form.

PETERSEN TEMPORARIES, INC.

Schedule of Land Holdings *

June 30, 19--

Location	Current Market Value	Original Purchase Price	% Increase in Value
11891 East Bannister Avenue	$17,500	$13,000	34.62
10735 Barat	8,300	7,500	10.67
3106 Euclid Avenue	5,500	5,000	10.00
8436 Kentucky Avenue	13,000	10,750	20.93
6931 Rockhill Road	10,000	8,750	12.50
Totals	$54,300	$45,000	

* Exclusive of buildings.

Job 4: Funds Flow Statement

PETERSEN TEMPORARIES, INC.
Funds Flow Statement
For the Year Ended June 30, 19--

Source of funds:
Operations:
Net income. $22,476
Add expense not requiring funds:
Depreciation. 1,947
Flow of funds from operations. . . $24,423

LESSON 40

40A Preparatory Practice [7] each line 3 times SS; DS between three-line groups

Alphabet	Ben Jackson will save the money required for your next big cash prize.
Figure/symbol	The 6½% interest of $81.08 on my $1,247.35 note (dated May 29) is due.
Rule for word division	Never divide contractions like "don't," "didn't," "wasn't," and so on.
Fluency	If you wish to write well, use those words that we all can understand.

| 1 | 2 | 3 | 4 | 5 | 6 | 7 | 8 | 9 | 10 | 11 | 12 | 13 | 14 |

40B Technique Practice: STROKING [5] each line at least twice

1	One hand	In my opinion, it was foolish to race up that hill as fast as you did.
2	Balanced hand	Did the chairman say the visit of the men will aid the endowment fund?
3	Combination	We mailed your statement to the address given on the card you sent us.
4	Adjacent keys	As Sadie said, few are they who excelled the points Portia Powers won.
5	Double letters	Lynn will see that Jill accepts an assignment in the office next week.

| 1 | 2 | 3 | 4 | 5 | 6 | 7 | 8 | 9 | 10 | 11 | 12 | 13 | 14 |

40C Growth Index [8] one 5′ writing; determine GWAM and errors

All letters are used.

		GWAM 2′	GWAM 5′
¶ 1 1.5 SI 5.6 AWL 80% HFW	The most alive, engaging, and capable people of every age are those	7	3
	with the clearest view of their personal as well as business goals. Ask	14	6
	anyone who fits this description, and he will probably be able to tell	21	8
	you exactly what he intends to do. Most people can achieve reasonable	28	11
	goals, so why not set yours high enough to keep your mind and body alert	35	14
	and flexible? The most satisfactory goal must be well beyond your pres-	43	17
	ent ability. It must be one, however, that you can attain with the	49	20
	right kind of planning and effort. A goal should make you acquire in-	56	23
	sights into new situations; it should make you use some unique talents.	64	25
¶ 2 1.5 SI 5.6 AWL 80% HFW	To make goal setting a really meaningful project, why not start by	6	28
	writing a comprehensive story of the rest of your life? You will dis-	14	31
	cover much from this exercise. Turn your imagination loose, but be	20	34
	practical. Write an honest report of the direction you want your life	27	37
	to take. As you write, ask yourself some penetrating questions: What	34	39
	kind of person do I want to be? What type of occupation do I want to	41	42
	pursue? What do I expect to get from it? Will I be satisfied with	48	45
	myself when I fulfill my expectations? What are the things I really	55	48
	want to accomplish? Answers to these puzzling questions will help you	62	50
	to formulate your goals.	65	51

2′ GWAM | 1 | 2 | 3 | 4 | 5 | 6 | 7 |

5′ GWAM | 1 | 2 | 3 |

Leave a 1" top margin.

PETERSEN TEMPORARIES, INC.

Balance sheets

June 30, 19--

Assets

Current asset:
    Cash on hand and in bank . . . . . . $ 30,871
    Accounts recievable   55,296
    Notes recievable   1,960
       Total current asset . . . . . . $ 87,767

Long lived asset:
    Office Furniture . . . . $ 2,675
      Less depreciaton . . .   1,266 $ 1,410
    Lands   45,000
    Buildings $50,495
      Less depreciaton . . .   4,877   45,618
      Total long lived asset   92,028

Total asset $179,885

Liabilities and Capitol

Current liability:
    Accounts payable $1,946
    Payroll taxes payable . . .   2,675
    Insurance Payable   263
      Total current liability . . . . $ 4,857

Long-term liabilities:
    Mortgage Payable   32,679

Total liability . . . . $ 37,636

Capital:
    Common stock, $55 par (2,000 shares
      authorized and issued) $110,000
    Retained Earnings   32,349

Total Capital   142,349

Total liability and Capital $179,885

40D   Problem Typing Measurement ㉚

Get Ready to Type . . .	4'
Timed Production . . .	20'
Proofread	6'

In the problems below, punctuation marks have been omitted in the opening and closing lines. Add those needed. Correct your errors.

Materials Needed. 2 letterheads, 1 plain sheet; 3 copy sheets, 2 sheets of carbon paper; 2 large and 1 small envelopes

Problem 1: Personal/Business Letter

Plain sheet; modified block, block ¶s, mixed punctuation; 60-space line; return address on Line 16; address a small envelope

Words

8005 Stewart Street | Albany, New York   8
12205 | June 10, 19-- | Mr. Howard F. Greg- 15
ory | 5829 Thornton Street | Albany, New 23
York   12206 | Dear Mr. Gregory | (¶ 1) You 29
asked me to let you know the nature of the 38
interview and | tests that I took at the Ham- 46
mond Electronics Company. I am | pleased 54
to comply. The tests were practical. They 63
covered | typewriting, English, spelling, and 72
arithmetic. I think I | did well on the tests. 81
(¶ 2) I was also asked about my club activi- 89
ties, hobbies, and | interests. Several times 98
during the interview, I was told | that my 106
attitude toward my job and co-workers would 115
be very | important. The Company fully be- 123
lieves in teamwork. I felt | relaxed and con- 131
fident during the interview. (¶ 3) If I get a 139
call from the Company, I shall let you know 148
the | results. Thank you for all the help you 157
have given me. | Yours sincerely | Miss Mar- 165
sha Siebert

Problem 2: Business Letter *(WB p. 41)*

Modified block style, block ¶s; open punctuation; 1 cc; 60-space line; date on Line 17; center the all-cap statement; address an envelope

Words

Current date | Fordham Manufacturing Co | 109 9
Northeastern Boulevard | Nashua NH 03060 | 17
Gentlemen (¶ 1) High-speed microfilming can 25
change the way you look at filing. | The Reli- 34
able 600 Microfilmer records more than 200 42

letters a | minute. (¶ 2) Microfilming is the 50
practical alternative to paper filing. | Micro- 59
filming is fast, accurate, and safe. The Reliable 69
600 | makes "filing" almost as easy as taking a 78
snapshot. 80

TAKE A CLOSER LOOK 84

(¶ 3) Return the enclosed card for our infor- 92
mative booklet on the | Reliable 600, or ask to 101
have a representative call. There is | no obli- 110
gation. | Yours very truly | John D Marvin | 118
Sales Manager | xx | Enclosure 123/137

Problem 3: Business Letter *(WB p. 43)*

Modified block style, block ¶s, open punctuation; 2 cc's; 60-space line; address an envelope

Words

Current date | Miss Mabel Lampel President | 9
Mobile Filing Systems Co | 1467 Coral Way | 17
Miami FL   33145 | Dear Miss Lampel (¶ 1) 24
A master key that can be copied for 50 cents 33
means that your | security is worth even less. 42
You can change your locks, but | this takes 51
time and costs money. (¶ 2) Safecard Elec- 58
tronic Keys can't be copied. They can be can- 67
celed | by simply pushing a button. A Safecard 76
is an invisibly coded | plastic card that opens 85
your doors when it is inserted into a | mag- 93
netically controlled slot. This card is rewriting 103
the book | on security systems. (¶ 3) For a 111
free demonstration of this amazing device, 119
write or call | toll free: (800) 423-4100. | Sin- 128
cerely yours | Mrs Maxine Strong | Security 137
Systems | xx | cc Mr H L Stone 143/160

Production Typing: LESSONS 111-115

In this section you will be a typist for the firm of Smith, Smith and Andersen (a public accounting partnership), 11891 East Bannister Road, Kansas City, MO 64138. The jobs you will type are typical of those you might type in any public accounting office.

The first 6 jobs you will type cover portions of an accounting report that Smith, Smith and Andersen are preparing for their client, Petersen Temporaries, Inc.

This report is to be bound at the left. Type each job with 2 cc's. Use the current year with all June 30 dates; use last year with all July 1 dates. In typing letters, use modified block style with indented paragraphs and open punctuation.

Bind Jobs 1-4 according to the instructions in Jobs 5 and 6. Then hand in the forms typed in the first 4 jobs placed correctly in three folders.

Job 1: Auditor's Statement (WB p. 29)

Remember to plan for binding at the left for this letter and all other parts of the report.

August 21, 19-- Board of Directors Petersen Temporaries, Inc. 3907 North Denver Avenue Kansas City, MO 64117 Gentlemen (¶1) We have examined the balance sheet of Petersen Temporaries, Inc., as of June 30, 19--, and the related statements of earnings and retained earnings for the year then ended. Our examination was made in accordance with generally accepted auditing standards and accordingly included such tests of the accounting records and such other auditing procedures as we considered necessary under the circumstances. (¶2) In our opinion, the accompanying balance sheet and statements of earnings and retained earnings present fairly the financial position of Petersen Temporaries, Inc., on June 30, 19--, and the results of its operations for the year then ended in conformity with generally accepted accounting principles applied on a basis consistent with that of the preceding year. Respectfully submitted

all caps——> Smith, Smith and Andersen Suzanne R. Smith, Partner Certified Public Accountant

(Words in body: 154)

SECTION 7 Tables and Simple Reports

LESSONS 41-48

Goals. When you complete these lessons, you should be able to type a variety of tables and simple reports. You will also improve your typing speed and control.

Errors. Correct errors in problem solutions as noted in directions. Your instructor will tell you how to handle errors in other problems.

Machine Adjustments. 70-space line; SS sentence drills; DS and indent ¶s 5 spaces; space problem copy as directed. For problems and ¶ copy use an adjusted right margin.

LESSON 41

41A Preparatory Practice [7] each line 3 times SS; DS between three-line groups

Alphabet	Maude Parker will visit the Chicago zoo before joining Alexis Quigley.
Figure	Paul typed page 29 on May 7, page 30 on May 14, and page 65 on May 18.
Figure/symbol	Baxter & Moore's check for $974.20 (check #1305) was cashed on July 7.
Fluency	He will do well to try one or more of the very fine pens for the work.

| 1 | 2 | 3 | 4 | 5 | 6 | 7 | 8 | 9 | 10 | 11 | 12 | 13 | 14 |

41B Technique Practice: STROKING [5] each line 3 times

Home row	Hal Skaggs had a bad fall as he made a gallant dash to raise the flag.
1st row	Zeal or zest can bring much more success next time than luck ever can.
Double letters	Ella was puzzled by the letter that followed the offer of a free book.
Adjacent keys	Last Wednesday, Lew Polk threw the ball to Sam Hopper for an easy out.

41C Technique Practice: RESPONSE PATTERNS [5] each line at least 3 times

Letter response	The executive expects the expert to explain his actions to an auditor.
Word response	The aid the men got from us did much to help them get their work done.
Combination	Nine seniors pointed to the easy quiz questions to support their case.
	A good many workers of this world surely need to have a faith lifting.

| 1 | 2 | 3 | 4 | 5 | 6 | 7 | 8 | 9 | 10 | 11 | 12 | 13 | 14 |

41D Speed/Control Building [10] twice on the EXPLORATION LEVEL; then twice on the CONTROL LEVEL; compare number of errors on the 4 writings

All letters are used.

1.4 SI
5.4 AWL
85% HFW

	GWAM 1'	2'	
Tabulating is just an extension of centering, which you have been	13	6	49
doing for quite some time; so it is not new to you. When you were typing	28	14	57
words or figures in columns in past lessons, you were told the number of	43	21	64
spaces to leave between the columns. You will likely use guides for the	57	28	71
horizontal placement of columns until you learn to plan a table without	72	36	79
help; then you will use your own judgment in typing an attractive table.	86	43	86

1' GWAM | 1 | 2 | 3 | 4 | 5 | 6 | 7 |
2' GWAM | 1 | 2 | 3 | 4 | 5 | 6 | 7 | 8 | 9 | 10 | 11 | 12 | 13 | 14 |

LESSONS 111-115

Lessons 111, 113, 115

Use the following daily lesson plan for Lessons 111, 113, and 115. Retain all jobs until you have completed Lesson 115.

Preparatory Practice (5′). Type 111A below, as directed.

Production Typing (45′). Type the jobs on pages 224-229. Follow the directions for each job; where specific directions are not given, use your own good judgment. Proofread carefully; correct all errors.

Lessons 112, 114

Use the following daily lesson plan for Lessons 112 and 114. Retain all jobs until you have completed Lesson 115.

Preparatory Practice (5′). Type 111B, below, as directed.

Technique Mastery (5′). Type 111C, below, as directed.

Production Typing (40′). Continue typing the jobs on pages 224-229. Follow the same general directions given for Lessons 111, 113, and 115.

111A Preparatory Practice (5) each line at least 3 times

Alphabet	Guy Crumley planned to review the book and relax just before the quiz.
Figure/symbol	The only fee for a 102-week course covering 63 basic areas is $754.98.
One hand	Only Edward Linny saw Fred Street win the award at the bazaar in Lyon.
Fluency	Hold your wrists not more than an inch from the frame of your machine.

| 1 | 2 | 3 | 4 | 5 | 6 | 7 | 8 | 9 | 10 | 11 | 12 | 13 | 14 |

111B Preparatory Practice (5) each line at least 3 times

Alphabet	My half dozen flavorful new soup mixes are in big, quick-to-open jars.
Figure/symbol	His letter of August 21 states, "I shall ship 40 #978 files @ $35.68."
Double letters	Billie Williams is planning to accept all offers for swimming lessons.
Fluency	The key to earning the respect of your friends is to respect yourself.

| 1 | 2 | 3 | 4 | 5 | 6 | 7 | 8 | 9 | 10 | 11 | 12 | 13 | 14 |

111C Technique Mastery (5) each line at least twice without error

Direct reaches	I must include in my article the data from that issue of the magazine.
Stroke response	Procedures announced yesterday include regulations regarding absences.
Left hand	After a date was set for the meeting, a secretary addressed the cards.
Right hand	It is my opinion, not our policy, that we must limit our oil supplies.
Combination	The regulation of television is of particular importance to all of us.

| 1 | 2 | 3 | 4 | 5 | 6 | 7 | 8 | 9 | 10 | 11 | 12 | 13 | 14 |

41E Problem Typing: TWO- AND THREE-COLUMN TABLES (23)

Guides for horizontal placement of columns (backspace-from-center method)

1. Move margin stops to ends of scale. Clear all tabulator stops.

2. Move carriage (carrier) to center of paper.

3. Decide on spacing between columns (if spacing is not specified)—preferably an even number of spaces (4, 6, 8, 10, etc.).

4. From center of paper, backspace once for *each 2 strokes* in the longest line of each column and for *each 2 spaces* to be left between columns.

As you backspace, count any extra stroke (that may occur at the end of the longest line of a column) with the space between columns. Likewise, if an extra space occurs at the end of an intercolumn, count it with the next column.

5. Set the left margin stop at the point where you complete the backspacing.

6. From the left margin, space forward *once for each stroke* in the longest line of the first column and for each space to be left between the first and second column.

7. *Set the tab stop at this point for the second column.*

8. Follow this procedure for each column in the table.

Problem 1: Two-Column Table

Use an 8½″ by 5½″ half sheet; DS; leave 20 spaces between columns. Center the problem vertically (see p. 55). Center the columns horizontally (see guides above).

NOTE: After setting the margin and tab stops by backspacing from center, check the placement by using the boxed key below the problem.

		Words
OFFICERS OF HORIZON INDUSTRIES		6
Victor Potter	President	11
Ben F. Edwards	Vice President	17
Eva M. Baker	Vice President	23
Kenneth Hoffman	Treasurer	28
Axel Hansen	Secretary	32
Melvin Hauser	Asst. Secretary	38

| 15 | 20 | 15 |

Problem 2: Three-Column Table

Full sheet; DS; 14 spaces between columns; center the problem vertically, the heading horizontally, and the columns horizontally

Technique Cue. Tabulate from column to column without looking up from the copy. Reach to the tab bar or key without moving the hand out of typing position.

Evaluate Your Work. Use your stroke and line-space ruler to check top, bottom, and side margins and the number of spaces between the columns.

			Words
SOME STATE NAMES AND THEIR ABBREVIATIONS			8
		TS	
Arizona	Ariz.	AZ	11
California	Calif.	CA	15
Connecticut	Conn.	CT	19
Delaware	Del.	DE	22
Illinois	Ill.	IL	25
Indiana	Ind.	IN	28
Louisiana	La.	LA	32
Michigan	Mich.	MI	35
New York	N.Y.	NY	38
Pennsylvania	Penn.	PA	42
Tennessee	Tenn.	TN	46
Washington	Wash.	WA	50

| 12 | 14 | 6 | 14 | 2 |

110C Statistical Timed Writing ⑮ three 3' writings; record GWAM of the best writing

All letters and figures are used.

¶ 1
1.6 SI
5.8 AWL
75% HFW

    In 1974 our company invested over $1.5 million in secured inden- 13 | 4 | 60
tures; this represented over 10% of our accumulated surplus. This year 27 | 9 | 64
we shall invest nearly $2.25 million at an average return of 6% per annum. 42 | 14 | 69
Our total investments will be in excess of $8.5 million, which is about 57 | 19 | 74
13.4% of our total assets of $63.4 million. We have been directed by 71 | 24 | 79
the Board of Directors not to let our investments exceed 15% of assets. 85 | 28 | 84

¶ 2
1.6 SI
5.8 AWL
75% HFW

    All prospective investments are given a good inspection; if they do 14 | 33 | 88
not meet positive analysis, they are rejected. The size of the offering 28 | 38 | 93
is not a factor if it meets SEC rules. A quick check of the prospectus 43 | 42 | 98
will identify those that qualify. Only about 4% of all stock offerings 57 | 47 | 103
will meet our rigid requirements. An anticipated return of at least 71 | 52 | 107
5.5% per annum must be evident; 6.5 to 7% is better. 81 | 55 | 111

1' GWAM | 1 | 2 | 3 | 4 | 5 | 6 | 7 | 8 | 9 | 10 | 11 | 12 | 13 | 14 |
3' GWAM | 1 | | 2 | | 3 | | 4 | | 5 |

110D Control Building ⑮ two 5' writings; record GWAM of the better writing

All letters are used.

¶ 1
1.7 SI
6.0 AWL
70% HFW

    The accounting profession is divided into three basic areas: pub- 13 | 3 | 49
lic, private, and governmental sectors. If a woman wants to be a public 28 | 6 | 52
accountant, she will find that she will be doing annual audits of her 42 | 8 | 55
client's books. She is charged with the responsibility of saying that 56 | 11 | 57
the records and financial statements do or do not reflect a true finan- 70 | 14 | 60
cial picture. 73 | 15 | 61

¶ 2
1.7 SI
6.0 AWL
70% HFW

    Private accounting means that there is a loyalty to a private 12 | 17 | 63
group; in other words, a woman who is this type of accountant is in the 27 | 20 | 66
employ of a business for the explicit purpose of handling or supervising 41 | 23 | 69
that company's financial records. She will be expected to supervise, 55 | 26 | 72
design, evaluate, and implement all new procedures; she analyzes, reviews, 70 | 29 | 75
and interprets all the financial data. 78 | 30 | 76

¶ 3
1.7 SI
6.0 AWL
70% HFW

    Government accounting offers a person a broad variety of employment 14 | 33 | 79
choices. One may be an accountant in a government department, bureau, 28 | 36 | 82
or agency; then the person may be moved to the auditing area of a gov- 42 | 39 | 85
ernmental auditing department. A government accountant is a civil servant 57 | 42 | 88
much like all other civil servants. To qualify for a civil service job 72 | 44 | 91
means that one must pass a civil service exam. 81 | 46 | 93

1' GWAM | 1 | 2 | 3 | 4 | 5 | 6 | 7 | 8 | 9 | 10 | 11 | 12 | 13 | 14 |
5' GWAM | 1 | | 2 | | 3 |

42A Preparatory Practice ⑦ each line 3 times SS; DS between three-line groups

Alphabet	Dr. Robert Wachs received a quaint onyx ring from Jack Pelz of Venice.
Figure/symbol	Did Ned pay $4.81 to $4.95 (less 6% discount) for 37 ft. of #260 wire?
Long words	Today, car buyers are knowledgeable about performance characteristics.
Fluency	Hand the proxy forms to the chairmen so that they can sign the titles.

| 1 | 2 | 3 | 4 | 5 | 6 | 7 | 8 | 9 | 10 | 11 | 12 | 13 | 14 |

42B Speed/Control Building ⑬ type each ¶ twice; then type one 3′ writing on both ¶s on the SPEED level and one 3′ writing on the CONTROL level

All letters are used.

		GWAM		
		1′	3′	

¶ 1
1.4 SI
5.4 AWL
85% HFW

You would not expect a sizable response to a mailing late in the — 13 | 4 | 41
spring of a letter promoting snow tires. Nor should you expect a letter — 28 | 9 | 46
written in less than standard language to be effective if it has been — 42 | 14 | 51
mailed to a group of college professors. — 50 | 17 | 54

¶ 2
1.4 SI
5.4 AWL
85% HFW

A good knowledge of words is vital to a writer, but so is a clear — 13 | 21 | 58
knowledge of the reader. To style your message to your reader's taste — 27 | 26 | 63
and to direct it to his vocabulary range are basic requirements of good — 42 | 30 | 67
writing. The writer is just the first half of the communication process. — 57 | 35 | 72
The reader is the other. — 61 | 37 | 74

1′ GWAM | 1 | 2 | 3 | 4 | 5 | 6 | 7 | 8 | 9 | 10 | 11 | 12 | 13 | 14 |
3′ GWAM | 1 | 2 | 3 | 4 | 5 |

42C Aligning Figures in Columns ⑩

To align columns of figures at the right

Follow the backspace-from-center method (page 79) to determine the left margin stop, backspacing once for each 2 strokes in the longest item in each column and intercolumn.

For the remaining columns, set a tab stop for the digit in each column that will require the least forward or backward spacing. To type the columns, tabulate and space forward or back as appropriate.

Type the drill below twice as shown; 60-space line.

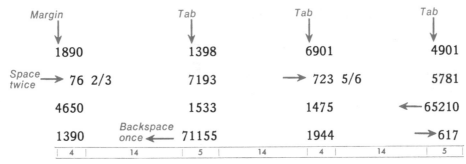

Margin	Tab	Tab	Tab
1890	1398	6901	4901
76 2/3	7193	723 5/6	5781
4650	1533	1475	65210
1390	71155	1944	617

| 4 | 14 | 5 | 14 | 4 | 14 | 5 |

SECTION 21 Typing in an Accounting Office

LESSONS 110-116

Section 21 provides opportunity to type problems normally encountered in an accounting office.

Drill Copy. SS; 70-space line

¶ Copy. DS; 70-space line; 5-space ¶ indentions; full sheets

Production Typing. Follow directions as to spaces between columns and DS or SS. Use reading position for financial reports. DS all multiple-line headings.

Supplies Needed. Letterheads (or full sheets); carbon paper; second sheets; folders or binders for reports; gummed labels; envelopes

LESSON 110

110A Preparatory Practice (5) each line at least 3 times

Alphabet	Jodie Quinwall packages frozen vegetables for shipment by REA Express.
Figure/symbol	Make your payment of $6,579.48 in 3 days (May 10) for the 2% discount.
One hand	In effect, we agree with his opinion regarding the great oil monopoly.
Fluency	The future of the company may depend on the sales they make this year.

| 1 | 2 | 3 | 4 | 5 | 6 | 7 | 8 | 9 | 10 | 11 | 12 | 13 | 14 |

110B Communication Aid: CAPITALIZATION AND PUNCTUATION (15)

1. Read the ¶s below and then type them with correct capitalization and punctuation.

2. Check your corrected ¶s with your instructor. Using your corrected copy, type two 1′ writings on each ¶.

3. Using the book, type two 1′ writings on each ¶. Record GWAM of the better writing.

		GWAM 1′	GWAM 3′	
¶ 1 1.7 SI 6.0 AWL 70% HFW	of the seventeen men who started on the well reported january	11	4	45
	second voyage to the estuary of the amazon three were natives of guaya-	23	8	49
	quil ecuador five had lived at one time or another in rio de janeiro	36	12	54
	eight were bostonians and one although few of the others actually	49	16	58
	believed him indicated reykjavik was his birthplace and hometown.	62	21	62
¶ 2 1.7 SI 6.0 AWL 70% HFW	all were veteran travelers. none of them had ever visited macapa	13	25	67
	an interesting old city of approximately twenty eight thousand citizens	25	29	71
	spread over the equator on the northern bank of the amazon. each person	39	34	75
	was filled with the excitement of his venture to this area of the larg-	53	38	80
	est and most mysterious river--the great and mighty amazon.	63	42	83

1′ GWAM | 1 | 2 | 3 | 4 | 5 | 6 | 7 | 8 | 9 | 10 | 11 | 12 | 13 | 14 |

3′ GWAM | 1 | 2 | 3 | 4 | 5 |

42D Problem Typing: ALIGNING FIGURES IN COLUMNS ⑳

Problem 1

Half sheet; SS; 16 spaces between columns; center the problem vertically, the headings and columns horizontally; proofread by comparing

		Words
MANPOWER NEEDS IN THE 1970'S		6
DS		
Annual Average by Office Occupations		13
TS		
Accountants	31,200	17
Bank tellers	14,700	21
Bookkeepers	74,000	25
Cashiers	64,000	28
Office machine operators	20,800	34
Programmers	34,700	38
Stenographers/secretaries	247,000	45
Systems analysts	22,700	50
Typists	61,000	53

25	16	7

Problem 2

Half sheet; SS; 20 spaces between columns; center the problem vertically, the headings and columns horizontally; proofread by comparing

		Words
FIRST SEMESTER ENROLLMENTS--1975		7
DS		
By Colleges and Schools		11
TS		
Art	218	13
Business Administration	1,505	19
Education	980	22
Engineering	453	25
Letters and Science	5,225	30
Library Science	91	34
Music	174	36
Public Health	47	40
Theater Arts	117	43

23	20	5

LESSON 43

43A Preparatory Practice ⑦ each line 3 times SS; DS between three-line groups

Alphabet	Jane Fox owns a copy of the book Zelma Quade has given to all members.
Figure	Please turn to page 530 and answer Items 2, 4, 6, 7, 8, 9, 10, and 16.
Apostrophe	Is the notation on this memorandum Bob's, Dick's, Ralph's, or R. J.'s?
Fluency	A good student knows: the brighter he is, the more he needs to learn.

| 1 | 2 | 3 | 4 | 5 | 6 | 7 | 8 | 9 | 10 | 11 | 12 | 13 | 14 |

43B Centering Columnar Headings ⑩

To determine the center of a column

From the beginning point of a column, space forward once for each two strokes (letters, figures, or spaces) in the longest line in the column. Disregard a leftover stroke.

To type the columnar heading

From the center of the column, backspace once for each two spaces in the heading. Disregard a leftover stroke. Begin to type where the backspacing ended.

Type the drill below on a half sheet; DS; 10 spaces between columns; center the columnar headings over the columns, underlined.

Name	Birthday
George Washington	February 22, 1732
Ulysses Simpson Grant	April 27, 1822

N-PRAM. N-PRAM (net production rate a minute) refers to the rate on production copy on which errors are erased and corrected.

$$\text{N-PRAM} = \frac{\text{Gross (total) words} - \text{Penalties}}{\text{Length (in minutes) of writing}}$$

Penalties for Uncorrected Errors. Deduct the following penalties for errors not corrected during the production period:

Deduct 10 words ..... for each error not erased on an original copy

Deduct 5 words ...... for each error not erased on a carbon copy

Job 1: Letter *(WB p. 25)*

Modified block with indented ¶'s; open punctuation; 2 cc's

	Words
january 15, 19-- ms annette v bushman 905	9
palm avenue jacksonville fl 32205 dear ms	18
bushman subject: employment offer (¶ 1) I	25
have reviewed your resume and feel that your	34
background and training would be valuable to	43
our organization. (¶ 2) Your references have	51
been checked and found to be very compli-	59
mentary and entirely satisfactory. Your em-	68
ployment test results were in the top 10 per-	77
cent of all applicants tested by our Personnel	86
Department. We would like to offer you a	94
position as management trainee; this position	103
will provide you with ample opportunity to	112
learn our management policies and techniques.	121

	Words
After a one-year training period, you will be	131
assigned to one of our Jacksonville offices as	140
a middle manager. (¶ 3) Please give us a	147
written letter of acceptance by January 31.	156
If you elect to join our organization, we would	166
like you to report for work on February 15.	175
Please call the Personnel Department prior to	184
February 15 to set up a pre-employment inter-	193
view on the date you are to report to work.	202
(¶ 4) If you have any questions about this	208
offer, please call me. sincerely hampton in-	217
surance company p. john hampton, president	226
cc mr r zaugg, personnel director (Words in	233/246
body: 189)	

Job 2: Agenda

Full sheet; center vertically; DS with SS indented lines; 70-space line; use leaders between columns

		Words Job 2	Job 3
FRANKLIN DISTRIBUTING COMPANY		6	6
Agenda for Board of Directors Meeting		14	14
September 30, 19--		17	17
1. Call to Order	E. Sherman Franklin	32	32
2. Reading and Approval of Minutes	Thomas A. Pope	45	45
3. Reports of Officers		50	50
President's Report	Karl T. Chambers	62	62
Treasurer's Report	Truman C. King	74	74
4. Dividend Declaration	Samuel R. Corning	88	87
5. Stock Option Plan Report	Sandra R. Chipman	102	102
6. Adjournment		105	105

Job 3: Revised Agenda

Retype Job 2, above, with the following changes: substitute William K. Jones for Samuel R. Corning; Harold W. McFarland for Sandra R. Chipman.

Problem 1

Full sheet; DS; 32 spaces between columns; reading position (p. 55); proofread by verifying

		Words
U.S. PERSONAL AND PER CAPITA INCOME		7
DS		
Ten Highest by State--1971		13
TS		
State	**Amount**	17
Tab stop → DS		
New York	$5,000	21
Connecticut	4,995	24
Alaska	4,875	27
Nevada	4,822	30
New Jersey	4,811	33
Illinois	4,775	36
Hawaii	4,738	39
Delaware	4,673	42
California	4,640	45
Massachusetts	4,562	49

| 13 | 32 | 6 |

Problem 2

Full sheet; DS; 24 spaces between columns; center vertically; proofread by verifying

		Words
TEN LARGEST COUNTRIES		4
DS		
In Square Miles (1970 Data)		10
TS		
Country	**Area**	15
Tab stop → DS		
Soviet Union	8,647,249	20
Canada	3,850,789	23
Mainland China	3,690,546	28
United States	3,614,254	33
Brazil	3,294,110	36
Australia	2,967,108	40
India	1,261,482	43
Argentina	1,071,879	47
Sudan	967,243	51
Algeria	919,352	54

| 14 | 24 | 9 |

Problem 3

Full sheet; DS; 18 spaces between columns; exact center; proofread by verifying

			Words
TWELVE MOST POPULOUS CITIES			6
DS			
Figures Given for Latest Year Available			13
TS			
City	**Population**	**Year**	21
Tokyo	9,005,000	1969	26
New York	7,798,757	1970	30
London	7,703,400	1969	35
Moscow	6,942,000	1970	39
Shanghai	6,900,000	1957	44
Bombay	5,700,358	1970	48
Sao Paulo	5,684,706	1968	53
Cairo	4,961,000	1970	57
Rio de Janeiro	4,206,332	1968	64
Peking	4,010,000	1957	68
Seoul	3,794,959	1966	72
New Delhi	3,772,457	1970	77

| 14 | 18 | 9 | 18 | 4 |

LESSON 109

109A Preparatory Practice (5) each line at least 3 times

Alphabet	Jack and Marge Sawyer explored the queer caves in Arizona before dawn.
Figure/symbol	She noted the price change of item #452 from 10 @ $6.97 to 12 @ $8.39.
Balanced hand	If they qualify, special aid may be given to the citizens of the city.
Fluency	The mind gets rusty with disuse; you can keep it sharp with new ideas.
	| 1 | 2 | 3 | 4 | 5 | 6 | 7 | 8 | 9 | 10 | 11 | 12 | 13 | 14 |

109B Growth Index (15) two 5′ control-level writings; record GWAM of better writing

All letters are used.

		GWAM 1′	5′	
¶ 1 1.5 SI 5.6 AWL 80% HFW	Generally, a typist will find that most businesses use one or more	13	3	60
	of the three basic business letter formats. Perhaps these letter for-	27	5	63
	mats have been institutionalized more as a result of the education that	42	8	66
	the typist receives in school than a decision from an executive of the	56	11	69
	company. If a company does not have its own letter style, the typist	70	14	71
	is usually free to choose the style that she prefers; and, of course, the	85	17	74
	style will be one of the "basic three" that she knows.	95	19	76
¶ 2 1.5 SI 5.6 AWL 80% HFW	There are two modified block styles commonly used in most of the	13	22	79
	business organizations today; one has the paragraphs indented and the	27	24	82
	other style has them blocked at the left. Both of them require that	41	27	85
	the dateline begin at the horizontal center of the paper. The address,	55	30	87
	salutation, and all of the final notations are placed at the left, but	69	33	90
	the complimentary close is started a double space below the body and	83	36	93
	typed in a block format at the center of the paper.	93	38	95
¶ 3 1.5 SI 5.6 AWL 80% HFW	The third letter style is labeled the "block style." The simplic-	13	40	98
	ity of this particular format is noted by the single characteristic that	28	43	101
	all elements of the letter begin at the left margin; there are no inden-	42	46	104
	tions used. The popularity of this style is due primarily to the ease	56	49	106
	of typing; only the right and left margin stops are required to be set.	71	52	109
	Of course, the typist must still be able to use good judgment in the	85	55	112
	vertical placement of the parts of the letter.	98	57	115
1′ GWAM	| 1 | 2 | 3 | 4 | 5 | 6 | 7 | 8 | 9 | 10 | 11 | 12 | 13 | 14 |			
5′ GWAM	| 1 | 2 | 3 |			

LESSON 44

44A Preparatory Practice [5] each line twice

Alphabet	Jenny Saxon left my squad last week and gave back a prize she had won.
Figure/symbol	Is that last-minute (!) report on bill #6753-48 due on April 19 or 20?
Quotation marks	"Have 'sunglow' all winter," I typed, "with a Magic Sunlamp by Solco."
Fluency	The civic group may ask for a formal audit of the records in February.
	| 1 | 2 | 3 | 4 | 5 | 6 | 7 | 8 | 9 | 10 | 11 | 12 | 13 | 14 |

44B Technique Practice: COMBINATION RESPONSE [5] each line twice

which is | of these | of course | amount of | number of | some of | part of | on our
it will | have to | for this | that this | at this | on this | to this | this letter
this matter | this time | that this | that it | so that | hope that | it was | if we
there are | it would | for this | that it | in order | will not | as you | thank you
as well | as well as | as soon | as soon as | we will | we will be | thank you for

44C Speed/Control Building [15]

1. Type each of the following ¶s twice, once for speed and once for control.

2. Type a 5′ writing on the 3 ¶s. Proofread by comparing. Determine *gwam*.

All letters are used.

		GWAM 2′	5′	
¶ 1 1.4 SI 5.4 AWL 85% HFW	In this class--and likely in your English classes as well--you have	7	3	35
	been taught the importance of selecting just the right word to convey	14	6	38
	the meaning you are after. You may have put the idea into practice in	21	8	41
	composing papers that are to be graded.	25	10	42
¶ 2 1.4 SI 5.4 AWL 85% HFW	You should also realize how important it is that you choose care-	31	13	45
	fully the words that you use in your daily conversation. Not only will	39	15	48
	such a habit help you to build a larger and more interesting vocabulary,	46	18	51
	but it will also require you to pause and think a bit before you speak.	53	21	54
¶ 3 1.4 SI 5.4 AWL 85% HFW	How can we expect our heads of state to communicate perfectly when,	60	24	56
	as most of us learn, a good friend at a casual get-together may react in	67	27	59
	some surprising way to a remark that, to the speaker, has been clearly	74	30	62
	stated? Better communications should start at the one-to-one level.	81	32	65

2′ GWAM | 1 | 2 | 3 | 4 | 5 | 6 | 7 |
5′ GWAM | 1 | 2 | 3 |

Job 9: Cost Sheet

Prepare an approval copy of the cost sheet shown below. Side margins of 1½″ are suggested. You might also set the right margin to lock the machine where you want your lines to end. Center vertically. Indent the *total* line 10 spaces from the left margin.

TYPEWRITING PRODUCTION COST SHEET

TS

Name of Typist _____

TS

Date _____ Job Number _____ Page _____

TS

Class Designation _____

SS

DS

Cost of all paper used to complete job:

DS

_____ sheets at .02 a sheet $_____

TS

Cost of carbon paper:

DS

_____ sheets at .03 a sheet   _____

TS

Charges for working time:

DS

Time job was started: _____

DS

Time job was finished: _____

DS

Total minutes: _____ x .05   _____

TS

Cost of writer's time (standardized):   4.50

TS

Miscellaneous costs (standardized):   .05

TS

Other costs (estimated):   _____

TS

TOTAL JOB COST $_____

2 DS

Signature of Typist _____

44D Problem Typing: THREE-COLUMN TABLES (25)

Problem 1

Full sheet; DS; reading position; 10 spaces between columns

In a money column, use a dollar sign before the top item and a total, if given. If the top item is not the longest number in the column, the dollar sign may be placed 1 space to the left of the horizontal starting point of the longest number (which may be the *total* number).

Underline the last item; DS and type the total, indenting the word *Total* 5 spaces.

			Words
OGLETHORPE COLLEGE BUILDING FUND			7
Contributions Received in First Quarter			15
Name	State	Amount	21
George Anderson	New York	$ 1,750.00	29
Edward O. Babcock	Idaho	500.00	35
Myron D. Bailey	Maryland	1,500.00	42
Marilyn O. Cross	Indiana	200.00	49
D. Wesley Dodds	Ohio	15,000.00	55
Allien Gratz	Iowa	1,250.00	60
N. R. Howell	Utah	75.50	65
Arthur McDonald	Illinois	2,500.00	72
Sylvia Schwartz	Indiana	1,250.00	79
Oscar P. Sweeney	Maine	560.00	85
Edward O. Welsh	Vermont	1,500.00	94
		DS	
Total		$26,085.50	97

Problem 2

Full sheet; DS; reading position; 10 spaces between columns

			Words
DEL MONACO PRODUCTS, INCORPORATED			7
Annual Conference Costs			12
Item	1974	1975	17
Conference rooms	$ 1,200	$ 1,200	23
Demonstration materials	.750	620	30
Exhibits	1,940	1,450	35
Entertainment	470	675	40
Handouts	92	140	45
Hotel accommodations	11,430	12,740	50
Meals for conferees	17,840	18,820	54
Travel	10,690	10,870	61
Total	$44,412	$46,515	66

Type the following letters for Mr. Harold Bringhurst, Chairman of the Board, to the five other members of the board; their names and addresses are listed at the right.

Type a REGISTERED AIRMAIL notation on both the letter and the envelope. Date the letter June 7, 19––; SUBJECT: Board of Directors Meeting–– June 30, 19––; Enclosure.

(¶ 1) Our next H. B. Import-Export Co. Board of Directors meeting will be held on June 30 at 7 p.m. in the Conference Room. Because two very important reports will be presented concerning our imports from a very large Japanese firm and a proposal to expand our exports to Nepal, your attendance is important. (¶ 2) Although we shall not vote on these two major proposals at this Board of Directors meeting, we must discuss them thoroughly so that a final decision can be made at our July meeting. (¶ 3) We must also make final recommendations concerning our letters of credit. I would hope that after limited discussion we could make a final decision. Please review last month's minutes and come prepared to finish this item of business. (¶ 4) A copy of the tentative agenda for the meeting is enclosed. (*Use the person's first name here.*) , if you would like to make any changes in the agenda, please let me have your comments no later than June 20. (Words in body: 180)

Mr. Cannon L. Jones
1309 Appleby Avenue
Baltimore, MD   21209

Ms. Ruth Ann Castleton
1875 Cherokee Avenue
Baton Rouge, LA   70802

Dr. Theodore M. Davis
1309 Kamehameha Avenue
Honolulu, HI   96822

Dr. Annette R. Thurman
669 Hunters Point Blvd.
San Francisco, CA   94124

Mrs. Susan T. Faulkner
2508 Adobe Falls Place
San Diego, CA   92120

Job 8: Final Copy of Agenda for Meeting

Mr. Bringhurst asks you to make the necessary changes on the tentative agenda (Job 6). Type a final copy of the agenda to be used in the Board of Directors meeting on June 30.

Change the presentation order of the two reports under #3 – "Special Reports." The Nepal report will be given by Carol S. Johnson. Eliminate the topic "Fluctuation of International Money Market"; in its place, add the topic "Review of Current Pricing Formula," to be presented by J. Hamilton Clay.

LESSON 45

45A Preparatory Practice [7] each line 3 times SS; DS between three-line groups

Alphabet	Prizes for Albuquerque's next track meet will be given by Judson Hall.
Figure	Dial 649-5718 or 649-5709 to obtain your copy of this 32-page booklet.
Figure/symbol	Should the 6½% rate on Long's $3,250 note (dated May 18, 1974) be 8¼%?
Fluency	The auditor said the profit due you should have been paid much sooner.

| 1 | 2 | 3 | 4 | 5 | 6 | 7 | 8 | 9 | 10 | 11 | 12 | 13 | 14 |

45B Technique Practice: STROKING [5] each line twice

1	Long words	The unit has synthesized circuitry for clear, dependable transmission.
2	Left hand	A few extra seats were set up on the vast stage as dessert was served.
3	Right hand	Jimmy Polk pulled the oily junk down the hill, but Jon only looked on.
4	Direct reaches	A hundred unusual designs made the celebrated decorator justly famous.
5	Adjacent keys	Except for Bert and Ernie, we saw very poor relations between members.
6	Hyphen	He drew the step-by-step, door-to-door plans for our all-purpose soap.

| 1 | 2 | 3 | 4 | 5 | 6 | 7 | 8 | 9 | 10 | 11 | 12 | 13 | 14 |

45C Proofreading: READING FOR MEANING [8] Half sheet; 65-space line; 1½″ top margin; DS

Type the following paragraph, filling in the blank spaces with the appropriate words selected from those listed at the left.

vis-a-vis
expenditure
concrete
decade
money
company
growing
leaders
dialogue
measure
life
expected
obligations
financial

There has been a ________ tendency in the past ________ for corporate ________ to use art in terms of their overall image ________ the complex requirements of today's society. The ________ of large sums of ______ may be difficult to justify because ________ results are difficult to ________. On the other hand, the ________ between management and society at large does emphasize some of the social ________ of modern capitalism. Is it not ________ to improve the quality of ________ for both the employees of a ________ and its public? Businessmen who look further than the next dividend recognize their responsibility to contribute more than mere ________ success.

Production Typing Information: TYPING LEADERS

Leaders are a series of periods (. . . . .) that are typed between 2 items. The purpose of leaders is to aid the reader by "leading" him from 1 place to the next. Leaders are used only when the distance between the 2 items is great enough to cause some difficulty for the reader to follow from 1 item to the next.

Leaders are made by alternating the period (.) and a space. If more than 1 row contains leaders, all the periods used for leaders should be aligned vertically. To align leaders vertically, type the periods on either the odd or the even numbers on the cylinder scale, guided by the first row of leaders.

Begin the first row of leaders at the second space after the first item and stop the row of leaders at a point 2 or 3 spaces short of the item to which the leaders point. If the leaders point to a column, as shown in the top illustration at the right, end all rows of leaders at the same point. If the leaders point to a *justified column* (see the lower illustration), end all rows of leaders at the same point, determined by the longest item in the column.

```
3.  Reports of Officers
       President's Report . . . . . . . . . .  Ralph A. Williams
       Vice President's Report  . . . . . . .  Helen R. Carlson
       Treasurer's Report . . . . . . . . . .  Peter Adams
4.  Reports of Special Committees
       Report on Personnel Policy . . . . . .  Roy C. Downs
       Report on Sales Promotion  . . . . . .  Frances Dietrich
       Report on Advertising Increase . . . .  Mary Lane
5.  New Business
       Plans for Expansion  . . . . . . . . .  George Hamilton
```

Leaders used in nonjustified material

```
3.  Reports of Officers
       President's Report . . . . . . . . . .  Ralph A. Williams
       Vice President's Report  . . . . . . .  Helen R. Carlson
       Treasurer's Report . . . . . . . . . .      Peter Adams
4.  Reports of Special Committees
       Report on Personnel Policy . . . . . .      Roy C. Downs
       Report on Sales Promotion  . . . . . .  Frances Dietrich
       Report on Advertising Increase . . . .       Mary Lane
5.  New Business
       Plans for Expansion  . . . . . . . . .  George Hamilton
```

Leaders used in justified material

NOTE: The number of leaders in each line in your solutions may not be the same as the number of leaders in the problems printed in the textbook.

Job 6: Tentative Agenda for Meeting

Type the following agenda on a full sheet. Use a 70-space line and leaders; center both horizontally and vertically.

H. B. IMPORT-EXPORT CO.
DS
Tentative Agenda for Meeting of the Board of Directors
DS
June 30, 19––
TS

1. Call to Order . . . . Harold Bringhurst

2. Statement of Purpose . . . . Shauna P. Maloney

3. Special Reports
       Proposal to Purchase Nippon Franchise . . . Philip Q. Franz
       Proposal to Expand Exports to Nepal . . . . Ruth R. Frampton

4. Discussion of Special Reports . . . . Shauna P. Maloney

5. Current Business
       Letters of Credit . . . . Samuel A. Holmes
       Fluctuation of International Money Market . . Carol W. Blood

6. Discussion of Current Business . . . . Shauna P. Maloney

7. Adjournment

45D Problem Typing: SIMPLE REPORT FORM (25)

Problem 1: Report with the Line Length Specified

Full sheet; 65-space line (center − 33, + 32, + 3 to 7; center heading on Line 10 (pica), Line 13 (elite); TS; then DS the ¶s with 5-space ¶ indentions; proofread by comparing

Words

SIMPLE REPORT STYLE
TS
4

To this point, you have typed most of your papers with a line 16
length specified (60 or 70 spaces), regardless of whether your 29
machine had pica- or elite-size type. You will now learn to type 42
reports according to standard conventions of manuscript layout, 55
based on the number of inches in the margin instead of the number 68
of spaces in the writing line. 74

When standard conventions are followed, pica and elite solu- 86
tions will differ somewhat. If one-inch side margins are used, 99
for example, an elite line will contain 78 spaces and a pica line 112
will contain but 65 spaces. As a result, more copy will fit on a 125
page of elite type. 129

If side margins of one inch are desired, ten pica spaces 141
should be allowed in each margin. On the other hand, users of 153
elite type should allow 12 spaces. 161

METRIC EQUIVALENTS	
Centimeters (cm)	
1 inch	2.5
1½ inches	3.75
2 inches	5
10 pica spaces	2.5
12 elite spaces	2.5
6 vertical line spaces	2.5
8½- by 11-inch paper	21.5 by 28

Problem 2: Report with the Margin Width Specified

Retype the report in Problem 1, using a top margin of 2″ (pica) and 2½″ (elite) and side margins of 1″ each.

Evaluate Your Work. With a stroke and line-space ruler, check top and side margins.

LESSON 46

46A Preparatory Practice (7) each line 3 times SS; DS between three-line groups

Alphabet	Dick will make a quick flight to La Paz, Bolivia, next July or August.
Figure	A 2-act play, held at 95 East 47 Street on June 16, began at 8:30 p.m.
Figure/symbol	Lehman & Warden's catalog lists item #482 at $960 (less 10% for cash).
Fluency	A man should want work enough to do and strength enough to do it well.

| 1 | 2 | 3 | 4 | 5 | 6 | 7 | 8 | 9 | 10 | 11 | 12 | 13 | 14 |

46B Special Characters and Symbols (6) each line twice; in Line 4, write the letter l with a pen

Abbreviations	The c.o.d. shipment to Maxwell & Bond, Inc., was sent f.o.b. New York.
Equation	Use x for <u>times</u>, − for <u>minus</u>, and = for <u>equals</u>: 450 x 7 − 670 = 2480.
Degrees	The melting point of gold is 1063° C.; but that of potassium, 63.5° C.
Formula	The beam loading formula she used was: $\dfrac{bdf^2}{6\ell} = W$ (W = load in pounds).

Job 3: Typing a Spirit Master

Type a spirit master from the approval copy of the memorandum prepared in Job 2. Proofread and correct errors. (If a spirit duplicator is available, run 10 copies.)

Job 4: Typing Index Cards *(WB pp. 9, 11)*

Type on cards the names and addresses of the exporters from which H. B. Import-Export Co. imports merchandise. Type the name of each exporter on a separate 5″ x 3″ index card. Transpose the name of an individual as shown in the illustration; type a company name as it appears. Finally, arrange the cards in alphabetic order.

```
↑ Gopal, Kapur N. (Mr.)        Line 3
3 spaces

  Mr. Kapur N. Gopal            Line 7
  12-M Bhagat Singh Market
  New Delhi, India
```

Fung & Son Exporters, Ltd.
315 Edinburgh House
G.P.O. Box 13327
Hong Kong

Hong Kong Exporters Co.
77 Nathan Road
Kowloon, Hong Kong

Mr. Kapur N. Gopal
12-M Bhagat Singh Market
New Delhi, India

African Exports
Independence Highway
P.O. Box 1168
Nairobi, Kenya

Piazza Import & Export Co.
29 Via di S. Maria dell'Anima
Rome, Italy

Spanish Leather Goods
17 Plaza Santa Ana
Madrid, Spain

Mr. Samir G. Khaleefy
Jeanne D'Arc Street
P.O. Box 33892
Beirut, Lebanon

Leather Exports, Ltd.
Nuruosmaniye Caddesi
Sokak 41/4
Istanbul, Turkey

Job 5: Letter on Executive-Size Letterhead (7¼″ x 10½″) *(WB p. 13)*

Type the following letter for Ms. Maloney on an executive-size letterhead to Fung & Son Exporters, Ltd., 315 Edinburgh House, G.P.O. Box 13327, Hong Kong. AIRMAIL notation on both the letter and the envelope; current date; cc Mr. Harlington C. Eddington; Subject: Import Agreement.

Gentlemen (¶ 1) Thank you for your hospitality during my recent visit to Hong Kong. I am confident that our import-export negotiations will prove to be beneficial to both our firms. (¶ 2) Our Hong Kong attorneys, Wong Associates, will deliver copies of our import agreement to you within two weeks. We would appreciate it if you would promptly sign all six copies and forward them to us by registered airmail. After we have received and signed the copies, we shall return two copies to you. (¶ 3) As soon as we receive the signed import agreement, our Purchasing Agent, Mr. Harold P. Quinn, will forward to you our first import order. (¶ 4) We are looking forward to a long and prosperous association with your firm. Sincerely (Words in body: 137)

46C Aligning and Typing Over ② Type the following line; remove the paper; reinsert and align.
Type over the first and last word in the line.

Our earnings are rising as the move from blue-collar jobs accelerates.

46D Problem Typing: MANUSCRIPTS AND REPORTS ㉟

Read the problem and study the illustrations below and on the next page. Then type the unbound manuscript as directed below. Indent the numbered items (*enumerations*) 5 spaces from the left and right margins (*double indention with blocked lines*), spaced as illustrated.

> Make a light pencil mark at the right edge of the page about 1″ from the bottom and another about 1½″ to remind yourself to leave a 1″ bottom margin.

Full sheets; DS and indent ¶s 5 spaces; 1½″ top margin for pica, 2″ for elite; 1″ side and bottom margins; position page number as indicated in the manuscript

First page of unbound manuscript (pica type)

MANUSCRIPT ON REPORT PREPARATION
An Acceptable Style

Manuscripts or reports may be either single- or double-spaced, depending upon the type of report. School reports, formal reports, and manuscripts to be submitted for publication should be double-spaced. Business reports may be single-spaced.

Margins

Leave a bottom margin of about one inch. Leave one-inch top and side margins on all pages with these exceptions:

1. For the first page of an unbound or left-bound manuscript, leave a top margin of one and a half or two inches.

2. On all pages of a leftbound manuscript, leave a left margin of one and a half inches.

3. For the first page of a topbound manuscript, leave a top margin of two or two and a half inches; the second and subsequent pages, one and a half inches.

Indent the first line of a paragraph either five, seven, or ten spaces. Quoted matter of four lines or more is single-spaced and indented five spaces from the left and right margins, preceded and followed by one blank line space.

Headings

Main headings. The main heading is typed in all capitals and centered over the line of writing. Secondary headings are typed a double space below in capitals and lowercase, followed by a triple space. If no secondary heading is used, the main heading is followed by a triple space.

Side headings. Side headings (like Margins and Headings in this manuscript) are typed at the left margin with no terminal punctuation and are underlined. Main words are started with a capital letter. Two blank line spaces precede and one blank line space follows a side heading.

Job 2: Approval Copy of Memorandum to Be Duplicated

(WB p. 7)

The following memorandum explaining a new procedure regarding the duplication of company publications is to be distributed to all typists in the H. B. Import-Export Co. office. Type only an approval copy.

TO: All typists
FROM: Rose Swensen, Office Manager
DATE: Current
SUBJECT: Justifying the Right Margin

(¶ 1) Publications of the H. B. Import-Export Co. will now be duplicated within our own office. All typists must become experts in the process known as "justifying the right margin." This process gives duplicated copies the appearance of a printed page. (¶ 2) Except for the last line of a paragraph, the words in each line are carefully spaced so that the right margin will be even. The process is very simple but time-consuming since all material to be justified must be typed twice. As you type a line to be justified, come as close to the right margin as possible (avoid extending beyond the margin). All unused spaces between the last letter typed and the right margin should be filled with diagonals (/); for example, with a 43-space line of writing, you would type:

for making from one to ten copies. Copy///
machines are especially useful in making///
additional copies of incoming documents////
such as customers' orders and bills of lad-

(¶ 3) When typing the material in final copy, the typist must use good judgment and distribute the unused spaces throughout the line so they are least noticeable:

for making from one to ten copies. Copy
machines are especially useful in making
additional copies of incoming documents
such as customers' orders and bills of lad-

(¶ 4) If the justified material is to be placed on a stencil, type a reminder at the end of each justified line on the final copy as to the number of spaces that must be distributed when the stencil is typed:

for making from one to ten copies. Copy	3
machines are especially useful in making	3
additional copies of incoming documents	4
such as customers' orders and bills of lad-	0

Work copy of page in company manual

Final copy of page in company manual

2

<u>Side headings</u>. Side headings (like <u>Margins</u> and <u>Headings</u> in this manuscript) are typed at the left margin with no terminal punctuation and are underlined. Main words are started with a capital letter. Two blank line spaces precede and one blank line space follows a side heading.

<u>Paragraph headings</u>. You have just typed a paragraph heading. It is indented, followed by a period, and underlined. Usually, only the first word or proper nouns and adjectives are capitalized.

<u>Page Numbers</u>

The first page need not be numbered; if it is, the number is centered a half inch from the bottom edge. On leftbound and unbound reports, the second and subsequent pages are numbered on Line 4 at the right margin. On topbound reports, all pages are numbered in first-page position.

Partial second page of unbound manuscript (pica type)

<u>Paragraph headings</u>. You have just typed a paragraph heading. It is indented, followed by a period, and underlined. Usually, only the first word or proper nouns and adjectives are capitalized.

<u>Page Numbers</u>

The first page need not be numbered; if it is, the number is centered a half inch from the bottom edge. On leftbound and unbound reports, the second and subsequent pages are numbered on Line 4 at the right margin. On topbound reports, all pages are numbered in first-page position.

LESSON 47

47A Preparatory Practice (5) each line twice SS; DS between two-line groups

Alphabet	Jackie Bigsby is acquainted with an expert on Venezuelan family names.
Figure/symbol	Mr. Brook's note (due October 19) for $390 was discounted at 7% today.
Fractions	Is it correct for her to type 5¼ with 6 3/8, or should she type 5 1/4?
Fluency	Freedom is not worth having if it does not give us the freedom to err.

| 1 | 2 | 3 | 4 | 5 | 6 | 7 | 8 | 9 | 10 | 11 | 12 | 13 | 14 |

47B Skill-Transfer Typing (5) 60-space line; each line twice

		Words
Straight copy	A majority of the club women questioned the chairman's authority.	13
Figure	Flight 746 left Copenhagen at 9:35 a.m. and arrived at 10:28 p.m.	13
Script	When you write, relax; the real secret is to talk to your reader.	13
Corrected copy	He ~~said~~ maintains that a # wide voc a bulary i s vital tof forc e fulf writ f ing.	13
Proofreading	[Is] a letter [does'nt] [found] just like [your], change it until [if] does.	13

47C Spread Headings (5)

Half sheet; 2" top margin; DS; center each heading at the right as a spread heading as shown in the first heading

Centering spread headings

1. To center a spread heading, from the center point backspace once for each stroke in the heading.

2. From this point, type the heading, spacing once between the letters and 3 times between the words.

C E N T E R I N G   H E A D I N G S

MANUSCRIPT ON REPORT PREPARATION

SIMPLE REPORT STYLE

LEFTBOUND MANUSCRIPTS

SPACING OUTLINES

Production Typing:

In this section you will be a typist for the H. B. Import-Export Co., Suite 402, 1803 Market Street, San Diego, CA 92102. You will be typing for Mr. Harold Bringhurst, Chairman of the Board; Ms. Shauna P. Maloney, President; Ms. Rose Swensen, Office Manager; and Mr. Harold P. Quinn, Purchasing Agent. The company style manual specifies that all company letters are to be typed in modified block style with indented paragraphs and open punctuation. The closing lines of all letters should include the typed name on the first line and the person's title or position on the second line.

The jobs you will be typing are typical of those you might be asked to do in any general office situation. Address envelopes for all letters; proofread carefully by using the comparing method; correct all errors. All items that are to leave the company should be "mailable"—technically correct with all errors corrected neatly. All items to be used within the company should be "usable"—content correct with only minor format errors.

Follow the job directions carefully; when specific instructions are not given, make basic decisions yourself. Use the following guide.

1. **Common Sense.** Let your artistic sense of balance and taste help to indicate how a job should be placed on a page for the utmost in attractiveness and utility. Learn to use margins and spacing to your advantage. Visualize how a job should look before you begin typing. Don't be satisfied just to finish a job; accept responsibility for the job and do it well. Learn to work independently.

2. **Basic Knowledge.** You have learned much about typewriting procedures by carefully following the directions given you. Now is the time to rely on what you have learned and put it to use. Trust your knowledge.

3. **References.** When seriously in doubt, check your textbook or ask your instructor for suggestions. For example, you may be directed in a job to use a subject line; but you are uncertain about just which forms are acceptable. Your textbook will explain that you may block it, indent it to paragraph point, or center it; you may type it in all caps or simply capitalize the first letter. The typist usually makes such decisions unless directed otherwise.

If you make some procedural mistakes as you type the jobs for the H. B. Import-Export Co., learn from your mistakes; in so doing, you will learn to be a professional typist.

Job 1: Interoffice Memorandum (WB p. 5)

Type the following memorandum to the new typist. His or her typing responsibilities will include the preparation of materials for duplication. This memorandum will give helpful suggestions.

TO: John K. Gunn
FROM: Rose Swensen, Office Manager
DATE: Current
SUBJECT: Preparing Material for Duplication

(¶ 1) An import-export office worker must prepare some items for duplication; therefore, will you please follow these general guidelines in preparing a job for duplication. (¶ 2) As a rule, type an approval copy of a letter or report to be duplicated, especially if the material is to be stenciled. Check the copy twice--once for accuracy of typing and once for accuracy of style. (¶ 3) For best results in typing copy for duplication, clean the type; then type with a normal, staccato touch. Errors can be corrected, but correcting procedures depend upon the supplies being used. The Office Procedures Manual contains a step-by-step procedure for making corrections on stencils, spirit masters, and copy to be used in the direct-copy process. If you are still in doubt after referring to the Office Procedures Manual, please ask your immediate supervisor for assistance. It is better to take a few minutes in which to learn the correct procedures than to use an incorrect procedure that requires an hour or two for correcting or completely redoing a job. Remember, "Haste makes waste."

47D Problem Typing: OUTLINES AND LEFTBOUND MANUSCRIPT ㉟

Problem 1: Outline Style

Full sheet; 2″ top margin; spread heading; 65-space line; vertical spacing and indentions from left margin as indicated

Words

T O P I C   O U T L I N E   5
TS

Reset margin ———→   I. IDENTIFYING DIVISIONS OF OUTLINES   16
DS
A. Roman Numerals for Major Divisions   24
B. Capital Letters for Subheadings (First Order)   34
C. Arabic Numerals for Items Under Subheadings (Second Order)   47
D. Lowercase Letters for Third Order Subheadings   57
DS

2 spaces

Align at right ———→   II. CAPITALIZATION OF HEADINGS IN OUTLINES   66
Backspace into margin

A. Major Headings in All Caps   72
B. First-Order Subheadings with Important Words Capped   83
C. Second-Order Subheadings with Only First Word Capped   94
D. Third-Order Subheadings with Only First Word Capped   105

III. SPACING AND PUNCTUATION IN OUTLINES   114

A. Spacing   117
Set tabs ———→   1. Horizontal spacing   121
a. Title typed either solid or as spread heading   131
b. Other headings typed solid   138
c. Two spaces after identifying designation   147
2. Vertical spacing as indicated in this outline   157
B. Punctuation   160
1. Except for abbreviations, no end-of-line punctuation   171
in topic outlines   175
2. Appropriate end-of-line punctuation in sentence out-   186
lines   187

Problem 2: Outline of Manuscript Style

Words

Full sheet; 2½″ top margin; 65-space line; follow Problem 1 directions

L E F T B O U N D   M A N U S C R I P T S   8

I. MARGINS FOR LEFTBOUND MANUSCRIPTS   16

A. Top Margin   19
1. First page 1½″ for pica, 2″ for elite type   29
2. Other pages, 1″   33
B. Side and Bottom Margins (All Pages)   41
1. Left margin, 1½″   45
2. Right and bottom margins, 1″   51

II. SPACING   54

A. Manuscripts for Publication, School Reports, Formal Reports   67
Double-Spaced   69
B. Business Reports Often Single-Spaced   78
C. Quoted Material of 4 or More Lines Single-Spaced   88
1. Indented 5 spaces from both margins   96
2. Quotation marks permissible but not required   106
D. Enumerations   109
1. Double-indented with blocked lines   117
2. Single-spaced with a double space between items   128

LESSONS 104-108

Lessons 104, 106, 108

Use the following daily lesson plan for Lessons 104, 106, and 108. Retain all jobs until you have completed Lesson 108.

Preparatory Practice (5′). Type 104A, below, as directed.

Production Typing (45′). Type the jobs on pages 213-218. Follow the directions for each job; where specific directions are not given, use your own good judgment. Proofread carefully; correct all errors.

Lessons 105, 107

Use the following daily lesson plan for Lessons 105 and 107. Retain all jobs until you have completed Lesson 108.

Preparatory Practice (5′). Type 104B, below, as directed.

Technique Mastery (5′). Type 104C, below, as directed.

Production Typing (40′). Continue typing the jobs on pages 213-218. Follow the same general directions given for Lessons 104, 106, and 108.

104A Preparatory Practice [5] each line at least 3 times

Alphabet	Max and June Zachary saw the aquatic show in Bigsville Park on Friday.
Figure/symbol	Invoice #406-839, due on January 27, gave the discount for cash @ 15%.
Shift keys	J. T. Kane will visit Binford, N.D.; Altoona, Pa.; and Lake Shore, Md.
Fluency	The citizens of the town claim that the problems have not been solved.
	| 1 | 2 | 3 | 4 | 5 | 6 | 7 | 8 | 9 | 10 | 11 | 12 | 13 | 14 |

104B Preparatory Practice [5] each line at least 3 times

Alphabet	After Wade bought the zinnias, June quickly put them in an extra vase.
Figure/symbol	Book #P-64037 (which once sold for $24.95) contains 281 illustrations.
3d, 4th fingers	A person who never makes a mistake is not checking his work very well.
Fluency	Consider the chance to do a major job a chance to grow in proficiency.
	| 1 | 2 | 3 | 4 | 5 | 6 | 7 | 8 | 9 | 10 | 11 | 12 | 13 | 14 |

104C Technique Mastery [5] each line at least 2 times without error

Word response	When he finds that he has to pay on time, he will find a way to do it.
Letter response	The manager heartily subscribes to the philosophy expressed yesterday.
Combination	The type of flexible equipment that we all need is the hydraulic lift.
Direct reaches	I must include in my article the data from that issue of the magazine.
	| 1 | 2 | 3 | 4 | 5 | 6 | 7 | 8 | 9 | 10 | 11 | 12 | 13 | 14 |

GENERAL GUIDES FOR TYPING FOOTNOTES

In a report, all statements of fact or of the opinions of someone other than the writer and all direct quotations taken from articles or books must be acknowledged with a foot-note. Footnotes in full form give complete information on the references being cited, preferably typed with standard abbreviations to conserve space.

Generally, footnotes are placed at the foot of the page on which reference to them is made; or they may be grouped at the end of the report. Footnotes are single-spaced with one blank line between them. They are numbered consecutively throughout a report or starting anew with "1" on each page. These numbers are typed as reference numbers a half space above the line at the end of a quotation, after the author's name, or at the end of a statement of fact.

Although footnotes vary in length, the following system works well for determining the placement of footnotes:

1. Roll the platen down so that a one-inch bottom margin remains.

2. From this point, roll the platen up three spaces for each footnote, plus another for its blank line space. Make a pencil mark where you stop.

3. When you have typed the page to the pencil mark, single-space; type an underline one and a half inches long; double-space; indent to paragraph point; type the raised footnote number and the footnote.

4. Use the roll-back procedure even on pages only partially full.

Pica

GENERAL GUIDES FOR TYPING FOOTNOTES

In a report, all statements of fact or of the opinions of someone other than the writer and all direct quotations taken from articles or books must be acknowledged with a footnote. Footnotes in full form give complete information on the references being cited, preferably typed with standard abbreviations to conserve space.

Generally, footnotes are placed at the foot of the page on which reference to them is made; or they may be grouped at the end of the report. Footnotes are single-spaced with one blank line between them. They are numbered consecutively throughout a report or starting anew with "1" on each page. These numbers are typed as reference numbers a half space above the line at the end of a quotation, after the author's name, or at the end of a statement of fact.

Although footnotes vary in length, the following system works well for determining the placement of footnotes:

1. Roll the platen down so that a one-inch bottom margin remains.

2. From this point, roll the platen up three spaces for each footnote, plus another for its blank line space. Make a pencil mark where you stop.

3. When you have typed the page to the pencil mark, single-space; type an underline one and a half inches long; double-space; indent to paragraph point; type the raised footnote number and the footnote.

4. Use the roll-back procedure even on pages only partially full.

Elite

Problem 3: Leftbound Manuscript

NOTE: Miniature models of both the pica and elite solutions are given above. *Do not type from the models.* Study them; then type from the copy given below.

Top margin for pica type, 1½″, for elite type, 2″; left margin, 1½″; right margin, 1″; bottom margin, at least 1″; type enumeration as indicated on p. 89.

Because of the wider left margin, the center point will be 3 spaces to the right of the point normally used.

GENERAL GUIDES FOR TYPING FOOTNOTES

(¶ 1) In a report, all statements of fact or of the opinions of someone other than the writer and all direct quotations taken from articles or books must be acknowledged with a footnote. Footnotes in full form give complete information on the references being cited, preferably typed with standard abbreviations to conserve space. (¶ 2) Generally, footnotes are placed at the foot of the page on which reference to them is made; or they may be grouped at the end of the report. Footnotes are single-spaced with one blank line between them. They are numbered consecutively throughout a report or starting anew with "1" on each page. These numbers are typed as reference numbers a half space above the line at the end of a quotation, after the author's name, or at the end of a statement of fact. (¶ 3) Although footnotes vary in length, the following system works well for determining the placement of footnotes: (*Enumerate*) 1. Roll the platen down so that a one-inch bottom margin remains. 2. From this point, roll the platen up three spaces for each footnote, plus another for its blank line space. Make a pencil mark where you stop. 3. When you have typed the page to the pencil mark, single-space; type an underline one and a half inches long; double-space; indent to paragraph point; type the raised footnote number and the footnote. 4. Use the roll-back procedure even on pages only partially full.

103D **Action Typing** (10) Type twice; as you type, follow the instructions of the ¶.

When you finish typing this sentence, center horizontally, by the backspace-centering method, the following items in all capitals:

Modified Block Style
AMS Simplified Style
Block Style

Center and type as a spread heading in all capitals the following titles (underline the second title):

Business Education Alliance
Zone Improvement Program--ZIP Code

103E **Paragraph Guided Writings** (20) The superior figures are the GWAM for the ½′ writings.

1. Choose a ¶ to use as a speed goal. Type two ½′ writings at the speed indicated in the ¶.
2. Use the next succeeding ¶ for three ½′ writings at the speed indicated.

3. Type your first ¶ again for two ½′ writings. Type with improved accuracy.
4. Type two 5′ writings; strive for accuracy.

		GWAM 1′	5′
¶ 1	In a general office, a typist might be expected to perform a variety	14	3 / 45
1.6 SI 5.8 AWL 75% HFW	of typing jobs--letters, memos, outlines, and many other jobs that re-	28	6 / 47
	quire good typing skill.	33	7 / 48
¶ 2	Letters that are typed in a general office represent a very wide	13	9 / 51
1.6 SI 5.8 AWL 75% HFW	spectrum--extremely long and complicated to the very short and simple.	27	12 / 54
	Usually a typist must know all the letter styles.	37	14 / 56
¶ 3	Memos are high-frequency items in the daily activity schedule of the	14	17 / 59
1.6 SI 5.8 AWL 75% HFW	typist who performs the duties as an employee of a large general office.	29	20 / 62
	Good typing speed and efficiency are required for all typing jobs.	42	22 / 64
¶ 4	An outline is often prepared before a formal presentation is given	13	25 / 67
1.6 SI 5.8 AWL 75% HFW	to the board of directors. An outline is sometimes prepared for a long	28	28 / 70
	manuscript, even before the author has had the chance to write any ele-	42	31 / 73
	ment of the manuscript.	47	32 / 74
¶ 5	A typist in a modern general office is often required to type the	13	34 / 76
1.6 SI 5.8 AWL 75% HFW	manuscript of a report. Knowing and understanding the requirements of	27	37 / 79
	the three basic report format styles is a duty of every typist; there	41	40 / 82
	are rules for margins, spacing, and page numbers.	51	42 / 84

1′ GWAM | 1 | 2 | 3 | 4 | 5 | 6 | 7 | 8 | 9 | 10 | 11 | 12 | 13 | 14 |
5′ GWAM | 1 | 2 | 3 |

LESSON 48

48A Preparatory Practice [7] each line 3 times SS; DS between three-line groups

Alphabet	The grave fire hazards of the job were quickly explained to three men.
Figure/symbol	McNeil's invoice #4296 (our order #750B dated 10/18) comes to $942.30.
Hyphen/dash	Hyphenate a multiword modifier preceding a noun--a hard-and-fast rule.
Fluency	The authority of those in power should be used for the benefit of all.
	| 1 | 2 | 3 | 4 | 5 | 6 | 7 | 8 | 9 | 10 | 11 | 12 | 13 | 14 |

48B Technique Practice: RESPONSE PATTERNS [5] each line twice

Letter response	Afterwards, we all saw him get an award for addressing the most cards.
Word response	If they can find the right guide, they may all go to the ancient city.
Combination	Believe only half of what you hear, but be sure it is the better half.
	Only a few of the members signed the sales contract that was prepared.
	| 1 | 2 | 3 | 4 | 5 | 6 | 7 | 8 | 9 | 10 | 11 | 12 | 13 | 14 |

48C Growth Index [8] one 5′ writing; determine GWAM and errors

All letters are used.

		GWAM 1′	GWAM 5′	
¶ 1	Many people believe that their dreams can have unique results.	13	3	45
1.5 SI	Thoreau said that if one moved in the direction of his dreams and really	27	5	48
5.6 AWL	tried to live the life he had imagined, he would meet with unexpected	41	8	51
80% HFW	success. A dream can make the impossible possible if you do work dili-	56	11	54
	gently. You must stay awake and make it come true, however.	67	13	56
¶ 2	A right idea consciously and persistently held in mind tends to be	13	16	59
1.5 SI	realized. Frequently, time is needed to have an idea develop; but it	27	19	61
5.6 AWL	will be realized--of that you can be sure. The power of positive thought	42	22	64
80% HFW	is far more than a clever slogan: It is latent power that can make the	57	25	67
	unusual happen. Clear thinking underlies this power.	67	27	69
¶ 3	Things that happen to us are consequences, not coincidences. Once	13	30	72
1.5 SI	a person believes that he can control circumstances by learning to apply	28	33	75
5.6 AWL	his thinking powers consciously, he can become master of his fate. No	42	35	78
80% HFW	one is justified in feeling that opportunity comes only by chance. "As	57	38	81
	a man thinks in his heart, so is he" is a principle that has been tested	71	41	84
	many times by men of every nation.	78	43	85
1′ GWAM	| 1 | 2 | 3 | 4 | 5 | 6 | 7 | 8 | 9 | 10 | 11 | 12 | 13 | 14 |			
5′ GWAM	| 1 | 2 | 3 |			

SECTION 20 Typing in a General Office

LESSONS 103-109

Section 20 provides opportunity to type problems normally encountered in a general office situation.

Drill Copy. SS; 70-space line

¶ Copy. DS; 70-space line; 5-space ¶ indentions; full sheets

Production Typing. Directions about paper size, line length, line spacing, ¶ indentions, carbons, and other instructions will be given with each problem if required. For no directions, you decide what must be done. Correct all errors. Address envelopes as needed.

Supplies Needed. Letterheads (or full sheets); interoffice communication forms; executive-size stationery; carbon sheets; second sheets; envelopes of appropriate size; stencil; spirit masters

LESSON 103

103A Preparatory Practice (5) each line at least 3 times

Alphabet	When judging books and movies, she frequently awarded exciting prizes.
Figure/symbol	On April 2, 1973, the rate on Joe's $5,460 note went up from 7% to 8%.
Long words	They organized symposiums for the programming of electronic computers.
Fluency	The quality of the work done is much more important than the quantity.
	| 1 | 2 | 3 | 4 | 5 | 6 | 7 | 8 | 9 | 10 | 11 | 12 | 13 | 14 |

103B Skill-Comparison Typing (5) each line of 103A, above, for a 1′ writing; compare GWAM

103C Manipulative Drill: CORRECTING; SQUEEZING AND EXPANDING WORDS; TYPING SYMBOLS (10)

Follow the directions given in the left column. Type each line twice.

1. **Erasing and Correcting Errors.** Type the line as given; then erase and correct errors.	A typist msut be conscious of errors and proofreed projects carefully.
2. **Squeezing Words to Correct Errors.** Type the sentence; then erase and squeeze the letters *ave* and *cor* to type the words *have* and *correct*.	Hav you made any typing errors on this paper? If so, corect them now.
3. **Expanding Words to Correct Errors.** Type the sentence; then erase and spread the letters *met* and *an* in place of *meet* and *and*.	She meet her boss at the office for and appointment with Mr. Williams.
4. **Typing Special Symbols.** Type the sentence using special symbols.	The formula to convert 45° F. to Celsuis is: (45° − 32) × 5/9 = 7° C.

48D Problem Typing Review ㉚

Problem 1: Leftbound Report with Table

Full sheet; leftbound manuscript style; DS; SS the table; 10 spaces between columns (Reference: pages 87-89)

Words

WHO DECIDES ON TELEVISION PROGRAMS? 7

(¶ 1) Many people play a part in planning the 15
programs that appear on your television 23
screen: producers, advertising specialists, and 33
network leaders. Except for the news, how- 41
ever, no sponsored program is shown without 50
the approval of the company paying the bill. 59
The common practice is for the sponsor of the 68
program or his advertising agency to endorse 77
each program before it is telecast. (¶ 2) The 86
net result of the practice of sponsor approval 95
is that a very small number of companies de- 104
cides what you can see. About one third of 112
all the money spent on television programs 121
in a recent year came from a mere ten com- 129
panies. Together they spent $538,740,200 on 138
television advertising. These companies thus 147
decide to a considerable extent what programs 157
you can turn on. (¶ 3) A list of the top five 165
companies, with the amounts they spent on 173
sponsored programs during the aforemen- 181
tioned year, follows: 185

Procter & Gamble Co.	$116,032,400	192
American Home Products		197
Corp.	61,195,800	200
Sterling Drug, Inc.	56,398,200	207
Bristol-Meyers Co.	55,901,100	213
General Foods Corp.	50,578,300	220

(¶ 4) While the sponsor does approve the 227
programs, it is the viewer who really decides 236
what he sees. If he doesn't like a program, he 245
turns it off. The sponsor must consider this 255
in deciding what he will approve. 261

Problem 2: Second Page of an Unbound Report with Table

Type the problem as the second page of an unbound report. Number the page; DS; SS the table; leave 12 spaces between columns (Reference: page 88)

Words

(¶) The Age of the Industrial Revolution, 8
with its assembly lines and fragmented 16
tasks, built the greatest corporations 23
and nations the world has ever known. 31
Regardless of how we attempt to view this 40
age, one idea rises above all others. That 48
idea is the worth and dignity of the individual. 58
What has been employee reaction to our 66
recent preoccupation with technology? What 75
do employees really want? (¶) One company 83
making a study of this problem concluded 91
that wages are rarely at the bottom of any 99
discontent. The company rated job-satisfaction 109
factors in this order: 113

Factor	Rank	
Individual recognition	1	123
Interesting job	2	127
Job security	3	130
Company growth	4	134
Salary and related benefits	5	140

Problem 3: Table from Corrected Copy

Half sheet; DS; center vertically; 6 spaces between columns

all caps		Words
Work Improvement Committee		5
1975-76 ← DS		7
← TS		
Name	Dept (spell out)	Room	15
Crowder, Enos (chairman)	Sales	1640	22
Glenwood, Denis	Purchasing	287	29
LeClaire, Marie	Accounting	2104	35
Sanchez, Norbert	Advertising	1744	42
Yuen, Henry	Data Processing	159	48

Problem 1: Two-Page Letter with Subject Line and Table

Block style; open punctuation; 2 cc's; current date

Words

mr william q rodewald office manager, p & t 12
associates 1935 east indian school road phoe- 21
nix az 85016 dear mr rodewald subject weston 31
office furniture and equipment (¶ 1) In your 39
recent letter you asked about different kinds 48
of office furniture and equipment produced by 57
us with a view to placing an order. (¶ 2) **We** 65
manufacture various kinds of furniture and 74
office equipment, but we distribute our prod- 83
ucts only through retail dealers. Therefore, 92
we could not fill your order directly. We 100
would, however, be happy to work with you 109
through one of our several dealers in Phoenix, 118
a list of which follows: 123

(Indent items from both margins; leave 6 spaces between columns; align right-hand column at the right.)

Clinton Office Supply	733 North Central	131
Newton Office Supply	1058 East Van Buren	140
Quik Shop Supply	15 East 7th Avenue	147
Dome Office Supply Co.	4986 East McDowell	155
General Office Supply	9 East Camelback	163
Percie's Office Center	6420 East Thomas	171
Carter Company	2488 Grand Avenue	177

(¶ 3) If you will get in touch with one of 185
these dealers, he will be happy to fill your 194
order for furniture or equipment. (¶ 4) You 202
also asked for information about the manu- 210
facturing process used for our filing cabinets. 220
We use a process known as "Thermol-Drive." 228
This simply means that each filing cabinet 237
undergoes a special process that makes it fire- 246
proof, waterproof, airtight, and virtually theft- 256
proof. The special finish will not allow high 265
temperatures to penetrate; therefore, papers 274

Words

are not damaged by fire. The drawer fronts 283
are constructed to seal airtight when closed; 292
water cannot seep into the cabinet and dam- 301
age its contents. Our filing cabinets have 309
proved to be airtight and waterproof in every 319
case in which they were involved in a flood. 328
We have not had one cabinet returned to us 336
as being defective during the five years that 346
we have been using our "Thermol-Drive" 353
process. Also, the special locks and combina- 362
tions used on our filing cabinets make them 371
especially safe for valuable papers and docu- 380
ments. Depending on your security require- 388
ments, additional security devices can be in- 397
stalled at a reasonable cost. (¶ 5) If you have 406
any further questions or would like more 414
information, you may either contact us directly 424
or visit any of the dealers in the Phoenix area. 434
sincerely the weston company martin s blake 443
sales representative cc mr arnold p johansen 452/473

Problem 2: Table

Full sheet; reading position; 10 spaces between columns; DS body; no rulings.

Words

AMSTERDAM BUDGET HOTELS 5

Hotel Name	Address	
Hotel Groot	134 Henegracht	17
Hotel Debeurs	7 Beursstraat	23
Hotel Anja	97 Singel	27
Hotel Visser	86 Bloemgracht	33
Hotel de Lantaerne	111 Leidsegracht	40
Hotel Beekhof	114 Leidsegracht	46
Hotel Adorama	27 Nic. Witsenkade	53
Hotel Marianne	107 Nic. Malsstraat	60
Hotel de la Poste	3 Reguliersgracht	67

(Address header row: 12)

Machine Adjustments. 70-space line; SS sentence drills; DS and indent ¶s 5 spaces; correct errors in all problem copy as you type. Circle uncorrected errors.

Goal. In this section you will see how well you type problems similar to those in prior lessons. Follow directions. Move quickly from one problem to the next.

LESSON 49

49A   Preparatory Practice ⑦ each line 3 times SS; DS between three-line groups

Alphabet	Ezra and John Voight played a number of quiet games with Clark Baxter.
Figure/symbol	Interest accumulated in 1975 to $436.08 when the rate increased by 2%.
Long words	Probability studies are particularly helpful in effective forecasting.
Fluency	You may find that some elements of their problems are hard to analyze.

| 1 | 2 | 3 | 4 | 5 | 6 | 7 | 8 | 9 | 10 | 11 | 12 | 13 | 14 |

49B   Speed/Control Building ⑬

1. Type two 5' writings on the ¶s; the first for speed, the second for control.

2. Compare the *gwam* and number of errors on the 2 writings.

3. Proofread by comparing. Check with the original such words as *affect*, *success*, and *analyze*.

All letters are used.

		GWAM 1'	5'
¶ 1 1.4 SI 5.4 AWL 85% HFW	What we say and how we say it can influence those to whom we talk	13	3 | 36
	and write. The language that we use influences the reactions of our	27	5 | 39
	reader to us and to our thoughts. Therefore, how we think and express	41	8 | 41
	our ideas will significantly affect the success of our daily lives.	55	11 | 44
¶ 2 1.4 SI 5.4 AWL 85% HFW	All the top jobs in the modern world of business require an ability	14	14 | 47
	to write well--and the bigger the job, the more vital the writing skill.	28	17 | 50
	Sooner than you foresee, you may find yourself in a high-ranking job	42	19 | 53
	writing high-level letters and reports. Will you be ready and able?	56	22 | 55
¶ 3 1.4 SI 5.4 AWL 85% HFW	The writing flair that some people show is usually the result of	13	25 | 58
	years of careful effort. If you make a habit of analyzing the letters of	28	28 | 61
	others and also compose some yourself, you can develop a flair of your	42	30 | 64
	own. In fact, flair may be little more than word skill well applied.	56	33 | 66

1' GWAM | 1 | 2 | 3 | 4 | 5 | 6 | 7 | 8 | 9 | 10 | 11 | 12 | 13 | 14 |
5' GWAM | 1 | 2 | 3 |

Get Ready to Type	4'
Timed Production	20'
Proofreading	6'

49C   Problem Typing Measurement ㉚

On page 94, punctuation has been omitted in opening and closing lines. Provide those needed.

Type an original and 1 carbon copy of each letter. Correct errors; circle uncorrected errors.

Supplies Needed. Letterheads or plain paper; carbon paper; second sheets; appropriate envelopes.

LESSON 102

102A Preparatory Practice ⑤ each line at least 3 times

Alphabet Marcia Jacques will be taking the plane back to Vera Cruz next Friday.

Figure/symbol Order 36 pens @ 27¢ each, 50 pencils @ 4¢ each, and 1 stapler @ $2.98.

Double letters Bill cannot succeed unless he applies the rule to all those attending.

Fluency Try to keep the front of your machine even with the edge of your desk.

| 1 | 2 | 3 | 4 | 5 | 6 | 7 | 8 | 9 | 10 | 11 | 12 | 13 | 14 |

102B Skills Checkup: STRAIGHT COPY ⑮ two 5' writings; record GWAM of the better writing

All letters are used.

	GWAM 1'	5'

¶ 1
1.5 SI
5.6 AWL
80% HFW

Since the beginning of time, man has tried to make his labor less · 13 | 3 | 63
tiring, his mental and physical efforts more endurable, his heavy work · 27 | 5 | 66
load more bearable. Over the years, he has been using his keen senses · 42 | 8 | 69
to guide him along the way to a more useful and productive life. From · 56 | 11 | 72
a very simple hand tool to a complex model, man developed more intricate · 70 | 14 | 75
tools and has now made machines that can run by themselves. The more · 84 | 17 | 77
recent developments have become known as automation. · 95 | 19 | 80

¶ 2
1.5 SI
5.6 AWL
80% HFW

The advent of automated equipment is now changing the modern office · 14 | 22 | 82
just as surely as did the invention of the typewriter more than one cen- · 28 | 25 | 85
tury ago. The new data processing machines are helping to solve the · 42 | 27 | 88
problems of handling the tedious, day-to-day, routine--though highly · 56 | 30 | 91
vital--jobs that must be done in our offices today. As the use of the · 70 | 33 | 94
typewriter eliminated the need for long hours of effort with a pen, the · 84 | 36 | 96
new equipment will do away with scores of similar low-level jobs. · 97 | 38 | 99

¶ 3
1.5 SI
5.6 AWL
80% HFW

Even as business the world over has grown at a fantastic rate, so · 13 | 41 | 102
the need for more data has mushroomed. Business executives in most parts · 28 | 44 | 105
of the world want massive amounts of information upon which to base their · 43 | 47 | 108
major decisions; they want and must receive the data faster. Data must · 57 | 50 | 110
be recorded rapidly. Just as automation in the factory helped to pro- · 71 | 53 | 113
duce goods more efficiently, now it is helping to keep the office in · 85 | 55 | 116
pace with the large demand for more and more paper work. · 96 | 58 | 118

1' GWAM | 1 | 2 | 3 | 4 | 5 | 6 | 7 | 8 | 9 | 10 | 11 | 12 | 13 | 14 |
5' GWAM | 1 | 2 | 3 |

Problem 1: Letter with Centered Line *(WB p. 49)*

Modified block style; block ¶s; open punctuation; 60-space line; date on Line 16

Words

Current date | Mrs Isabel Del Conte | 1728½ 9
Simmons Avenue | Brockton MA 02401 | Dear 17
Mrs Del Conte (¶ 1) We can't promise to 24
make moving a picnic. No mover can. But if 33
a snag should develop during your move, we 41
guarantee you'll get more than a shoulder to 50
cry on. You'll get action, and you'll get it fast 60
because we want our service to live up to *(DS;* 69
center) YOUR EXPECTATIONS (¶ 2) The first 75
thing to do if you need help is to get in touch 84
with your Blue Star agent and tell the prob- 93
lem. Nine times out of ten the solution can 102
be worked out quickly. (¶ 3) If you need 109
more than local help, our toll-free hot line is 119
open to you. Pick up a phone––anywhere in 127
the country––and dial direct to Blue Star 136
Movers. We'll do our best to help you. So 144
when you need help or perhaps just a kind 153
word from people who care, call us. We want 162
to hear from you. | Yours very truly | LeRoy 170
R Fisher | Customer Relations | xx 177/189

Problem 2: Letter in Modified Block Style *(WB p. 51)*

Modified block; block ¶s; mixed punctuation; 60-space line; date on Line 15

Words

Current date | The Honorable George Dens- 8
more | Mayor of the City of Scranton | City 16
Hall | Scranton PA 18510 | Dear Mr Mayor 25
(¶ 1) Used aluminum cans are worth as much 32
as $200 a ton. Unfortunately, many communi- 41
ties are just throwing them away; and that's 50
what we think should be stopped. (¶ 2) In 57
1970, we started a "Yes We Can" campaign 65

Words

to reclaim aluminum cans in the San Diego 74
and Dallas-Fort Worth areas. Since then, over 83
200 million cans have been reclaimed for re- 92
cycling in those cities alone. (¶ 3) We shall 100
pay as much as $200 a ton to any community 109
reclamation center for all the aluminum cans 118
it collects. We'll pay it because aluminum is 127
a practical packaging material for recycling. 136
(¶ 4) Read the enclosed brochure. Find out 144
how one community established its collection 153
center. We'll also send you a list of reclama- 162
tion centers. Just tell us you're interested. | 172
Respectfully yours | Lewis Archibald Man- 180
ager | Reclamation Division | xx | Enclosure 187/205

Problem 3: Personal Business Letter

Modified block style, block ¶s, mixed punctuation; 60-space line; start return address on Line 17; list enumerated items (see page 87, if necessary)

Words

10930 Waterman Street | Fort Worth Texas 8
76102 | November 17 19–– 13

Allen & Howell Inc | 297 Causeway Boule- 21
vard | New Orleans LA 70212 | Gentlemen 29
(¶ 1) I am interested in buying a movie pro- 36
jector for general home use. Because I am 45
not an expert projectionist, the projector must 54
be easy to operate. In addition, I am inter- 63
ested in the following features: *(Enumerate)* 70
1. It should have instant playback, just like 79
TV. 2. It should be able to handle cassettes, 89
thus eliminating splicing and threading. (¶ 2) 97
Do you make a movie projector meeting the 106
foregoing requirements? If you do, please 114
send me a descriptive folder and let me know 123
where I may see a demonstration. | Yours 131
very truly | Miss Mary Ann Fielding 138/151

101C Production Skills Checkup ㉚ Use plain sheets.

Problem 1: Letter Parts

Type correctly the copy in the right column as directed
in the left column. Begin on Line 4; DS between items.

1. **Address and Salutation.** Use open punctuation (see pages 65 and 67).

mrs florence p coleman vice president anderson & jones lumber co inc 3409 himebaugh street omaha ne 68111 dear mrs coleman

2. **Address with Attention Line.** Use mixed punctuation (see pages 67 and 125).

johnson & johnson inc 1011 east orange street tempe az 85281 attention mr james p whitmore jr gentlemen

3. **Letter with Blocked Subject Line.** Use open punctuation (see pages 67 and 125).

dear mr wilson subject budget for fiscal 1977

4. **Letter with Centered Subject Line.** Use open punctuation (see pages 67 and 125).

gentlemen subject capital gains benefit

5. **Closing Lines.** Block style; mixed punctuation; enclosure notation (see pages 67 and 127).

sincerely yours gordon engineering inc samuel kaye executive vice president bj enclosures 2

6. **Closing Lines with Carbon Copy Notation.** Modified block style; mixed punctuation (see pages 67 and 129).

very truly yours president r v jones/khp cc mr frank c williams mr orlando p frederick

7. **Second-Page Heading.** Use the horizontal form (see page 111).

dr anthony w garcia 2 current date

8. **Second-Page Heading.** Use the block form (see page 111).

united states steel corporation 2 current date

Problem 2: Letter in Block Style

Block style; mixed punctuation (see page 107); capitalize and punctuate heading and closing lines

	Words
september 5, 19-- mr jay p king safety super-	9
visor kerr-malone corporation 268 stewart	18
reno nv 89501 dear mr king (¶ 1) We received	26
your film request but will be unable to sup-	35
ply this particular film. The film entitled	44
"How to Use Your Fire Extinguisher" is	52
badly worn and outdated; it is no longer avail-	61
able for distribution. (¶ 2) Another film cov-	69
ering the same basic information can be	77
obtained on a loan basis from the McGee Com-	86
pany. This company's address is enclosed.	94
sincerely educational films inc neil barker	104
manager (*your initials*) enclosure	108/125

Problem 3: Composing at the Typewriter

Modified block style; block ¶s; open punctuation (see page 67).

Today is October 10. You are Mr. King's assistant. You have been instructed by Mr. King to prepare a letter ordering the film "Proper Use of Safety Apparel"; its catalog number is FX-278. Request the film for November 3-10. Enclose a check for $8.20 (rental fee of $5.95 plus $2.25 for shipping and handling). Be sure to include a "thank you" for Mr. Barker's help in locating the film "Use That Extinguisher." Mr. King would like you to request that Mr. Barker send a copy of the latest film catalog and a supply of order forms. Also request that this film order be acknowledged. Address this letter to Mr. Neil Barker, Manager | Educational Films, Inc. | 1324 Bruckner Boulevard | Bronx, NY 10459.

LESSON 50

50A Preparatory Practice [5] each line twice SS; DS between two-line groups

Alphabet	Judge Vray promised to bring the portable screen for next week's quiz.
Subscripts	They asked each of us to type these formulas: H_2O, H_2SO_4, and Na_2CO_3.
Figure/symbol	Serial #81547 was stamped on the engine; Model #2093 (6) was below it.
Fluency	Both speed and control will improve if you do your work well each day.

50B Technique Practice: STROKING [7] each line twice

1	Long words	Government agencies and associations give help in developing programs.
2	Double letters	Will Bill and Jess Phillips do well to pass up the offer from Russell?
3	Adjacent keys	Twelve folk singers hope to buy an excellent bass viol and new guitar.
4	3d/4th fingers	Polly was puzzled by six quaint wax dolls in an antique dealer's shop.
5	Direct reaches	Young Lord Cecil received a large grant of undeveloped land in Africa.
6	Home row	Did Dale Flagg laugh after Sally asked that she look at the joke book?

| 1 | 2 | 3 | 4 | 5 | 6 | 7 | 8 | 9 | 10 | 11 | 12 | 13 | 14 |

50C Growth Index [8] one 5′ writing; determine GWAM and errors

		GWAM 1′	5′	
¶ 1	Almost anyone who works in an office needs special skills. They	13	3	50
1.5 SI	are basic to success on the job. Equally prized are such qualities as	27	5	53
5.6 AWL	tact, loyalty, and enthusiasm. Because he does not attach enough impor-	42	8	56
80% HFW	tance to them, a worker will often fail to realize his aims. They are	55	11	58
	needed, and they can be developed--just as the skills needed for a job	70	14	61
	can be developed.	73	15	62
¶ 2	"Tact," said Lincoln, "is the ability to describe others as they see	14	17	65
1.5 SI	themselves." It is the lubricant that makes people work as a team, and	28	20	67
5.6 AWL	teamwork is an essential quality in getting through the complex affairs	43	23	70
80% HFW	of a busy office on time. Also needed is discretion. What one hears or	57	26	73
	sees in an office must be held in the strictest of confidence. Remember,	72	29	76
	you cannot be criticized for what you did not say.	82	31	78
¶ 3	Generally, anyone expecting to advance in his company must like his	14	34	81
1.5 SI	work. He must be willing to climb over an annoying hurdle or two to com-	28	37	84
5.6 AWL	plete his job; for as one writer said, "In matters pertaining to enthusi-	43	40	87
80% HFW	asm, no man is sane who does not know how to be insane on the proper	57	42	90
	occasion." Few factors are so damaging to company morale as the worker	71	45	92
	who moves through his responsibilities in low gear.	81	47	94

1′ GWAM | 1 | 2 | 3 | 4 | 5 | 6 | 7 | 8 | 9 | 10 | 11 | 12 | 13 | 14 |
5′ GWAM | 1 | 2 | 3 |

SECTION 19 Basic and Production Skills Checkup

LESSONS 101-102

Section 19 provides a checkup of basic and production skills. If a task is difficult, refer to the Reference Guide page in the directions for the problem.

Drill Copy. SS; 70-space line

Paragraph (¶) Copy. DS; 70-space line; 5-space ¶ indentions; full sheets

Production Skills Checkup. Directions about the paper size, line length, line spacing, ¶ indentions, carbon copies, and other special instructions come with each problem *when required*. In the absence of directions, you make the decision.

Supplies Needed. Plain sheets

LESSON 101

101A Preparatory Practice (5) each line at least 3 times

Alphabet	Viewed by many as lazy speech, excessive jargon shows lack of quality.
Figure/symbol	Trade discounts of 10%, 20%, and 15% were given on invoice #398-64078.
Shift keys	Zelmo, Fred, Helen, and Ruth went to the World's Fair at Osaka, Japan.
Fluency	Experience is a great teacher and also part of the pay I get for work.

| 1 | 2 | 3 | 4 | 5 | 6 | 7 | 8 | 9 | 10 | 11 | 12 | 13 | 14 |

101B Timed Writing (15) three 3′ writings; record GWAM of best writing

All letters are used.

		GWAM 1′	GWAM 3′	
¶ 1 1.5 SI 5.6 AWL 80% HFW	A letter is one of the truly strong elements that may be utilized	13	4	55
	in modern business. The men in the companies that use letters and fol-	27	9	60
	low them up promptly are most certain to reap many rich rewards. A man	42	14	65
	who aspires to a self-satisfying business career should take full advan-	56	19	70
	tage of the extra benefits that quickly accrue as a result of writing	70	23	74
	good business letters.	75	25	76
¶ 2 1.5 SI 5.6 AWL 80% HFW	Writing a good letter that is friendly in tone and has the correct	13	29	80
	correlation of thoughts and words is just as important in a business as	28	34	85
	being polite and proper in public. The effective letter is prepared	42	39	90
	with a general sense of how the reader will react. It conveys the idea	56	44	94
	it intends to convey with a minimum of words and without violating the	70	48	99
	rules of good grammar and punctuation.	78	51	102

1′ GWAM | 1 | 2 | 3 | 4 | 5 | 6 | 7 | 8 | 9 | 10 | 11 | 12 | 13 | 14 |
3′ GWAM | 1 | 2 | 3 | 4 | 5 |

50D   Problem Typing Measurement ㉚

Get Ready to Type . . . . . 4'
Timed Production . . . . . . 20'
Proofreading . . . . 6'

Apply the standard rules for problems learned in earlier lessons. Erase and correct errors as you type.

Problem 1: One-Page Unbound Report

Full sheet; DS; SS table; leave 10 spaces between columns; last line of table is longest

	Words
COMPETENCIES OF BEGINNING	5
OFFICE WORKERS	8

(¶ 1) The following table shows the office competencies rated as essential for a beginning office worker, as reported by 161 organizations. Only the top five competencies are shown here. *(Tabulate)*

	Words
	16
	24
	33
	42
	45

		Words
File alphabetically	84.5%	51
Handle telephone communications	80.7	58
Type envelopes	75.2	62
Use appropriate office procedure	74.5	70
Use manual or electric typewriter	73.3	78

(¶ 2) The ability to file alphabetically and the ability to use the telephone were rated highly by four out of five organizations in the survey. Nearly three out of every five of the organizations stated that the ability to use a manual or electric typewriter was essential. Fewer than one out of a hundred, however, stated that the ability to use an electric typewriter was more important than the ability to use a manual machine.

	Words
	86
	95
	104
	114
	123
	132
	141
	150
	159
	164

Problem 2: Second Page of Leftbound Report

Full sheet; DS; SS and center the table with 6 spaces between columns; number the page

	Words
(¶) While no one can forecast the future,	8
some aspects of the job market can be pre-	16

dicted quite accurately. According to the U.S. Labor Department's Bureau of Statistics, the five occupations with the most openings each year during the 1970's are as follows:

		Words
		26
		35
		44
		51
Stenographers/secretaries	247,000	58
Retail sales people	131,000	64
Hospital attendants	111,000	70
Mechanics/repairmen	89,200	75
Bookkeepers	74,000	79

(¶ 3) Apparently, automation has not affected the need for secretaries. They are in great demand today, and this demand will remain with us.

	Words
	85
	96
	105
	106

Problem 3: Two-Column Table

Full sheet; DS; reading position; SS heading; 12 spaces between columns; SS 2-line item and indent second line of an item 2 spaces

	Words
ESTIMATED RESEARCH AND DEVELOPMENT	7
EXPENDITURES | IN COLLEGES AND UNI-	13
VERSITIES	15

		Words
(In Thousands)		18
Department or Agency	Amount	29
Health, Education, and Welfare	$ 874,000	38
National Science Foundation	374,000	45
Defense--Military Functions	212,000	53
National Aeronautics and Space		59
Administration	119,000	65
Atomic Energy Commission	85,000	72
Agriculture	88,000	76
All other	116,000	82
	$1,868,000	84

Division 3 | Advanced Typewritten Communications

Introduction

The general teaching/learning goals of this division of the book are to enable you:

• To continue developing your basic typewriting skills through the use of effective skill-development materials.

• To gain some meaningful typewriting experience in applying your typewriting skill to practical on-the-job activities in staff offices (such as a general office, an accounting office, and an executive office) and in service offices (such as a technical office, a professional office, and a government office).

• To develop a keen responsibility for high-quality typewritten work.

• To develop the ability to make decisions without direct supervision.

This division of the book will give you ample opportunity to achieve these goals. However, in order to succeed in Advanced Typewritten Communications, you must develop a high degree of internal motivation.

The arrangement of this division of the book is different from that of the two previous divisions. Only 19 of the 50 lessons are structured for an entire class period; the remaining 31 lessons are grouped into blocks of 4 to 6 class periods to provide you with a better opportunity to develop your production skills. Each production block is designed around a specific office, and the jobs you will type are typical of the jobs you would expect to find in that particular office.

This division provides for about 30 percent of your classroom time to be devoted to skill-development activities and 70 percent to production jobs.

How well you succeed in Advanced Typewritten Communications will depend to a large extent on your ability to apply directions given in earlier sections of the book, to organize your work properly, and to strive for high-quality performance at all times.

Division 2 | Intermediate Typewritten Communications

Introduction

Now that you have achieved basic typing skill, you are ready to learn to apply that skill to a variety of problems. In Division 2, you will be shown how to use what you have learned in order to make your skill more meaningful as both a personal and a business tool.

Division 2 is devoted to the technicalities of typing business letters and reports. Commonly used styles and forms are illustrated and explained, and you will have an opportunity to type selected samples of each style. You will also learn how to position a letter attractively on a page, how to punctuate it uniformly, and how to position properly any special features it may have. Grammar and composition will be stressed to help you better express in typewritten form your own thoughts and to assist others in presenting theirs.

As you begin each new section of lessons, be sure to read carefully the directions given before the first lesson in the section. These directions will tell you the standard procedures you are to follow and the specific supplies you will need.

As you complete the lessons in Division 2, be aware of suggestions for improving your efficiency through the use of shortcuts and improved handling of machine parts. Above all, learn to be the most serious critic of your work. Study what you have done. Learn from a mistake when you make one. Notice what makes a problem look businesslike and attractive. Develop an eye for professional-looking work, and you will be on your way toward becoming a professional.

Problem 1: Last Page of a Topbound Manuscript

This is page 4 (the last page) of a report; reference, page 166

(¶) True to predictions, women in the 70's have continued to seek and to | 13
find employment in the clerical ranks, where they are genuinely needed | 28
to satisfy the increasing demand for efficient, knowledgeable office | 42
workers. Opportunities for advancement in the office have increased, | 56
too; and it is not uncommon today to find women in responsible management | 71
positions. (¶) The Woman of Today, however, is also carving new places | 84
for herself in the world of work. Having rejected the idea that certain | 99
jobs are "more suitable" for women, she has shown that she can find suc- | 113
cess in a variety of occupations that were formerly considered exclu- | 127
sively the realm of the male worker. The Woman of Today might just | 140
decide that she wants to be, for example, a truck driver, a traffic cop, | 155
a rabbi, a veterinarian, a sports writer, a highway builder, an engineer, | 170
or a welder.[6] (¶) On the other hand, though, she might decide to be a | 183
housewife. Or a schoolteacher. Or an office worker. But the Woman of | 198
Today has indicated that the choice of her career is going to be hers. | 212
| 216

[6] Patricia Marshall, "Look Who's Wearing Lipstick," Manpower | 228
(December, 1972), p. 2. | 232

Problem 2: Interoffice Memorandum with Table *(WB p. 225)*

Words

Reference: p. 138

TO: Sandra M. Hayes FROM: Andrew J. Rikerson DATE: *Current* SUBJECT: | 7
Information for Financial Statement (¶ 1) Listed below are the first of the | 21
figures you will need to complete the annual report for our stockholders. | 36
The figures given in the first column represent our accounting for the | 50
current year; and it would be most meaningful, I think, if you were to | 64
set them up in a way that would invite direct comparison with last year's | 79
figures, which are shown in the second column. | 89

	This Year	Last Year	
Revenues	$ 5,049,669	$1,994,766	103
Net income	503,255	692,981	109
Total assets	10,800,993	5,237,264	116
Stockholders' equity	5,258,145	4,751,596	125

(¶ 2) We shall send you other figures as soon as we finish computing them. | 139

Problem 3: Typing Envelopes

Address an envelope for each address. Give a title, Mr. or Ms., to each. Count 11 words for each envelope typed. Disregard return addresses.

J. E. Marcos   198 Liberty Road   Wilmington, DE   19804
Mary Bine   1980 Highway 99   San Bernardino, CA   94208
Leroy Trone   37 Isis Street   San Francisco, CA   94103
Dirk E. Napoletini   798 Haven Lane   Tucson, AZ   84719
Ella Arnet   393 Highcrest Drive   Nashville, TN   37211
Richie E. Brent   796 Crawford Lane   Mobile, AL   36617
Louella McGown   192 Brighton Road   Trenton, NJ   08638
Frank Mead   18 Country Club Drive   Spokane, WA   99318

SECTION 9 Basic and Problem Skills Checkup

LESSONS 51-53

Purpose. This section will check your ability to operate a typewriter, to adjust to a typewriter that is perhaps unfamiliar to you, and to recall various types of problems that are included in basic typewriting lessons.

Machine Adjustments. Unless otherwise directed, use a 70-space line and single spacing (SS) for drill lines; 70-space line, double spacing (DS), and 5-space paragraph (¶) indentions for paragraph copy. Follow problem directions carefully.

LESSON 51

51A Preparatory Practice (5) each line 3 or more times

Alphabet	A grizzly bear jogged through the pine woods after a quick-moving fox.
Direct reaches	Fred tried to decide just how much of the old junk might be destroyed.
Figure/symbol	A & D's memo #894-673-2 (dated May 20) requests a 15½ or 16% discount.
Fluency	A good criticism has a positive goal for it is meant to help someone.

| 1 | 2 | 3 | 4 | 5 | 6 | 7 | 8 | 9 | 10 | 11 | 12 | 13 | 14 |

51B Technique Improvement: FIGURES AND SYMBOLS (5) each line 3 or more times

1 The * on page 358 of THE STORY OF 1760 refers you to pages 76 and 209.

2 The 19 vessels--labeled "Circa 780 B.C.--were 245 to 360 years older.

3 The blue sedan (Model 950--315 hp) has a BLUE BOOK value of $2,786.40.

| 1 | 2 | 3 | 4 | 5 | 6 | 7 | 8 | 9 | 10 | 11 | 12 | 13 | 14 |

51C Typewriter Operation Checkup (10) Perform each operation as directed below.

1. **Paper Guide.** Set the paper guide at 0 (or whatever setting is appropriate for the typewriter you are using). See page iii if your typewriter needs a different setting.

2. **Margins.** Set the margin stops for a 50-space line; then a 60-space line; then a 70-space line.

3. **Paper Bail; Card Holders.** If your machine has adjustable card holders, be sure they are in "up" position. Raise the paper bail; twirl a sheet of paper into the typewriter; replace the paper bail.

4. **Line-Space Regulator.** Set the line-space regulator for double spacing, then for single spacing.

5. **Touch Regulator.** (a) Set the touch regulator at its lowest setting; then type the following sentence.

   A sheet of paper that is 11 inches long
   will hold 66 lines of typewritten copy.

   (b) Set the regulator at a medium setting and retype the sentence. (c) Set the regulator at its highest setting. Type the sentence again. (d) Set the regulator at the point you prefer.

6. **Paper Release.** Operate the paper release and remove the paper from the typewriter. Return the release to its normal position. Practice inserting and removing the paper several times.

100A Preparatory Practice (5) each line at least 3 times

Alphabet
Figure/symbol
One hand
Fluency

Mary Turner quickly ate the extra pizza we had saved for Jane Boering.
That policy, #7639-838-42-RJ* (issued February 16, 1970), has expired.
A date has been set to create an estate of the acreage in Cedar Hills.
Is it not true that, relative to the snail, the turtle is a jet plane?
| 1 | 2 | 3 | 4 | 5 | 6 | 7 | 8 | 9 | 10 | 11 | 12 | 13 | 14 |

100B Growth Index (15) two 5' writings; compute GWAM for both writings

All letters are used.

		GWAM
		1' / 5'

¶ 1
1.5 SI
5.6 AWL
80% HFW

Men who know how a skill is acquired do not deny the vital need
for rapid finger action. It is wrong, however, to think that motions
alone can develop typewriting speed. Smooth typing at a fast rate is
an end result of many things done extremely well. A typing student
will soon learn that reading habits, posture, and attitude are necessary
parts of a total performance. Without them, rapid finger action has
little effect on the rate of speed.

¶ 2
1.5 SI
5.6 AWL
80% HFW

An expert typist will, for example, read copy very carefully. His
eyes follow the lines at an even rate. Typists who look away from the
copy frequently lack the requisite continuity in typing, and speed is
reduced materially. Do not read too far ahead. Focus on just a word
or two at a time. When you come to a long, hazardous word, type as you
read each letter or syllable. Good reading habits can help to produce
better typewriting results.

¶ 3
1.5 SI
5.6 AWL
80% HFW

Odd as it may seem, an individual who is practicing to perfect a
skill--trying to become really good in an activity like swimming, golf,
or typing--can defeat his own best efforts by just plain going at it too
hard. A good and conscientious effort is required, but a little smile
of confidence can do more for skill achievement than the clenched teeth
and set jaw of determination. You are more likely to win the big prizes
in skill with relaxed, coordinated, and rhythmic control than you are
with a great amount of frantic, fast-moving, power-charged action.

GWAM column values (1' | 5'):
13 | 3 | 61
27 | 5 | 64
41 | 8 | 67
55 | 11 | 69
69 | 14 | 72
83 | 17 | 75
90 | 18 | 76
14 | 21 | 79
28 | 24 | 82
42 | 26 | 85
56 | 29 | 88
70 | 32 | 90
84 | 35 | 94
90 | 36 | 94
13 | 39 | 97
27 | 41 | 100
42 | 44 | 103
56 | 47 | 106
71 | 50 | 109
85 | 53 | 111
99 | 56 | 114
112 | 58 | 117

1' GWAM | 1 | 2 | 3 | 4 | 5 | 6 | 7 | 8 | 9 | 10 | 11 | 12 | 13 | 14 |
5' GWAM | 1 | 2 | 3 |

51D Problem Checkup: ONE-PAGE STATISTICAL REPORTS (30) Read both problems before typing them.

Problem 1: Unbound Report

Top margins 2″ elite, 1½″ pica; side margins 1″; DS; 5-space ¶ indention; circle errors

	Words
SETTING SIDE MARGINS	4

TS

(¶ 1) The space allowed for side margins is usually stated in either (a) inches of space in the margins or (b) number of spaces in the line itself. A skilled typist can interpret directions given in either fashion. (¶ 2) To set side margin stops when directions are given in inches ("2-inch margins," for example), convert the number of inches into spaces according to the size of type being used. For pica, multiply by 10; for elite, by 12. For 2-inch margins, the left margin stop on a machine with elite type will be set at 24 (0 plus 24); the right margin stop setting will be calculated at 78 (102 minus 24), to which 3 to 7 spaces will be added to permit the bell to ring at the margin point. On a machine with pica type, the left margin stop will be set at 20 and the right margin stop at from 68 to 72 (85 minus 20 plus 3 to 7). (¶ 3) When a specific line length is requested (for example, a "70-space line"), the line is centered on the page by placing half of it on either side of the centering point--50 or 51 with elite type, 42 or 43 with pica--and setting the margin stops ac-

cordingly. Thus, margins for a 70-space line on a machine with elite type will have settings as follows: Half of 70 (35) is deducted from the centering point (50 or 51) for the left margin (15 or 16); the other half (35) is added to the centering point (50 or 51) for the right stop and adjusted 3 to 7 spaces farther to permit the bell to ring at the margin point.

Problem 2: Unbound Report

Top margins 2″ elite, 1½″ pica; side margins 1″ DS; 5-space ¶ indention; circle errors; spread heading

	Words
T Y P E W R I T E R T Y P E S I Z E S	4

TS

(¶ 1) Pica type is larger than elite type; 10 pica or 12 elite characters can be typed in a horizontal inch. A little quick arithmetic tells us that, using an elite scale, paper 8½ inches wide will accommodate 102 strokes (8½ inches times 12 strokes to an inch). Measured on a pica scale, 8½-inch paper will hold but 85 characters (8½ inches times 10 spaces to an inch). When paper is inserted at 0 on the paper-table scale or the paper-bail scale, the reading at the right edge of the paper will indicate the size of type on the typewriter. (¶ 2) On standard-model typewriters, both sizes of type allow 6 lines to a vertical inch; therefore, a 1-inch top or bottom margin will be 6 lines deep, a 2-inch margin will be 12 lines deep, and so on. A sheet of paper 11 inches long will accommodate 66 lines (11 inches times 6 lines to an inch).

LESSON 52

52A Preparatory Practice (5) each line at least 3 times

Alphabet	After a week's probe, the lazy jury acquitted 27 men of evading taxes.
Figure/symbol	About 17 2/3 percent of the 16,450 men have read George Orwell's <u>1984</u>.
Long words	He is likely to influence the next generation of intellectual leaders.
Fluency	A grin can cut a big load in half; a frown just heaps the load higher.

| 1 | 2 | 3 | 4 | 5 | 6 | 7 | 8 | 9 | 10 | 11 | 12 | 13 | 14 |

99D Production Measurement [35] 25′ typing; current date; 1 cc; type envelopes; compute N-PRAM

Problem 1: Modified Block Letter *(WB p. 219)*

Mixed punctuation; indented ¶s

Words

Mrs. Della Stevens Jackson Personnel 7
Agency 721 Dalton Street Jackson, MS 15
39203 Dear Mrs. Stevens: (¶ 1) Recently I 22
learned that my secretary, Olga Leonard, will 31
be leaving the city with her husband, who has 40
been transferred to Ogden, Utah. Her resig- 49
nation becomes effective the end of this 57
month. She has been a most effective secre- 66
tary, and I shall be sorry to lose her. (¶ 2) 74
Because your agency helped us find Mrs. 82
Leonard, I should like you to help find her 91
replacement. As you know, we want a person 99
with above-average skills, one who works well 109
with people and who enjoys meeting the 116
public. We are, of course, an equal-opportunity 126
employer. (¶ 3) Please call my office as soon 134
as possible to arrange interviews. I shall be 144
available all next week. Sincerely, Seth T. 153
Bruce President xx 157/173

Problem 2: Block Letter *(WB p. 221)*

Use the letter given as Problem 1, but add in the appropriate positions the following features:

Subject line: Secretarial Replacement

Company name in closing lines: ADOLPH, ADLER, AND BRUCE *(Add 11 words for these lines.)*

Problem 3: AMS Simplified Letter Executive-Size Paper *(WB p. 223)*

Words

Miss Eileen Greenside One Mark Twain 7
Circle Chattanooga, TN 34706 YOUR JOB 15
APPLICATION (¶ 1) Thank you for your ap- 22
plication for our secretarial vacancy. I have 31
examined your qualifications and consulted 40
with Mr. Stein. He is interested in discussing 50
the matter in a personal interview with you. 59
Can you meet with us next Monday morning 67
at 10:15 in my office? (¶ 2) Should you have 75
any question or if the date or time is incon- 84
venient, please call my office; we can arrange 93
another appointment. K. P. BENTON, PER- 101
SONNEL DIRECTOR xx 105/118

Problem 4: Outline

2″ top and left margins

Words

SECOND NATIONAL BANK 4

Orientation Meeting for New Employees 12

I. INTRODUCTION 15

A. Message from the President 21
B. Agenda for the Meeting 27

II. BANK SERVICES 31

A. Checking Accounts 35
B. Savings Accounts 39
C. Safe Deposit Boxes 44
D. Loans and Credit 48
E. Travel Assistance 53
F. Investments 56
G. Other Services 60

Words

III. SPECIAL DEPARTMENTS 65

A. Bank Loans 68
B. Trusts 70
C. Commercial Development 75
D. Travel 78

IV. SPECIAL INFORMATION 83

A. Correspondent Banks 87
B. Federal Deposit Insurance Corpora- 95
tion 96
C. Federal Reserve System 101
D. American Banking Association 108
E. Magnetic Ink Character Recognition 116
F. Bank-Related Legal Problems 122

V. INCENTIVE PROGRAM 126

A. Teller of the Month 131
B. Century Club 135
C. The President's Club 140

52B Typewriter Operation Checkup [5] Perform each operation.

1. **Carriage Release and Tab Clear Key.** Locate these parts on your typewriter. Use them to clear any tabulator stops now set on your machine.

2. **Tab Set Key.** Set a tabulator stop at the centering point for 8½- by 11-inch paper.

3. **Tabulator and Backspace Key.** Tabulate to the center of a full sheet of paper; backspace to center horizontally each of the following 4 titles. DS.

Pride	Excellence in Communications
Self-Expression	The Development of Word Processing

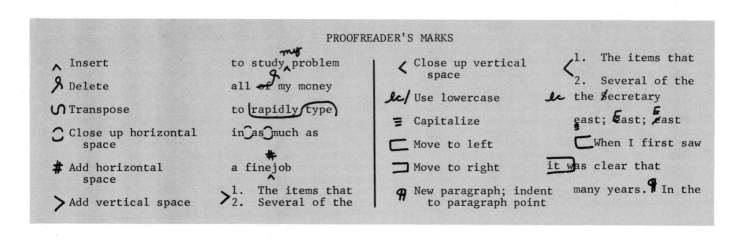

PROOFREADER'S MARKS

Mark	Example	Mark	Example
^ Insert	to study ^ problem (my)	< Close up vertical space	1. The items that / 2. Several of the
Delete	all ~~of~~ my money	lc/ Use lowercase	the ~~S~~ecretary (lc)
Transpose	to rapidly type	≡ Capitalize	east; East; east
Close up horizontal space	in as much as	[Move to left	[When I first saw
# Add horizontal space	a finejob	] Move to right	it was clear that
> Add vertical space	> 1. The items that / 2. Several of the	¶ New paragraph; indent to paragraph point	many years. ¶ In the

52C Problem Checkup: CORRECTED COPY; TABULATION; COMPOSITION [40]

Problem 1: Memorandum from Corrected Copy

Half sheet; 1″ top and side margins; SS; correct errors

Words

August 9, 19-- Insert year 3

> 3 blank lines

subject: communications 8

~~Good~~ Effective communications begins with a clear, well-expressed thoughts. (and ideas) 24

When such thoughtsand ideas are reduced to writing, care must be 52

exercised of insure that words are spelled correctly, that punctuation 66

is ~~correct~~ accurate and adequate ~~to make easy reading~~, and that the work 80

is neat enough to invite the reader's attention. The ~~job of the~~ expert typist 94

~~is~~ does not just make a ~~to~~ copy; he ~~must~~ also accepts responsibility for a certain 108

~~degree~~ amount of editing, for proofreading, and for preparing copy. 112

(eye-pleasing, easy-to-read)

SECTION 18 Basic and Production Skills

LESSONS 99-100

Machine Adjustments. Proceed as follows: SS drill copy on a 70-space line. Indent ¶ copy 5 spaces, DS, 70-space line. In production copy, when directions are incomplete, use your judgment. Correct errors. If you finish before time is called, begin Problem 1 again. When appropriate, reference is given for a review of problem procedures but no extra time is allowed for this.

Supplies Needed. 8 small envelopes for chain feeding.

LESSON 99

99A Preparatory Practice [5] each line at least 3 times

Alphabet	Major Forbes quickly recognized the power of an auxiliary naval force.
Figure/symbol	She traveled about 726,894 miles, logging $1,530\frac{1}{4}$ hours of flying time.
Long words	Vehicular traffic commenced utilizing the enormous structure Thursday.
Fluency	To be able to type is fine, but it is the end product that is primary.

| 1 | 2 | 3 | 4 | 5 | 6 | 7 | 8 | 9 | 10 | 11 | 12 | 13 | 14 |

99B Communication Index [5] each sentence twice

1. Use a full sheet; 2″ top margin; 70-space line; SS; DS between sentence groups.
2. Read each sentence for meaning before typing it.
3. Capitalize and punctuate as you type. Do not number the lines.

1 on june 7 1974 carl haas who was then our representative resigned
2 he asked bob parker his agent to visit our office today mr taylor
3 if its true the company made no profit its reports should show none
4 the man we hire for this position must be alert reliable and honest
5 bobs racquet is in the mens locker room but jean has hers with her
6 if lizas telephone rings while she is out will you please answer it
7 mr randall ellis name had been omitted from our hostess guest list
8 his car equipped for low lead gasoline is dark blue he ordered red

99C Technique Improvement: RESPONSE PATTERNS [5] each line twice on the control level. Alternate directions: a $\frac{1}{2}'$ writing on each line

1 **Letter response** New concepts and techniques are being tested to deal with the project.
2 Decision-making capability demands considerable insight and foresight.
3 **Word response** The man who knows and knows that he knows is a man who will do things.
4 We must all learn that here is a right time and a right place to act.
5 **Combination** Either you or I can go. Neither of us has a session during that hour.
6 The power of positive thought is, moreover, more than a clever slogan.

| 1 | 2 | 3 | 4 | 5 | 6 | 7 | 8 | 9 | 10 | 11 | 12 | 13 | 14 |

Guides for horizontal placement of columns (backspace-from-center method)

1. Move margin stops to ends of scale. Clear all tabulator stops. Move carriage (carrier) to center of paper.

2. From center of paper, backspace once for *each 2 strokes* in the longest line of each column and for *each 2 spaces* to be left between columns.

NOTE: As you backspace, count any extra stroke (that may occur at the end of the longest line of a column) with the space between columns. If an extra space occurs at the end of an intercolumn, count it with the next column.

3. Set the left margin stop at the point where you complete the backspacing.

4. From the left margin, space forward *once for each stroke* in the longest line of the first column and for each space to be left between the first and second column.

5. *Set the tab stop at this point for the second column.*

6. Follow this procedure for each column in the table.

Problem 2: Tabulation

Half sheet; 1½″ top margin; DS; 10 spaces between columns; circle errors

1. If necessary, review the steps for horizontal placement of columns given above.
2. Tabulate the words; study spellings as you type.

advice	convenient	chagrin
commitment	judgment	personnel
muscle	vertical	recognize
losing	beacon	similar
permitting	personal	missile
subtle	separate	promptly
privileges	traveled	misspelling

Intercolumns

Problem 3: Composition

Half sheet; 1″ top and side margins; 3 blank lines between subject and date; SS; correct errors

Using the current date, compose a short memorandum on a half sheet.

After SUBJECT: type your own name.

In the body of the memorandum, describe yourself briefly and give several reasons why you are taking a course in typewriting. Include, if you wish, any information you think might be helpful or of general interest to your instructor.

Using the proofreader's marks shown on page 100, revise your preliminary copy; then type a final copy.

LESSON 53

53A Preparatory Practice [5] each line at least 3 times

Alphabet	Al Gray became exhilarated as we kept justifying his five quiz scores.
Figure/symbol	At the meeting, 289,356 stockholders (70%) voted "No" on proposal #14.
One hand	As Johnny Carver asserted, Fred was regarded as carefree and careless.
Fluency	A right approach to work that must be done cuts the size of most jobs.
	1 | 2 | 3 | 4 | 5 | 6 | 7 | 8 | 9 | 10 | 11 | 12 | 13 | 14

I. PUNCTUATION FORMS

A. *Mixed Punctuation*
1. Colon follows salutation
2. Comma follows complimentary close
3. Possibly most popular form
B. *Open Punctuation*
1. No special marks of punctuation
2. Possibly most efficient form

II. MARGINS

A. *Average Letter*
1. 1½" side margins
2. Date on about Line 15
B. *Short Letters*
1. 2" side margins
2. Date on about Line 20
C. *Long Letters*
1. 1" side margins
2. Date on about Line 12

III. SPECIAL PARTS (SHOWING ORDER WHEN USED)

A. Date
B. Mail Notation
C. Letter Address
D. Attention Line
E. Salutation
F. Body
G. Complimentary Close
H. Company Name
I. Signer's Name and/or Title
J. Reference Initials
K. Enclosure (or Attachment) Notation
L. Carbon Copy Notation
M. Postscript

IV. STYLES

A. *Block*
1. All special parts placed at left margin
2. Paragraphs not indented
B. *Modified Block*
1. Date and closing lines placed at center point (or left of center to accommodate long company name)
2. Paragraphs might or might not be indented
C. *AMS Simplified Style*
1. Block format
2. Omits salutation and complimentary close
3. Has subject line typed in all caps
4. Signer's name and title typed in all caps

53B Straight-Copy Checkup ⑬ two 5' control-level writings; figure GWAM on both writings

GWAM (gross words a minute) =	$\dfrac{\text{Gross (total) words typed}}{\text{Length (in minutes) of writing}}$

All letters are used.

GWAM

	1'	5'

¶ 1
1.4 SI
5.4 AWL
85% HFW

It is often easy to locate the person who has confidence in his | 13 | 3 | 53
ability to typewrite well. He looks confident. His typing is quick | 27 | 5 | 56
and fluent. He spends little time looking back and forth from desk copy | 41 | 8 | 59
to the problem in his machine. He does not worry about making an error. | 56 | 11 | 62
He realizes that he is working easily within the range of his ability | 70 | 14 | 64
and that all should be well if he does not lose control of himself. | 83 | 17 | 67

¶ 2
1.4 SI
5.4 AWL
85% HFW

One of the most difficult things to learn is how to relax; yet to | 13 | 19 | 70
be able to stay calm through a tense moment is an important part of any | 28 | 22 | 73
typewriting-improvement program. When we relax, we have more confidence | 42 | 25 | 75
to face problems without undue nervousness. To remain calm when we face | 57 | 28 | 78
problems is certainly not an easy thing to do; but if we really try to | 71 | 31 | 81
relax while we type, the effort is likely to pay big dividends. | 84 | 33 | 84

¶ 3
1.4 SI
5.4 AWL
85% HFW

Learning to pace ourselves will help us to cope with our jobs. It | 13 | 36 | 86
will help us build confidence. To be fast is not always to be good; so | 28 | 39 | 89
it is frequently better for us to slow our pace deliberately, to be cau- | 42 | 42 | 92
tious, than to press on without giving sufficient attention to what we | 56 | 45 | 95
are doing. Caution is not the same thing as confidence--but they work | 71 | 48 | 98
well together, for we become more confident when we make fewer errors. | 85 | 50 | 101

1' GWAM | 1 | 2 | 3 | 4 | 5 | 6 | 7 | 8 | 9 | 10 | 11 | 12 | 13 | 14 |
5' GWAM | | 1 | | 2 | | 3 |

53C Typewriter Operation Checkup ⑦

1. **Margin-Release Key.** Type Sentence 1 below. Turn the cylinder forward about 5 lines; depress the margin-release key; move the carriage to the extreme left. Erase *may*. Return to original typing position; type *can* in the erased space.

2. **Ratchet Release.** Type Sentence 2. Operate the ratchet release; turn the cylinder forward about 3". Operate the ratchet release and turn the cylinder back to the line of writing. Type over the sentence.

3. **Variable Line Space**r. Type Sentence 2. Use the variable line spacer and turn the cylinder forward about 3". With the variable line spacer depressed, return to the line of writing; release the variable line spacer. Type over the sentence.

4. **Bell and Margin Lock.** Space forward 10 spaces from your left margin stop. Type Sentence 3 until the bell rings. As you continue to type, count the number of strokes between the ringing of the bell and the locking of the machine. On most machines, this number will be between 3 and 7. Remember it, and consider it when you set your right margin stop.

1 Both pica and elite type may be measured six lines to a vertical inch.

2 Use 50 or 51 as the centering point whenever you type with elite type.

3 For a 1-inch top margin on a page, you should begin to type on Line 7.

98B Control Building [5]

4 errorless copies of each line. Alternative directions: three ½′ control-level writings on each line; avoid pauses.

Add 123 and 456 and 789; divide this by 123. The result is 11.121951.

If item #57483 costs 97 cents a pound, 18 pounds will cost you $17.46.

Five percent, sometimes written .05 (or 5%), is equal to 1/20 of 100%.

| 1 | 2 | 3 | 4 | 5 | 6 | 7 | 8 | 9 | 10 | 11 | 12 | 13 | 14 |

98C Straight-Copy Timed Writing [20] Repeat 96B, page 197.

98D Communication Aid: COMPOSITION [20]

As part of its interviewing process, the Acme Manufacturing Company asks you to prepare a statement responding to each of the questions given below.

1. Compose an answer in statement form to each of the questions.
2. Proofread your responses carefully and mark any corrections.
3. With your responses inserted, type the statement in final form.

ACME MANUFACTURING COMPANY

Employment Questionnaire

Specifically, what kind of a job do you think you would most enjoy? Why?

In about a year, there will be an opening as supervisor of a group of ten people working on special projects. There will also be an opening in one of our European offices. Will either one of these positions interest you? Why or why not?

The Company has a management-training program that involves two years of training. The salary is somewhat lower than that of another position for which you are also qualified, but chances for advancement after training are better. Which position interests you more? Why?

What personality traits do you possess that you think will make you a valuable employee? Why should we be interested in hiring you?

What salary do you expect? List six items with amounts that you believe will be (or are) your major expenses for a typical month.

53D Problem Checkup: ENUMERATIONS; OUTLINE; COMPOSITION ㉕

Problem 1: Enumerated Items

2″ top and 1″ side margins; SS items with DS above and below; indent items 5 spaces from left margin (indention with blocked lines); correct errors

	Words
GUIDES TO WORD DIVISION	5
TS	

Divide––   7

   1. Words between syllables only   13

   2. After the double letters in a word when   22
it ends in double letters and has a syl-   30
lable added to it   34

   3. Words between double consonants   41

   4. Between double letters when the final   49
consonant is doubled in adding a suffix   57

   5. Hyphenated compounds only at the point   66
of the hyphen   69

Do not––   70

   6. Divide a word of one syllable or of five   79
or fewer letters   83

   7. Separate a one-letter syllable at the be-   92
ginning or end of a word   97

   8. Separate a two-letter syllable at the end   106
of a word   108

   9. Divide the last word on a page   115

Avoid if possible––   119

   10. Dividing words at the ends of two or   127
more consecutive lines or a word at the   135
end of the last complete line of a para-   143
graph   144

Problem 2: Outline

Full sheet; 2″ top margin; 40-space line; vertical spacing as shown; correct errors

	Words
COMMUNICATIONS AND THE BUSINESSMAN	7
TS	

  I. BASIC PROCESSES INVOLVED   13
      DS
    A. Reading   15
    B. Writing   18
    C. Speaking   20
    D. Listening   23

  II. THE BUSINESSMAN AS A READER   30
    A. Mail   31
      1. Letters   34
      2. Catalogs, brochures, etc.   39
    B. Reports   42
    C. Notes and References   47

  III. THE BUSINESSMAN AS A WRITER   54
    A. Letters   56
    B. Reports   59
    C. Notes   61

  IV. THE BUSINESSMAN AS A SPEAKER   67
    A. Reports   70
    B. Speeches   72
    C. Directions   75
    D. Dictating   78
    E. Presiding   81

  V. THE BUSINESSMAN AS A LISTENER   88
    A. Reports   90
    B. Requests   93
    C. Directions   96

Problem 3: Composition

Half sheet; 1″ top and side margins; correct errors

This is the end of the 3-lesson review section. If time permits, type a brief paragraph about your readiness to begin the next section. Do you feel confident? Do you believe your skill is increasing? In what areas do you need to concentrate future efforts: building speed, increasing accuracy? improving techniques? gaining technical information? Be as specific as you can.

LESSON 97

97A Preparatory Practice [5] each line at least 3 times

Alphabet	The jumpy gazelle often runs off quickly when excited by human voices.
Figure/symbol	Ray Cook sent 530 bills in 1974, reducing his bad-debts losses $8,268.
i, o	Four million citizens of Ohio voted to organize the school of biology.
Fluency	When we do little jobs well, big jobs also tend to work out all right.
	| 1 | 2 | 3 | 4 | 5 | 6 | 7 | 8 | 9 | 10 | 11 | 12 | 13 | 14 |

97B Communication Aid: SPELLING [10] 3 times; SS; DS between groups

Full sheet; 2″ top margin; decide spaces between columns

belief	Duluth	reins	analyze
relieve	Winston-Salem	receive	questionnaire
believe	Albuquerque	conceive	accommodate
friend	Cincinnati	deceive	separate
sieve	Paterson	receipt	a lot
convenience	Tallahassee	seine	inasmuch

97C Technique Improvement: COMBINATION RESPONSE [10] each line 5 times; flowing rhythm

1 The past is of use to us only as it can make fuller the life of today.
2 Being a leader is largely a matter of knowing how to work with people.
3 It makes a difference whether they go into a thing to win or to drift.
4 The will to win is a big aid to all those who want to do great things.
5 The final games are to be played by two of the best teams in the city.

97D Production Typing [25] Continue typing the problems in 95C.

LESSON 98

98A Preparatory Practice [5] each line at least 3 times

Alphabet	Max took his quiet journey through Switzerland before moving to Capri.
Figure/symbol	The tags marked * say: "Sell @ $17.89 each or @ $5,326.40 a carload."
Double letters	My committee arrived too soon; the innkeeper cannot accept us at noon.
Fluency	Do we worry more about curing problems than we do about avoiding them?
	| 1 | 2 | 3 | 4 | 5 | 6 | 7 | 8 | 9 | 10 | 11 | 12 | 13 | 14 |

SECTION 10 Basic Business Letter Styles

LESSONS 54-60

Machine Adjustments. Unless otherwise directed, proceed as follows: SS drill copy on a 70-space line. Indent ¶ copy 5 spaces, DS, 70-space line.

Letterhead or plain paper for production copy; current date unless given, your reference initials; correct errors; letter style and envelopes as shown.

LESSON 54

54A Preparatory Practice (5) each line at least 3 times

Alphabet	All of his money exhausted, lazy Jacques is now verging on bankruptcy.
Figure/symbol	*Billed as "385 sets @ 76¢ a set," the listing caused a $194.02 error.
1st row	Can Mr. Van Bux, the banker, visualize our volume six months from now?
Fluency	Anybody can be wrong. Can being wrong not be a beneficial experience?

| 1 | 2 | 3 | 4 | 5 | 6 | 7 | 8 | 9 | 10 | 11 | 12 | 13 | 14 |

54B Speed Building (15) Type on the exploration level.

1. Type two 1′ writings on each ¶.
2. Type two 3′ writings on all ¶s.
3. Compute *gwam* for each writing.

Exploration Level. Type rapidly. Try for a few more words a minute with each writing. Temporarily ignore errors.

All letters are used.

		GWAM 1′	3′	
¶ 1 1.5 SI 5.6 AWL 80% HFW	A business letter is uniquely representative of its writer. It	13	4	72
	should be neat and well centered on a page, or it will seem that it has	27	9	76
	been typed with little care. Any error should be repaired so that it	41	14	81
	cannot be seen. Accurate spelling and grammar are also vital to a let-	55	18	86
	ter. A good dictionary is a correspondent's best friend.	67	22	90
¶ 2 1.5 SI 5.6 AWL 80% HFW	The letters we write are extensions of our own personalities, so	13	27	94
	each one should say to the reader that we are capable of acting in a	27	31	99
	judicious and businesslike way. A letter that is well done is one good	41	36	103
	indication of our ability. The importance of proofreading is apparent;	56	41	108
	all errors must be found before a business letter is mailed.	68	45	112
¶ 3 1.5 SI 5.6 AWL 80% HFW	There are a few specific guides and tables that can be useful in	13	49	116
	typing a business letter. Such guides indicate how a letter can be	27	54	121
	placed attractively on a page and how its special lines can be punctu-	41	58	126
	ated. If the guides are followed, letter forms become standardized;	54	63	130
	and a reader is less likely to be distracted by vagaries of style.	68	67	135

1′ GWAM | 1 | 2 | 3 | 4 | 5 | 6 | 7 | 8 | 9 | 10 | 11 | 12 | 13 | 14 |

3′ GWAM | 1 | 2 | 3 | 4 | 5 |

LESSON 96

96A Preparatory Practice (5) each line at least 3 times

Alphabet | Jud might have exchanged all those quaint toy zebras for a pink clown.

Figure/symbol | Policy #35-482 is due March 12; the premium is $164.70, or 39% higher.

3d row | Our pitcher, Quentin, threw three powerful pitches and won the series.

Fluency | Not much happens to our boat if we wait for someone else to launch it.

| 1 | 2 | 3 | 4 | 5 | 6 | 7 | 8 | 9 | 10 | 11 | 12 | 13 | 14 |

96B Straight-Copy Timed Writing (20) Type a 5′ and a 10′ writing.

All letters are used.

GWAM

		1′	5′	10′

¶ 1
1.5 SI
5.6 AWL
80% HFW

There are a number of aspects to the job-selection process that can be overlooked; and to be assured that there is a pleasing and self-satisfying job situation in your own future, you ought probably to think early in your career about a few of these aspects. For example, finding the right position will surely involve, among other things, choosing a geographical area in which you think you will want to make your home.

13 3 2 35
27 5 3 36
42 8 4 38
56 11 6 39
70 14 7 41
84 17 8 42

¶ 2
1.5 SI
5.6 AWL
80% HFW

Sixty years ago, geography limited our vocational choices. People did not move far from the family home; therefore, they learned a skill that would be needed in that region. We live in a more mobile society today, but geography is still important. Our occupational choices have widened to match our mobility, and a person is left with two questions instead of one: What shall I do for a living and where shall I do it?

13 20 10 43
28 22 11 45
42 25 13 46
56 28 14 48
70 31 16 49
84 34 17 51

¶ 3
1.5 SI
5.6 AWL
80% HFW

Most people, happily, can combine their geographic and professional goals; a few cannot. Certainly an Easterner can become a cowboy if he wishes, or a Midwesterner an oceanographer; but each will likely have to settle in a new place to do it. On the other hand, the person who has his mind set on living in some particular spot, say Alaska or Florida, might have to choose a profession that is wanted and needed there.

14 36 18 52
28 39 20 53
42 42 21 55
57 45 23 56
71 47 24 58
84 51 25 60

¶ 4
1.5 SI
5.6 AWL
80% HFW

There is something extremely comfortable about living in a familiar area, and some people hesitate to move away. Others, however, sense adventure in new places and new faces. To some degree, it is important that the individual planning his career recognize that it is all right to want to be something and that it is all right to want to be somewhere, but that the two, sooner or later, must somehow be put together.

14 53 27 61
27 56 28 62
42 59 29 63
56 62 31 65
70 64 32 66
84 67 34 67

1′ GWAM | 1 | 2 | 3 | 4 | 5 | 6 | 7 | 8 | 9 | 10 | 11 | 12 | 13 | 14 |
5′ GWAM | 1 | 2 | 3 |
10′ GWAM | 1 | 2 |

96C Production Typing (25) Continue typing the problems in 95C.

54C Technique Improvement: RESPONSE PATTERNS [5] each line at least twice

Letter Response. See, think, and type difficult combinations letter by letter.
Word Response. See, think, and type short, easy words as word wholes.

Combination Response. Type short, easy words as word wholes. Type difficult combinations letter by letter. Blend the two responses into a smooth typing rhythm.

Letter response Fifteen prominent businessmen regularly attend those Toronto meetings.
Several inspectors hesitantly gestured toward certain rejected crates.

Word response If they know the way to do it, I do not think they should wait for us.
If you will try to do the best job you can, we know you will not fail.

Combination The next time you are in our town, we invite you to stop at our plant.
He has been a member of the area Chamber of Commerce for a year or so.
It does not seem likely that many freight shipments will arrive today.

| 1 | 2 | 3 | 4 | 5 | 6 | 7 | 8 | 9 | 10 | 11 | 12 | 13 | 14 |

54D Communication Pretest: CAPITALIZATION AND PUNCTUATION [10] full sheet; DS; 3″ top margin

Type each sentence once as you capitalize and punctuate it. Do not number the sentences. Later lessons of this division contain rules and other aids to help you build skill in communications. Attempting to provide the capitalization and punctuation required in these sentences will enable you to assess your present knowledge of capitalization and punctuation.

1 they sold 3276 tickets between january 1 1974 and january 13 1975
2 their answers were short concise and very accurate don't you think
3 they say that they want to hire an alert capable person for this job
4 these letters most of which were received this morning must be read
5 when you have finished typing the letters begin typing the envelopes
6 i could mail all those letters today but i do not have enough stamps
7 in 1974 35 books were added to our price list in 1975 15 pamphlets
8 mr roy leff the noted lecturer discussed his latest book outcries
9 after explaining his proposal mr hegl outlined it on the chalkboard
10 we must request therefore that full payment be sent with each order

54E Technique Improvement: FIGURES AND SYMBOLS [5] two or more times with fewer than 3 errors; carefully compare your ¶s with book copy

1′ GWAM

Odd-lot customers at the New York Stock Exchange purchased 68.8 13
million shares in 1972 (4% below 1971) and sold 121.9 million shares 27
(8% below 1971). The sale balance of 53.1 million shares was the second 41
largest in history, exceeded only by 1971's 60.3 million shares. The 55
value of odd lots in 1972 was $8.7 billion; in 1971, $8.6 billion. 68

| 1 | 2 | 3 | 4 | 5 | 6 | 7 | 8 | 9 | 10 | 11 | 12 | 13 | 14 |

SALARIED PERSONNEL APPLICATION FOR EMPLOYMENT

PLEASE PRINT WITH BLACK INK OR USE TYPEWRITER

Inform receptionist or interviewer before completing this form if you have been tested or have completed an employment application here within the last twelve months.

NAME (LAST, FIRST, MIDDLE INITIAL) (MAIDEN NAME)	SOCIAL SECURITY NUMBER	BIRTH DATE (MO-DAY-YR)	PRESENT DATE
Bennett, Dale C.	360-14-9068	Feb. 1, 1955	March 26, 1975

ADDRESS (NUMBER, STREET, CITY, STATE, ZIP CODE)	YEARS AT PRESENT ADDRESS	HOME PHONE NO.	WORK PHONE NO.
2110 Forest Drive, Oconomowoc, WI 53916	2	885-5650	--

HEIGHT	WEIGHT	U.S. CITIZEN?	SINGLE	MARRIED	WIDOWED	DIVORCED	SEPARATED	IF MARRIED IS SPOUSE EMPLOYED? YES NO	WHAT COMPANY?
5'10"	165	YES X NO ☐	X	☐	☐	☐	☐	☐ ☐	

NO. OF MINOR CHILDREN	AGES OF MINOR CHILDREN	RENT HOME ☐ OWN HOME ☐ LIVING WITH RELATIVES ☐	FATHER'S OR GUARDIAN'S OCCUPATION	ARE YOU A FORMER EMPLOYE? YES NO
			Toolmaker	☐ X

ARE YOU PRESENTLY EMPLOYED? YES NO	AMOUNT OF TERMINATION NOTICE REQUIRED BY YOUR PRESENT EMPLOYER	COMMUTING DISTANCE IN MILES TO THIS LOCATION	0-5	6-10	11-20	21-30	31-40	OVER 40	DO YOU HAVE A DRIVERS LICENSE? YES NO
X ☐	Has been given		☐	☐	☐	☐	☐	☐	X ☐

TYPE OF WORK DESIRED:

1. Administrative secretarial   2. Secretarial

SALARY REQUIRED $ Your schedule

IF YOU ARE DIRECTLY RELATED TO AN EMPLOYE OF THIS COMPANY, GIVE NAME, POSITION OR OCCUPATION, AND RELATIONSHIP: None

DO YOU HAVE ANY PHYSICAL CONDITION THAT MAY PREVENT YOU FROM PASSING A PHYSICAL EXAMINATION, OR THAT SHOULD BE CONSIDERED IN YOUR PLACEMENT?   YES ☐ NO X   IF YES, EXPLAIN:

HAVE YOU EVER BEEN CONVICTED OF A CRIME (OTHER THAN TRAFFIC VIOLATIONS)?   YES ☐ NO X   IF YES, EXPLAIN:

E D U C A T I O N	EDUCATIONAL INSTITUTION	LOCATION (CITY, STATE)	DATES ATTENDED FROM MO. YR.	DATES ATTENDED TO MO. YR.	DIPLOMA, DEGREE, OR CREDITS EARNED	CLASS STANDING (CHK QUARTER) 1	2	3	4	MAJOR SUBJECTS STUDIED
GRADE SCHOOL	Wilson Elementary	Hartford, Wis.	9 60	6 69						
HIGH SCHOOL	Watertown High	Hartford, Wis.	9 69	6 73	Diploma	x				Math, Eng. business
COLLEGE	Waukesha Community	Oconomowoc, Wis.	6 73	4 75	A.B.S.	x				Admin. secretary
OTHER	None									

LIST BELOW THE POSITIONS THAT YOU HAVE HELD (LAST POSITION FIRST)

1. NAME AND ADDRESS OF FIRM	DESCRIBE POSITION RESPONSIBILITIES
Dyer Motors, Inc. South Stateway Oconomowoc, WI 53916	a. Assistant to president's secretary b. Dictation/transcription of correspondence and minutes of board meetings
POSITION TITLE Assistant to president's secretary	c. Crew member, warehouse labeling mchn.

FINAL MO SALARY $ 150	AV. OVERTIME AND/OR COMM. --	EMPLOYED (MO-YR) FROM: 7/73	TO: Present part time	REASON FOR LEAVING Graduating and leaving the area

2. NAME AND ADDRESS OF FIRM	DESCRIBE POSITION RESPONSIBILITIES
Watersby Canning Company Hartford, WI 54203	a. b.
POSITION TITLE None	c.

FINAL MO SALARY $ 450	AV. OVERTIME AND/OR COMM. --	EMPLOYED (MO-YR) FROM 6/71	TO 9/72	REASON FOR LEAVING Summer employment

3. NAME AND ADDRESS OF FIRM None	DESCRIBE POSITION RESPONSIBILITIES
	a. b.
POSITION TITLE	c.

FINAL MO SALARY $	AV. OVERTIME AND/OR COMM.	EMPLOYED (MO-YR) FROM	TO	REASON FOR LEAVING

NUMBER OF ADDITIONAL FULL-TIME POSITIONS YOU HAVE HELD WITHIN THE PAST FIVE YEARS.

I UNDERSTAND THAT I SHALL NOT BECOME AN EMPLOYE OF BENTURA UNTIL I HAVE SIGNED AN EMPLOYMENT AGREEMENT WITH THE FINAL APPROVAL OF THE EMPLOYER AND THAT SUCH EMPLOYMENT WILL BE SUBJECT TO VERIFICATION OF PREVIOUS EMPLOYMENT, DATA PROVIDED IN MY APPLICATION, AND ANY RELATED DOCUMENTS OR RESUME, AND WILL BE CONTINGENT ON MY PASSING A REQUIRED PHYSICAL EXAMINATION BY THE EMPLOYER. I KNOW THAT A REPORT MAY BE MADE THAT WILL INCLUDE INFORMA- TION CONCERNING MY CHARACTER, GENERAL REPUTATION, PERSONAL CHARACTERISTICS AND MODE OF LIVING, AND THAT I CAN MAKE A WRITTEN REQUEST FOR ADDITIONAL INFORMATION AS TO THE NATURE AND SCOPE OF THE REPORT IF ONE IS MADE.

SIGNATURE *Dale C. Bennett*

AN EQUAL OPPORTUNITY EMPLOYER

Stationery. Before starting to type letters, check your stationery supply. Business letters are usually typed on 8½- by 11-inch letterhead paper. For a multipage letter, plain paper of the same size, color, and quality as the letterhead is used after page 1. Onionskin or manifold paper is used for carbon copies.

Letter Length. To know where to type the dateline of a letter, estimate its length; that is, *short, average, long,* or *2-page.* This decision also indicates the width of the side margins. For business letters in the sections that follow, start the letter address on the fourth line below the date.

Margins. For short letters, 2-inch side margins are appropriate, with the date typed on about Line 20. For an average-length letter, use 1½-inch side margins; type the date on about Line 15. For long 1-page and multipage letters, use 1-inch side margins; type the date on about Line 12. Although some offices use standard margins for all letters, the side margins in this and ensuing sections will vary with letter lengths.

Letter Placement. Office typists position letters by quick judgment; and the placement table given below will, with practice, help you develop this sense. *The table is merely an aid, however. You should discontinue using it as soon as possible* and substitute your own judgment. Learn to work with approximations. The table gives word counts for letters only to help you visualize letter lengths. On the job, word counts are rarely available; your ability to judge will be vital.

Guides for Adjustment. As you learn to judge letter placement, consider 2 factors: (1) Is your type size pica or elite and (2) does the letter contain space-consuming special features like attention or subject lines, a table, or an enumerated list? Be alert for such items and allow for them by raising the dateline from 1 to 3 lines.

If the letter length is in the lower part of its range (for example, 102 words for average length), you probably will not need to adjust the dateline to achieve good placement even though the letter contains a space-consuming feature.

LETTER PLACEMENT TABLE

Body of Letter	Letter Length	Side Margins	Dateline on
Up to 100 words	Short	2″	Line 20
101 to 300 words	Short-average	1½″	Line 17
	Average	1½″	Line 15
	Long-average	1½″	Line 13
301 to 350 words	Long	1″	Line 12
Over 350 words	2-page	1″	Line 12

PUNCTUATION STYLES

Mixed punctuation: Use a colon after the salutation and a comma after the complimentary close.

Open punctuation: Omit these marks.

MODERN FURNITURE, INC.
623 S.W. Morrison Street / Portland, Oregon 97204
Telephone 503-732-3264

Current date

Ms. D. R. Jacobs, President
Jacobs & Orwant, Inc.
945 - 33d Street, S.E.
Grand Rapids, MI 49506

Dear Ms. Jacobs:

Subject: Weatherwise Garden Furniture

Thank you for meeting with me yesterday to discuss our new line of Weatherwise Garden Furniture.

When I returned to the main office, I told John Barton, our sales manager, that your store was giving serious consideration to taking on our Weatherwise line. He was, of course, pleased; in fact, he authorized me to offer you a five percent discount on your initial order.

I shall be in Grand Rapids in a week or two and shall telephone ahead for an appointment to see you. In the meantime, let me know if there is any information or service I can provide regarding our Weatherwise line.

Sincerely yours,

Hale Streeter
Hale Streeter
Sales Representative

xx

A copy of our manufacturer's warranty is enclosed.

Block style: All lines start at the left margin.

With a personal business letter of either style, type your return address on the two lines above the dateline.

Modified block with block paragraphs: Dateline and complimentary close start at midpage. Enumerations indented 5 spaces from left (or both) margins.

AKRON CONTRACTORS INC.
16 VAN COURT
AKRON, OHIO 44307
(216) 333-2097

Current date

Mr. Jay Kernan
Morris, Kernan, and Crowell
2271 Ridgewood Road
Akron, OH 44303

Dear Mr. Kernan

This letter confirms our telephone conversation of this morning in which we appointed you our legal representative in the case of Armstrong versus Dettmer.

I am having a complete list of our transactions with both litigants documented. Upon its completion, I shall send you a copy of the list. If you need still further information, let me know personally.

Sincerely yours

H. Gage Hall
H. Gage Hall
President

xx

cc Mr. McLean Stewart

Letter of application

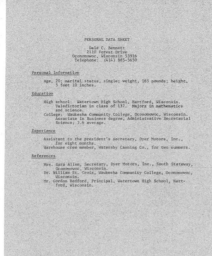

Personal data sheet

On plain paper, compose and type a letter to Mr. Samuel S. Sawyer, Bentura Enterprises, at the address given in Problem 1. Use the current date and your choice of letter and punctuation style. Apply for a position for which you think you are now or will later be qualified. Proofread and edit your first draft; then type a final copy.

Problem 5: Personal Data Sheet

Construct and type a personal data sheet, using your own data arranged attractively on the page.

Problem 2: Personal Data Sheet

From the copy shown below, type the data sheet. Use a 2″ top margin and 1″ side margins. Indent each order 5 spaces.

Problem 6: Application Form (WB p. 211)

Complete a Bentura Enterprises application form to accompany your letter of application and your personal data sheet.

Problem 3: Application Form (WB p. 209)

Type the application form on page 251. Align your typing just above the printed lines. Accommodate the copy to the space.

	Words
PERSONAL DATA SHEET	4
DS	
Dale C. Bennett	7
2110 Forest Drive	11
Oconomowoc, Wisconsin 53916	15
Telephone: (414) 885-5650	21
TS	

Personal Information   29

Age, 20; marital status, single; weight, 165 pounds; height, 5 feet 10 inches.   44

Education   48

High school: Watertown High School, Hartford, Wisconsin. Valedictorian in   63
class of 137. Majors in mathematics and science.   74
College: Waukesha Community College, Oconomowoc, Wisconsin. Associate   88
in Business degree, Administrative Secretarial Science; 3.6 average.   102

Experience   106

Assistant to the president's secretary, Dyer Motors, Inc., for eight months.   122
Warehouse crew member, Watersby Canning Co., for two summers.   134

References   138

Mrs. Sara Allen, Secretary, Dyer Motors, Inc., South Stateway, Oconomowoc,   153
Wisconsin.   156
Dr. William St. Croix, Waukesha Community College, Oconomowoc, Wisconsin.   171
Mr. Gordon Redford, Principal, Watertown High School, Hartford, Wisconsin.   185

Communications Design Associates

801 JACKSON STREET, WEST   CABLE: COMDA
CHICAGO, ILLINOIS 60607   TELEPHONE: (312) 342-9753

		Words in Part	Total Words
Dateline	February 14, 19-- *Date on Line 18*	4	4
	Operate return 4 times		
Letter address	Mr. Martin McKensie	8	8
	McKensie Brothers, Inc.	12	12
	7829 Robertson Street	17	17
	Abilene, TX 79606 DS	21	21
Salutation	Dear Mr. McKensie DS	24	24
Body of letter	This letter is typed in block style with open punctuation.	36	36
	The simplicity of this style has made it increasingly popular	49	49
	among business firms. The streamlined appearance seems to	60	60
	typify today's modern, streamlined world--yet the style in-	72	72
	cludes all the elements of information normally found in	84	84
	business letters.	87	87
	Observe that all lines, including the date, inside address,	12	99
	salutation, and closing lines, begin at the left margin. The	24	111
	spacing between letter parts is standard. As in the modified	37	124
	block letter style, the number of line spaces left in the top	49	136
	margin varies with the length of the letter. DS	58	145
Complimentary close	Sincerely yours	61	148
	Operate return 4 times		
	Charles Harley Chambers		
Typed name	Charles Harley Chambers	66	153
Official title	Public Service Director	71	158
Reference initials	mew	72	159

Style Letter 3: BLOCK STYLE, OPEN PUNCTUATION

Note that with open punctuation, the salutation and complimentary close have no terminal punctuation.

LESSON 95

95A Preparatory Practice [5] each line at least 3 times

Alphabet The judges realize that six quick verdicts would benefit my plaintiff.
Figure/symbol Pam & Kim, Inc., 238 Main (Suite #7), raised their bid 10% to $19,560.
Shift keys Tessa, Tina, Ronald, and Ruth met in Toronto, Ontario, on a Wednesday.
Fluency Is my single purpose in life to haul myself up the hill of prosperity?
| 1 | 2 | 3 | 4 | 5 | 6 | 7 | 8 | 9 | 10 | 11 | 12 | 13 | 14 |

95B Communication Aid: COMPOSITION [15]

1. Type the ¶ below.
2. In a responding ¶, grant the appointment on the date specified. Set a time for the appointment and indicate that it can be changed if necessary.
3. Proofread your typed copy of the first ¶; mark any necessary corrections.
4. Edit and correct your ¶s; then retype both ¶s in final form.

I shall be graduated in June from Bradley University with a major in marketing, and I am frankly interested in opportunities for a career with your company. My qualifications, I believe, will interest you. I shall be in Austin on Monday, May 5. May I see you on that day?

95C Production Typing [30]

Problem 1: Letter of Application

Decide on letter and punctuation style

Words
2110 Forest Drive Oconomowoc, Wisconsin 53916 March 20, 19-- Mr. Sam- 14
uel S. Sawyer Personnel Manager Bentura Enterprises 1012 Kewanee Street 29
Racine, Wisconsin 53404 Dear Mr. Sawyer (¶ 1) Will you please consider me 43
an applicant for the position of secretary to your Vice President of Marketing 58
and Research. Dr. William St. Croix suggested that I write you, for he believes 75
I have the necessary qualifications for the position. (¶ 2) On April 9, I shall be 90
graduated from Waukesha Community College with an Associate in Business 105
degree with a major in administrative secretarial science. My grade point average 121
has been 3.6 or better, and I have developed to a superior level the stenographic 138
skills necessary for an administrative secretarial position. (¶ 3) I am presently 153
employed on a part-time basis as assistant to Mrs. Sara Allen, secretary to the 169
president of Dyer Motors, Inc. This position has provided excellent experience 185
in using my shorthand and transcription skills. (¶ 4) You will find enclosed with 201
this letter a personal data sheet, which will give you more complete information 217
about my background and qualifications. At your convenience, I shall be glad to 233
come to your office to discuss the position and the reasons for my interest in a 249
career with Bentura Enterprises. Sincerely yours Dale C. Bennett Enclosure 264/281

Communications Design Associates

801 JACKSON STREET, WEST   CABLE: COMDA
CHICAGO, ILLINOIS 60607   TELEPHONE: (312) 342-9753

		Words in Parts	5' GWAM
	Date and closing lines at center point	3	1
Dateline	Line 12 → January 17, 19--		
	Operate return 4 times		
Letter address	Miss Grace Dunham	7	1
	Kansas Academy	10	2
	2121 Holiday Square	14	3
	Topeka, KS 66607	18	4
Salutation	Dear Miss Dunham	21	4
Body of letter	Thank you for your letter complimenting the appear-	31	6
	ance of the sample business letters we sent you. We are	43	9
	sincerely pleased that you found them suitable for use	54	11
	in your classes.	57	11
	We stress these procedures to typists who prepare	10	13
	our letters:	13	14
	1. Know how to use standard letter styles. A letter	24	16
	typed in a standard style has a familiar appearance; there	35	18
	are fewer distractions from the message.	44	20
	2. Be alert for inaccuracies. If something in the	54	22
	letter doesn't look or sound right, ask about it.	64	24
	3. Check doubtful spellings and punctuation. Such	75	26
	errors raise doubts in the mind of the reader.	84	28
	4. Make certain any noted enclosures are actually	95	30
	included with the letter; otherwise, the Company will be	106	33
	embarrassed.	109	33
	5. Proofread carefully each letter before removing	119	35
	it from the typewriter. Verify all figures. Correct	130	37
	errors expertly.	134	38
	If we can be of further help to you, Miss Dunham, I	10	40
	hope you will write to us again.	17	41
Complimentary close	Sincerely yours	20	42
	Operate return 4 times		
	Charles Harley Chambers		
Typed name Official title	Charles Harley Chambers	25	43
	Public Service Director	29	44
Reference initials	stu	30	44

Style Letter 4: MODIFIED BLOCK STYLE, INDENTED PARAGRAPHS, OPEN PUNCTUATION

Note that in letters with indented paragraphs enumerated items are typed in the same style as the paragraphs and are not indented from the right margin. Notice too that space-consuming items may require special placement attention. The enumerations in this letter made placement on Line 12 more appropriate than on Line 15, as specified in the Letter Placement Table on page 106.

94D Communication Aid: PROOFREADING AND COMPOSITION ⟨20⟩ unbound manuscript style; provide title

1. Type the ¶s below, making changes as indicated. Be alert for—and correct as you type—any misspelled words or incorrect punctuation that may not be marked.
2. Proofread the ¶s carefully. Mark any additional

changes to be made when you type the final copy.
3. Compose 1 or 2 more ¶s that give additional reasons why people work. Proofread your composition carefully; then retype all the ¶s in final form.

	Words
There are several reasons why people work. One	10
reason hardly needs atating: To earn money. Since people	21
today are not self-sustaining, they must have money to	32
satisfy basic human needs ~~requi~~ for food, clothing, and shelter.	44
Many folks, of course want more than just basic needs,	56
and More money (and work) is ~~are~~ required to supply ~~all~~ extras.	67
Money also buys such needed forms of protection as savings in-	79
surance and medicle care.	85
People work, too, because they have the time for it.	96
They ~~can~~ find satisfaction in a well balanced division ~~balance~~ of	106
time between work and play ~~work~~. Too much ~~great~~ of either, they	117
believe, can contribute to Jacks dullness. "If I didn't	129
work, says Mr. A, "I'd sit at home lifting my feet while	140
my wife vacuumed the rug. "What would I do if I did not	152
work?" Mrs. A asks. "I'd probably vacuum the rug whether ~~if~~ it	163
needed it or not.	167

94E Control Building ⟨5⟩ two 2' control-level writings; compute GWAM

All letters are used.

1.5 SI
5.6 AWL
80% HFW

	GWAM		
	1'	2'	
Let there be no doubt on this one point: Efficiency in the basic	13	7	63
office skills is fundamental. Of course, a person who is unable to	27	13	69
type, spell, proofread, or solve simple arithmetic problems proficiently	41	21	77
is not likely to get a typing job in the first place; however, the idea	56	28	84
emphasized here is that typing ability alone is not enough. A typist is	70	35	91
expected to bring to the job a number of polished personal qualities	84	44	98
that permit him to use his skill in typing to best advantage. The more	99	49	105
polished the qualities, the better will be his chances for success.	112	56	112

1' GWAM | 1 | 2 | 3 | 4 | 5 | 6 | 7 | 8 | 9 | 10 | 11 | 12 | 13 | 14 |
2' GWAM | 1 | 2 | 3 | 4 | 5 | 6 | 7 |

LESSON 55

55A Preparatory Practice (5) each line at least 3 times

Alphabet Aquatic experts have judged my worn samples to be fossilized plankton.

Figure/symbol Bond #7365024 will not be called until 1978, and it pays 5¼% interest.

Hyphen Our vice-president is on a far-reaching trip to get all-round players.

Fluency A busy man may work until five--then work through a downtown auto jam.
| 1 | 2 | 3 | 4 | 5 | 6 | 7 | 8 | 9 | 10 | 11 | 12 | 13 | 14 |

55B Skill-Comparison Typing: STATISTICAL COPY (15) two 2' writings on each ¶; try to maintain skill on ¶ 1 (easy), ¶ 2 (average), and ¶ 3 (high average)

All letters are used.

	GWAM	
	2'	5'

¶ 1
1.3 SI
5.2 AWL
90% HFW

If we were to try to make a quick judgment from the 1974 annual   6 | 3 | 57
report of the Call Company, it would be a statement that would show how   13 | 5 | 60
this company and most others its size have strong ties with the national   20 | 8 | 63
economy. When in the last half of 1974 the national economy gave signs   27 | 11 | 66
of a general upswing, the fortunes of most of these firms started to   33 | 14 | 69
clamber back to the point where they had been at the first of that year.   40 | 17 | 72

¶ 2
1.5 SI
5.6 AWL
80% HFW

The Call Company sells up to 85 percent of its products in the   6 | 19 | 74
civilian sector of the national economy; so when a small economic slow-   14 | 22 | 77
down took place in the prior year, the outlook for 1974 did not seem to   21 | 25 | 80
be very bright. But when improvements were noted late in 1974, prices   29 | 28 | 83
firmed and earnings responded. Business started to pick up, and many of   36 | 31 | 86
the companies that had been holding back started to order. The economy   43 | 34 | 89
improved, and so did the position of most of the small business firms.   50 | 37 | 91

¶ 3
1.6 SI
5.8 AWL
75% HFW

The reversal in economic aspect came a trifle too late to allow   6 | 39 | 94
1974 to satisfy the promise the Call Company had expected of it. While   13 | 42 | 97
it is true that sales were the second highest in company history (pass-   20 | 45 | 100
ing the $1.5 million mark), they were 4 percent lower than the record   27 | 48 | 103
earnings of 1973. Hence, net income was lower. The economic lull, the   34 | 51 | 105
collapse in selling prices, and the upsurge in production costs all   41 | 53 | 108
contributed to lower profits for the year.   45 | 55 | 110

2' GWAM | 1 | 2 | 3 | 4 | 5 | 6 | 7 |
5' GWAM | 1 | 2 | 3 |

Machine Adjustments. Unless otherwise directed, SS drill copy on a 70-space line. Indent ¶ copy 5 spaces, DS, 70-space line. Letterhead or plain paper for production copy; current date unless given, your reference initials; correct errors; decide letter style unless indicated. You need not make cc of problems in this section.

LESSON 94

94A Preparatory Practice (5) each line at least 3 times

Alphabet	Jerry will exchange zinc for quicksilver because of price adjustments.
Figure/symbol	Our check #76921 for $340.68, covering your invoice #537, is enclosed.
Long words	The secured obligation includes extension of my original indebtedness.
Fluency	What makes a man laugh can tell you what sort of man he happens to be.

| 1 | 2 | 3 | 4 | 5 | 6 | 7 | 8 | 9 | 10 | 11 | 12 | 13 | 14 |

94B Technique Improvement: STROKING (10) 3 or more errorless copies of each line

1	1st/2d fingers	That jug got very heavy when Burt filled it and rushed to the bonfire.
2	3d/4th fingers	Will's pencils and paper are apt to disappear quickly as class closes.
3	3d row	A petty trick often turns out poorly, for we "reap what we have sown."
4	2d row	John is grateful; he asked Dan to thank us for filing his tax returns.
5	1st row	Can Mr. Mazer, my ex-boss, give me exactly 4/5 of my maximum benefits?
6	Shift keys	The Suburban Insurance Company is in the Fielder Building in Plymouth.
7	Left hand	The greatest act we ever saw was the Savage Lion of Sweetwater, Texas.
8	Right hand	The company union opposes my opinion, despite our June and July polls.

| 1 | 2 | 3 | 4 | 5 | 6 | 7 | 8 | 9 | 10 | 11 | 12 | 13 | 14 |

94C Skill-Transfer Typing (10) two 1' writings on each line; try to maintain GWAM

		Words
Goal	The star of a show sings one song too few, not one too many.	13
Figures	Their check for $137 brought the total collected to $892.50.	13
Script	*Counting time is not nearly so important as making it count.*	13
Corrected copy	An idea is not responsible for the people who believe it.	13

55C Production Orientation and Skill Building [30]

Problem 1 *(WB p. 59)*

1. Type the letter on page 108 in the style shown, using the machine adjustments given there.
2. Type on the exploration level; do not erase and correct errors.
3. Proofread by comparing; mark with a pencil any needed corrections.

Problem 2 *(WB p. 61)*

1. On plain paper, type a 5′ writing on the letter from your corrected copy. Do not correct your typing errors. Compute *g-pram* (gross production rate a minute) as shown below.
2. On a letterhead, type the letter again, but on the control level. Erase and correct your errors as you type.

$$\text{g-pram} = \frac{\text{Gross (total) words typed}}{\text{Length (in minutes) of writing}}$$

LESSON 56

56A Preparatory Practice [5] each line at least 3 times

Alphabet	Bob Frags quickly explained why we don't have zero weather in Jamaica.
Figure/symbol	By buying the stock at 124¼ and selling it at 86½, Lance lost $395.70.
Vowels	Despite his diet, he ate various pieces of chocolate candy and sweets.
Fluency	Be sure to vote; it is with our vote that we ensure and insure rights.

| 1 | 2 | 3 | 4 | 5 | 6 | 7 | 8 | 9 | 10 | 11 | 12 | 13 | 14 |

56B Control Building: STATISTICAL COPY [10]

1. Type the problem below; make the corrections indicated.
2. Use the problem for a 2′ writing on the control level. Compute *gwam*.
3. Use the problem for a 3′ control-level writing. Compute *gwam*.

¶ 1
1.5 SI
5.6 AWL
80% HFW

	GWAM 2′		GWAM 3′	
The Conference Board says that 75,~~000,000~~ drivers drove ~~their~~	6	52	4	35
52 million cars 485 billion miles in 1955. By 1971, 29 million	13	60	9	40
additional drivers and about ~~two times~~ as many cars were on	18	64	12	43
the road; and the cars were being driven a bit under a	23	70	16	47
trillion miles (the average number of miles acar is driven	29	76	20	51
every year is still withing a range of 9,500 to 10,000). Public	35	82	24	55
forms of transoprtation carried a total of 6 Billion people	41	88	28	59
in 1971, 5½ ibllion of them by mass transit system.	47	93	31	63

2′ GWAM | 1 | 2 | 3 | 4 | 5 | 6 | 7 |
3′ GWAM | 1 | 2 | 3 | 4 | 5 |

Problem 1: Interoffice Memorandum (WB p. 199)

Words

TO: Ralph Vincent FROM: Gilbert H. Roswell DATE: *Current* SUBJECT: Commissions Earned by Salesmen (¶ 1) As you know, the Company pays a 5% commission on all qualified sales exceeding the quota set for each salesman. The commissions are paid on net sales. The net figure used does not include amounts added for sales taxes, and discounts are deducted. (¶ 2) Commissions earned during the last year are as follows:

Salesman	Commission
Baylor, Claude	$250
Cassio, S. K.	425
Deltsos, Laurel	130
Farquar, Melody	325
Moony, William E.	250
Wallis, Maynard	325

10
22
36
52
66
78
85
89
93
97
101
105
109

Problem 2: Purchase Order (WB p. 201)

Words

TO: Bolgas Camera Supply Company, 45 Southgate Street, Worcester, MA 01610 ORDER NO. 866-R-32 DATE November 18, 19-- TERMS Net 30 days SHIP VIA Express

13
22
23

Quantity	Cat. No.	Description	Price	Total	
3	738-C	Instamatic lens attachments	9.95	29.85	33
8	818-L	Poster mounts, yellow	.45	3.60	41
5	819-L	Poster mounts, black	.45	2.25	48
3	777-C	Movie reel albums	2.99	8.97	56
4	721-C	Lucite photo frames	1.89	7.56	64
				52.23	65

Problem 3: Invoice (WB p. 203)

Prepare an invoice for the items included in Problem 2 above. The invoice number is 9610. The date is November 25, 19--.

Problem 4: Credit Memorandum (WB p. 205)

Prepare a credit memorandum for the return of the 4 lucite photo frames ordered in Problem 2. The memorandum number is 73; the date is December 5, 19--.

Problem 5: Voucher Check (WB p. 207)

Type a voucher check (#3855) to Bolgas Camera Supply Company for $44.67 in payment of their November 25 invoice for $44.67. The date is December 20, 19--.

Note that the original amount was $52.23; but $7.56, the amount of the credit memorandum, has been deducted.

56C Production Typing Information: ADDRESSING ENVELOPES

To hasten the sorting and distribution of first-class mail, the U.S. Postal Service Corporation uses Optical Character Readers to read electronically the ZIP Code and the name of the city and to sort the letters into appropriate bins. The Postal Service asks that the following directions be observed.

Address Placement. The city and state line is optically scanned. The address lines must be higher than ½″ from the bottom of the envelope but no higher than 3″ from the bottom. The "read zone" for the OCR is 8″ long and 2½″ deep. It cannot be closer than 1″ to either the right or the left edge of the envelope.

Extraneous information, regardless of its nature, will not interrupt the OCR if the information is placed above the read zone. The space below the read zone must be kept completely clear.

Spacing. The address lines should be blocked. Single spacing is recommended by the Postal Service.

The city and state names and the ZIP Code should appear in that sequence on the bottom line. Four-line addresses may be used as long as the city line lies within the read zone.

Personal Titles. Always use an appropriate personal title on a letter, envelope, or card addressed to an individual. When a woman's marital status is unknown, use *Miss* or *Ms.* as the personal title.

State-Name Abbreviations. The Postal Service recommends the use of approved 2-letter state-name abbreviations with ZIP Codes. The approved list is given on Reference Guide page viii. These abbreviations should be typed in all capitals without periods.

In typing state names in letter addresses, the recommended practice is to use the 2-letter abbreviations and the ZIP Codes. If the ZIP Code is unavailable, spell the state name in full or use the traditional abbreviation.

Mailing Notations. Directions to the Postal Service, such as AIRMAIL, SPECIAL DELIVERY, etc., are typed in capitals, below the stamp and at least 3 line spaces above the address.

Addressee Notations. Directions to the recipient, such as *Hold for Arrival, Please Forward, Personal*, etc., should be typed a triple space below the return address and 3 spaces from the left edge of the envelope. Addressee notations may be typed in either all capitals or caps and lowercase, underlined.

In Care of and Other Lines. If it is inconvenient to position such items as attention lines, in-care-of notations, and account numbers outside the read zone, type them on any line of the address block *above* the street name or box number.

Envelope Sizes. Some companies use large (No. 10) envelopes as standard practice; other companies use envelopes of various sizes and forms to meet different needs. The bulkiness of the contents usually indicates the appropriate size of envelope.

When a choice is available, use a small envelope for half-size stationery or onionskin sheets. For letters on regular-size stationery of one or more pages, use the large (No. 10) envelope.

On the small and large envelopes illustrated below, the addresses are typed in the read zones.

LESSON 93

93A Preparatory Practice (5) each line at least 3 times

Alphabet   The Maharajah's quixotic group visited Auckland, New Zealand, briefly.

Figure/symbol   Send check #23-79 for $522 ($580 less 10%) to 346 Day Drive by May 23.

Double letters It occurred to the committee that a fall meeting would be unnecessary.

Fluency   To double-check can take a little time, but it can pay huge dividends.

| 1 | 2 | 3 | 4 | 5 | 6 | 7 | 8 | 9 | 10 | 11 | 12 | 13 | 14 |

93B Growth Index (15) two 5′ control-level writings; compute GWAM on both writings

All letters are used.

		GWAM	
		1′	5′

¶ 1
1.5 SI
5.6 AWL
80% HFW

Many letters appear to click right away; many do not. Do you know — 13 | 3 | 53
why this is true? A letter can be short, clear, concrete, and correct; — 28 | 6 | 56
but it can lack the sparkle a good writer likes to get into a communica- — 42 | 8 | 59
tion. What is missing? Chances are good that the omitted quality is an — 57 | 11 | 62
evasive factor called the "personal touch." The letters that click have — 71 | 14 | 65
it; but those that do not are cold, impersonal, and unimaginative. — 85 | 17 | 68

¶ 2
1.5 SI
5.6 AWL
80% HFW

Good letters contain a skillful mix of fact and feeling. They can — 13 | 20 | 70
scarcely be otherwise; for they are written by people, to people, and — 27 | 22 | 73
about people and ideas that involve people. The tone quality a letter — 42 | 25 | 76
possesses has an important bearing on the way it will be received. It — 56 | 28 | 79
should be positive, friendly, and helpful. The ideal letter is one in — 70 | 31 | 82
which a writer puts part of himself in the envelope before he seals it. — 85 | 34 | 84

¶ 3
1.5 SI
5.6 AWL
80% HFW

Many effective correspondents realize the importance of basic sales — 14 | 37 | 87
principles. They have good ideas on how to use such principles to help — 28 | 39 | 90
them frame letters that win support. Initially, they try to gain the — 42 | 42 | 93
reader's attention; then they discuss the subject in a way that is apt — 56 | 45 | 96
to appeal to the reader and make him want to be involved. In the clos- — 70 | 48 | 99
ing, they suggest action to be taken and urge the reader to take it. — 84 | 51 | 101

1′ GWAM | 1 | 2 | 3 | 4 | 5 | 6 | 7 | 8 | 9 | 10 | 11 | 12 | 13 | 14 |
5′ GWAM | 1 | 2 | 3 |

93C Production Measurement (30) correct errors; figure N-PRAM

Type the problems on page 191 for 20′. Make 1 cc of each problem. You will be scored on the number of problems that you finish.

56D Production Typing: LETTERS IN MODIFIED BLOCK STYLE, MIXED PUNCTUATION ㉘

Before typing the problems in this lesson, read Production Typing Information: ADDRESSING ENVELOPES, on page 111. Type envelopes for the letters as requested.

In the 3 letters that follow, you are requested to use mixed punctuation (which has been omitted in the problem copy).

Problem 1: Long Letter (WB p. 63)

300 words; block ¶s; address envelope

	Words
Mr. Harmon Silverman, President | Acme	10
Manufacturing Company | 12537 Esplanade	18
Avenue | Davenport, IA 52803 | Dear Mr.	25
Silverman (¶ 1) Would you purchase a new	33
car from a salesman who was strolling around	42
in his bare feet? Would you buy cosmetics or	51
clothing from a saleslady with dirty smears	60
on her face and her dress? Would you leave	68
your money with a banker who tells you, "We	77
ain't open on Saturdays. We ain't open on	86
Monday mornings, neither"? (¶ 2) It is very	93
likely that you would not. Appearance and	102
impressions are quite important to us in decid-	111
ing where we should place our confidence, and	120
we don't do business with people in whom we	129
have no confidence. (¶ 3) That's why it is	137
important that the letters that leave your	145
office are just about perfect in every detail––	155
no smudges; no careless appearance; no incor-	164
rect spelling; no bad grammar; and, of course,	173
no misinformation. If any of these elements	182
are present, your reader loses confidence in	191
you. (¶ 4) The Morningside Secretarial Tray	199
can help your typist improve the appearance	208
of your letters. It contains an excellent ref-	217
erence book, a standard dictionary, and all the	226
implements necessary to make neat correc-	234
tions. Just show her this letter and ask for	244
her opinion of such a tray. We are certain she	253
will tell you how the tray can help her im-	262
prove the appearance of your letters. (¶ 5)	269
Don't let what you want to say get lost in the	279
way you say it. When you send out a less-	287
than-perfect business letter, you can be well	296
on your way to striking out. With the Morn-	305
ingside Secretarial Tray on your team, your	314
message has a much better chance of getting	323
exactly the reaction you want. Very truly	331
yours | Elva E. Briggs, President | xx	338/359

Problem 2: Average-Length Letter (WB p. 65)

153 words; block ¶s; address envelope

	Words
Mr. Walter L. Davis | 500 Mesker Park	10
Drive | Evansville, IN 47712 | Dear Mr.	18
Davis | (¶ 1) It was around ten o'clock in the	26
evening. It was cloudy and dark. Just at	34
the corner of Albert Smith's house, a prowler	44
lurked. He was watching the house. (¶ 2) It	52
was seven in the evening. A big delivery truck	61
from a local store was making a last-minute	70
delivery during the Christmas season. The	79
box the man carried was a big one. He	86
couldn't see very clearly. He missed his step.	96
(¶ 3) It was also sometime during a spring	104
evening that a prospective buyer arrived to	112
look at Mr. Smith's house. It looked rather	121
gloomy in the twilight. (¶ 4) In each of these	130
instances, Albert Smith wished that he had	138
installed a Clearvue gas lawn lamp. It would	148
have brightened these occasions considerably.	157
Maybe it isn't too late for you. Wouldn't it be	167
a good idea to call us for details? Sincerely	176
yours | Miss Mary Lauder | Sales Representa-	184
tive | xx	185/198

Problem 3: Short Letter (WB p. 67)

62 words; indent ¶s; address envelope

	Words
Primus Construction Company | 35854 Pine-	11
wood Road | White Plains, NY 10605 | Gen-	18
tlemen (¶ 1) We are planning to expand our	26
office facilities by adding a wing to our present	36
building. We are inviting area firms to submit	45
bids for this construction. (¶ 2) If your com-	53
pany is interested, please contact our office	63
before the end of the month; and we shall	71
send you a set of specifications for the job.	80
Yours truly | Gregory J. Talmeff | Secretary-	89
Treasurer | xx	91/105

LESSON 92

92A Preparatory Practice (5) each line at least 3 times

Alphabet   Jon Veming quenched the blaze by pouring sixty buckets of water on it.

Figure/symbol   Our $1,906.47 payment saved us 37¼ cents (.3725) on each of 138 items.

Double letters   I see a skillfully written letter with no misspelling or other errors.

Fluency   Why not make it a habit always to go just a bit further than is asked?

| 1 | 2 | 3 | 4 | 5 | 6 | 7 | 8 | 9 | 10 | 11 | 12 | 13 | 14 |

92B Communication Aid: QUOTATION MARKS (15) full sheet; 1½" top margin; 70-space line; SS; DS between items; heading, QUOTATION MARKS

Words

Rules   5

(1) Enclose a direct quotation with quotation marks.   16

(2) When a quotation is broken by such expressions as he said, enclose   30
both parts of the quotation with quotation marks.   40

(3) Place periods or commas inside the closing quotation mark.   53

(4) Place semicolons or colons outside the closing quotation mark.   67

(5) Place question marks or exclamation points inside closing quotation   81
marks when they are part of the quotation; place them outside when   95
they refer to the entire sentence, of which the quotation is but a   108
part.   109

(6) Enclose in quotation marks the titles of magazine articles, reports,   124
lectures, subdivisions of printed works, and theses. (Underline or   138
type in all capitals titles of books, magazines, and newspapers.)   151

Examples   154

(1) This man wrote, "Happiness is not the end of life; character is."   169

(2) "Great minds," Irving wrote, "have purposes; others have wishes."   183

(3) "What we need," Harry said, "is dirtier hands and cleaner minds."   197

(4) She said, "I listen for facts"; I know she concentrates on ideas.   211

(5) Did he read "A New Asia"? I called, "Strike while others sleep!"   225

(6) Chapter 3 of Management Today is entitled "Model Office Systems."   243

Application Paragraph   251

Did you read Jack's article entitled Life in the Suburbs? In it   265
he told the story of the city lady who said to the farmer, What is the   279
strange odor in your garden? That, said the farmer, is fertilizer.   294
For the land's sake! exclaimed the lady. Yes, said the farmer.   307

92C Production Typing: BUSINESS FORMS (30) Continue typing 91C, page 185.

LESSON 57

57A Preparatory Practice [5] each line at least 3 times

Alphabet	Brazilian Judge Frank Wavo is quietly confirming the risk of smallpox.
Figure/symbol	Call 875-0529 on May 9 to purchase volume #4 at a discount of 33 1/3%.
Direct reaches	Freddy needed his cooperation in order to start the logs rolling away.
Fluency	During August, he had some other work that had taken up time at night.
	1 2 3 4 5 6 7 8 9 10 11 12 13 14

57B Control Building: STATISTICAL COPY [10] Control Level. Relax. Adopt an attitude of typing 5-10 words slower than your usual rate.

1. Type the ¶ once untimed. Keep your eyes on the copy while you type.

2. Type two 3′ writings on the control level. Proofread by comparison. Compute *gwam*.

1.6 SI
5.8 AWL
75% HFW

	GWAM 1′	3′	
A recent edition of LIFE INSURANCE FACT BOOK reported a study of	13	4	32
life insurance coverage in the United States. It indicated that 86% of	27	9	37
the men studied had some type of life insurance (as compared with 74%	41	14	42
of the women). Wherever the "head of household" was in the 45-54 age	55	18	46
group, 92% of them were insured. Following retirement, 67% of American	70	23	51
families with heads of household 65 or over had one or more policies.	84	28	56

1′ GWAM 1 2 3 4 5 6 7 8 9 10 11 12 13 14
3′ GWAM 1 2 3 4 5

57C Production Typing Information: LETTERS OF TWO OR MORE PAGES [5]

In typing a multipage letter, do not end a page with a divided word. Leave at least 2 lines of a paragraph at the foot of a page and carry at least 2 lines to the next page. Use plain paper of the same color and quality as the letterhead for the second and subsequent pages of letters.

Begin the heading on Line 7 at the left margin in *block style* or in the one-line *horizontal style*, as illustrated at the right. Leave 2 blank lines between the heading and the first line of the resumed letter; use the same side margins as for the preceding page.

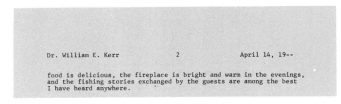

Dr. William E. Kerr
Page 2
April 14, 19--

food is delicious, the fireplace is bright and warm in the evenings,

Block style of second-page heading

Dr. William E. Kerr 2 April 14, 19--

food is delicious, the fireplace is bright and warm in the evenings,
and the fishing stories exchanged by the guests are among the best
I have heard anywhere.

Horizontal style of second-page heading

OMITTING WRITER'S NAME IN SIGNATURE LINE

When the letter writer's name is not typed in the signature line, type it before your reference initials at the left margin, thus: *DBLong:stu*.

Hastings Furniture Co.

1300 Garfield Avenue
Kansas City, KS 66104

18-186
1010

Words

September 26 19--   No. 4982   4

PAY to the order of Lex Tool Supply Co. $56.12   9

Fifty-six 12/100-- Dollars   23

MIDWEST NATIONAL BANK
Kansas City, Kansas

_____
Treasurer, Hastings Furniture Company

⑆1010⑈0186⑆ 143 0602 46⑈

Detach this stub before
cashing this check.

TO   IN PAYMENT OF THE FOLLOWING INVOICES:

Lex Tool Supply Co.   27
1012 Barnett Avenue   31
Kansas City, KS 66104   36

Date	Invoice	Amount
8/29/--	8692	56.12	39

Hastings Furniture Company

1300 Garfield Avenue
Kansas City, KS 66104

Individuals ordinarily pay for merchandise, medical or legal service, and the like,
when they receive a statement of their account. A business, however, customarily
pays for an invoice or a number of invoices, using a voucher check. The voucher
is the detachable portion showing the invoice numbers covered by the check.

Statement of Account

Words

Date Sept. 30, 19--   3

To

┌
    Hastings Furniture Co.   ┐
    1300 Garfield Avenue
    Kansas City, KS 66104
└   ┘

LEX
TOOL SUPPLY CO.
1012 Barnett Avenue
Kansas City, KS 66102
Telephone: (913) 661-3631

8
12
16

Date	Items	Debits	Credits	Balance	
Sept.					
1	Balance			56.12	21
18	Invoice #8771	33.25		89.37	27
26	Credit memo #391		5.25	84.12	33
27	Payment on account		56.12	28.00	39

Even when payments have covered individual invoices, a common practice is to
send customers end-of-month statements that show the month's transactions.

57D Production Typing: MODIFIED BLOCK STYLE WITH VARIATIONS ㉚

Problem 1: Two-Page Letter (WB p. 69)

535 words; use date of April 14, 19--; open punctuation; block ¶s; address envelope

	Words
Dr. William E. Kerr ǀ 9032 St. James Place ǀ	11
New York, NY 10038 ǀ Dear Dr. Kerr (¶ 1)	18

Dr. William E. Kerr ǀ 9032 St. James Place ǀ New York, NY 10038 ǀ Dear Dr. Kerr (¶ 1) Early last month I had the opportunity of presenting to your service club our story about Arctic fishing at Great Pine Lodge, Great Bear Lake, in the Northwest Territories of Canada. It was great fun for me to be with your club and give them the exciting details about fishing in the fourth largest freshwater lake in all North America, and I enjoyed meeting and talking with you. (¶ 2) As you know, Dr. Kerr, Canada's Northwest Territories is one of the few remaining frontier areas that are completely accessible by automobile, airplane, and boat. For the true sportsman, it probably holds more genuine appeal than any other area in North America; and our Great Pine Lodge is right in the middle of it. (¶ 3) The fishing is unsurpassed. Grayling and Arctic char of trophy size can be taken from the local waters with a minimum of effort; and since the lake covers 12,000 square miles, you don't need to worry about other fishermen crowding you out of a good fishing spot. (¶ 4) For those days when a rest from fishing is desired, there is nothing more inspiring than to take a boat or trail trip from the Lodge. The scenery is truly beautiful, and it is not unusual to see a bear or moose at the water's edge. At Great Pine Lodge, the camera is second in importance only to the fishing rod.

(¶ 5) When I spoke with you following our meeting in New York, you indicated that you annually took a fishing trip, usually in Canada, and that you had not yet made definite arrangements for this year's trip. We want you to come to Great Pine Lodge, Dr. Kerr; and we want you to come this year. With your intense interest in sport fishing, Great Bear Lake has to be the lake for you to fish this year. (¶ 6) My wife and two sons, who help me operate Great Pine Lodge, join me in inviting you and your family to spend a week or two with us. While we have no facilities for swimming, your family are sure to enjoy Great Pine Lodge if they enjoy the outdoors. Our living accommodations are complete, and they are reasonably priced. The food is delicious, the fireplace is bright and warm in the evenings, and the fishing stories exchanged by the guests are among the best I have heard anywhere. (¶ 7) We have prepared a new 20-page full-color brochure about Great Pine Lodge, and I will send you a copy just as soon as it comes from the printer. This brochure will give you more information about our Lodge. Questions about rates, license fees, transportation, clothing, equipment, guides, and seasons are answered in detail. (¶ 8) We are receiving requests for reservations now; so we hope to hear from you soon, Dr. Kerr. Sincerely yours ǀ Andrew Fitzgerald ǀ xx 543/555

Problem 2: Writer's Name Omitted (WB p. 71)

83 words; mixed punctuation; indent ¶s; address envelope

Mr. John B. Boyd ǀ 2745 Bondcroft Drive ǀ Buffalo, NY 14226 ǀ Dear Mr. Boyd (¶ 1) The Black Businessmen's Association of Utica met last month to hear a talk by Clifton Duclos on urban redevelopment. The message was so well received that the BBA decided to have it printed for distribution. (¶ 2) Copies are now available; and if you would like a supply to use with appropriate groups in your area, let us know how many you will need and we shall be happy to send them to you. Cordially yours ǀ Executive Secretary DBLong:*your initials* 105/117

Problem 3:

Invoice

(WB p. 191)

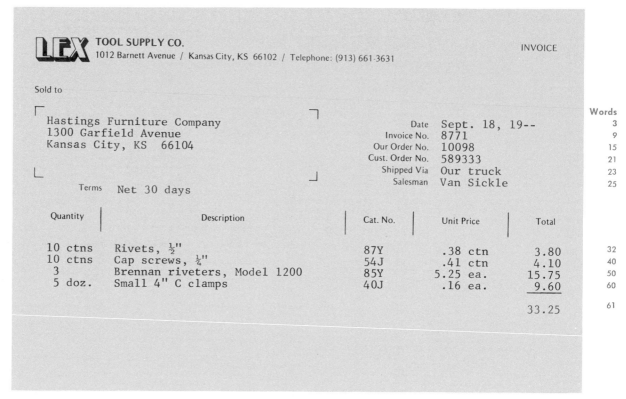

						Words
LEX TOOL SUPPLY CO. 1012 Barnett Avenue / Kansas City, KS 66102 / Telephone: (913) 661-3631					INVOICE	

Sold to

Hastings Furniture Company
1300 Garfield Avenue
Kansas City, KS 66104

		Words
Date	Sept. 18, 19--	3
Invoice No.	8771	9
Our Order No.	10098	15
Cust. Order No.	589333	21
Shipped Via	Our truck	23
Salesman	Van Sickle	25

Terms   Net 30 days

Quantity	Description	Cat. No.	Unit Price	Total	Words
10 ctns	Rivets, ½"	87Y	.38 ctn	3.80	32
10 ctns	Cap screws, ¼"	54J	.41 ctn	4.10	40
3	Brennan riveters, Model 1200	85Y	5.25 ea.	15.75	50
5 doz.	Small 4" C clamps	40J	.16 ea.	9.60	60
				33.25	61

An invoice usually accompanies a shipment of merchandise.

Problem 4:

Credit Memorandum

(WB p. 193)

LEX TOOL SUPPLY CO.
1012 Barnett Avenue / Kansas City, KS 66102 / Telephone: (913) 661-3631

		Words
Hastings Furniture Company	Credit Memorandum No. 391	5
1300 Garfield Avenue		10
Kansas City, KS 66104	Date Sept. 26, 19--	18
	Your Order No. 589333	19

YOUR ACCOUNT HAS BEEN CREDITED FOR:

Quantity	Description	Cat. No.	Unit Price	Amount	
1	Brennan riveter, Model 1200	85Y	5.25	5.25	28

A credit memorandum notifies a buyer that his account has been credited, usually for returned goods.

LESSON 58

58A Preparatory Practice [5] each line at least 3 times

Alphabet	Daniel Joyer's macabre mask, "Banquo's Ghost," won five or six prizes.
Figure/symbol	Compute: 640 pairs @ $38\frac{1}{2}$¢ and 975 sets @ $12\frac{1}{2}$¢; allow a $14\frac{1}{4}$% discount.
Shift keys	D. H. Ochs, P. G. Hasko, and R. I. Quinn live in Salt Lake City, Utah.
Fluency	Habits--the more we use them, the more difficult it is to change them.
	| 1 | 2 | 3 | 4 | 5 | 6 | 7 | 8 | 9 | 10 | 11 | 12 | 13 | 14 |

58B Communication Aid: COMMA [20] full sheet; 1½" top margin; 70-space line; SS; DS between items

1. For the heading, type COMMA.

2. Type the rules and the examples given below. (Type the figures in parentheses. Space once after the closing parenthesis. Underline the side headings.)

3. Type the application paragraph ss, inserting the proper punctuation as you type.

Words

Rules 3

DS

Space once after parenthesis

(1) In citing a date within a sentence, set off the year with commas. 18

(2) When two or more adjectives modify a noun, separate them by commas 32
if they bear equal relationship to the noun. 41

(3) Separate by commas a series of words or a series of phrases. 54

(4) Use a comma after a dependent clause that precedes a principal 68
clause. (Do not set off a clause used as a subject or predicate.) 81

(5) Use commas to set off a nonrestrictive appositive, but do not set 95
off a restrictive appositive. 101

(6) Separate with a comma two consecutive, unrelated numbers. 114

TS

Examples 117

(1) On May 24, 1975, we transferred our account to a bank in Phoenix. 131

(2) A brilliant young lecturer gave an interesting, informative talk. 145

(3) They like to receive letters that are short, clear, and friendly. 160

(4) When we are angry, what we say may not be precisely what we mean. 174

(5) Mr. Poe, our professor of English, reviewed the book AUTUMN WIND. 188

(6) In 1969, 135 firms used this plan. During 1974, 32 discarded it. 202

TS

Application Paragraph *(Capitalize and punctuate as you type.)* 211

our firm was founded on may 22 1898. in 1965 12 branch offices 224
were opened in mayville leeton and bowson. when there is sufficient 238
demand our president earl t o'keefe intends to open more branches. our 254
company is known for its dynamic progressive leadership. 265

Problem 1:

Purchase Requisition

(WB p. 187)

Hastings Furniture Co.   PURCHASE REQUISITION

Deliver to: Paul Woods   Requisition No. 58163

Location: Dock 14   Date Sept. 10, 19--

Job No. AZ-7   Date Required As soon as possible

Quantity	Description
10 ctns	$\frac{1}{2}$" rivets
10 ctns	$\frac{1}{4}$" cap screws
3	Brennan riveters
5 doz.	Small 4" C clamps
5	Drag lights, 50' cord
1 doz.	60-watt light bulbs
1 doz.	75-watt light bulbs

Requisitioned by: _____

Words
3
8
13
17
21
25
30
35
40
45

A purchase requisition is completed by the company unit that needs the supplies or equipment.

Problem 2:

Purchase Order

(WB p. 189)

Hastings Furniture Co. 1300 Garfield Avenue   PURCHASE ORDER
Kansas City, KS 66104
Telephone: (913) 472-4047

Lex Tool Supply Co.   Purchase Order No. 589333
1012 Barnett Avenue   Date Sept. 12, 19--
Kansas City, KS 66102   Terms n/30
                                Ship Via Your truck

Quantity	Cat. No.	Description	Price	Total
10 ctns	87Y	Rivets, $\frac{1}{2}$"	.38 ctn	3.80
10 ctns	54J	Cap screws, $\frac{1}{4}$"	.41 ctn	4.10
3	85Y	Brennan riveters, model 1200	5.25 ea.	15.75
5 doz.	40J	Small 4" C clamps, drop forge	.16 ea.	9.60
				33.25

By _____ Purchasing Agent

Words
1
8
12
18
20
27
35
46
57
58

A purchase order is used by a company to order materials.

58C Production Typing Information: PLACEMENT OF OFFICIAL TITLES [5]

Beginning with this lesson, vertical lines will no longer indicate line endings; therefore, you will need to decide in the letters that follow how to type such lines.

Depending upon what will give better balance to lines in the letter address, an official title may follow the name of the addressee on the same line; it may precede the company name on the next line; or it may go on a line by itself. Punctuate the lines appropriately. Notice the balance and punctuation in the lines at the right.

Similarly, the official title of the letter writer may appear on the same line as his name; or, if an unbalanced line results, the title may be blocked on the typed name of the writer. These styles are shown at the right.

Placement of Official Titles

Letter addresses

Mr. Leon R. Gray, President
Vanguard Trucking Company

Miss Emily J. Evenson
Administrative Secretary
Braemmer and Simpler, Inc.

Mr. Howard J. Fenstermacher
Treasurer, Reliance Van Lines

Signature lines

P. E. Maxwell, President

Raymond E. Manguelo
Chairman of the Board

58D Production Typing: AMS SIMPLIFIED LETTER STYLE [20]

Problem 1: AMS Style Letter *(WB p. 73)*

Type the letter on page 117 in the style shown. *There are 175 words in the body of the letter.*

Problem 2: AMS Style Letter *(WB p. 75)*

There are 178 words in the body of the letter.

Words

Mr. E. E. Eyre, Sales Manager Akko Manu- 11
facturing Company 3300 Woodlawn Avenue 19
Columbus, GA 31904 PREPARATION OF A 26
MARKET SURVEY (¶ 1) Furniture store 32
owners, managers, and buyers need to know 40
the names of reputable companies that are 49
making furniture today. To supply this ser- 57
vice, we are preparing a MARKET SURVEY 65
that will be distributed to stores subscribing 75
to our service. (¶ 2) A similar survey was 82
sent to our subscribers two years ago. Many 91
furniture manufacturers found this survey to 100
be instrumental in acquiring new business. 109
There is no expense involved on your part; 118
our services are paid for by the stores we 126
represent. (¶ 3) If your company wishes to 134
be listed in the MARKET SURVEY, please give 143
us the following information: 1. A complete 152
description of furniture manufactured 2. Pat- 161
terns and designs recently developed 3. Dates 170
and terms of delivery; services rendered (¶ 4) 178
We should like to have this information soon 187
because we intend to go to press in six weeks. 197
Your cooperation in this matter will be deeply 206
appreciated. ROBERT ADAIR, PRESIDENT xx 214/233

Evaluate Your Work. Before removing a job from the typewriter, proofread it carefully for errors. After removing it, study its general appearance to form judgment on which to base adjustments for similar jobs in the future.

91C Communication Aid: NUMBER USAGE [10]

full sheet; 1½″ top margin; 70-space line; SS; DS between items; heading, NUMBER USAGE

Words

Rules 5

(1) Numbers preceded by nouns of designation are usually expressed in 19
figures. 21

(2) Express measures, weights, and dimensions in figures. 33

(3) In business letters, the percent sign (%) is preferred when it is 47
preceded by definite figures. With approximations and in most formal 61
writings, percent is preferred. 67

(4) Spell names of small-numbered avenues and streets (ten and under). 82
Type house numbers in figures, except for house number One. 94

Examples 97

(1) We found the exact quotation in Volume VIII, Section 4, page 191. 111

(2) The box Ralph sent measured 7 ft. 6 in. and weighed 45 lbs. 3 oz. 126

(3) About 85 percent of all loans will bring a return of 8% interest. 140

(4) They have moved from One 125th Street to 8130 North First Street. 154

Application Paragraph 163

At this time, six % of the firm's mail is comprised of packages; 176
and about eighty-five percent of these packages are correctly delivered 188
to our 165th Street office. All COD packages and first-class mail must 202
be delivered to our main office at Two North Fourth Street. 213

91D Production Typing Information: TYPING BUSINESS FORMS [5]

Centering data in columns. No hard-and-fast rule on centering data in columns applies. Generally, in each column except the description column, the longest line is centered by eye measurement under the column heading. Centering by exact methods is neither required nor recommended.

Tabulation. Make full use of the tabulator mechanism to insure proper alignment of figures in the columns when typing business forms like requisitions, purchase orders, and invoices. Well-designed forms have various items positioned so that the left margin setting and each tab stop will serve most items. When you set tab stops, plan settings that can be used repeatedly.

Abbreviations. Because of limited space, periods may be omitted after abbreviations and in columnar tables of figures where a rule separates dollars from cents. It is customary, also, to use such abbreviations as *gal.*, *ft.*, *ea.*, %, and # for *No.* Names of months may also be abbreviated to save space.

Spacing. Single-space insertions on forms unless you have three or fewer lines and ample room, in which case use double spacing. With multiline items, single-space and indent the second and ensuing lines three spaces.

Communications Design Associates

801 JACKSON STREET, WEST **CABLE:** **COMDA**
CHICAGO, ILLINOIS 60607 **TELEPHONE: (312) 342-9753**

	Words in Parts	5' GWAM	

Begin all major lines at left margin

October 5, 19--
(3 | 1 | 41)

Address at least 3 blank line spaces below date

Mr. T. B. Gregory, Manager *(9 | 2 | 42)*
Northern Publishing Company *(14 | 3 | 44)*
16500 Florence Avenue *(19 | 4 | 44)*
Duluth, MN 55811 *(22 | 4 | 45)*

Salutation omitted

Subject line in all capital letters with a triple space above and below it

AMS SIMPLIFIED STYLE *(26 | 5 | 46)*

This letter is typed in the timesaving simplified style *(38 | 8 | 48)*
recommended by the Administrative Management Society. *(49 | 10 | 50)*
To type a letter in the AMS style, follow these steps: *(60 | 12 | 53)*

Enumerated items at left margin; indent unnumbered items 5 spaces

1. Use block format. *(5 | 13 | 54)*

2. Omit the salutation and the complimentary close. *(15 | 15 | 56)*

3. Include a subject heading and type it in ALL CAPS a *(27 | 17 | 58)*
   triple space below the address; triple-space from *(37 | 19 | 60)*
   the subject line to the first line of the body. *(46 | 21 | 62)*

4. Type enumerated items at the left margin; indent un- *(58 | 23 | 64)*
   numbered items five spaces. *(63 | 25 | 65)*

5. Type the writer's name and title in ALL CAPS at least *(75 | 27 | 67)*
   four line spaces below the letter body. *(83 | 29 | 69)*

6. Type the reference initials (typist's only) a double *(95 | 31 | 72)*
   space below the writer's name. *(101 | 32 | 73)*

Correspondents in your company will like the AMS simpli- *(11 | 34 | 75)*
fied letter style not only for the eye appeal it gives *(22 | 37 | 77)*
letters but also for the resultant reduction in letter- *(33 | 39 | 79)*
writing costs. *(36 | 39 | 80)*

Complimentary close omitted

E. David Bonnette

Writer's name and title in all caps at least 3 blank line spaces below letter body

E. DAVID BONNETTE, PRESIDENT *(42 | 41 | 81)*

akb *(43 | 41 | 81)*

Style Letter 5: AMS SIMPLIFIED LETTER STYLE (Typed in Pica Type)

The Administrative Management Society has adopted a simplified letter style for business letters. Study the letter above, which is typed in the recommended style. The enumerated items list the distinctive features of the style. Study also the marginal notations and guides for correct placement of letter parts.

Problem 2: Interoffice Memorandum *(WB p. 185)*

Words

TO: John E. Sheard FROM: Lars E. Jensen 6
DATE: September 22, 19-- SUBJECT: SM7 11
Alloy Tests (¶ 1) Hastings Furniture has 18
requested that we exert our earliest energies 27
on tests of SM7 flexibility. I suggest, there- 36
fore, that the testing schedule you sent me be 45
revised so that flexibility tests can be con- 54
ducted on both Monday and Tuesday. If Dr. 63
Shell is not available, schedule the tests with 72
Dr. Sokar. Stress tests should follow. (¶ 2) I 81
believe you will agree that we cannot endorse 90
SM7 for furniture components on the basis of 99
flexibility tests alone. Stress, for example, 108
must exceed 300# under a variety of condi- 117
tions without breaking (if Springmetal breaks, 126
some nice lady or some irate gentleman is 134
going to end up on the floor). Flexibility, of 144
course, is desirable for comfort in the type of 154
furniture Hastings is planning; on the other 163
hand, acceptable stress and tensile factors are 172
vital for safety. The other tests have mainly 182
to do with durability. (¶ 3) Do not the follow- 190
ing minimum standards seem reasonable? 198

Test	Minimum Standard	Priority	Words
			210
Flexibility	5% at angles	1	215
Stress	300# per sq. in.	1	220
Thermal	Firm, −90° to 150° F.	2	227
Tensile	Fatigue resistant	1	232
Corrosion	Normally resistant	3	239

(¶ 4) I shall study the Rosenthal report care- 247
fully as soon as I receive it. xx 253/259

LESSON 91

91A Preparatory Practice (5) each line at least 3 times

Alphabet	Jim quickly played the exciting pizzicato movement from Boccio's work.
Figure/symbol	Operator 26 in Reno wants you to call Area Code 703, 643-8591 at once.
e, i	Neither friend visited me while I lay ill in Reider Infirmary in Erie.
Fluency	What is my potential to contribute to the world through the work I do?

| 1 | 2 | 3 | 4 | 5 | 6 | 7 | 8 | 9 | 10 | 11 | 12 | 13 | 14 |

91B Technique Improvement: TYPING FIGURES AND SYMBOLS (5) each line 2 or more times

On May 3, 1975, I leased Apartment 204 at 6868 Putt Road (for $1,600).

Your memo #83-40 (dated May 25) mistakenly cites "16 prs. @ 79¢ a pr."

The problems are 276 ÷ 13 and 845 ÷ 90; set them up this way: 13)276.

Type on Line 49, "137 pens @ $36.80 ea., less 5½%. Ship immediately."

To work this problem: Add (+) 186,549 to 327,060; subtract (−) 3,672.

| 1 | 2 | 3 | 4 | 5 | 6 | 7 | 8 | 9 | 10 | 11 | 12 | 13 | 14 |

LESSON 59

59A Preparatory Practice (5) each line at least three times

Alphabet	Dank fog hid unlit objects; expressway driving became quite hazardous.
Figure/symbol	Corley & Wellman sent us check #723 (dated November 19) for $4,867.50.
1st row	Can Victor Zorn cleverly recover much extra evidence and deceive them?
Fluency	He is a man who profits from the work of firms that make our machines.
	| 1 | 2 | 3 | 4 | 5 | 6 | 7 | 8 | 9 | 10 | 11 | 12 | 13 | 14 |

59B Communication Aid: COMMA (15) full sheet; 1½″ top margin; 70-space line; SS; DS between items

1. For the heading, type COMMA.

2. Type the rules and examples given below. (Type the figures in parentheses. Space once after the closing parenthesis. Underline the side headings.)

3. Type the application paragraph, inserting the proper punctuation as you type.

Words

Rules 3

(1) Use commas to set off a nonrestrictive clause. 13

(2) Use a comma to separate coordinate (independent) clauses joined 27
by one of the coordinating conjunctions (and, but, for, nor, or, 43
and sometimes so and yet). 49

(3) Use a comma to set off an introductory phrase containing a verb. 63

(4) Use commas to set off words and phrases that are parenthetic (not 77
essential to the sentence structure). 85

(5) Use commas to set off words of direct address. 96

(6) Use a comma to separate a city and a state name. 106

Examples 110

(1) This trip, which is recommended in all guide books, costs little. 124

(2) A position is open, but I cannot yet interview anyone to fill it. 138

(3) To qualify for this job, applicants must write effective letters. 152

(4) Learning to typewrite, for example, requires consistent practice. 167

(5) Thank you, Mr. Cole, for sending the portraits to me so promptly. 181

(6) Our annual meeting will be held in Cleveland, Ohio, on August 21. 195

Application Paragraph *(Capitalize and punctuate as you type.)* 204

we know for example of several job openings in cleveland ohio. 217
one of them which we want to fill by april 1 is for a typist. the 231
applicant must be able to type rapidly but accuracy is also important. 245
to apply for this job you should contact us at once miss dellings. 259

90C Communication Aid: NUMBER USAGE (10) full sheet; 1½" top margin; 70-space line; SS; DS between items; heading, **NUMBER USAGE**

Words

Rules — 5

(1) Numbers ten and under are generally spelled out; numbers eleven and — 19
above are written in figures––except for conformity, as in this sen- — 33
tence. (See Rule 2.) — 37

(2) When several numbers are used in the same context, all numbers should — 52
be typed in the same way, either in figures or spelled out, except — 65
that any number that begins a sentence must be spelled out. — 78

(3) As a general rule, spell out the shorter of two numbers used together. — 93

(4) Isolated fractions are usually spelled out, but a series of fractions — 108
is typed in figures. — 112

Examples — 115

(1) He bought six bananas and two pints of cream to make the dessert. — 130

(2) Sixty-five people (57 men, 5 boys, and 3 women) climbed Mt. Hood. — 144

(3) Order No. 135 was for two 50-gallon drums and 27 ten-gallon cans. — 158

(4) Almost one fourth of the job is finished. Add 1/2, 3/7, and 5/8. — 172

Application Paragraph (Type all numbers in correct usage.) — 181

Our team won six of its games last year. Three of the games were — 194
won by just one run. The score of the last game was 13 to 12, and we — 208
won it in the last half of the final inning. In that game, a batter — 222
broke two nine ounce bats, one fourth of the bats the team owned. — 234

90D Production Typing: INTEROFFICE MEMORANDUMS WITH SYMBOLS AND TABLES (30)

Problem 1: Interoffice Memorandum (WB p. 183)

Words

TO: Lars E. Jensen FROM: John E. Sheard — 6
DATE: September 21, 19–– SUBJECT: Retest- — 11
ing Springmetal Alloy (SM7) (¶ 1) Accord- — 18
ing to Dr. Rosenthal's report, the failure of — 27
our tests on SM7 was due to an error in for- — 36
mula application. Dr. Rosenthal says that the — 45
correct formula for use in our basic procedure — 54
(Step 6) should have been the Linz formula: — 63
$M^2/M \div 1.4^s = P_s$. The thermal exposure — 72
should have been 1900° F. instead of 1750° F. — 81
Dr. Rosenthal explains: (Double-indent ¶ 2.) (¶ 2) — 86
An attempt to apply the Craig-Towne formula — 95
[the one we used] in tests such as this is — 105
understandable; but the difference between — 113
the formulas [the Linz and the Craig-Towne], — 123
although small, was critical in the SM7 tests. — 132

(¶ 3) The complete Rosenthal report is in my — 140
office, and copies of it will be sent to you as — 150
soon as they can be made. Will you please — 158
review all computations for SM7 as soon as — 167
you can. (¶ 4) The staff and the materials will — 176
be ready for new tests at 9:30 on the follow- — 184
ing mornings next week. — 189

TS

SM7 REVISED TEST SCHEDULE — 195

TS

Test	Day	Director	
Stress	Monday	Dr. Kurtz	— 206
Thermal	Tuesday	Dr. Ogden	— 211
Flexibility	Wednesday	Dr. Shell	— 218
Tensile	Thursday	Dr. Parsons	— 223
Corrosion	Friday	Dr. Sokar	— 229/235

DS (row header) — 201

The following 3 letters are to be typed in different styles. Make all decisions regarding placement and punctuation style (open or mixed).

NOTE: For a personal business letter, block the return address on the 2 lines above the dateline.

Problem 1: AMS Style Letter (WB p. 77)

	Words
Mr. Samuel T. Underhill 660 Folkstone Way	11
York, PA 17402 WE ARE WORRIED, MR.	19
UNDERHILL (¶ 1) Exactly 90 days ago we	25
sent you a statement of account showing a	34
balance of $98.15. Since then we have sent	42
you three more statements, but we have had	51
no reply from you. (¶ 2) Now we have really	59
become concerned. Ordinarily we are patient,	68
for there are legitimate reasons why a person	77
cannot always pay his bills on time. Company	86
policy, however, does not permit us to allow	95
unpaid balances to remain on our books longer	105
than 120 days. (¶ 3) Your credit record with	113

	Words
us is excellent. The yellow edge on your	121
credit card indicates that you have a top credit	131
rating with us. That's what puzzles us. Why	140
should a person with your credit reputation	149
not pay his bills? (¶ 4) You have been a good	157
customer, and we have appreciated your patronage.	165
We don't want to turn this account	174
over to a collection agent. (¶ 5) If you have	182
a complaint, tell us about it; if not, just send	192
us your check. Your credit rating has not yet	202
been affected. I know you want to keep it	210
that way. MAX W. RADKE, PRESIDENT xx	218/249

Problem 2: Personal Business Letter in Modified Block Style

	Words
1775 Sheridan Street Honolulu, Hawaii	8
96814 (current date) Miss Mary Carter Big	16
Mountains Insurance Co., Inc. 450 Silver	24
Avenue Albuquerque, New Mexico 87101	31
Dear Miss Carter (¶ 1) Thank you for your	39
comments about the article I wrote for The	48
Office. My original manuscript contained answers	58
to your questions about typing envelopes,	66
but space limitations did not allow them	76
to be included. I can, however, summarize my	85
recommendations for you. (¶ 2) On a small	92
envelope type the address (blocked and single-	101
spaced) on Line 11 or 12, 2½ inches from the	110
left edge. On a large envelope type the address	119
in this style on Line 15 or 16, 4 inches	128
from the left edge. (¶ 3) On plain envelopes	136
type the return address (blocked and single-	145
spaced) on Line 2, 3 spaces from the left edge.	155
(¶ 4) Type addressee notations (such as	162
Please Forward) a triple space below the	173
return address and 3 spaces from the left edge.	183

	Words
Type mailing notations (AIRMAIL, for example)	191
below the stamp and at least 3 line spaces	200
above the envelope address. (¶ 5) I hope the	208
guides are helpful. Please write me again if	218
I can provide any further information. Very	227
truly yours Henry S. Chung	232/260

Problem 3: Personal Business Letter in Block Style

	Words
2400 Brookside Drive Niagara Falls, NY	8
14304 (current date) Mr. George W. Packard	17
1305 Niemeyer Road Erie, Pa. 16509 Dear	25
Mr. Packard (¶ 1) I regret that I cannot	32
attend the retirement dinner honoring Helen	41
Mauer. The project on which I am now working	49
in Niagara Falls will keep me here for at	58
least another month. (¶ 2) My assistant, Cletus	66
Towler, will be able to attend, however,	75
and will send his reservation in a day or two.	85
(¶ 3) Please extend to Mrs. Mauer my sincere	91
best wishes for a happy retirement. Sincerely	100
Brenda Jones	104/125

Problem 2: Business Letter *(WB p. 179)*

Words

August 18, 19-- Mr. L. Patrick Cavanaugh 8
President Hastings Furniture Company 1300 17
Garfield Avenue Kansas City, KS 66104 25
Dear Mr. Cavanaugh (¶ 1) The necessary 31
materials have arrived, and the tests you re- 40
quested on the new Springmetal alloy are 48
ready to begin. Dr. John Sheard, of our staff, 58
will direct the experiments. (¶ 2) We shall 66
follow your specifications carefully to deter- 75
mine whether this alloy is appropriate for use 84
in home furniture. It would be helpful to us 93
if one of your engineers would consult with 102
us in a week or ten days to double-check your 111
figures against our findings. Would this be 120
possible? (¶ 3) Our tests should take approxi- 128
mately three weeks. Dr. Sheard will issue a 137
full report at that time. Sincerely Lars E. 146
Jensen Director xx 150/171

Problem 3: Letter with an Internal Table *(WB p. 181)*

Words

August 25, 19-- Dr. Lars E. Jensen Direc- 8
tor Independent Laboratories, Inc. 3519 16
Floyd Boulevard Sioux City, IA 51105 23
Dear Dr. Jensen (¶ 1) Thank you for your 30
prompt response to my letter. Our engineer- 39
ing staff feels somewhat reassured to know 48
that progress is being made with our testing 57
program. Deadlines are getting closer, how- 65
ever; and if we are to use the Springmetal 74
alloy in our new line of Airez furniture, we 83
must make definite plans within a matter of 92
weeks. (¶ 2) In view of the shortage of time, 100
we have decided to concentrate our efforts on 109
just four pieces of patio furniture to introduce 119
the Airez concept, rather than try to produce 128
a full line. These four products and their 137
metal requirements are shown below: 144

		Words
Airez Rocker	5′ flexible underpinning	152
Airez Recliner	4′ side supports, with	159
	4′ flexible underpinning	164
Airez Glider	4′ flexible side supports	172
Airez Hassock	6″ flexible underpinning	180

(¶ 3) The measurements correspond to 186
sketches we have furnished you. (¶ 4) Our 193
immediate needs, as you can see, involve flexi- 203
bility; and your tests in the immediate future 212
will, we hope, reflect this need. All other tests 222
should go forward as time permits. Sincerely 231
yours HASTINGS FURNITURE COMPANY 238
L. Patrick Cavanaugh President xx 245/265

LESSON 90

90A Preparatory Practice [5] each line at least 3 times

Alphabet	Jim Flack was required to pay the tax on the zinc souvenirs he bought.
Figure/symbol	On November 3, 1974, Richard paid $50.68 (plus tax) for 125# of nails.
1st row	Mr. Newman discovered zinc, bauxite, and miscellaneous minerals there.
Fluency	Let me, if I criticize, be more critical of myself than of my friends.

| 1 | 2 | 3 | 4 | 5 | 6 | 7 | 8 | 9 | 10 | 11 | 12 | 13 | 14 |

90B Technique Improvement: STROKING [5]

Type 3 times on the control level. Hold your arms and hands quiet. Center the stroking action in your fingers.

1	**3d/4th fingers**	The six dazed, weary antelopes walked slowly down the westward slopes.
2	**Double letters**	Miss Poole, from Tallahassee, will see Mississippi and Tennessee soon.
3	**One hand**	John Plum traced the baggage to my street address there in Sweetwater.
4	**Shift keys**	Senator John Poe visited the United States Naval Academy in Annapolis.
5	**m, n**	One mild morning in March, nine men ran ten miles from Niles to Milan.

| 1 | 2 | 3 | 4 | 5 | 6 | 7 | 8 | 9 | 10 | 11 | 12 | 13 | 14 |

LESSON 60

60A Preparatory Practice [5] each line at least 3 times

Alphabet	Eliza quit both her jobs, packed six bags, and moved far away to Nome.
Figure/symbol	Cody & Dee's checks #381 ($176.89) and #407 ($154.72) are outstanding.
a, e	These ears of corn are easier to eat than were the ears I ate earlier.
Fluency	It can be an amazing experience to find that work can be a lot of fun.
	1 | 2 | 3 | 4 | 5 | 6 | 7 | 8 | 9 | 10 | 11 | 12 | 13 | 14

60B Growth Index [15] two 5′ control level writings; figure GWAM on better writing

All letters are used.

		GWAM 1′	GWAM 5′	
¶ 1	The words that we use are effective whenever they enable others to	13	3	52
1.5 SI	understand precisely what it is we mean. There are certain rules of	27	5	55
5.6 AWL	grammar, of course, that justify the decision to use a particular word;	42	8	58
80% HFW	and we should adhere to such rules. However, an essential point to keep	56	11	61
	in mind in choosing that word is that it must help convey clearly and	70	14	64
	accurately to others the meaning of our written or spoken message.	83	17	66
¶ 2	Choosing with care the words we use provides us with the power to	13	19	69
1.5 SI	express ourselves more effectively and gives others clearer insight as	27	22	72
5.6 AWL	to our meaning. We must try to be aware of the importance of using the	42	25	75
80% HFW	right word, the specific one that conveys what we really want to say.	56	28	78
	This practice not only helps us express ourselves; it also adds richly	70	31	81
	to our ability to think keenly, with precision and with clarity.	83	33	83
¶ 3	If we want to talk and to write more effectively, we must acquire	13	36	86
1.5 SI	an adequate supply of words. A large vocabulary is a definite advantage	28	39	89
5.6 AWL	for a businessman. It allows him to use one word rather than several to	42	42	92
80% HFW	express his ideas. It helps him add zest and meaning to his speech and	57	45	94
	his writing. The personal satisfaction derived more than repays him for	72	48	97
	the labor involved in acquiring a useful stock of words.	83	50	100
1′ GWAM	1 | 2 | 3 | 4 | 5 | 6 | 7 | 8 | 9 | 10 | 11 | 12 | 13 | 14			
5′ GWAM	1 | 2 | 3			

60C Production Measurement: BLOCK AND AMS STYLE LETTERS [30] 20′ timing; compute N-PRAM

For the letters on page 121, decide the placement and style, correct errors, use the current date, make a carbon copy, and type an envelope of appropriate size.

Supplies needed: Letterheads (or full sheets); carbon sheets; second sheets; envelopes.

N-PRAM (net production rate a minute)

N-pram refers to the rate on production copy when a number of items are to be typed and when errors are to be erased and corrected. *N-pram* measures both typing and nontyping activities; therefore, it is good procedure to have all supplies ready before beginning to type.

Penalties: Deduct 10 words for each unerased error on original; 5 words for each unerased error on a carbon copy

$$\text{n-pram} = \frac{\text{Gross (total) words} - \text{penalties}}{\text{Length (in minutes) of writing}}$$

Tables in written communications

For letters up to 200 words (containing a table), use 1½″ side margins; for letters over 200 words, use 1″ side margins. In addition, raise the date-line by 1 or 2 lines for each line in the table. This is a rough guide; your judgment should prevail.

When space permits, indent a table from both margins. Single-space. For a table with a centered heading, triple-space before and after the heading and after the last line of the table. For a table without a centered heading, double-space before the first and after the last lines.

As a rule, position the columns by the backspace-from-center method.

Shortcut placement of simple 2-column tables

Set a tab stop for the first column 5 to 10 spaces to the right of the left margin. For the second column, set a tab stop a like number of spaces *plus* 1 for each stroke in the longest columnar entry (backspacing from the right margin). Adjust the side indentions as necessary to prevent having the columns too far apart for easy reading.

Adjustments in vertical placement of letters

You may occasionally find that you have misjudged the length of a letter and that it is going to be either too high or too low on the page. The following suggestions for condensing or expanding the depth of a letter can help you solve such letter-placement problems.

Condensing. To condense a letter that is longer than expected:

1. Reduce the space allowed for the signature.

2. Omit the company name (if one is used) in the closing lines.

3. Type the reference initials on the same line as the writer's typewritten name.

Expanding. To expand a letter that is shorter than expected:

1. Leave 2 blank lines between the body of the letter and the complimentary close.

2. Increase the space allowed for the signature.

3. Type the reference initials 4 to 6 spaces below the writer's typewritten name.

89E Production Typing: LETTERS AND TABLES (25)

Problem 1: Three-Column Table

DS; decide spaces between columns

			Words
HASTINGS FURNITURE COMPANY			5
Designer Notes—Airez Line			11
Name	Description	Colors ⁕	20
Airez Table	12″ legs; 3′ square surface	W	28
Airez Rocker Chair	S-shaped supports	W, Y, G	37
Airez EZ Chair	Padded; S-shaped supports	W, Y, G	47
Airez Recliner	Adjusted S shape; high back	W, Y, G	57
Airez Glider	Supported 2-seat swing	W, Y, G	66
Airez Hassock	6″ legs; 1′ square top; padded	W	76
Airez Chairs	4 legs; padded; firm	W	83
			86

⁕W, white; Y, yellow; G, green.   93

Problem 1: Letter in Block Style (WB p. 79)

Words

Mr. J. C. Burdett President Transpex Air 12
Transportation Company 3075 Dwyer Ave- 19
nue Utica, NY 13501 Dear Mr. Burdett 27
(¶ 1) On Wednesday afternoon, September 33
27, I was a first-class passenger on your jet 43
Flight 71 from Philadelphia to Pittsburgh. 51
The plane left Philadelphia on time, but we 60
were no sooner aloft than the stewardess told 69
me that Cleveland would be our first stop. 78
No stop in Pittsburgh was scheduled. Some- 87
one had made a mistake in my ticket. (¶ 2) 94
Of course, I should have done some checking. 103
If I had read the signs and listened to the 112
announcement, I would not have found myself 121
in Cleveland when I wanted to be in Pitts- 129
burgh. I'm sure you will agree, however, that 138
the fault was mostly yours. (¶ 3) Your people 146
in Cleveland thought so, too; they arranged 155
prompt transportation for me back to Pitts- 164
burgh. They even bought me a delicious din- 172
ner. What impressed me most, however, was 181
the fact that there was no wrangling about 189
who had made the mistake. Everyone was 197
interested in my welfare and in getting the 206
job done. (¶ 4) My compliments to you, sir, 214
and to your airline. I look forward to flying 223
with you again. Sincerely Paul Rawls Trea- 232
surer xx   234/253

Problem 2: Letter in AMS Style (WB p. 81)

Words

February 18, 19-- Mrs. Olive McGarrity 8
2557 Havemeyer Street Brooklyn, NY 11211 16
OUR PRESEASON SALE (¶ 1) Two weeks ago 23
we sent you a copy of our new spring catalog 32
containing illustrations of the newest in 40
fashions and an invitation to enter a preseason 50
order at preseason prices. We waited pa- 58
tiently, but we didn't hear from you. (¶ 2) 66
The opening of the season is getting closer, 75
and the time within which we can offer pre- 83
season discounts is getting shorter. In fact, 92
the price list we sent you will be discontinued 102
the first of next month. That's just about ten 112
days from now. (¶ 3) Ten days should be 119
enough, however, for you to browse through 127
the catalog again. Notice the vibrant colors 136
that are in vogue now and will continue to be 146

smart this spring. Notice the wide range of 155
sizes that we are offering in each model. 163
Notice the variety of accessories available with 173
each model, accessories that enable you to 182
personalize your selections. (¶ 4) Last, but 190
not least, we do want you to notice our prices. 199
Never before could we offer such high-quality 209
merchandise with such low price tags. They 217
simply cannot be matched anywhere. (¶ 5) 225
We urge you to act now, Mrs. McGarrity. We 233
can't accept your order at these prices after 243
the first of the month. MRS. MARY FLINN, 251
MANAGER xx   253/265

Problem 3: Letter in Block Style (WB p. 83)

Words

Bridegall and Martin, Inc. 2900 Edgar Ave- 11
nue Dayton, OH 45410 Gentlemen (¶ 1) 18
As you requested, we are sending you our 26
new full-color catalog with a complete listing 35
of our high-quality merchandise. We hope it 44
will help you select the equipment you need 53
for your playground, park, or school. (¶ 2) 61
Our three basic sales standards--quality, ser- 70
vice, and price--are our guidelines for each 79
sale; and we promise complete satisfaction. 88
(¶ 3) Our services include such assistance as 96
budget counseling, final installation, and 104
follow-up. (¶ 4) We should appreciate an 112
opportunity to discuss our products with you 121
and to assist you in planning your future 129
equipment requirements. Very truly yours 138
Ted Lovett Sales Manager xx   144/156

Problem 4: Letter in AMS Style (WB p. 85)

Words

Ms. Doris Thigpen 2721 Kerr Avenue 10
Berkeley, CA 94707 THE TIME HAS COME, 18
THE MANAGER SAID (¶ 1) When we turn 24
out the lights and lock the doors next Satur- 33
day night, one of the biggest sales in Roger's 42
history will be over. (¶ 2) There is still time, 51
however, to hurry in to see the many beautiful 60
items in every department. Late-model suits, 69
coats, sportswear, furnishings, hats, and shoes 79
--all at low, low prices--are waiting for you. 89
Bargains abound at every counter. (¶ 3) But 98
it will all be history on Monday morning; and 106
if you don't get here before Saturday night, 115
it will be (sob) too late. MRS. LOIS ELSON, 124
MANAGER xx   126/136

LESSON 89

89A Preparatory Practice [5] each line at least 3 times

Alphabet	Jeff York amazed us by stating his quixotic view of the labor problem.
Figure/symbol	On May 26, 1974, George paid Sedge-Brown $513.02, just $4.98 too much.
Shift keys	Mr. Smith's itinerary included Tulsa, Dallas, Fort Worth, and Houston.
Fluency	We ought not to tell her to go to the store for just a box of oatmeal.

| 1 | 2 | 3 | 4 | 5 | 6 | 7 | 8 | 9 | 10 | 11 | 12 | 13 | 14 |

89B Communication Aid: SYMBOLS [10]

Full sheet; DS; 10 spaces between columns; reading position

OTHER MEANINGS FOR CONVENTIONAL CHARACTERS

Caret (insert)	Diagonal	his for/pictures
Times, by	x (lowercase)	62 x 18
Minus	Hyphen	25 - 15
Signed	Diagonals, s	/s/ J. R. Stout
Pounds	Number sign	100# of coal
Feet	Apostrophe	9' x 12'
Minute	Apostrophe	5' writing
Inch or inches	Quotation mark	8½" x 11"
Second	Quotation mark	3" warning
Ditto	Quotation mark	John Bellen, Erie E. S. Brior, "

89C Technique Improvement: STROKING [5] each line twice on the control level

Double letters	Unnecessary commissions allocated to Mr. Pratt were finally corrected.
Double letters	Jeff succeeded in connecting excessive fees with current difficulties.
1st/2d fingers	Judith Ney finished tying bright red ribbons on more than fifty gifts.
1st/2d fingers	The rugged and mighty Matterhorn and Jungfrau jut to majestic heights.
3d/4th fingers	Six small shops in an old piazza ask low prices for antique clay pots.
3d/4th fingers	Paul X. Waxo passed the quiz; he knew (at last) "Vox populi, vox Dei."
Long reaches	Cluny Braun, my niece, brought many excerpts from my column on nerves.
Long reaches	My uncle, Jimmy Brocklyn, mumbled sadly, "My TV must be broken again."

| 1 | 2 | 3 | 4 | 5 | 6 | 7 | 8 | 9 | 10 | 11 | 12 | 13 | 14 |

SECTION 11 Business Letters with Special Features

LESSONS 61-66

Machine Adjustments. Unless otherwise directed proceed as follows: SS drill copy on a 70-space line. Letterhead or plain paper for production copy; current date unless given, your reference initials. Correct errors. Prepare at least one carbon copy and an envelope. Decide the margin settings (most letters are average or short) and the form of punctuation to use. Block all paragraphs.

LESSON 61

61A Preparatory Practice (5) each line at least 3 times

Alphabet	Elizabeth Jacks should mix five quarts of gray paint for Hugh Budwell.
Figure/symbol	Didn't invoice #87456-901 allow us a 3 1/5% discount--or was it 3 2/5%?
Adjacent reaches	There were three points on Kili's eastern slope free of rough weather.
Fluency	It is difficult for me to guide somebody further than I myself can go.

| 1 | 2 | 3 | 4 | 5 | 6 | 7 | 8 | 9 | 10 | 11 | 12 | 13 | 14 |

61B Communication Pretest: PUNCTUATION MARKS (10) full sheet; 2" top margin; DS

The following sentences will pretest your knowledge of capitalization and punctuation to be studied in this and later sections. As you type, make all necessary corrections so that the sentences will be complete and accurate. The column at the left indicates the item of punctuation being pretested.

1	Terminal punctuation	will you please take appropriate steps to rectify this matter quickly
2	Terminal punctuation	does your representative plan to be in macon sometime in april or may
3	Exclamation point	swing into action hurry the contest is not over yet you can win
4	Semicolon	mr lynn is in cleveland we do not expect him to return until friday
5	Semicolon	i expected a call from them this morning however i was disappointed
6	Semicolon	if the phone rings answer it and if it is ellen tell her i am here
7	Hyphen	twenty three of the men will complete the end of the day computations
8	Hyphen	i know that the machine is available for a 10 20 or 30 day period
9	Hyphen	any up to date equipment should be able to do a first rate job for us
10	Dash	perfection the best that can be accomplished is what we all aim for

88C Manipulative Drill: DRAWING RULES (LINES); TYPING WITH RULES ⑮

Drawing rules

Position the typewriter carriage at the point desired for a rule (line). Brace a pencil against some part of the typewriter near the ribbon; hold the pencil firmly against the paper.

Horizontal Rules. To draw horizontal rules, depress the carriage-release lever and move the carriage for the length of rule desired.

Vertical Rules. To draw vertical rules, release the ratchet; then turn the cylinder the distance of the desired rule. Reengage the ratchet.

1. Draw an approximate 4″ horizontal rule. Remove the paper; reinsert it; align with the drawn rule; center and type the following sentence:

Mail the purchase order today.

2. Note the relationship of the letters to the line. The words should be close to the line, but letters with down stems should not cut it. Repeat Drill 1.

3. Draw a square with approximate 4″ sides. Center your name in the square.

4. Draw 2 vertical rules approximately 3″ long and 1½″ apart. Between the rules, center and type in columnar fashion these figures:

$127.14   25.09   8.98   40.35

88D Manipulative Drill: CONSTRUCTING A BUSINESS FORM ⑮ Make a copy of the form below.

1. Use a 1″ top margin and a 69-space line. The carriage should lock after the sixty-ninth stroke.

2. For the first through the fourth lines, center the heading and type the title at the left margin. Backspace from the right margin and type the *Job No.* line.

3. For the fifth through seventh lines, compute placement line by line on the basis of 69 strokes in each

line. Allow a certain number of spaces for words and a certain number for underline.

4. The form is to have 3 equal-width columns. Draw vertical lines with a pencil 23 spaces from the left and right edges of the 69-space lines.

5. **Eighth line:** Center each column heading in its 23-space block.

				Words
1st line	GHESTON CABINET BUILDERS			5
2d line	Dahill Road			7
3d line	Silver Spring, MD 20906			12
4th line	Job Production Cost Sheet	Job No._____		22
5th line	Constructed for_____	Article_____		34
6th line	Description_____			50
7th line	Quantity____Date Started_____Date Completed_____			64
				92
8th line	Materials	Direct Labor	Manufacturing Expense	101
				115
				129
				143
				157
				171
				185

61C Manipulative Drill: CORRECTING COPY BY SQUEEZING AND EXPANDING WORDS

Procedures for correcting copy by squeezing and expanding words

Occasionally, a word must be corrected because a letter has been omitted or an unneeded one added. The correction involves erasing the error and either squeezing more letters into the space left by the erasure or spreading fewer letters over the space. This can be accomplished in three ways:

1. If your typewriter has a half-space key, hold it down as you strike the individual letters.

2. Hold down the space bar as you type the individual letters (unless your machine has an electric repeat bar).

3. Position the carriage by hand or with the backspace key. (Center the alignment indicator *between* the marks on the alignment scale.)

SQUEEZING WORDS

> The bys left for the footbal game.

When you have omitted a letter in a word, erase the entire word (or use chalked paper or opaque white ink). Because 1 more letter must be inserted than the erased space contained, only ½ space will be available before and after the corrected word if the spacing of the word is to be normal.

Positioning with Half-Space Key or Space Bar: Move the carriage to the first blank space of the area. Depress and hold down the half-space key or space bar while you type the corrected word, as:

> The boys left for the football game.

Positioning by Hand: Move the carriage to the second blank space of the area; for example, 32 on your cylinder scale. With your left hand, hold the carriage with the indicator centered between 31 and 32 and type the first letter of the correction. Continue in this way, centering the indicator between the marks on the alignment scale, as:

> The boys left for the football game.

EXPANDING WORDS

When a correction involves deleting an unneeded letter, erase the entire word. Then accommodate the extra space by leaving 1½ spaces before and after the word. You can do this by following the steps for squeezing words, except that you must position the carriage 1 space to the right of the point for squeezing words. The result will appear thus:

> The students left.

NOTE: When a correction involves the insertion or deletion of more than one letter, consider carefully whether correction by squeezing or expanding is feasible. For further information, see Reference Guide page xii.

Type the problem sentences exactly as shown at the right and make the corrections needed by **squeezing** or **expanding** the words. Compare your corrected copy with the illustration of corrections below.

1. My invitation cam in he afternoon mail.
2. Do you knoww if the others aare going, too?
3. Perhaps we can leave wrk early tht day.
4. All our ork can be completed by four o'clock.

> My invitation came in the afternoon mail.
> Do you know if the others are going, too?
> Perhaps we can leave work early that day.
> All our work can be completed by four o'clock.

61D Speed/Control Building

1. Type four 1' writings on the EXPLORATION LEVEL. Record the highest GWAM achieved.

2. Type three 1' writings on the CONTROL LEVEL. Record GWAM for the most accurate writing.

6.0 AWL
70% HFW
1.7 SI

Your ability to type will be beneficial in numerous ways. Type is easier to read; and for that reason, if for no other, typing is usually preferred over handwriting for personal, official, and collegiate use. Moreover, typing saves time. Work can be done rapidly and efficiently, allowing extra time for leisure. It saves space, also; for more typed material can be arranged on a page than is feasible with handwriting.

Machine adjustments

Drill Copy. Full sheet, 70-space line, SS.

¶ Copy. Full sheet, 70-space line, DS, 5-space ¶ indention.

Production Copy. Letters: modified block style, open punctuation. Interoffice memorandums: refer if necessary to page 139. Provide reference initials. Envelopes and cc: if requested. Business forms: Use printed forms if available; if not, use half sheets and type the material as you would on a printed form. (Do not type the form itself.)

LESSON 88

88A Preparatory Practice ⑤ each line at least 3 times

Alphabet	The jarring impact of the earthquake paralyzed six old Bavarian towns.
Figure/symbol	O'Dell paid $729.38 (less 10%) for model #4560 at Birtwell & Smothers.
Double letters	Kelly will succeed in getting the committee's letters to their office.
Fluency	Man's culture lies in his ability to prize that which is good in life.

| 1 | 2 | 3 | 4 | 5 | 6 | 7 | 8 | 9 | 10 | 11 | 12 | 13 | 14 |

88B Communication Aid: SPECIAL SYMBOLS (FROM CORRECTED COPY) ⑮

Full sheet; DS; 4 spaces between columns; reading position

			Words
	Constructing SPECIAL SYMBOLS		6
Plus	Diagonal; backspace; hyphen	$+$	13
Divided by	Hyphen; backspace; colon	$\div$	21
Left bracket	Diagonal; backspace; underline; roll cylinder back one line; underline	$\lfloor$	32 / 49
Right bracket	Underline; diagonal; backspace; roll cylinder back one line; underline	$\rfloor$	50 / 56
Exponent	Ratchet release; figure	10^5	64
Degrees	Ratchet release; o (lowercase)	32°	73
Superior	Ratchet release; figure or letter	below.^{3}	83
Inferior	Ratchet release; figure or letter	H_2SO_4	93
Equals	Ratchet release; hyphens	$=$	100

61E Composition (10)

Compose a block-style letter to your instructor. Use the college address. Tell how your ability to type is improving, or explain how any difficulties might be overcome.

LESSON 62

62A Preparatory Practice (5) each line at least 3 times

Alphabet	Examine Herb's work; judge for quality; recognize needed improvements.
Figure/symbol	Felt & Blane's address is 7290 East 356th Street (Telephone 452-8134).
One hand	Drews was requested to decrease the minimum number of pollution tests.
Fluency	Many elements must be combined to produce work in which we take pride.

| 1 | 2 | 3 | 4 | 5 | 6 | 7 | 8 | 9 | 10 | 11 | 12 | 13 | 14 |

62B Communication Aid: TERMINAL PUNCTUATION (15) full sheet; 1½" top margin; 70-space line; SS; DS between items

1. For the heading, use TERMINAL PUNCTUATION.
2. Type the rules and examples (with figures).

3. Type the application paragraph, inserting the proper terminal punctuation as you type.

	Words
Rules DS	6
(1) A complete sentence has a period for terminal punctuation.	19
(2) A request in the form of a question is usually punctuated with a period.	33 / 35
(3) Use a question mark after a direct question—not after an indirect question.	49 / 51
(4) Use an exclamation point after a word, a phrase, or a sentence to indicate strong emotion or to carry sharp emphasis.	65 / 76
Examples	79
(1) The mastery of an art requires insight and technical proficiency.	93
(2) Will you please have Mr. Johns sign the six copies of the report.	107
(3) He asked how long she has worked for you. When did you hire her?	122
(4) Your sales met your quota! Congratulations! You earned a bonus!	136
Application Paragraph	145

Congratulations You have solved the problem After three days of hard work, I feel you have earned a rest You may leave early on Friday if you like Will that be suitable If so, will you please inform Miss Lee before you leave She asked when you would be finished

159
174
188
200

NOTE: Proofread work carefully before you take it from the typewriter. Don't be satisfied that a quick glance will find obvious errors, and don't be misled into believing that you will "know" when you type an error. Reread what you have typed as if you had not read it before. Check spelling, punctuation, and all figures. If you find an error, realign your work and make the correction neatly.

	Words
A GOOD MANAGER IS A GOOD LEADER	6

(¶ 1) To be a manager is to be a leader. One 14
can be a manager of things or a manager of 23
people, but it is the latter that usually brings 33
greater satisfaction––or frustration. (¶ 2) The 41
good manager is a team worker; for it is obvi- 50
ous that if he could do the thing alone, he would 60
not need a team. He works closely with his 69
subordinates; and their accomplishments, their 79
concerns, and their failures he accepts as his 88
accomplishments, his concerns, and his failures. 98
The team of a good manager pulls together 106
and, like as not, enjoys the effort. (¶ 3) A 114
good manager is tolerant of those who have 123
sincerely tried and is firm with those who 132
haven't. He tries to lead democratically by 141
group decision making; for it is difficult, if not 151
impossible, to lead anybody who does not want 160
to be led. His power to convince, he knows, 169
stands him in better stead than does his power 178
to convict. 181

(¶ 4) The degree of involvement can 187
be either a full-blown democratic style, 195
in which the group literally decides by 203
consensus and/or majority opinion, or 211
the more common consultative style in 218
which the group members discuss, de- 225
bate, argue, test, and recommend ideas 233
with the understanding that, after the 241
coals of dialectic have cooled, it is the 249
manager who reserves to himself the 256
right and responsibility to make the 264
final decision and stand clearly account- 272
able for it.[1] 275

(¶ 5) A good manager knows the strengths 282

and weaknesses of subordinates. When he 290
delegates authority, as he must, he makes his 299
assignments with the assurance that they can 308
and will be carried out. (¶ 6) The good man- 316
ager, too, has developed confidence in his own 325
ability to be a leader; and his confidence en- 334
ables him to ride out most storms––even 342
storms of criticism. In doing so, he earns the 353
respect that other managers feel they must 361
demand. (¶ 7) He has trained himself to be 370
maturely sensitive to "people problems." He 379
takes pride in his team, and they in him; and 388
this esprit de corps, in the long run, is one of 398
the truest tests of mature leadership. 406

(¶ 8) A man's emotional maturity 412
determines his ability to work effec- 419
tively with other people. There is no 427
credit due you for being old in years; 434
that is something that just happens. 442
But to be mature in thinking is a credit 450
to you because you have worked toward 458
it and developed it. Maturity is a state 466
of mind, not a date on a calendar.[2] 474

(¶ 9) To be a manager is to be a leader; and 482
the quality of leadership is determined by abil- 491
ity to initiate action, make sound decisions, 500
exercise fairness, and accept ultimate responsi- 510
bility. Leadership is often a big job. It al- 519
ways takes a unique person. 524
528

[1] James Owens, "Participation––Prove It 536
Works," Training in Business and Industry, 551
Vol. 10, No. 2 (February, 1973), p. 56. 559
[2] "To Become a Manager," The Royal Bank 570
of Canada Monthly Letter, Vol. 52, No. 1 583
(January, 1971), p. 4. 587

Problem 2: Topbound Manuscript
Retype Problem 1. Use topbound manuscript style.

62C Production Typing Information: MAILING NOTATIONS AND ATTENTION LINES IN LETTERS ③

Mailing notation in a letter

If a special mailing notation is used in a letter, type it at the left margin midway between the dateline and the first line of the letter address.

Attention line in a letter

While the attention line is still used, there is a growing preference for addressing an individual or a department in the first line of the letter address. When using the attention line, type it a double space below the letter address and a double space above the salutation, preferably at the left margin. Note that the salutation must agree with the letter address, not with the attention line.

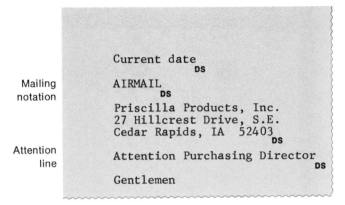

62D Production Typing: LETTERS WITH MAILING NOTATIONS AND ATTENTION LINES ㉗

Problem 1: Block Style Letter with Mailing Notation and Attention Line (WB p. 87)

Words

AIRMAIL Priscilla Products, Inc. 27 Hillcrest Drive, S.E. Cedar Rapids, IA 52403 — 20
Attention Purchasing Director Gentlemen (¶ 1) What would you do if you had a — 34
roomful of something you couldn't use? Try to clear the place out, right? Well, we — 51
are in that position. (¶ 2) We actually have a warehouse full of Lex electronic cal- — 66
culators that must be moved out right away to make room for next year's models. — 82
They are excellent machines, but--like last year's dress--they probably lack some — 99
of the "pizzazz" that model changes do provide. (¶ 3) I don't need to tell you — 114
about the outstanding performance of the Lex. It was a bargain at its original — 130
price! Nevertheless, we are sending you airmail a special price list for these — 146
calculators and are offering a discount on even these reduced prices. (¶ 4) We plan — 161
to install our new stock early next month. If you are interested in buying ten (our — 178
minimum order at these prices) or more Lex calculators--with satisfactory per- — 194
formance guaranteed--act quickly! Sincerely yours Raymond J. Spadafore Sales — 209
Manager xx — 211/228

Problem 2: Modified Block Letter with Mailing Notation (WB p. 89)

Words

AIRMAIL Mr. Neil E. Belskus Director of Sales Priscilla Products, Inc. 27 Hill- — 19
crest Drive, S.E. Cedar Rapids, IA 52403 Dear Neil (¶ 1) Thank you for your — 33
recent letter confirming our appointment in Chicago for Monday of next week at — 49
the Hotel DeSoto. (¶ 2) In response to your inquiry about the use of electronic — 64
calculators by our field personnel, I can assure you that our people use them and — 80
use them very successfully. (¶ 3) We decided to buy calculators last year after — 95
conducting a survey in which our field personnel were asked to tell us frankly — 111
whether they thought such equipment would be a good investment. In convincing — 127
numbers they enthusiastically supported a plan to purchase calculators. (¶ 4) If you — 143
want further information about the plan we use, Neil, let's discuss it further in — 159
Chicago. I look forward to meeting with you. Sincerely yours Kenneth L. Rostow — 176
Sales Manager xx — 179/201

LESSON 87

87A Preparatory Practice (5) each line at least 3 times

Alphabet	James Forrest's proxy quickly voted to recognize the required by-laws.
Figure/symbol	"My rate of return," he said, "can be 32½% ($1,385 + $4,260) by 1979."
Direct reaches	Dee longed to troll for muskellunge, so Polly swerved to deeper water.
Fluency	We can't find time to do a job right--but we find time to do it twice.
	| 1 | 2 | 3 | 4 | 5 | 6 | 7 | 8 | 9 | 10 | 11 | 12 | 13 | 14 |

87B Growth Index (15) two 5′ writings; compute GWAM for both writings

All letters are used.

		GWAM 1′	GWAM 5′	
¶ 1 1.5 SI 5.6 AWL 80% HFW	It has been stated that to know abundance is to tolerate extrava-	13	3	53
	gance. After all, what is so wrong about wasting what we have much of?	28	6	56
	The problem seems to be that wastefulness can become habitual. We stop	42	8	59
	being careful. We waste time, energy, money, and natural resources. We	57	11	62
	waste in little ways and big. We waste what is our own and what belongs	71	14	64
	to others.	73	15	65
¶ 2 1.5 SI 5.6 AWL 80% HFW	There seems to be a kind of joyous quality that goes with being	13	17	68
	wasteful, a kind of reckless abandon that implies that we do not need	27	20	71
	to be careful or thoughtful about what we do. Logically, waste can be	41	23	73
	tolerated when and where there is unlimited supply; unhappily, though,	55	26	76
	most of the things that we need or enjoy are in limited supply--things	69	29	79
	like time, energy, goods, money, and resources.	79	30	81
¶ 3 1.5 SI 5.6 AWL 80% HFW	It is well, therefore, to be economical in the use of all things.	13	33	84
	Regardless of where waste is found--in the home, in business, or in the	28	36	87
	political world--it is generally a sign of inefficiency. Waste is con-	42	39	89
	trolled only when people become concerned about it, watch for it, and	56	42	92
	eliminate it. In other words, waste stops when people care enough to	70	44	95
	stop it. When waste is not stopped and is allowed to go unchecked, it	84	47	98
	immediately jeopardizes all chances for success of any venture of which	99	50	100
	it is part.	101	51	101
1′ GWAM	| 1 | 2 | 3 | 4 | 5 | 6 | 7 | 8 | 9 | 10 | 11 | 12 | 13 | 14 |			
5′ GWAM	| 1 | 2 | 3 |			

87C Production Measurement: MANUSCRIPTS (30)

Type for 20′. Correct all errors. When you are finished, compute *n-pram*. Use margins appropriate for your typewriter. Refer to page 166 if necessary.

Problem 3: Modified Block Letter with Mailing Notation and Attention Line *(WB p. 91)*

Words

AIRMAIL American Business Machines, Inc. 11
1570 Armstrong Street New Haven, CT 19
06511 Attention Sales Manager Gentlemen 27
(¶ 1) We are considering the purchase of 34
about 100 small electronic calculators for field 43
use. These machines would be nonmemory 51
models capable of handling the basic arith- 60
metic processes. (¶ 2) If you care to submit 68
a bid for our consideration, you are invited to 77
do so. Your bid must be received within the 86
next ten days, however; for we want to move 95
quickly. Yours very truly Ms. Claudia de 103
Vries Purchasing Director xx 109/126

Problem 4: Modified Block Letter with Mailing Notation and Attention Line *(WB p. 93)*

Type a copy of the letter in Problem 3. Address it to: V-E-M Company 9 La Sorbona San Juan, PR 00927.

LESSON 63

63A Preparatory Practice [5] each line at least 3 times

Alphabet	The exact propinquity of the moving red object was quickly recognized.
Figure/symbol	Exactly 25 7/16 of the solids (384 pounds) must be added at 10:29 a.m.
Long words	Management development must challenge the manager to question success.
Fluency	Lucky is the man with workable plans for what he wants his life to be.

| 1 | 2 | 3 | 4 | 5 | 6 | 7 | 8 | 9 | 10 | 11 | 12 | 13 | 14 |

63B Communication Aid: SEMICOLON AND COLON [15] 1½″ top margin; 70-space line; SS; DS between items

1. For the heading, use SEMICOLON AND COLON.
2. Type the rules and examples (with figures).
3. Type the application paragraph, inserting the appropriate punctuation as you type.

Words

Rules 6

(1) Use a semicolon between independent clauses of a compound sentence 20
when no conjunction is used. 26

(2) Use a semicolon between independent clauses of a compound sentence 41
that are joined by a conjunctive adverb (however, therefore, etc.). 54

(3) Use a semicolon to separate independent clauses of a compound sen- 68
tence if any of the clauses are punctuated with commas. 80

(4) Use a colon to introduce an enumeration or listing. 91

Examples 95

(1) The statements did not come with his letter; they may come today. 109

(2) We had engine trouble; consequently, we could not arrive in time. 123

(3) You can take Fay, Helen, and John; and the others will go by bus. 137

(4) Please ship us the following parts: fuse box, light, and switch. 151

Application Paragraph 160

The amount was due last week but it has not been paid The goods 173
have been received therefore there is no reason for delay We cannot 188
claim the discount which was five percent but we can avoid the penalty 203
Please type these items a letter a check and an airmail envelope 217

Unpublished report

"Commentary." A daily analysis of news broadcast on Radio Station
KDKA, Pittsburgh, Pennsylvania, January 11, 1974.

16
26

"Don't Drink the Water." _Newsweek_ (July 23, 1973), p. 48.

40

Magazine articles

Grant, Patricia S. "The Lot of a Latter-Day Edison." _Money_, Vol.
2, No. 8 (August, 1973), p. 40.

54
61

Two-author book

Keithley, Erwin M., and Philip J. Schreiner. _A Manual of Style
for the Preparation of Papers & Reports_, 2d ed. Cincinnati:
South-Western Publishing Co., 1971.

77
98
105

Lecture notes

Kerwin, E. R. "Will the Real Office Expert Please Stand Up." From
a talk given before the Portland, Maine, Chamber of Commerce,
September 15, 1974.

119
131
136

One-author book

Lawrence, T. E. _Seven Pillars of Wisdom_. Garden City: Doubleday
& Company, Inc., 1935.

154
158

"A" disregarded in alphabetizing

A Manual of Style, 12th ed. Chicago: The University of Chicago
Press, 1969.

175
178

Author and editors cited

Perrin, Porter G. _Writer's Guide and Index to English_, 4th ed.,
prepared and edited by Karl W. Dykema and Wilma R. Ebbitt.
Chicago: Scott, Foresman and Company, 1965.

198
209
219

No author cited

Savings and Loan Fact Book. Chicago: United States Savings and
Loan League, 1971.

237
241

Edition number

Turabian, Kate L. _A Manual for Writers of Term Papers, Theses,
and Dissertations_, 3d ed., Rev. Chicago: The University
of Chicago Press, 1967.

262
277
282

Government publication

U.S. Department of Commerce, Bureau of the Census, _Statistical Abstract of the United States, 1972_, 93d ed. Washington: U.S.
Government Printing Office, 1972.

298
317
324

Problem 2: Title Page

1. Center on a full sheet of paper the items as shown at
the right. Follow the vertical spacing directions (6 vertical lines to an inch).

2. When you have the title page, assemble your papers
in this order:

> Title page (this problem)
> Manuscript pages (83C, pages 169-171)
> Bibliography page (Problem 1, above)

3. Fasten the sheets together across the top edge, ½″
from the top of the paper.

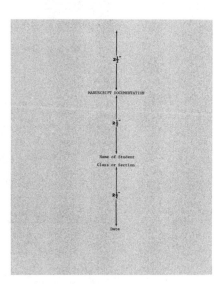

63C Production Typing Information: SUBJECT LINE AND REPLY REFERENCE NOTATION [5]

Subject line

A *subject line*, when used, is typed a double space below the salutation. In the block style or the AMS simplified letter style (page 117), the subject line is typed at the left margin. In other styles it may be typed (1) at the left margin, (2) at paragraph point, or (3) centered. The word *Subject*, when used in the subject line, is followed by a colon and is typed in all capitals or with only the first letter capitalized. It may also be omitted (as in the AMS simplified letter style).

Centered subject line

```
Ms. Claudia de Vries
Purchasing Director
Priscilla Products, Inc.
27 Hillcrest Drive, S.E.

Dear Ms. de Vries

          SUBJECT:  Your Request for Quot

We can quote you a price of $11,500, f.o
```

Reply reference notation

Some writers ask that a reply to a letter mention a file or case number. If the letterhead provides a printed position for this information (usually at the top of the letterhead), supply it there. If not, type the reply reference notation as you would type a subject line. The word *Reference* or *Re* may be typed before the notation.

Blocked reply reference notation

```
Mr. L. E. Martinez
Sales Manager
V-E-M Company
9 La Sorbona
San Juan, PR  00927

Dear Mr. Martinez

Reference:  #3289

Thank you for your prompt response to ou
```

63D Production Typing: LETTERS WITH SUBJECT LINES AND REPLY REFERENCE NOTATIONS [25]

Problem 1: Modified Block Letter with Blocked Subject Line (*WB p. 95*)

Words

Ms. Claudia de Vries Purchasing Director Priscilla Products, Inc. 16
27 Hillcrest Drive, S.E. Cedar Rapids, IA 52403 Dear Claudia 29
SUBJECT: The Premier SL Electronic Calculator (¶ 1) In response to 41
our telephone conversation yesterday afternoon, I'm happy to quote 54
you a firm price of $12,150 for 100 Premier SL Electronic Calcula- 67
tors. This is $10.50 (each) less than our regular price. (¶ 2) We 79
shall furnish certificates of warranty, good for two years, autho- 92
rizing repair or replacement of parts lost, worn, or damaged in normal 107
use. These certificates can be used at any authorized repair shop 120
listed on the warranties. We also guarantee delivery within 60 133
days of receipt of order. (¶ 3) We appreciate your support of local 145
business, Claudia. Let's keep Cedar Rapids growing. Cordially yours 159
Grant A. Lidke Manager xx 164/187

LESSON 86

86A Preparatory Practice [5] each line at least 3 times

Alphabet	Joel quickly extinguished the blazing fire in the powerful locomotive.
Figure/symbol	My new figures show a 1,235,780 increase, or 469¼% more than expected.
e, i	Desiring to lose weight, I used my weird diet until the eightieth day.
Fluency	Change can be beneficial, but no elemental law says that it always is.
	| 1 | 2 | 3 | 4 | 5 | 6 | 7 | 8 | 9 | 10 | 11 | 12 | 13 | 14 |

86B Technique Improvement: STROKING [5] each line at least twice

1	Direct reaches	Myron Trumble tried to unlock the gate in front of the deserted house.
2	Direct reaches	John Price agreed to pay the invoice if he received a receipt from us.
3	1st/2d fingers	Five Navy tugs tried to enter the harbor before fog ruined visibility.
4	1st/2d fingers	Frederick Hunt informed them they might apply for the jobs on Tuesday.
5	3d/4th fingers	As Alex pointed out in his paper, the essay questions were quite easy.
6	3d/4th fingers	Our annual contract renewal calls for adequate provisions for storage.
7	Long reaches	I may prepare a summary of my lumber and linoleum purchases this year.
8	Long reaches	Many young people ate their lunch at Lenny Brigg's cafe in Huntsville.
		| 1 | 2 | 3 | 4 | 5 | 6 | 7 | 8 | 9 | 10 | 11 | 12 | 13 | 14 |

86C Sentence Guided Writings [10]

Type four or more errorless copies of each line.

Alternative Directions:
Type 2 or more 1′ writings on each sentence with the guide called each 15″, 12″, or 10″.

		GWAM 15″	12″	10″
Long reaches	We filed an application for the funds before reading the announcement.	56	70	84
Figure/symbol	In 1974, storms delayed delivery of 6,380 tons (25% of all shipments).	56	70	84
Long reaches	Under this new system, all their employees receive annuities annually.	56	70	84
Figure/symbol	The report for 1975 showed a profit of $327,460, or a net gain of 18%.	56	70	84
	| 1 | 2 | 3 | 4 | 5 | 6 | 7 | 8 | 9 | 10 | 11 | 12 | 13 | 14 |			

86D Production Typing: BIBLIOGRAPHY AND TITLE PAGE [30]

Problem 1: Bibliography

Type the bibliography shown on page 175 as the last page of the topbound manuscript typed as 83C, pages 169-171. Use the same margins that you used for page 1 of the manuscript. SS; DS between items. Transpose the name of only the first of 2 or more authors.

A bibliography is arranged alphabetically by the first word of an entry (disregarding *A*, *An*, and *The*). Start the first line of each entry at the left margin; set a tab stop and indent the second and subsequent lines 5 spaces. Number the page appropriately.

Problem 2: Modified Block Letter with Mailing Notation and Centered Subject Line *(WB p. 97)*

Words

AIRMAIL—SPECIAL DELIVERY Ms. Claudia de Vries Purchasing Director 17
Priscilla Products, Inc. 27 Hillcrest Drive, S.E. Cedar Rapids, IA 30
52403 Dear Ms. de Vries SUBJECT: Your Request for Quotation (¶ 1) 42
We can quote you a price of $11,500, f.o.b. Cedar Rapids, for 100 Vulcan 57
Electronic Calculators, Model 7-D. The regular price of this model is 71
$139 each; thus we are offering a discount of over 17 percent. (¶ 2) The 85
Vulcan 7-D will give you many years of top-quality service. Yesterday 99
afternoon we asked Arnold & Company, our representatives in your area, 113
to demonstrate the 7-D for you. We also airmailed to you a complete set 128
of literature on this model. Read it carefully; then give the machine 142
itself a thorough testing. (¶ 3) Arnold & Company will call you for an 155
appointment for the demonstration. Please call or write me personally 170
when I can be of further assistance. Sincerely yours Paul P. Wither- 183
spoon Sales Manager xx 188/216

Problem 3: Modified Block Letter with Mailing Notation and Reply Reference Notation *(WB p. 99)*

Words

AIRMAIL Mr. L. E. Martinez Sales Manager V-E-M Company 9 La 12
Sorbona San Juan, PR 00927 Dear Mr. Martinez Reference: #3289 28
(¶ 1) Thank you for your prompt response to our request for a price 40
quotation on electronic calculators. (¶ 2) The ROMY Model BP-738 seems 53
to meet our requirements. It will be helpful to us, therefore, if you will 69
(1) quote us final prices for 100 of these machines, (2) ship us a machine 84
for trial or have a local representative demonstrate one for us, and (3) indi- 99
cate possible delivery dates. (¶ 3) A prompt response will again be appre- 113
ciated. Yours truly Ms. Claudia de Vries Purchasing Director xx 125/143

LESSON 64

64A Preparatory Practice [5] each line at least 3 times

Alphabet	Equip the tug Zyma B for work and expect her to be judged serviceable.
Figure/symbol	Employee #4870 at B-P-W & Company worked from 1:30 to 5:27 for $36.89.
Double letters	All his possessions have been transferred to your home in Tallahassee.
Fluency	Let us always play the game fairly, the way it was meant to be played.

| 1 | 2 | 3 | 4 | 5 | 6 | 7 | 8 | 9 | 10 | 11 | 12 | 13 | 14 |

LESSON 85

85A Preparatory Practice [5] each line at least 3 times

Alphabet — Clark now realizes that his brusque expletives frightened my dog Jinx.

Figure/symbol — My May 14 receipt (#5302) was stamped, "Note that Rule 76-98 applies."

Home row — Jason thanked the Highland laddies and lassies for dancing the flings.

Fluency — I shall be the captain of my own future; nobody else can do it for me.

| 1 | 2 | 3 | 4 | 5 | 6 | 7 | 8 | 9 | 10 | 11 | 12 | 13 | 14 |

85B Speed Building: STATISTICAL COPY [15] Goals are marked in the copy.

1. Type three copies of the ¶. Strive for smooth, even stroking.
2. Type three 1½″ writings; each for 90 or more words in that time (60 wam).

Alternate:

1. Type three ½″ writings; reach for 30 or more words in that time.
2. Type three 1½′ writings; reach for 90 or more words

1.5 SI
5.6 AWL
80% HFW

1′ GWAM

Serious accidents happen all over the house: 30 percent in the 13
kitchen or dining area; 24 percent on the porch or in the yard; 18 per- 27
cent in the living room or bedroom; 12 percent on steps; 3 percent in 41
the bathroom; 3 percent in the cellar; 2 percent in the hall; 1 percent 55
in the garage; and 7 percent in other places. They can happen in all 69
sorts of ways: 38 percent result from a fall on the level; 14 percent 84
from a fall from above; 13 percent from an object that is hot or afire; 98
9 percent from the handling of materials; 2 percent from falling mate- 112
rials; and 10 percent from yet other causes. 121

1′ GWAM | 1 | 2 | 3 | 4 | 5 | 6 | 7 | 8 | 9 | 10 | 11 | 12 | 13 | 14 |

85C Technique Improvement: CORRECTING COPY [10] Type each line DS exactly as it appears; then take appropriate steps to correct the errors.

1 Several important inventions and discoervies changed their operations.
2 A plan will help you do th things you should when you should do hem.
3 Mr Rusella wasnt able to offer us any assistance at that exact time.
4 Who can know the great things he can do untl he tries to do his best.
5 There is nothng dangerous about he great movement that is udnerway.

85D Production Typing: TOPBOUND MANUSCRIPT WITH FOOTNOTES [20] Continue typing 83C, pages 169-171.

64B **Communication Aid:** COLON AND HYPHEN [15] **1½″ top margin; 70-space line; SS; DS between items**

1. For the heading, use COLON AND HYPHEN.
2. Type the rules and examples (with figures).
3. Type the application paragraph, inserting the appropriate punctuation as you type.

Words

Rules 6

(1) Use a colon to introduce a question or long quotation. 18

(2) Two spaces follow a colon except when used between sets of reference 32
initials in a letter or to separate hours and minutes. As a rule, 46
use figures with a.m. and p.m. 52

(3) Use a hyphen in compound numbers from twenty-one to ninety-nine. 66

(4) Retain the hyphen in a series of compounds with the same ending or 81
beginning; this is called suspended hyphenation. 95

Examples 99

(1) The question is this: What experience is necessary for the jobs? 113

(2) We finished the tour at 12:45 p.m. and left the city at 5:26 p.m. 127

(3) Approximately thirty-seven of the forty-eight delegates attended. 141

(4) Each 2- and 3-day tour is taken in a school-owned or -leased bus. 155

Application Paragraph 164

The question that puzzles me is this With nearly forty two of 177
the forty five freight cars unloaded why is it necessary to assign 190
another two or three man team to them The cars I believe can be 204
unloaded by 2 30 p m today and then they can be shifted to a siding 218

64C **Production Typing Information:** COMPANY NAME IN CLOSING LINES; ENCLOSURE NOTATION [5]

Company name in closing lines

If the company name appears in the closing lines, type it in all capitals, a double space below the complimentary close as shown in the illustration at the right. The writer's name is then typed on the fourth line below the company name.

Enclosure notations

When items other than the letter itself are included in the envelope, the word *Enclosure* or *Enclosures* is typed a double space below the reference initials. If desired, a colon may be placed after the word *Enclosure* and the number of enclosures, the serial number of an enclosure, or a few identifying words typed, as:

Enclosures: 3

Enclosures: Contract No. 762-1-A
Contract No. 762-1-B

Enclosure: Operating Manual

```
Meanwhile, we have shipped a ROM
freight for trial in your office
favorable reply from you soon.
                    DS
Cordially yours
                    DS
V-E-M COMPANY                          (Company name)
                    3 blank lines


L. E. Martinez
Sales Manager

xx

Enclosure                              (Enclosure notation)
```

LESSON 84

84A Preparatory Practice [5] each line at least 3 times

Alphabet	Our quiz grades improved quickly, but we failed the June examinations.
Figure/symbol	My May 7 memo read, "386 rulers @ 49¢; 5 1/3% if paid within 20 days."
Shift keys	Mary, Jack, and Sarah Jane visited St. Paul, Minnesota, last November.
Fluency	We can always do more good by being good than we can in any other way.
	| 1 | 2 | 3 | 4 | 5 | 6 | 7 | 8 | 9 | 10 | 11 | 12 | 13 | 14 |

84B Technique Improvement: STROKING [5] each line 3 times or two ½′ writings on each line

3d/4th fingers	Professor Lopez' quiz in law was two hours long; still, we all passed.
One hand	My secretary addressed every card for the union assembly on Wednesday.
Long words	Mr. Tryon outlined economic implications and technical specifications.
Double letters	Miss Farrell will issue free passes to all of Bill Lee's office staff.
	| 1 | 2 | 3 | 4 | 5 | 6 | 7 | 8 | 9 | 10 | 11 | 12 | 13 | 14 |

84C Communication Aid: CAPITALIZATION [10]

1. For the heading, type CAPITALIZATION.
2. Type the rules and examples given below (with figures); underline the side headings.
3. Type the application paragraph, inserting the proper punctuation as you type.

Words

Rules 8

(1) Usually, capitalize nouns that immediately precede a number stated 19
in figures. The word page is not ordinarily capitalized unless it 34
begins a sentence. Common nouns are not capitalized if No. or # 47
is used. 49

(2) Capitalize only the first word of a complimentary close. 61

(3) Capitalize all titles used in the address and closing lines of busi- 75
ness letters. 78

(4) Capitalize a title preceding a name if used as part of the name. In 93
business usage, titles that follow a name are not usually capitalized. 107

Examples 111

(1) Payment of our invoice No. 372 is recorded in Journal 4, page 56. 125

(2) Capitalize first words of complimentary closes: Sincerely yours. 139

(3) Capitalize titles in letter addresses: Mr. John Lowe, Treasurer. 153

(4) The club manager met President Don Fox and Cy Lee, the secretary. 167

Application Paragraph 176

i asked the assistant librarian to help me find professor william 189
webers book on english grammar. he referred me to room 103 shelf 8. 204
the book indicates on page 33 that the following capitalization is 217
correct very truly yours dear dean hill paragraph 6 policy #85. 231

84D Production Typing: TOPBOUND MANUSCRIPT WITH FOOTNOTES [30] Continue typing 83C, pages 169-171.

64D Production Typing: LETTERS WITH COMPANY NAME IN CLOSING; ENCLOSURE NOTATION [25]

Problem 1: Block Style Letter; Company Name in Closing Lines; Enclosure *(WB p. 81)*

Because of the special lines in this letter, type the date 3 lines higher than usual.

Words
AIRMAIL Ms. Claudia de Vries Purchasing 11
Director Priscilla Products, Inc. 27 Hillcrest 20
Drive, S.E. Cedar Rapids, IA 52403 Dear 29
Ms. de Vries SUBJECT: ROMY Electronic 34
Calculators (¶ 1) We can offer a price of 44
$12,000 (f.o.b. Cedar Rapids) for 100 ROMY 52
BP-738 Electronic Calculators, with a 5 per- 61
cent discount if paid within 30 days of invoice 70
date. (¶ 2) The ROMY BP-738 carries a 77
2-year warranty. If for any reason a ROMY 85
BP-738 fails to perform properly during that 94
period, it will be repaired without charge if 104
returned to us in San Juan. (¶ 3) We have 111
received notice from one of our correspondent 120
companies of a new calculator they are about 129
ready to place on the market. This calculator 138
is hand-size, runs on either AC current or a 148
built-in battery, and carries a warranty similar 157
to the one offered with the ROMY. We shall 166
be able to offer this machine to you at less 175
than $70 per unit; but I doubt that we shall 184
have them in stock for several months yet. 193
Additional information on this machine is en- 202
closed. (¶ 4) Meanwhile, we have shipped a 209
ROMY BP-738 to you via airfreight for trial 218
in your office. We hope to have a favorable 227
reply from you soon. Cordially yours V-E-M 236
COMPANY L. E. Martinez Sales Manager 244
xx Enclosure 246/270

Problem 2: Block Style Letter with Enclosure Notation *(WB p. 103)*

Words
AIRMAIL Priscilla Products, Inc. 27 Hill- 11
crest Drive, S.E. Cedar Rapids, IA 52403 19
Attention Ms. Claudia de Vries Gentlemen 28
(¶ 1) We regret that we must withdraw our 35
recent sales offer on quantities of Lex elec- 44
tronic calculators. Our complete stock has 52
been sold. (¶ 2) We are pleased to announce, 60
however, that the new Model LEX J/K cal- 68
culator is now in stock. It has features that 78
surprise even us, and we have been working 86
with electronic calculators for a long time. 95
(¶ 3) Take a few minutes to examine the 102
brochure we have enclosed. We believe it will 112
convince you that the LEX J/K is the NOW 120
machine. No modern office can afford to be 129
without it. Sincerely yours Raymond J. 137
Spadafore Sales Manager xx Enclosure: 144
LEX J/K brochure 148/170

Problem 3: Modified Block Style Letter with Special Lines *(WB p. 105)*

Provide necessary commas and semicolons.

Words
Ms. Claudia de Vries Purchasing Director 11
Priscilla Products, Inc. 27 Hillcrest Drive 20
S.E. Cedar Rapids IA 52403 Dear Ms. 28
de Vries SUBJECT: Your Request for Bid 36
(¶ 1) Thank you for your letter inviting us 43
to submit a bid on 100 electronic calculators. 53
(¶ 2) At the present time we do not stock 60
electronic calculators. We have been in busi- 69
ness only nine months therefore we have re- 78
stricted our initial stock to a fine offering of 88
Orion typewriters as well as a complete line 97
of Spartan metal office furniture. Literature 106
describing this outstanding office equipment 115
is enclosed. (¶ 3) We regret that we cannot 123
bid now however we should appreciate hear- 132
ing from you when you again have need for 140
office furnishings. Very truly yours RAM- 148
PARTS OFFICE SUPPLY COMPANY Miss 155
Tommie R. Smith Manager xx Enclosures 162/185

LESSON 65

65A Preparatory Practice [5] each line at least 3 times

Alphabet	Bud's dog isn't lazy; he quickly makes five extra jumps to win prizes.
Figure/symbol	For $274.31 (plus tax), Mr. Stone can take UAL Flight 580 at 6:19 a.m.
Shift keys	Bob and Jim Smith visited the Hillsdale County Fair in July or August.
Fluency	Now is the time to find out how I can contribute to the world of work.

| 1 | 2 | 3 | 4 | 5 | 6 | 7 | 8 | 9 | 10 | 11 | 12 | 13 | 14 |

on which some authorities disagree. (¶13) 735
Short form. There is a generally accepted brief 747
form of footnote that can be used when a com- 756
plete bibliography is provided with a report. 765
The form is shown as Footnote 3, below.[3] 773
(¶14) Complete form. The complete footnote 783
for a book reference is given in Footnote 1. 793
When no author's name is given for a refer- 801
ence, the style shown in Footnote 4 is used.[4] 810
(¶15) When reference is made to a magazine 818
article, the style used in Footnote 5 is recom- 827
mended.[5] When no author is named for a 835
magazine article or when volume and issue 843
numbers are not given, however, the style 852
shown as Footnote 6 is preferred.[6] (¶16) 859
Governmental agencies acting as authors are 868
listed with the largest body first, followed by 877
its division and subdivision in order. For 886
printed works available from the U.S. Govern- 895
ment Printing Office, the facts of publication 904
are as shown.[7] (¶17) Unpublished reports, 911
minutes, letters, and the like are documented 920
informally by showing available facts in logi- 929
cal order without parentheses.[8] For references 939
to lectures and speeches, the pertinent avail- 948
able facts are placed in parentheses after the 957
name of the speaker and the title of the lecture 967
or speech.[9] 969

Special Short Forms of Footnotes 982

(¶18) Subsequent footnotes that would repeat 990
most or all of one already used are not re- 999
peated in their entirety. For example, when 1008
two footnotes contain references to the same 1017
work and one follows the other without inter- 1025
vening footnotes, use ibid., the abbreviation 1035
for ibidem (in the same place). Include the 1046
page number if it differs from the original 1054
footnote.[10] (¶19) When a footnote refers to 1062
a different page in a work already cited and 1071
one or two footnotes separate it from the 1080
original one, use the author's name and the 1088
notation op. cit., the abbreviation for opere 1100

citato (in the work cited), with the page num- 1110
ber. Repeating the name of the publication 1119
and other identifying data is unnecessary.[11] 1128
(¶20) A footnote reference to the exact mate- 1136
rial cited previously--but with interrupting 1145
footnotes--needs no page reference, only the 1154
author's name and loc. cit. (for loco citato, in 1167
the place cited).[12] 1171
SS 1174
DS

[1] Erwin M. Keithley and Philip J. Schreiner, 1183
A Manual of Style for the Preparation of 1199
Papers & Reports (2d ed.; Cincinnati: South- 1211
Western Publishing Co., 1971), p. 38. 1219

[2] Kate L. Turabian, A Manual for Writers of 1232
Term Papers, Theses, and Dissertations (3d 1248
ed., Rev.; Chicago: The University of Chi- 1257
cago Press, 1967), p. 27. 1262

[3] T. F. Lawrence, Seven Pillars of Wisdom, 1275
p. 295. 1277

[4] Savings and Loan Fact Book (Chicago: 1289
United States Savings and Loan League, 1297
1971), p. 9. 1300

[5] Patricia S. Grant, "The Lot of a Latter-Day 1309
Edison," Money, Vol. 2, No. 8 (August, 1973), 1319
p. 40. 1321

[6] "Don't Drink the Water," Newsweek (July 1331
23, 1973), p. 48. 1335

[7] U.S. Department of Commerce, Bureau of 1343
the Census, Statistical Abstract of the United 1359
States, 1972 (93d ed.; Washington: U.S. Gov- 1370
ernment Printing Office, 1972), p. 63. 1378

[8] Quoted from "Commentary," a daily analy- 1386
sis of news broadcast on Radio Station KDKA, 1395
Pittsburgh, Pa., January 11, 1974. 1402

[9] E. R. Kerwin, "Will the Real Office Expert 1411
Please Stand Up." (From a talk given before 1420
the Portland, Maine, Chamber of Commerce, 1428
September 15, 1974). 1432

[10] Ibid., pp. 19-20. 1437

[11] Lawrence, op. cit., p. 192. 1445

[12] Turabian, loc. cit. 1450

65B Communication Aid: HYPHEN AND DASH [15] full sheet; 1½″ top margin; SS; DS between items; 70-space line

1. For the heading, use HYPHEN AND DASH.
2. Type the rules and examples (with figures).
3. Type the application paragraph, inserting the appropriate punctuation as you type.

Words

Rules 5

(1) Use a hyphen to join compound adjectives preceding a noun. 18

(2) Use a dash (--) to indicate a sudden change in thought. 30

(3) Use a dash (--) for emphasis to set off an appositive. 42

(4) Use a dash (--) to introduce the name of an author when it follows 56
a direct quotation. 61

Examples 64

(1) The well-known statesman has been appointed for a four-year term. 78

(2) The best way--perhaps the only way--to have friends is to be one. 92

(3) Your stars--freedom, opportunity, faith--are bright and constant. 107

(4) "The road to freedom, while narrow, is a two-way street."--Gross. 121

Application Paragraph 129

Our last minute instructions indicate that all B rated equipment 142
must be replaced. Our annual budget the one we prepared last fall 156
does not provide for this expense. There is one way and only one for 171
us to do this: "Make a decision and follow it through." Dewey 183

65C Production Typing Information: CARBON COPY NOTATION AND POSTSCRIPT [5]

Carbon copy notation

A carbon copy notation (cc) indicates for whom copies of the letter were made. It is typed a double space below the reference initials or the enclosure notation, if one is used. If this or some other notation is to appear on the carbon copy only (blind carbon copy), type the notation (bcc or other) on a piece of paper held between the typewriter ribbon and the original (top) sheet.

Postscript

Type a postscript a double space below the last item at the end of a letter. The letters *P.S.* need not be used. A postscript should be blocked or indented to agree with the style used in other paragraphs of the letter.

```
By the way, Paul Chapman, mid
Premier Equipment Company, wi
Tuesday.  He and I would like
with you and your associates.

Cordially yours



Grant A. Lidke, Manager

xx

Enclosure

cc Mr. Paul Chapman

I shall call your office on M
```

Carbon copy notation

Postscript

MANUSCRIPT DOCUMENTATION 5

TS

(¶1) When, within a manuscript, a writer cites 13
material that did not originate with him, he 22
must acknowledge the source of the informa- 31
tion. This obligation is usually satisfied with 41
footnotes, a process of documentation. Foot- 49
notes serve other purposes as well. 57

(DS; then double-indent and SS the quoted ¶.)

(¶2) Footnotes provide the most versa- 63
tile method for referring the reader to 71
information outside the text material. 79
They may be used for these purposes: 87
(1) acknowledge the source of infor- 94
mation, (2) support arguments, (3) 101
provide additional material for the 108
reader, (4) identify quoted material, 115
(5) elaborate on the meaning within 123
the text, or (6) refer the reader to 130
other parts of the text.[1] 135

TS

Placement of Footnote Reference Figures 151

(¶3) Footnotes are indicated by typing a ref- 159
erence figure as a superior figure following 168
the material being documented, placed where a 177
minimum interruption of thought results. Four 186
placements of footnote reference figures in 195
common use are described below. (¶4) <u>After</u> 204
<u>the quotation</u>. The preferred position of the 216
reference figures is at the end of material 224
that is directly or indirectly quoted or para- 233
phrased. (¶5) <u>After the introductory state-</u> 247
<u>ment</u>. An almost equally accepted placement is 257
at the end of the statement that introduces 266
directly quoted material. (¶6) <u>After the name</u> 277
<u>of the author</u>. A less accepted practice, but one 289
enjoying considerable use, is to place the refer- 299
ence figure after the name of the author of the 309
cited work. A major disadvantage of this prac- 318
tice is the inconsistency that results if refer- 328
ences are made to materials without mention- 336
ing the author's name in the body of the 344
manuscript or when reference is made to ma- 353
terials without a named author. (¶7) <u>After a</u> 362

side or a paragraph heading. If most or all of 377
the material following the heading is based 386
on source material, it is acceptable to place 395
the reference figure following the side or para- 405
graph heading. The side heading that intro- 413
duces the next paragraph illustrates this 421
procedure. 424

Placement of Footnotes [2] 433

(¶8) Although footnotes may be typed in the 441
body of a manuscript directly below the line in 450
which the reference occurs, the preferred place- 459
ment is in numerical order to end approxi- 468
mately one inch from the foot of the page (even 478
on a page not completely full, such as the last 487
page of a chapter). A single space and an inch- 497
and-a-half divider line separate the footnotes 506
from the body of the report. 512

Numbering and Spacing Footnotes 525

(¶9) Each footnote should be preceded with- 532
out spacing by a reference figure raised one- 541
half line space. Footnotes should be single- 550
spaced with a double space between them. The 559
first line of a footnote should be indented to 569
paragraph point. Footnotes should preferably 578
be numbered consecutively throughout a 586
short manuscript. If a report is divided into 595
chapters, numbering can be consecutive within 604
chapters. (¶10) Two or more short footnotes 612
may be typed on one line if they are separated 622
by at least two blank spaces. In no instance, 631
however, may a footnote so begun be contin- 639
ued on a second line. (¶11) A lengthy foot- 647
note of explanatory material may be continued 656
at the foot of the next page, above any other 665
footnotes for that page. A divided footnote 674
should be broken in the middle of a sentence 683
to make it obvious that the footnote is 691
incomplete. 694

Forms of Footnotes 701

(¶12) The footnotes that follow represent the 709
consensus of authorities for basic style and 718
defensible compromises of differences on points 728

65D Production Typing: LETTERS WITH CARBON COPY NOTATIONS AND POSTSCRIPTS ㉕

Problem 1: Modified Block Style Letter with Carbon Copy Notation and Postscript (WB p. 107)

Prepare a typewritten copy of the style letter illustrated on page 133.

Problem 2: Modified Block Style Letter with Postscript (WB p. 109)

	Words
Mr. K. L. Rostow Sales Manager Lighthouse Plastics, Inc. 685 Grandview Ave-	18
nue Sioux Falls, SD 58103 Dear Ken (¶ 1) Replies have now been received	31
from each of our branch offices; and, as you predicted, the results of our survey	48
compare with those obtained from the survey your company conducted. Nearly	63
90 percent of our field personnel who responded (about 12 percent didn't) say they	79
are interested in owning a calculator to help with paperwork. (¶ 2) Accordingly,	95
we have decided to proceed with plans to purchase 100 electronic calculators and	111
to make these calculators available to field personnel at half the cost price. (¶ 3)	127
Thank you for your continued interest in our "calculator problem," Ken. Your	142
advice has indeed been helpful. Sincerely yours Neil E. Belskus Director of Sales	159
xx Clint DeLoach, who had lunch with us in Chicago, is our new Director of Adver-	175
tising. Our search ended at home!	182/202

Problem 3: Modified Block Style Letter with Enclosure Notation and Postscript (WB p. 111)

	Words
Type the date a line higher than usual. Ms. Claudia de Vries Purchasing Director Priscilla Products, Inc. 27 Hillcrest	19
Drive, S.E. Cedar Rapids, IA 52403 Dear Ms. de Vries SUBJECT: Request for	24
Bid on Electronic Calculators (¶ 1) Although we wrote you several days ago	48
declining to enter a bid for the sale of electronic calculators, we find that we can	65
now do so. (¶ 2) We are representing Vulcan Electronics, Inc., which has autho-	79
rized us to offer you a firm bid of $13,500 for an order of 100 Vulcan 7-D calculators.	97
This is a substantial reduction from the retail price, and this price is f.o.b. Cedar	114
Rapids. We can make delivery within 30 days of receipt of your order. (¶ 3) Com-	129
plete details about this fine calculator are contained in the brochure we have	145
enclosed. Notice the versatility of this machine; notice its attractiveness; notice	162
the generous warranty statement; then notice the price we are offering you.	178
(¶ 4) Please let us hear from you soon, for this offer cannot be held open indefinitely.	194
Very truly yours RAMPARTS OFFICE SUPPLY COMPANY Tommie R. Smith	208
Manager xx Enclosure If your sales manager wishes to contact us, we might	223
be able to feature a line of your products in our store.	234/257

83B Communication Aid: CAPITALIZATION ⑩

1. For the heading, type CAPITALIZATION.
2. Type the rules and examples given below (with figures); underline the side headings.

3. Type the application paragraph, inserting the proper punctuation as you type.

Full sheet; 1½" top margin; 70-space line; SS; DS between items; underline side heads

	Words
### Rules	5

(1) Capitalize the first word of a complete quotation. Do not capitalize the first word of a quotation resumed within a sentence. — 19, 32

(2) Capitalize the first word of a sentence that follows a colon. — 45

(3) Capitalize adjectives and nouns that are used as part of proper names except for geographic terms in plural form that are used with a series of proper names. — 60, 74, 78

(4) Capitalize words derived from proper nouns unless these words have acquired independent, common meanings. — 92, 100

Examples — 103

(1) "He is suffering," the critic said, "from paralysis of analysis." — 118

(2) Use this rule: Capitalize principal words in titles of articles. — 132

(3) We camped on Cedar and Moon lakes on our way to Ellis State Park. — 146

(4) He could not seem to orient himself as he traveled in the Orient. — 160

Application Paragraph — 169

after reading his paper entitled the orient today the student joked that he had not seen a turkey in turkey. young man said the professor are you trying to teach this class? no said the fellow. the professors classic reply: Then dont talk like an idiot. — 182, 196, 211, 223

83C Production Typing: TOPBOUND MANUSCRIPT WITH FOOTNOTES ㉟

1. Read the manuscript on pages 170-171 carefully so that you will understand its content before you type it.

2. Type the manuscript in topbound style (Reference: page 166). Use a 5-space ¶ indention. Number the pages.

3. Even though the problem presents all footnotes at the end of the report, type each footnote on the page on which its reference figure appears. Plan ahead to leave 5 to 7 spaces at the foot of a page for a margin, at least two lines of the paragraph, and the footnotes. At least two lines of the paragraph must be carried over to the top of the next page.

4. Number the footnotes consecutively throughout the manuscript.

5. The illustration at the right shows the second page of the manuscript typed in pica type.

NOTE: You will not finish the problem in this lesson; you will be given additional time in Lessons 84 and 85.

<u>After the name of the author</u>. A less accepted practice, but one enjoying considerable use, is to place the reference figure after the name of the author of the cited work. A major disadvantage of this practice is the inconsistency that results if references are made to materials without mentioning the author's name in the body of the manuscript or when reference is made to materials without a named author.

<u>After a side or a paragraph heading</u>. If most or all of the material following the heading is based on source material, it is acceptable to place the reference figure following the side or paragraph heading. The side heading that introduces the next paragraph illustrates this procedure.

<u>Placement of Footnotes</u>[2]

Although footnotes may be typed in the body of a manuscript directly below the line in which the reference occurs, the preferred placement is in numerical order to end approximately one inch from the foot of the page (even on a page not completely full, such as the last page of a chapter). A single space and an inch-and-a-half divider line separate the footnotes from the body of the report.

<u>Numbering and Spacing Footnotes</u>

Each footnote should be preceded without spacing by a reference figure raised one-half line space. Footnotes should be single-spaced

[2]Kate L. Turabian, <u>A Manual for Writers of Term Papers, Theses, and Dissertations</u> (3d ed., Rev.; Chicago: The University of Chicago Press, 1967), p. 27.

2

Page 2 of a topbound manuscript

METRO PUBLISHING COMPANY

3642 Sheridan Road, North
Chicago, IL 60613

Cable: Metrop
Telephone: (312)671-9842

		Words in Parts	5' GWAM	
	Current date	3	1	48
Mailing notation	AIRMAIL	5	1	49
	Priscilla Products, Inc.	10	2	49
	27 Hillcrest Drive, S.E.	15	3	51
	Cedar Rapids, IA 52403	19	4	52
Attention line	Attention Office Manager	24	5	53
	Gentlemen	26	5	53
Subject or reference line	SUBJECT: Special Features in Business Letters	36	7	55

Mr. Edward Pierce has asked me to write you about our new booklet, LETTER CONSTRUCTION, that illustrates some of the special features that are from time to time found in modern business letters. These features, as illustrated in this letter, serve special functions that can improve the efficiency of correspondence.

	47	9	57
	58	12	59
	69	14	62
	80	16	64
	91	18	66
	99	20	68

Except for certain limitations imposed by the AMS Simplified Letter, style and punctuation do not restrict the use of these features. Postscripts, however, are indented in the same manner as the paragraphs in the letter. A subject line may, if desired, also be indented to match paragraph indentions; or it may be centered.

	11	22	70
	22	24	72
	34	27	74
	45	29	77
	56	31	79
	65	33	81

Although the purposes of these features are special and their use limited, a good typist understands their functions and how and when to use them. The enclosed copy of LETTER CONSTRUCTION gives you further information.

	11	35	83
	22	37	85
	34	40	87
	44	42	89

	Sincerely yours	47	42	90
Company name	METRO PUBLISHING COMPANY	52	43	91
	M. J. Trussel			
	M. J. Trussel, Editor	57	44	92
		57	44	92
	stu			
Enclosure notation	Enclosure	59	45	92
Carbon copy notation	cc Mr. Edward Pierce	64	46	93
Postscript	Additional free copies of the booklet are available.	74	48	95

Style Letter 6: MODIFIED BLOCK LETTER ILLUSTRATING SPECIAL FEATURES OF A BUSINESS LETTER (Typed in Pica Type)

Problem 1: Unbound Manuscript

A WOMAN OF DISTINCTION

(¶ 1) Mary McLeod Bethune devoted almost her entire life to the development of educational opportunities for members of her race. Born in South Carolina, the first member of her immediate family not born a slave, Mary was a gifted child; and when a missionary school for black children was started in her home area, her parents expected her to attend it. (¶ 2) Although remarkably adept at schoolwork, it was her leadership qualities that set her far above others and took her to Scotia Seminary in Concord, North Carolina, from which she was graduated in 1893. After attending the Moody Bible Institute in Chicago, she returned to her hometown to teach. At age 22 she married; and although her husband insisted that she give up her job following the birth of their son, she was just as adamant that she had--as she described it-- an even higher calling in life. (¶ 3) In 1904, with a down payment of only $1.50, she rented a two-story house in Daytona Beach, Florida, where she started the Daytona Literary and Industrial School for Girls. Her school was at once successful, and later it was merged with the Cookman Institute for Men to become Bethune-Cookman College. Until her retirement in 1942, Mrs. Bethune served as president of the college. She was honored with the Springarn medal in 1935, and in 1954 she was named by the Dorie Miller Foundation as "Mother of the Century." (¶ 4) Mary McLeod Bethune was indeed a Woman of Distinction.

Problem 2: Unbound Manuscript with Footnotes

COMMUNICATIONS

(¶ 1) It can be said with a degree of certainty that a thought is nothing more than a thought until it stimulates activity. Even if a person has a "bright idea," it will go unnoticed unless he can somehow communicate it to others --in writing, with spoken language, or through physical action. (¶ 2) In almost any area of work, the ability to communicate clearly and effectively is valuable--an important element in the package of skills that a worker offers for sale. Keithley says of it:

(¶ 3) The ability, therefore, to organize and analyze information to make it useful and to communicate such factual information in an orderly manner is one of the more important attributes of those who hope to advance their careers.[1]

(¶ 4) The ability to communicate well, however, is a skill that most of us must set about to learn conscientiously; and the acquisition of that skill should be a primary educational objective of every serious student. What at one time is measured in grades will later be measured in dollars.

[1] Erwin M. Keithley and Philip J. Schreiner, A Manual of Style for the Preparation of Papers & Reports (2d ed.; Cincinnati: South-Western Publishing Co., 1971), p. 1.

LESSON 83

83A Preparatory Practice (5) each line at least 3 times

Alphabet — Jack ordered a few very large zinnias and some quaint phlox from Bert.

Figure/symbol — Model #7006, marked $528.11, is selling for $435.99--a loss of $92.12.

Long words — The audio-visual environment offers unique opportunities for research.

Fluency — Until a problem confronts us, why must we worry about how to solve it?

| 1 | 2 | 3 | 4 | 5 | 6 | 7 | 8 | 9 | 10 | 11 | 12 | 13 | 14 |

LESSON 66

66A Preparatory Practice (5) each line at least 3 times

Alphabet	Explain quietly how Dickens vilified Ebenezer Scrooge or Jacob Marley.
Figure/symbol	He said, "Ship 14 #872 lamps, listed at $39.50 less 6% cash discount."
a, u	Thousands of us order sauerkraut to inaugurate an auspicious New Year.
Fluency	Judy is the auditor for the firm of Lee & Work in the downtown office.

| 1 | 2 | 3 | 4 | 5 | 6 | 7 | 8 | 9 | 10 | 11 | 12 | 13 | 14 |

66B Growth Index (15) two 5′ control-level writings; figure GWAM

All letters are used.

		GWAM 1′	5′	
¶ 1 1.5 SI 5.6 AWL 80% HFW	Whenever you compose a business letter (or any letter), write it	13	3	60
	as if you were speaking directly to the person to whom you are writing.	28	6	63
	Express your ideas clearly enough that there is scant reason for a re-	42	8	66
	cipient to be confused. Whether or not the recipient agrees with you	56	11	69
	is usually important, but rest assured he can do neither if he does not	70	14	71
	recognize what you are talking about. Whenever you have doubts about	84	17	74
	clarity, ask someone to scan the letter before you mail it.	96	19	77
¶ 2 1.5 SI 5.6 AWL 80% HFW	When we receive a reply that doesn't seem sensible, it could be	13	22	79
	that our own original letter is at the root of the difficulty. Did we,	27	25	82
	for example, try to be more impressive than expressive? Plain words,	41	27	85
	nicely chosen, usually allow little room for confusion. It is true,	55	30	88
	of course, that words are imperfect tools for conveying our ideas; how-	69	33	90
	ever, we just don't have anything else that works quite so well. We	83	36	93
	can't mail a gesture, a look, or an attitude. We must use words.	96	38	96
¶ 3 1.5 SI 5.6 AWL 80% HFW	However, the fact must be faced that words are meaningful only when	13	41	99
	put together in sentences; and a successful correspondent knows how to	28	44	101
	manufacture some good ones. He will also try to be brief without being	42	47	104
	miserly with facts. He knows that he is writing to another human, one	56	50	107
	who has all the strengths and frailties of humanity; so he uses a touch	71	53	110
	of psychology here and there. Above all, he writes the kind of letter	85	55	113
	he likes to receive. That makes his work enjoyable.	95	57	115

1′ GWAM | 1 | 2 | 3 | 4 | 5 | 6 | 7 | 8 | 9 | 10 | 11 | 12 | 13 | 14 |
5′ GWAM | 1 | 2 | 3 |

66C Production Measurement: BUSINESS LETTER WITH SPECIAL FEATURES (30) 20′ timing; correct errors; compute N-PRAM

Type the 4 letters on page 135 with block ¶s. Make 1 carbon copy (2 if a cc notation is used). Address an envelope for each letter. All letters are of average length. Choose punctuation styles; use current date.

LESSON 82

82A Preparatory Practice [5] each line at least 3 times

Alphabet	Jack and Beth Powell may take a quiz next week if the board gives one.
Figure/symbol	Memo #7091 said: Buy $25\frac{1}{2}$ dozen @ 46¢ and $38\frac{1}{4}$ dozen @ 27¢ immediately.
Double letters	Bill Hatten and Gregg Mann discussed a funny fellow from Apple Valley.
Fluency	Is he a speaker who tries to make up in length what he lacks in depth?
	| 1 | 2 | 3 | 4 | 5 | 6 | 7 | 8 | 9 | 10 | 11 | 12 | 13 | 14 |

82B Speed Building [5] Use 82A, above, for two 2′ writings; type sentences twice in each writing.

82C Communication Aid: CAPITALIZATION [10]

1. For the heading, type CAPITALIZATION.
2. Type the rules and examples given below (with) figures); underline the side headings.
3. Type the application paragraph, inserting the proper punctuation as you type.

Full sheet; 1½″ top margin; 70-space line; SS; DS between items; underline side heads

Words

Rules 5

(1) Capitalize names of the days of the week, months, and holidays; do 19
not capitalize names of seasons unless they are personified. 32

(2) Capitalize names of regions; do not capitalize nouns or adjectives 46
indicating mere direction. 51

(3) Capitalize names of organizations, clubs, and their derivatives. 65
Capitalize names that indicate specific individuality and that are 79
used as proper names. 83

(4) Capitalize names of specific courses; do not capitalize such names 98
when they are used to denote general divisions of knowledge. 110

Examples 113

(1) I can arrange for a showing of fall styles on Tuesday, August 28. 128

(2) I landed in eastern France after I had crossed the Arctic Circle. 142

(3) The Rotary Club met in the Jeffrey Room of the Continental Hotel. 156

(4) You must write shorthand well, so please enroll in Shorthand III. 170

Application Paragraph 179

early last spring, before i finished the geography course i was 192
taking (canadian regions), a friend and i drove north for a long weekend 206
visit to manitoba. although we left on a thursday evening, by saturday 221
we were still in north dakota; so we decided to turn south toward home. 235

82D Production Typing: UNBOUND MANUSCRIPTS; FOOTNOTES [30]

Type the 2 problems in this lesson as unbound manuscripts. Reread appropriate portions of the outline on page 166 before you begin to type.

Problem 1: Modified Block Style Letter (*WB p. 121*)

Words

AIRMAIL   Mr. Robert W. Nickerson   Assis- | 10
tant Vice President   Midway Supply Com- | 18
pany   3785 Hughes Road   Louisville, KY | 25
40207   Dear Mr. Nickerson   Re: Your Pur- | 33
chase Order 8-K-5133   (¶ 1) We regret very | 40
much the inconvenience caused you by the | 48
failure of your recent order to arrive as prom- | 58
ised.   (¶ 2) Our records indicate that ship- | 65
ment was made from our docks in ample time | 73
to arrive before the date specified in your | 82
order.   Interstate Truck Lines, Inc., was | 91
the carrier used; and the shipping memoran- | 99
dum clearly states that the order was to be | 108
given priority treatment.   (¶ 3) Mr. Henry | 115
Searfoss, of our sales department, will person- | 125
ally investigate the shipment and the circum- | 133
stances that may have caused its delay. In any | 143
event, we have shipped you a duplicate order. | 152
Please keep the first delivery that arrives and | 162
direct that the second one be returned to us | 171
by the delivering carrier.   Very truly yours | 180
ALLIED EQUIPMENT COMPANY   George L. | 187
Griffiths   President   xx   cc Mr. Henry Sear- | 195
foss | 196/219

Problem 2: Modified Block Style Letter (*WB p. 123*)

Words

SPECIAL DELIVERY   Mr. Stanton P. Farr | 10
1945 Field Avenue   St. Paul, MN   55516 | 18
Dear Mr. Farr   SUBJECT: Your Birthday | 26
(and Ours)   (¶ 1) Next Tuesday is your | 32
birthday. Congratulations! It will be our | 41
birthday, too; for it was exactly 25 years ago | 50
next Tuesday that Blenheim's served its first | 59
customer in St. Paul.   (¶ 2) As part of our | 67
celebration, we plan to give beautiful sport | 76
shirts to five area men who are our customers | 85
and who will be celebrating birthdays with | 94
us.   (¶ 3) One of these shirts is yours, Mr. | 102
Farr, if you will come in on Saturday and pick | 111
it out. While you are here, we shall take your | 121
picture and feature it in our birthday sale | 129
announcement that will appear in The Eagle | 140
on Tuesday.   (¶ 4) We shall watch for you | 147
on Saturday.   Cordially yours   BLENHEIM'S | 155
MEN'S STORE   Paul S. Rometo   Manager   xx | 163
If one of our new salespeople fails to recog- | 172
nize you, please show him this letter. | 179/194

Problem 3: Block Style Letter (*WB p. 125*)

Words

Flying Eagle Restaurants, Inc.   2514 Davis | 11
Avenue   Los Angeles, CA   90024   Attention | 19
Purchasing Officials   Gentlemen   (¶ 1) As | 26
the sole distributor in this area for Allen | 35
Equipment Company, we are happy to enclose | 44
the new 165-page Allen catalog.   (¶ 2) The | 51
Allen catalog contains some interesting items | 60
that are being introduced this year. Your | 69
attention is directed particularly to page 15, | 78
where the completely new line of Allen steam | 87
vats is illustrated and explained. These steam | 97
vats operate on an entirely new principle that | 106
has been proven both efficient and economical. | 116
(¶ 3) We know that the new catalog will be | 123
especially helpful to you if you are planning | 132
to redesign or rebuild any of your kitchens. | 142
We shall welcome the opportunity to discuss | 150
Allen products with you and to help you de- | 159
termine your specific requirements.   Sincerely | 168
yours   Larry J. Wingo   Sales Manager   xx | 176
Enclosure: The Allen catalog | 182/196

Problem 4: Modified Block Style Letter (*WB p. 127*)

Center the subject line.

Words

REGISTERED MAIL   Rothwell & Spahn   510 | 10
Reed Avenue   Boston, MA   02149   Attention | 18
Purchasing Director   Gentlemen   Subject: | 26
Your Order #56812   (¶ 1) On this date, a sec- | 34
ond unsuccessful attempt was made to deliver | 43
the above-listed order to your address. The | 52
goods are currently being held at our ware- | 60
house at 2175 Reservoir Road.   (¶ 2) You may | 68
claim them there during regular business | 76
hours if you will show your copy of the ship- | 85
ping order to the man in charge.   (¶ 3) We | 92
shall hold the goods there for 30 days. After | 102
that time, they will be transferred to our ware- | 111
house on Rhode Island Avenue; and a rental | 120
charge will be assessed for each day thereafter. | 130
Yours very truly   GREAT LAKES DELIVERY | 138
SERVICE   M. P. St. John   Dispatcher   xx | 145
Before acceptance, please examine the ship- | 154
ment carefully for damage. | 159/178

TYPING MANUSCRIPTS AND REPORTS

TS

I. MARGINS

DS

Reset margin→   A. Unbound Manuscripts and Reports   16

        Set tab→   1. Top, first page: $1\frac{1}{2}$ inches, pica; 2 inches, elite   27

            2. Subsequent pages: top and side, 1 inch; bottom, at least 1 inch   41

   B. Bound Manuscripts and Reports   47

            1. Topbound: same as unbound, but increase top margins $\frac{1}{2}$ inch   60

            2. Leftbound: same as unbound, but increase left margins $\frac{1}{2}$ inch   73

DS

Backspace into margin→   II. SPACING   76

   A. Body   78

            1. Double-spaced with 5-, 7-, or 10-space paragraph indentions (and   92

               more than 1 line of a paragraph at top or foot of a page)   103

            2. Quoted materials of 4 or more lines single-spaced and double-indented   118

               5 spaces (quotation marks optional)   125

            3. Tables single-spaced   130

   B. Footnotes   133

            1. Numbered consecutively throughout a short report   144

            2. Identified by superior figures typed $\frac{1}{2}$ space above the line of   157

               writing   159

            3. Separated from the last line of body by a divider line approximately   173

               $1\frac{1}{2}$ inches long, preceded and followed by 1 blank line   184

            4. Indented to paragraph point and single-spaced with a double space   198

               between footnotes   202

III. HEADINGS AND SUBHEADINGS   208

   A. Main Heading   211

            1. Centered in all capital letters over the writing line   223

            2. Followed by 1 blank line and a secondary heading or by 2 blank lines   237

               and the first line of the body   244

   B. Secondary Heading (Explains or Amplifies the Main Heading)   256

            1. Centered with all important words capitalized   266

            2. Followed by 2 blank lines   272

   C. First-Order Subheadings (Side Headings)   281

            1. Preceded by 2 blank lines and followed by 1 blank line   293

            2. Typed at the left margin, underlined, no terminal period   305

            3. Main words capitalized   310

   D. Second-Order Subheadings (Paragraph Headings)   320

            1. Preceded by 1 blank line   326

            2. Indented to paragraph point (usually only first word capitalized),   340

               underlined, and followed by a period   348

IV. PAGINATION (PAGE NUMBERING)   354

   A. Unbound and Leftbound Manuscripts and Reports   364

            1. First page: centered on line of writing $\frac{1}{2}$ inch from bottom   377

               of page (or omitted)   381

            2. Subsequent pages: on Line 4 at the right margin   392

   B. Topbound Manuscripts and Reports   399

            1. First page: centered $\frac{1}{2}$ inch from bottom of page (or omitted)   412

            2. Subsequent pages: centered $\frac{1}{2}$ inch from bottom of page   424

SECTION 12 Administrative Communications

LESSONS 67-72

Unless otherwise directed, proceed as follows:
Drill Copy: Full sheet; 70-space line; SS.
Paragraph Copy: Full sheet; 70-space line; DS; 5-space ¶ indention.
Production Typing: Follow directions given with each problem; correct errors; make a carbon copy.

For letters, use the modified-block style, open punctuation, and indented ¶s.

Materials Needed: Letterheads in executive and half sizes (or full sheets appropriately marked or folded), carbon sheets, interoffice communication forms, envelopes, and a postal card.

LESSON 67

67A Preparatory Practice [5] each line at least 3 times

Alphabet	The exquisite, azure blue water of some Japanese lakes gets very cold.
Figure/symbol	He wrote, "Sell 875 @ 63¼¢ ea., 130 @ 29½¢, and the remainder @ 49½¢."
Adjacent keys	We were assured Polk Power Saws were proper saws to cut sides 32 x 45.
Fluency	Our neighbor and his visitor may take a dirigible to the ancient city.

| 1 | 2 | 3 | 4 | 5 | 6 | 7 | 8 | 9 | 10 | 11 | 12 | 13 | 14 |

67B Control Building [10]

1. Try to type each ¶ one or more times without error.
2. Type a 3′ writing on the CONTROL LEVEL. Use all ¶s.

All letters are used.

		GWAM 1′	3′	
¶ 1 1.7 SI 6.0 AWL 70% HFW	Effective correspondents write in a manner that makes the reader	13	4	75
	believe a message was intended individually for him. Authorities allude	28	9	79
	to this approach as one emphasizing the You attitude; it stresses use	42	14	84
	of the pronoun You, not I or We.	48	16	86
¶ 2 1.7 SI 6.0 AWL 70% HFW	There is a widely recognized premise in the economic world that a	13	20	91
	firm will expand in ratio with its ability to communicate. As business	28	25	96
	letters are often the most vital link in such a chain of communications,	42	30	100
	concern about their quality is understandable.	51	33	103
¶ 3 1.7 SI 6.0 AWL 70% HFW	Because the tone of a letter often sets the tone for its answer,	13	37	108
	most successful business letters are considerate. An amicable letter	27	42	112
	is apt to be answered in an amicable fashion; an uncivil letter may be	41	47	117
	rejected totally. Politeness wins friends; lack of respect does not.	55	52	122
¶ 4 1.7 SI 6.0 AWL 70% HFW	So content can be easily comprehended, a letter should be specific,	14	57	126
	concrete, and directly on target. Many top-notch writers use a mental	28	62	131
	outline to make sure their ideas are logically organized. They discuss	42	67	136
	a topic fully before going on to another one. When finished, they stop.	57	72	141

1′ GWAM | 1 | 2 | 3 | 4 | 5 | 6 | 7 | 8 | 9 | 10 | 11 | 12 | 13 | 14 |
3′ GWAM | 1 | 2 | 3 | 4 | 5 |

SECTION 15 Technical Papers and Reports

LESSONS 81-87

Unless otherwise directed, proceed as follows:
Drill Copy. Full sheet; 70-space line; SS
¶ Copy. Full sheet; 70-space line; SS; 5-space ¶ indentions.

Production Copy. Follow directions for the problems. Erase and correct errors. Make any necessary decisions as to style or form.

LESSON 81

81A Preparatory Practice (5) each line at least 3 times

Alphabet	In her zany book, Madge Cowper says it is quite fair to tax juveniles.
Figure/symbol	Mark Invoice 118299 "350 sets @ 67¢ a set, less 2 4/5% cash discount."
d, e	Jed decided to heed me; he destroyed the weeds, then seeded the field.
Fluency	Some men and women plan their future; some just wait for it to happen.

| 1 | 2 | 3 | 4 | 5 | 6 | 7 | 8 | 9 | 10 | 11 | 12 | 13 | 14 |

81B Technique Improvement: STROKING (15) 3 or more correct copies of each line

Inside reaches	The Ghurka rug was torn five times before Mr. Hunter finally fixed it.
Long reaches	Myna's brothers, Brad, 16; Cedric, 17; and Muncell, 19, drove us home.
	Only the hungry baby's babbling disturbed the dignity of the ceremony.
	The men received a number of summaries of the stormy political report.
Outside reaches	Popular Queen Paula saw the purple azaleas on display at my dormitory.
3d row	We were there two weeks earlier; point out where you were living then.
m, n	Nominated in May, the winning candidate came from Menominee, Michigan.
	Ina and Min can never swim a nine-mile stint from Milan to Birmingham.

81C Production Typing: OUTLINE (35)

2 full sheets; top margin: 1½" for pica or 2" for elite; 1" side margins; at least 1" bottom margin; follow directions for vertical spacing

1. Type the outline on page 166. As a reminder to leave at least a 1" bottom margin, make a light pencil mark about 1½" from the bottom edge. (Erase the mark later.) For the first page, center the page number on the line of writing ½" from the bottom, which will leave 3 blank lines below the page number.

2. On the second page, type the page number in the upper right corner, even with the right margin, on Line 4. Begin typing the copy for the second page on Line 7. Two spaces follow the period after numbered or lettered divisions in an outline.

67C Communication Index: CAPITALIZATION AND PUNCTUATION ⑬ Capitalize and punctuate as you type.

1   i know however that we are holding about twenty six first row seats

2   her car bearing a washington license is parked in a no parking zone

3   stop that shipment at once mr fallone wants it to go by airfreight

4   do you know why we have not heard from mr fauser our agent in miami

5   i wonder whether the contests will be held in cleveland or charleston

6   joe who owns an old bus drives to tucson and it takes him 15 hours

7   a chemist in fact any scientist could analyze these strange fluids

8   when the returns have been counted we shall know who won the election

9   will you please ask about their low priced one and two bedroom units

10   in 1972 1830 ships entered and left the harbor in 1973 only 1501

67D Technique Improvement: STROKING ⑫ each line 3 times; correct errors

1 i, o   Ohio's position as a contributor to this nation's growth is improving.

2 l, o   Lola told Olga only to find the old wool stole and roll it in oilskin.

3 m, n   Many metropolitan managers meet annually in Maine to nominate members.

4 r, e   Mr. Fleer retired to Berlin, where he will reside after winter recess.

5 s, a   Please ask Asa if he has tasted sassafras, as Sally Mason says he has.

6 s, d   Sandy desired new sod; she dressed and seeded the fields on Wednesday.

7 s, w   There was a swish of wings; the swallows' sweet trills swelled upward.

8 t, r   It won't hurt to try a rinse on her hair, Gert; just don't try a tint.

9 u, i   Louis ruined my fruit when he bruised it, but it made delicious juice.

10 v, b   Several vibrations became obvious, but seven brave boys never wavered.

67E Manipulative Drill: ALIGNING COLUMNS AT THE RIGHT ⑩ full sheet; 2" top margin; SS

To align columns at the right

1. Type the first listed item in the position desired.
2. On the next line, position the carriage 1 space to the right of the last character of the item above.
3. Backspace once for each character in the second item.
4. Type the second item. Repeat procedure for any subsequent items.

1. Using the procedure given at the left, type the columns below, aligning the items at the right.

2. The first column is an acceptable heading for an interoffice memorandum. Position the column to leave a 1" left margin.

3. Position the second and third columns as indicated. Type each column individually; do not tabulate from column to column.

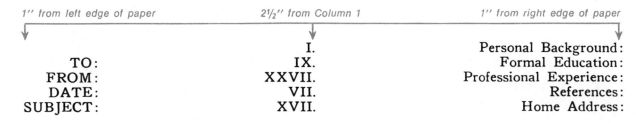

1" from left edge of paper	2½" from Column 1	1" from right edge of paper
	I.	Personal Background:
TO:	IX.	Formal Education:
FROM:	XXVII.	Professional Experience:
DATE:	VII.	References:
SUBJECT:	XVII.	Home Address:

80C Production Measurement �30 20′ writing; compute N-PRAM

Full sheet, reading position, DS; decide intercolumn spaces; correct errors

Problem 1

		Words
STATES WITH SPANISH-SPEAKING		8
POPULATION OF 75,000 OR MORE		12
Arizona	333,000	15
California	3,102,000	19
Colorado	286,000	23
Florida	451,000	27
Illinois	364,000	31
Michigan	121,000	34
New Jersey	310,000	39
New Mexico	407,000	43
New York	1,456,000	47
Ohio	95,000	50
Pennsylvania	107,000	54
Texas	2,060,000	57
		61

Source: Department of Labor, Manpower, Sep- 73
tember, 1972. 76

Problem 2

				Words
RULERS OF GREAT BRITAIN				5
Since 1714				7
Ruler	House	From	To	14
George I	Hanover	1714	1727	20
George II	Hanover	1727	1760	25
George III	Hanover	1760	1820	31
George IV	Hanover	1820	1830	37
William IV	Hanover	1830	1837	42
Victoria	Hanover	1837	1901	48
Edward VII	Saxe-Coburg and Gotha	1901	1910	56
George V	Windsor	1910	1936	62
Edward VIII	Windsor	1936	1936	68
George VI	Windsor	1936	1952	73
Elizabeth II	Windsor	1952	--	79

Problem 3

			Words
BRANCH MANAGERS' MEETING			5
June 4, 19--, 8:15			9
			30
Topic	Speaker	Time	34
			44
Introductions	Hostwith		49
Orientation	Crabill	8:30	54
President's message	Rossini	9:45	60
Maintaining schedules	Clemente	10:30	68
Territorial changes	Robinson	11:00	75
Filing reports	Clemente	11:30	81
Previewing new products	Robinson	1:00	88
New tax information	Hemphill	3:00	95
Sales quotas	Robinson	3:30	101
New policies	Rossini	3:45	106
			116

Problem 4

				Words
ASSETS OF U.S. LIFE INSURANCE COMPANIES				8
(000,000 Omitted)				12
				34
Asset	1971	1970	1961	38
				49
Total assets	$222,102	$207,254	$126,816	57
Government securities	11,000	11,068	12,045	66
Corporate bonds	79,198	73,098	48,887	73
Stocks	20,607	15,420	6,258	79
Mortgages	75,496	74,375	44,203	85
Other assets	35,801	33,293	15,423	92
				103

Source: Life Insurance Fact Book, 1972. 116

LESSON 68

68A Preparatory Practice [5] each line at least 3 times

Alphabet	The exultant jockey had won five bronze plaques and seven gold medals.
Figure/symbol	How can B/O & H, Inc., meet accounts of $27,463 and $58,900 by June 1?
Double letters	Ann can now notify all her classes that the 22 books will arrive soon.
Fluency	Our problem is that there is a right and a wrong way with any problem.

| 1 | 2 | 3 | 4 | 5 | 6 | 7 | 8 | 9 | 10 | 11 | 12 | 13 | 14 |

68B Speed/Control Building [10]

Type a 2′ EXPLORATION LEVEL writing; determine GWAM. Then type two 2′ CONTROL-LEVEL writings. Compare GWAM for each writing.

All letters are used.

1.5 SI
5.6 AWL
80% HFW

2′ GWAM

A man's ability to reason and his capacity to solve problems are 6
closely related to the quantity of words he knows. Most experts say, 13
however, that just memorizing new words will do little to add to your 20
mental stature. If word knowledge is retained, a large vocabulary will 27
make it possible for you to understand and assimilate more. Keep in 34
mind, though, that a man is not smart because he has a good vocabulary. 41
It is the other way around. 44

| 1 | 2 | 3 | 4 | 5 | 6 | 7 |

68C Production Typing: INTEROFFICE MEMORANDUMS [35]

Problem 1: Interoffice Memorandum *(WB p. 129)*

Type the memorandum on page 139 with 1″ side margins. Prepare 2 carbon copies

If interoffice memorandum forms are unavailable, use full sheets of plain paper. Type the headings as shown in the first column of 67E, page 137, but use double spacing. Leave a 1″ top margin.

Problem 2: Interoffice Memorandum *(WB p. 131)*

Type the memorandum on page 139. Address it to Nora E. Lindell, Purchasing Director. In the first line of the message, change Boise to Akron. Omit the last ¶ and cc notation.

Problem 3: Interoffice Envelopes

Following directions given in the memorandum on page 139 and illustrated below, address envelopes for the memorandums typed for Problems 1 and 2 and a third envelope for the extra carbon copy typed for Problem 1.

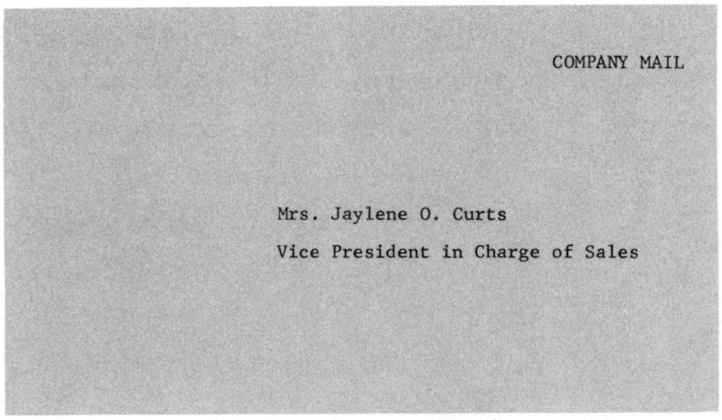

Company mail envelope

LESSON 80

80A Preparatory Practice [5] each line at least 3 times

Alphabet	In a truly amazing way, John's books quickly verified his tax reports.
Figure/symbol	*List does not include Day & Company's policy #87-6320-WE-1954 (paid).
1st row	Has Maxine Mazon or Bab Vanz, members of this club, climbed Mt. Blanc?
Fluency	To capitalize on the right to vote is the sign of a mature individual.
	| 1 | 2 | 3 | 4 | 5 | 6 | 7 | 8 | 9 | 10 | 11 | 12 | 13 | 14 |

80B Growth Index [15] two 5′ control-level writings; figure GWAM on better writing

All letters are used.

		GWAM 1′	5′	
¶ 1	Business letters are an effective form of communication, but they	13	3	60
1.5 SI	are an expensive form as well. One management consultant has calculated	28	6	63
5.6 AWL	the cost of a typical letter to run as high as fifteen dollars. Others	42	8	66
80% HFW	use a lesser sum, but it cannot be denied that letters cost money. Much	57	11	69
	of their cost is attributable to the wages of people engaged in letter	71	14	72
	writing. It seems reasonable to assume, then, that the less time it	85	17	74
	takes to get out a letter, the less expensive it will be.	96	19	77
¶ 2	When an executive writes a letter, a portion of his salary becomes	13	22	79
1.5 SI	part of its cost. The same principle applies to the work of a typist	27	25	82
5.6 AWL	or to anybody else who contributes to the letter. Of course, costs for	42	28	85
80% HFW	all other charges, such as paper, postage, light, heat, rent, and depre-	56	30	90
	ciation on machinery, must also be counted. Although none of these	70	33	91
	costs taken singly seems to be of major importance, together they add	84	36	93
	up to a significant figure as the cost for one letter.	95	38	96
¶ 3	Typically, an office function will at some time be stated as a	13	41	98
1.5 SI	dollar figure, as an expense item. Most businessmen assume that an	26	43	101
5.6 AWL	office function is an investment that will in time pay for itself. If,	41	46	104
80% HFW	upon analysis, a function is found to be so expensive that it is not	54	49	106
	returning an amount that is at least equal to its cost, that function	68	52	109
	will be ended and some other, more profitable activity substituted. A	83	55	112
	firm makes profit from efficient procedures as well as from its sales.	97	57	115
1′ GWAM	| 1 | 2 | 3 | 4 | 5 | 6 | 7 | 8 | 9 | 10 | 11 | 12 | 13 | 14 |			
5′ GWAM	| 1 | 2 | 3 |			

AMICOLA beverage, inc.
For a World of Refreshment

INTEROFFICE MEMORANDUM

Words

Printed headings
     TO: Jaylene O. Curts, Vice President in Charge of Sales   10

Omit personal title
     FROM: B. W. Draybicki, Office Manager   17

     DATE: January 23, 19--   20

     SUBJECT: Company Correspondence   25

Omit salutation   TS

Although you may have used many of the same procedures at the Boise 38
branch office, I shall from time to time illustrate for you some 51
standard forms and procedures we use here in the home office. If 65
you have suggestions, I shall be happy to have them. 75

1″ side margins
Correspondence within our company is typed on this special inter- 88
office form. It provides a rapid, convenient means of communi- 101
cating between various members of the organization. As you can 113
see from the printed headings, information can be set up quickly. 127
All lines start one inch from the left edge of the paper. Only 140
essential information is included. 146

SS; DS between ¶s
Full addresses, personal titles, the salutation, the complimentary 160
close, and the signature are omitted. The use of a subject head- 173
ing is recommended, however, because it immediately tells the 185
reader what is discussed in the memorandum. It is also an aid in 198
filing the communication. 203

Interoffice messages, regardless of length, should be typed with 216
one-inch margins. Generally, messages should be typed in block 229
form and single-spaced with double spacing between paragraphs. 242
Short messages, however, may be double-spaced; but, if of more 255
than one paragraph, the paragraphs must be indented. A triple 267
space separates the subject line and the body of the message. 279

The initials of the typist should be typed a double space below 292
the last line of the message; and notations regarding enclosures 305
and carbon copy distribution, when used, are typed in the same 318
position they occupy in regular letters. 326

When an envelope is needed, the notation COMPANY MAIL is typed in 339
the space normally used for a postage stamp. The address is typed 352
on the envelope in the position an address usually occupies. The 366
recipient's name and his department designation should be given. 378

I hope your new office is comfortable. If there is some way the 391
general office staff can be helpful, please let me know. 402

Omit complimentary
close and stu 403
signature

cc Paul McCary, Administrative Assistant 412
cc notation   Sales Department 415

Style Letter 7: INTEROFFICE COMMUNICATION (Typed in Pica Type)

Problem 2: Table with Uneven Columns and Total Lines

Words

Full sheet; DS; reading position; decide spaces between columns; align third column at the % symbol as shown

SALES FIGURES AND BONUSES EARNED

Week of July 8, 19—

Salesperson	Sales	Bonus Rate	Bonus	Words
				7
				11
				12
				23
Ben Wise	$ 1,750	5%	$ 87.50	29
Lois Grantham	1,480	4	59.20	35
Luther Gilson	1,320	5	66.00	40
Albert Belskus	1,980	3	59.40	46
Richard Shupe	1,200	2½	30.00	52
Beatrice O'Flynn	2,330	4	93.20	58
Elaine Malinowski	1,760	4	70.40	65
Hugh Churchill	3,400	3½	119.00	74
Totals	$15,220		$584.70	79

Problem 3: Table from Corrected Script

Full sheet; DS; reading position; decide spaces between columns

Words

	1974	1975	Words
Spanish Umbrella Boutique (all caps)			5
Pro-rated Advertising Costs			11
Item	1974	1975	16
Accessories	$ 450	$ 40	22
Women's clothing	3,008	4,120	26
cosmetics	80	68	30
Gloves, handbags	530	705	36
Jewelry	1,012	1,200	40
Lingerie	800	650	44
Notions	55	70	48
Rain wear	1070	125	55
totals	$5,697	$6,990	59

69A Preparatory Practice (5) each line at least 3 times

Alphabet	Ezra Weber likes the piquancy of orange juice mixed with clover honey.
Figure/symbol	In <u>1925</u>, A & E Company's net sales were $283,490; in <u>1974</u>, $6,708,351.
Left hand	Fears decreased as westward breezes gave six vessels access to a reef.
Fluency	Some "friends" find it more natural to be critical than to be helpful.

| 1 | 2 | 3 | 4 | 5 | 6 | 7 | 8 | 9 | 10 | 11 | 12 | 13 | 14 |

69B Communication Aid: PARENTHESES (15)

Full sheet; 1½″ top margin; 70-space line; SS with DS between items.

1. Type the heading, PARENTHESES.
2. Type the rules and examples given below (with figures); underline the side headings.
3. Type the application paragraph, inserting the proper punctuation as you type.

Words

<u>Rules</u>   5

(1) Use parentheses to set off parenthetical or explanatory matter.   18

(2) Use parentheses when an amount expressed in words is followed by   32
the same amount in figures.   38

(3) Parentheses may be used to enclose enumerations.   49

(4) A punctuation mark is placed inside the closing parenthesis if it   63
applies to the parenthetical material.   71

(5) A punctuation mark follows the closing parenthesis if it punctuates   85
the sentence itself.   89

(6) A reference in parentheses at the end of a sentence is placed before   104
the period. If the reference is a complete sentence, it is written   117
as a complete sentence and enclosed in parentheses.   128

<u>Examples</u>   131

(1) Ralph (my cousin) lives in the capital city of Arizona (Phoenix).   146

(2) I can sell my home to them for thirty thousand dollars ($30,000).   160

(3) We should all work for (1) speed, (2) control, and (3) good form.   174

(4) Bring the late report with you. (We have a copy of the old one.)   188

(5) I shall call him (the clerk, I mean), but I shall call you first.   202

(6) You will find the pictures you desire in the new book (page 137).   217

<u>Application Paragraph</u>   225

The house will cost forty thousand dollars $40,000. This price   238
includes 1 carpets, 2 draperies, and 3 storm windows. When we   252
close the deal within 1 week, I hope we shall change our address   266
(165 Hope Road. Our home at least so our realtor tells us has been   280
sold.   281

79C Communication Aid: APOSTROPHE ⑩

1. For the heading, use APOSTROPHE.
2. Type the rules and examples (with figures).

3. Type the application paragraph, inserting the appropriate punctuation as you type.

Words

Rules

4

(1) Add 's to form the plural of letters, words used as words, and numbers stated in figures.

19
24

(2) Use an apostrophe to show omission of figures (class of '75).

37

(3) Use the apostrophe to show omission of letters in contractions (Rob't, Marg't, Sec'y). No period follows such contractions.

51
63

(4) Use the apostrophe as single quotation marks for a quotation within a quotation.

78
81

Examples

84

(1) Miss Dunne gave F's to students who used too many and's or but's.

98

(2) The dinner meeting for the class of '66 will be held on Thursday.

112

(3) "Ira S. Clark, Sec'y" is how he signs the minutes of the meeting.

127

(4) Mr. Kromer said, "I heard them say to your sister, 'It is time.'"

141

Application Paragraph

149

Jacks article in the newsletter read, "The class of 27 held its reunion last week. Saml Snows antique car, a Model T Ford (no other Model Ts there) won a special prize. Sams acceptance speech was a model of brevity. He said simply, I accept.

163
177
191
200

79D Production Typing: TABLES ㉚

Problem 1: Three-Column Table

Half sheet; exact center; SS; 10 spaces between columns

Words

HIGHEST PEAKS IN NORTH AMERICA

6

Name	Location	Feet	
McKinley	Alaska	20,320	13
Logan	Canada	19,850	18
Citlatepec	Mexico	18,700	22
St. Elias	Alaska and		27
	Canada	18,008	31
Popocatepetl	Mexico	17,887	34
Foraker	Alaska	17,395	39
Iztaccihuatl	Mexico	17,343	44
Lucania	Canada	17,150	49
King	Canada	17,130	54
Blackburn	Alaska	16,523	58

62

69C Production Typing ㉚

Problem 1: News Release

Words

1½'' top and side margins; DS body with 5-space ¶ indentions; no cc

January 24, 19-- | 3

DS

FOR IMMEDIATE RELEASE | 8

3 blank lines

(Center) LOCAL DISTRIBUTOR GRANTED FRANCHISE | 15

TS

(¶ 1) The Shebazz Bottling Co., of 4909 Hoffman Road, has been granted local | 29
franchising rights for the distribution of a popular new soft drink, Crystal Ade, | 46
it was announced yesterday by Amicola Beverage, Inc., of Charlotte, North | 61
Carolina. (¶ 2) Crystal Ade is a lemon-flavored carbonated beverage. According | 76
to Amicola, its low caloric content and the addition of Vitamin C make it an | 91
excellent after-school drink for children. Tests are also reported to have shown | 108
that its thirst-quenching ability exceeds that of several of its leading soft drink | 124
competitors. (¶ 3) B. L. Green, President of Shebazz Bottling Co., says that | 139
Crystal Ade will be available in local stores within a few weeks. | 152
(DS and center) # # # | 153

```
Shebazz Bottling Co.
4909 Hoffman Road
Rochester, NY  14622




              Student's Name
              Street Address
              City, State  ZIP Code
```

Address side of card

Typing postal cards

SS and block both the return and the postal card addresses. The 2-letter state-name abbreviation for use with the ZIP Code is permissible.

Start the return address on Line 2, 3 spaces from the left edge. Start the address on about Line 10 or 11 and 2'' from the left edge.

On the message side, type the date on Line 3, TS, and type the message. TS and type the signature. On postal cards, the salutation and complimentary close are optional.

Problem 2: Postal Card (5½'' x 3¼'') *(WB p. 133)*

48-space line; block style; SS; use the return address of the Shebazz Bottling Co.; address the card to yourself

```
January 25, 19--

Dear Mailbox User

As you can see, I'm only a postal card.  Usually
the message I carry is not exactly earthshaking
in importance.  But the message I carry today is
one you are going to be glad to receive.  If you
take me to your local dealer, I'm worth a bottle
of CRYSTAL ADE.  No strings attached.  You don't
even need to return the empty bottle.


Postal Pete
```

Message side of card

Words

January 25, 19-- Dear Mailbox User (¶) As | 8
you can see, I'm only a postal card. Usually | 17
the message I carry is not exactly earthshak- | 26
ing in importance. But the message I carry | 34
today is one you are going to be glad to | 43
receive. If you take me to your local dealer, | 52
I'm worth a bottle of CRYSTAL ADE. No | 60
strings attached. You don't even need to re- | 69
turn the empty bottle. Postal Pete | 76

Multiline Column Headings. When counting the lines in a table for vertical centering, remember to count each line in multiline column headings. If the column headings vary in number of lines, align all headings at the bottom.

Problem 2: Table with Horizontal Rulings

Full sheet; DS; exact center; 8 and 4 spaces between columns; add horizontal rulings as in Problem 1; type source note below bottom rule

			Words
OCCUPATIONS OF YOUNG WORKERS, 16 TO 19 YEARS OLD			10
By School Status			13
Occupation	In School	Out of School	43 / 48
Clerical workers	17.5%	23.4%	68
Service workers except private household	26.3	15.1	78
Operatives	11.1	25.7	82
Nonfarm workers	14.8	13.7	88
Salesworkers	11.3	5.9	92
Private household workers	7.6	2.3	100
Farm workers	5.3	4.5	104
Craftsmen and foremen	2.4	6.4	111
Professional, technical, and managerial workers	3.7	2.9	122

Source: Department of Labor, Manpower Report of the President, 1972. 150

LESSON 79

79A Preparatory Practice [5] each line at least 3 times

Alphabet	I know that an extreme Quebec blizzard may be jeopardizing four lives.
Figure/symbol	Lee & Lee lost 36% on the sale of the 875 books they sold for $12,493.
One hand	Face the facts; you can win an award only if you exceed Jim's average.
Fluency	The wise man finds time for socializing; he finds time for quiet, too.

| 1 | 2 | 3 | 4 | 5 | 6 | 7 | 8 | 9 | 10 | 11 | 12 | 13 | 14 |

79B Control Building [5] each line 3 times; repeat lines in which an error was made

		Words
Goal	Nothing is so rare as the use of a word in its true meaning.	12
One hand	John Plum traced the baggage to my street address in Waseca.	12
Corrected copy	Weare ~~glad~~ (pleased) to wriet to your a bot this new, ~~unique~~ (unusual) bok.	12
Script	His success depends on his ability to work well with others.	12

| 1 | 2 | 3 | 4 | 5 | 6 | 7 | 8 | 9 | 10 | 11 | 12 | 13 | 14 |

Problem 3: Interoffice Memorandum *(WB p. 135)*

Make 4 cc, 3 to be sent to Alfred B. Graessel, Vice President; Jaylene Curts, Vice President in Charge of Sales; and Nora E. Lindell, Purchasing Director. Make appropriate cc notation.

DS heading; SS and block the ¶; indent enumerations 5 spaces and block lines; DS between items

Words

TO: Members of the Executive Committee 7
FROM: R. B. Proctor, President 12
DATE: January 25, 19-- 15
SUBJECT: Executive Committee Meeting 21

The Executive Committee will meet Monday, January 29, at 32
10 a.m. in the Board Room. Lunch will be served at 12:30. Items 46
to be discussed include the following: 54

1. Opportunities for foreign franchising 62
   Mr. Graessel and Mrs. Curts 67
2. Promotion plans for Crystal Ade 75
   Mrs. Curts 77
3. Disposition of the Sudan Street warehouse 86
   Miss Lindell 89
4. Expansion of office services 95
   Mr. Graessel 98

LESSON 70

70A Preparatory Practice [5] each line at least 3 times

Alphabet	The five dozen quarts of blackberry and grape juice mixture were mine.
Figure/symbol	In 1957, our profits were $37,461.05; this year, they are $189,227.13.
Shift keys	I moved from Elm Street, Orange, Texas, to Pine Avenue, Red Oak, Iowa.
Fluency	The future is not with a job; it is with the worker who does that job.

| 1 | 2 | 3 | 4 | 5 | 6 | 7 | 8 | 9 | 10 | 11 | 12 | 13 | 14 |

70B Speed/Control Building [10] Repeat 68B, page 138.

70C Production Typing [35]

Problem 1: Letter on Executive-Size Paper *(WB p. 137)*

Modified block style

Words

January 29, 19-- Mr. E. Page Gorman, Edi- 9
tor The Charlotte Post-News 1191 Summit 16
Avenue Charlotte, NC 28208 Dear Mr. 23
Gorman (¶ 1) Thank you for your recent 30
letter inquiring about the steps our company 39
is taking to help solve the ecology crisis. As 49
one of the leading bottling companies in the 58
United States, we have been especially inter- 66
ested in sponsoring research that will help to 76
alleviate the littering problem. (¶ 2) Our 83
present research efforts center upon two pos- 92
sible solutions: (1) changing the usual shape 102
of soft drink containers to provide a variety of 111
other practical uses (such as a cup or a vase) 121
and (2) developing a suitable plastic container 130
material that will be biodegradable when at- 139
tacked by ultraviolet rays from the sun. (¶ 3) 148
Please write me again if I can give you more 157
information. Feel free to quote from this let- 166
ter. Very truly yours Alfred B. Graessel 174
Vice President xx 178/196

Typing on executive-size stationery

Executive stationery is 7¼″ by 10½″. With stationery narrower than the regular 8½″, regulate the line length by setting appropriate margins, usually 1″. Type the date on about Line 15.

Examples

(1) She walked from Wilson's Department Store to Citizens State Bank. 95

(2) It's true that eight years' work was destroyed in one day's time. 110

(3) The office manager X'd out the last line; then he OK'd the cable. 124

(4) Fred has had ten years of experience as manager of Eckert Studio. 138

Application Paragraph 147

 Mr. Steel has had nineteen years experience as credit manager for 160
Manns Main Market. Prior to joining Manns, he had six years of similar 175
experience in one of Toledos leading stores. If Mr. Mann has OKd our 189
plan, Mr. Steels retirement dinner will be held with two weeks notice. 204

78C   Production Typing: TABLES WITH HORIZONTAL RULINGS ③⑤

Problem 1: Table with Horizontal Rulings

Full sheet; DS; reading position; decide number of spaces between columns

ACTUAL VERSUS BUDGETED EXPENSES

For Month of July, 19--

Expense	Budget	Actual
Data processing	$ 250	$ 250
Depreciation	210	210
Insurance	125	125
Light and heat	165	153
Postage and mailing	38	40
Printing and stationery	185	212
Rent	400	400
Salaries	5,380	5,320
Taxes	75	75
Telephone	75	110
Word processing	85	76

Words
6
DS
11
DS
22
33
DS
37
SS
48
54
58
62
66
72
78
81
85
88
92
96
SS
107

Problem 2: Minutes of a Committee Meeting

Words

1½" top, 1" side
margins; SS; 5-space
¶ indentions

MINUTES OF THE MEETING
OF THE EXECUTIVE COMMITTEE
DS

January 29, 19—
TS

A regular meeting of the Executive Committee of Amicola Beverages, Inc., was held on Monday, January 29, 19—, at 10 a.m. Members present were Mr. Graessel, Mrs. Curts, Miss Lindell, and Mr. Proctor, who presided. Mr. Caulder was absent because of illness.
DS

The minutes of the previous meeting were accepted as read.

Mr. Graessel and Mrs. Curts reported that plans for foreign distribution of Amicola, Pixie, and Crystal Ade were progressing satisfactorily. Franchises in Canada and Mexico have already been granted. Discussions with British and French representatives are now being held.

Promotion plans for Crystal Ade are being developed in conjunction with Frank, Beeman & Heinz. Franchise holders have been authorized to distribute free bottles of Crystal Ade to residents in their areas. The expense will be underwritten by the Company. Layouts for magazine advertising will be ready for discussion at the next meeting, according to Mrs. Curts.

Miss Lindell reported that the Sudan Street warehouse has been vacated in anticipation of renovation in that area. It was generally agreed that the disposal of the building should be put in the hands of the Company attorney.

Discussion of the expansion of office services was postponed at the suggestion of Mr. Graessel pending the arrival of new equipment that has been ordered.

There being no other business, the meeting was adjourned at 12 p.m.
DS

Respectfully submitted

3 blank lines

Secretary

Problem 3: Letter on Executive-Size Stationery *(WB p. 139)*

February 3, 19— Mr. John Yee, Attorney at Law Humpleston & Watson 500 West Stonewall Street Charlotte, NC 28208 Dear John (¶1) If you believe such action to be wise, I hereby authorize you to enter suit in the name of our Company against the appropriate parties engaged in the condemnation and appropriation of our warehouse and other property on Sudan Street. (¶2) Our accountants have advised me, however, that it might be a good idea to consider seriously allowing the property to be condemned and writing off the loss against what we anticipate will be a banner year for profits. (¶3) I suggest that you meet with our finance people to discuss the relative merits of these two proposals and to consider any other possibilities open to us at this time. Sincerely Alfred B. Graessel Vice President xx cc Lee Caulder Treasurer

Problem 2: Three-Column Table with Source Note

Full sheet; reading position; DS; 12 spaces between Columns 1 and 2, 6 spaces between Columns 2 and 3

Company	Listed Shares	Market Value	Words
			6
LEADING STOCKS IN MARKET VALUE			
(Stated in Millions)			10
			13
			21
Int'l Business Machines	115.3	$38,864	29
American Tel. & Tel.	549.3	24,582	35
General Motors	287.6	23,152	41
Standard Oil (N.J.)	226.6	16,712	48
Sears, Roebuck	155.4	15,931	53
Eastman Kodak	161.5	15,710	59
General Electric	184.9	11,581	65
Xerox Corp.	78.0	9,774	69
Texaco Inc.	274.3	9,429	74
Minnesota Mining & Mfg.	56.3	7,597	82

SS

1½" line → DS _____ 85

Source: New York Stock Exchange, <u>Fact Book</u>, 1972. 95

LESSON 78

78A Preparatory Practice (5) each line at least 3 times

Alphabet Howard Long paid the tax on five quarts of gray paint for Jack Bozman.

Figure/symbol Lee & Cowl's 14¼% discount applies to your $27,630 and $58,909 orders.

Adjacent keys We were excited and frightened; we looked like three dreaded warriors.

Fluency Individuality, one form of sensitivity, makes me proud that "I am me."

| 1 | 2 | 3 | 4 | 5 | 6 | 7 | 8 | 9 | 10 | 11 | 12 | 13 | 14 |

78B Communication Aid: APOSTROPHE (10)

1. For the heading, use APOSTROPHE.
2. Type the rules and examples (with figures).

3. Type the application paragraph, inserting the appropriate punctuation as you type.

Rules	Words
	4
(1) Company and organization names sometimes omit the apostrophe.	18
(2) It is better not to use the possessive form for inanimate objects; but business sanctions the possessive with <u>day</u>, <u>month</u>, <u>year</u>, etc.	32 / 48
(3) Use <u>'d</u> to form the past and past participle of coined words.	61
(4) Do not use an apostrophe with a possessive noun if a preposition follows it.	75 / 78

LESSON 71

71A Preparatory Practice (5) each line at least 3 times

Alphabet	Elizabeth requested that Marge and Jack pay to fix our vacuum sweeper.
Figure/symbol	In 1974, John Rolfe paid $2,438.65 for a boat and $150.92 for a motor.
Home row	Ask Gladys if she has a half tank of gas; she has less than she knows.
Fluency	The men may visit the walls of the ancient city if they can find them.

| 1 | 2 | 3 | 4 | 5 | 6 | 7 | 8 | 9 | 10 | 11 | 12 | 13 | 14 |

71B Communications Checkup (10)

1. Type a copy of the ¶. Insert commas as needed.
2. Check your copy with your instructor.

3. Type a 2" writing or two 1" writings from the book. Insert commas as you type.

All letters are used.

1.7 SI
6.0 AWL
70% HFW

Our current contract which expires in three years insures us a share of an expanding profitable marketing area. As you recall Mr. Enzo our original agreement was completed on July 15, 1973 when Maria Wingo who was then our agent in Iowa signed for us. Subsequent negotiations have usually not been easy but we have always profited from them.

	GWAM	
	1'	2'
	14	7	42
	28	14	49
	42	21	56
	57	28	63
	69	35	68

1' GWAM | 1 | 2 | 3 | 4 | 5 | 6 | 7 | 8 | 9 | 10 | 11 | 12 | 13 | 14 |
2' GWAM | 1 | 2 | 3 | 4 | 5 | 6 | 7 |

71C Production Typing Information: CHAIN FEEDING ENVELOPES (5)

Method 1: Back feeding

Stack the envelopes *face up* at the left side of the typewriter.

Insert the first envelope to typing position; place a second envelope behind the cylinder in the "feed" position.

Address the first envelope. As you twirl the first envelope out of the machine with the right hand, feed another envelope in the "feed" position with the left hand.

As the first envelope is removed, the second envelope will be moved into typing position. Continue the "chain" by placing a new envelope in the "feed" position each time the addressed envelope is removed.*

Method 2: Front feeding

Stack the envelopes face down, flap toward you, at the left side of the typewriter.

Address the first envelope; then roll it back (toward you) until ½" shows above the alignment scale.

Insert the next envelope from the front, placing it between the first envelope and the cylinder.

Turn the cylinder back to remove the first envelope and to position the second one. Continue the "chain" by feeding all envelopes from the front of the cylinder.

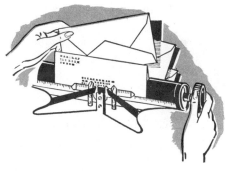

Back-feeding envelopes

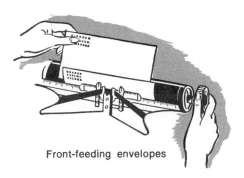

Front-feeding envelopes

* Some typewriters require three envelopes simultaneously around the platen for backfeeding. When this is necessary, insert an envelope between the bottom of the preceding envelope and the platen.

77B Communication Aid: APOSTROPHE (10) as directed in 76C, page 154; heading, APOSTROPHE

Words

Rules 4

(1) When common possession is to be shown for two or more persons, use 19
's with the last name only. 25

(2) Possessive pronouns do not take an apostrophe. (It's is the contrac- 40
tion of it is and thus requires an apostrophe.) 51

(3) When a one-syllable proper name ends in s or other sibilant, add 's 66
for possession. 69

(4) Add only an apostrophe to show possession with a multisyllable proper 84
name ending in s or other sibilant. 91

Examples 95

(1) Van and Bert's mother is here; Jan's and Pat's mothers have left. 109

(2) The book is hers. Its cover is torn, so wrap it with great care. 123

(3) Bess's talk on current events was better than Mr. Nance's report. 137

(4) Carl Williams' store is only one block from Vince Marquez' house. 152

Application Paragraph 160

Bob and Hollys station wagon is packed with Rosss bat and ball, 173
Rays badminton set, and Louis volleyball. Jeans sweater is packed; 187
Holly is not taking hers. If its a nice day, they will eat lunch on 201
one of Jesss picnic tables; if not, they will eat on Frances porch. 215

77C Production Typing Information: TABLES WITH TWO-LINE ITEMS; TABLES WITH FIGURE COLUMNS (5)

Two-Line Items. If a column in a table consists of items of even length with but 1 or 2 exceptionally long ones, break the long items into 2 or more lines and then determine which line is the longest in the column. Use that line to position the column in backspacing from center.

Figure Columns. Many tables have a descriptive column that accompanies 2 or more columns of related figures. The descriptive column is called the *stub*. For eye appeal and ease of reading, leave a greater number of spaces between the stub and the first figure column than between the figure columns.

77D Production Typing: TABLES (30)

Half sheet; short side at left; exact center; SS; 12 spaces between columns

Problem 1:

HALLARON CORPORATION DS

Branch Offices TS

Location	Manager	Words
		4
		7
Location	Manager	14
Albany, New York	E. P. Ward	19
New Brunswick, New Jersey	Louise Rosenberg	28
Sioux City, Iowa	G. B. Lockhardt	35
Omaha, Nebraska	Tallie V. Harris	41
Cleveland, Ohio	Lucien Prentiss	48
South Bend, Indiana	Paul M. Fuentes	55

71D Production Typing (30)

Problem 1: Chain Feeding Envelopes

Chain-feed 16 small envelopes, typing 2 for each of the following addresses. Feed 8 envelopes by method 1 (back feeding) and 8 by Method 2 (front feeding). Reference: page 142.

Ocean Beverages
17 French Street
Atlantic City, NJ 08401

Indiana Bottlers, Inc.
1599 Arsenal Avenue, North
Indianapolis, IN 46201

Metro Distributors
1565 Ozark Street
Springfield, MO 65803

New England Products Company
212 Calvin Street
Springfield, MA 01104

Cliff House Bottling Company
655 Cliff Avenue
Binghamton, NY 13905

Capital Beverages, Inc.
19 Rhode Island Avenue, N.E.
Washington, DC 20002

Dixie Beverage Company
467 Buchanan Street
Greensboro, NC 27405

Al's Friendly Service
787 Monitor Road
Poughkeepsie, NY 12603

Problem 2: Interoffice Memorandum *(WB p. 141)*

		Words
TO:	Ralph Bemis Proctor	4
FROM:	Jaylene O. Curts	7
DATE:	February 2, 19--	11
SUBJECT:	Advertising Program for Crystal Ade	18

(¶ 1) We are making progress with the advertising plans for Crystal Ade. Frank, Beeman & Heinz promise that we shall have sample magazine layouts soon. They are also planning some radio and television packages for our consideration. As our budget for the Crystal Ade promotion is only $150,000 for this year, however, we shall need to be selective; that is, we must decide soon whether we want to concentrate our advertising in one medium or whether it might be wiser to use a shotgun approach through a variety of media. (¶ 2) A few members of our sales staff have sug- 25 34 43 51 60 68 77 87 96 105 114 121 130

gested that some sort of catchy slogan might help catch the imagination of the public. Do any of the following ideas appeal to you? 139 148 156

(SS and indent each line 12 spaces.)

Crystal Ade: Your own private iceberg — 164
Crystal Ade: Just a hint of lemon — 171
Crystal Ade: It's a y-u-m-m-m drink — 179
Crystal Ade: When everything else goes wrong — 187 188
Crystal Ade: All it needs is you — 195

(¶ 3) If you think the idea of a slogan is a good one, perhaps we could sponsor a contest in conjunction with our other advertising. 202 211 220
(¶ 4) The merits of these suggestions can, of course, be discussed at our next Executive Committee meeting; but I should like to include in our present planning any suggestions you might want to make. xx 228 237 245 254 260/266

Problem 3: Composition *(WB p. 143)*

Assume you are the assistant advertising manager. Compose an interoffice memorandum to Mrs. Curts. In it, indicate either (1) your preference for one of the slogans in Problem 2 or (2) suggest one or two other slogans that you think might be considered. Give reasons for your choice(s). Proofread; mark any necessary corrections; then type a final copy.

76E Production Typing: TWO-COLUMN TABLE [15]

			Words in Columns	Total Words
Main heading	APOSTROPHE USAGE			3
Secondary heading	Examples of Possessive Forms			9
Column headings	Singular	Plural		15
	mouse's	mice's	3	18
	gentleman's	gentlemen's	8	23
	girl's	girls'	11	26
	rose's	roses'	13	29
	month's	months'	17	32
	lady's	ladies'	20	35
	deer's	deer's	22	38
	boss's	bosses'	25	41
	child's	children's	29	44
	my	our	31	46
	foreman's	foremen's	35	50

11	14	11

Problem 1: Table on Half-Size Paper

After studying the information on page 155 and the placement of the various parts of the table illustrated above, type the table in exact center as shown.

Problem 2: Table with Changes

In the remaining time, type the illustrated table again, omitting the secondary heading and leaving 10 spaces between columns. (*47 words*)

LESSON 77

77A Preparatory Practice [5] each line at least 3 times

Alphabet	His proclivity to work explains his fine grade on a major botany quiz.
Figure/symbol	L/P, Inc., 7521½ Hone Road, grossed 2¼% more ($2,348.60) than in 1974.
d, e	Eddie decided to deed the feedlot to Fred; he indeed needed the money.
Fluency	Time is such a costly element, we ought to use it as wisely as we can.

| 1 | 2 | 3 | 4 | 5 | 6 | 7 | 8 | 9 | 10 | 11 | 12 | 13 | 14 |

LESSON 72

72A Preparatory Practice [5] each line at least 3 times

Alphabet	Five zebras will quietly make appearances in this dark, exotic jungle.
Figure/symbol	Invoice #267-095, dated May 23, read: "140 ctns. (Grade 8) @ 12¢ ea."
c, d	Dick deduced the cold wind could induce Cedric to decal the goods COD.
Fluency	A woman is entitled to equal pay when she does the same work as a man.
	| 1 | 2 | 3 | 4 | 5 | 6 | 7 | 8 | 9 | 10 | 11 | 12 | 13 | 14 |

72B Growth Index [15] two 5′ control-level writings; figure GWAM for each writing

All letters are used.

		GWAM 1′	GWAM 5′	
¶ 1 1.5 SI 5.6 AWL 80% HFW	It would be unusual for a conscious person to get through a day	13	3	60
	and not make a decision of one sort or another. Each day's activity	27	5	62
	presents alternatives and comparisons that demand of us a choice. Such	41	8	65
	choices are usually not of equal value; that is, in most cases one choice	56	11	68
	will result in better consequences than the other. A good choice is	70	14	71
	based on logic drawn from education and experience; and the better deci-	84	17	74
	sions we make, the better judgment we are said to have.	95	19	76
¶ 2 1.5 SI 5.6 AWL 80% HFW	Although our modern world surrounds us with a sense of urgency, an	13	22	79
	important decision ought not to be made in haste. When we face such a	28	25	82
	decision, we need time to deliberate about our alternatives, to discrimi-	42	27	85
	nate between this and that idea, to distinguish the plausible from the	56	30	87
	unlikely, and to check carefully all of the facts. What we deposit away	71	33	90
	in our minds becomes our "data bank," to which we turn for the solutions	86	36	93
	to problems. We can do this--or we can guess.	95	38	95
¶ 3 1.5 SI 5.6 AWL 80% HFW	Other factors can, and should, be part of our deliberations. Each	13	41	96
	of us, for instance, needs to develop and to use the personal touch of	28	43	101
	beauty, of symmetry, and of compassion; for emotions, as well as logic,	42	46	103
	are a vital part in making a decision. But we should avoid the hazard	56	49	106
	of looking for absolutes, of believing that we must always decide one	70	52	109
	way or another. When we face problems that involve people, a small	84	55	112
	compromise is often a better solution than a large decision.	96	57	114
1′ GWAM	| 1 | 2 | 3 | 4 | 5 | 6 | 7 | 8 | 9 | 10 | 11 | 12 | 13 | 14 |			
5′ GWAM	| 1 | 2 | 3 |			

Vertical placement of tables

Exact. Count total lines to be used, including any blank lines; subtract total from lines available; divide remainder by 2 (disregarding a fraction). Leave this number of blank lines in the top margin.

Reading Position. Start the material 2 lines above the computed exact center.

Roll-Back Method. Insert the paper; roll it to the vertical center. Roll the cylinder back (toward you) once for every 2 lines in the table. This will place the copy in exact vertical center. For reading position, roll the cylinder back 2 additional lines.

Spacing After Headings. Leave 1 blank line between a main and a secondary heading and between a column heading and its column. Leave 2 blank lines below a main heading, if a secondary heading is not used, or after a secondary heading when both a main and a secondary heading are used.

Horizontal placement of tables

Centered Headings. After determining the top margin and spacing down to the starting line, center the main heading; DS and center a secondary heading, if used; then TS--as noted above.

Columns (Backspace-from-Center Method). Note the longest item in each column. If a column heading is the longest item, count it as such unless judgment indicates otherwise. Decide the number of spaces to leave between columns (preferably an even number).

Backspace from the center of the paper once for every 2 strokes in the longest line of each column and once for every 2 spaces between the columns (the *intercolumns*). Count any odd or leftover stroke with the next column or intercolumn. At the point where you complete the backspacing, set the left *margin* stop for the first column.

From the left margin, space forward once for each stroke in the first column and once for each space between the first and second columns. Set the first *tab* stop. Follow this procedure to set tab stops for the remaining columns.

Column Headings. Center column headings over the columns. When you have counted a column heading as the longest item in a column, you may need to reset the tab stop to center the *column* below the *heading*.

There are several methods of centering a column heading over a column, but probably the easiest is to add

the cyclinder-scale figures for the first and last strokes in the column. Dividing this sum by 2 will result in the center point of the column.

Column headings are usually underlined.

Horizontal rulings

Horizontal lines or *rulings* are often used in tables to set off the column headings. Usually, a full-width double ruling is typed above the column headings and a single ruling below them. A single ruling is also typed below the last line of the table.

These rulings can be the exact width of the table, or they can extend several spaces on each side of it. To type rulings the exact width of the table, first determine the placement of the columns. After setting the tab stop for the last column, continue spacing forward once for each stroke in the last column. Immediately after stroking for the last stroke, set the right margin stop to lock the carriage at that point. You can then type rulings across the page until the carriage locks.

Double Rulings. DS from the last line of the centered heading; type the first of the double rulings; then operate the variable line spacer and move the cylinder forward slightly; type the second ruling. DS between this double ruling and the column headings.

Single Rulings. SS from the column headings; type a single ruling; DS and type the first items in the columns. After typing the last items in the columns, SS and type a single ruling.

Source Note (If Used). DS from the last single ruling; type the source note at the left margin or indent 3 to 5 spaces.

Tab stops for columns of figures

Uneven Columns. When a column contains items uneven in length, set the tab stop at a point that will suit the greatest number of entries. After tabulating, backspace for longer items or space forward for shorter ones.

Dollar Signs. In a money column, type a dollar sign before the first amount in the column and before the total, if one is shown. Type the dollar sign before the first amount aligned 1 space to the left of the longest amount in the column, which might be the total.

Totals. Totals are treated as a part of the column. For easier reading, totals are usually separated by a blank line from the last item in the column.

Problem 1: Letter on Executive-Size Paper (WB p. 145)

	Words
February 5, 19-- The Honorable Albert S.	8
Banks Mayor, The City of Charlotte, Char-	16
lotte City Hall, Charlotte, North Carolina	24
Dear Mayor Banks (¶ 1) Thank you for your	32
kind invitation to serve on the Charlotte Com-	41
munity Action and Growth Committee. I am	49
happy to accept this appointment. (¶ 2) As	57
you know, I have long been interested in the	66
civic development of our community. As a	74
former chairman of the Treasure Chest Drive,	83
I am well aware of the crucial needs of the	92
Charlotte area and of a few of the ways in	100
which those needs can best be met. (¶ 3) I	108
am particularly pleased to be working with	117
Dr. Lawrence. I have worked with him on	125
various projects, and I know and appreciate	134
his philosophy. He is an outstanding person,	143
and Charlotte is certainly fortunate that he is	152
free to work with us at this time. As the	161
chairman of the Community Action and	168
Growth Committee, he will provide the type	177
of leadership that will accomplish the most in	186
the shortest time. (¶ 4) Thank you for your	194
expression of confidence in the work I have	203
been trying to do. I am pleased to contribute	212
my services to your administration, Mr.	220
Mayor, and to the people of Charlotte. Sin-	229
cerely yours Alfred B. Graessel Vice Presi-	237
dent xx	239/259

Problem 2: Interoffice Memorandum (WB p. 147)

	Words
TO: B. W. Draybicki, Office Manager FROM:	6
Nora E. Lindell, Purchasing Director DATE:	14
February 5, 19-- SUBJECT: Typewriting	20
Services	21
(¶ 1) Our office is preparing a number of re-	29
ports and letters relating to Company prob-	37
lems with the Sudan Street warehouse. Would	46
it be possible to have a typist from the gen-	55
eral office assigned to us full time until the	65
present crush of work is over? (¶ 2) We	72

	Words
want someone who can type well, of course;	80
but it is just as important that the person you	90
send be able to (1) type from a variety of	98
source notes, (2) provide us with necessary	107
editorial services (who can and will proof-	116
read; who can spell and punctuate), and (3)	124
be knowledgeable about typing items in ac-	133
ceptable form. (¶ 3) In other words, Brad, we	141
want a typist who can do more than just type;	150
we are asking for a genuine professional who	159
knows how to communicate. (¶ 4) Can you	166
help us? xx	169/177

Problem 3: Letter on Half-Size Paper (WB p. 149)

Half sheet, long side at left; modified block style; date on Line 12; side margins approximately ¾″

	Words
February 5, 19-- Mrs. Viviann Cushman	8
5422 Skycrest Lane Charlotte, NC 28210	16
Dear Mrs. Cushman (¶ 1) On behalf of its	23
employees, officers, and Board of Directors,	32
I am happy to inform you of this Company's	40
decision to donate the amount of $5,000	48
toward the development of playground and	56
park facilities in the Sleepy Hollow area.	65
(¶ 2) As a corporate resident of this city, we	73
welcome this opportunity to express our in-	82
terest in and concern for Charlotte. It is a	91
great city, and we take pride in the small part	100
we have been able to play in its development.	110
(¶ 3) We await your instructions for the deliv-	118
ery of our check. Very truly yours Ralph	126
Bemis Proctor President xx	131/143

Problem 4: Chain-Feeding Small Envelopes

Type an envelope for Problems 1-3, above; then type an envelope for each of the Charlotte residents listed below. Provide appropriate personal titles.

Rachel Hayes	2784 Sherbrook Drive	28210
Enzo Gabruci	6301 Sherbourne Road	28210
David Lansky	5942 Sherrill Avenue	28208
James E. Lee	3567 Sherwood Avenue	28207
Edna Parkman	1235 Shirhall Street	28208
Monette Lieb	2456 Shoreline Drive	28214
Bette Grants	4678 Silabert Avenue	28205

76B Paragraph Guided Writing [5] two 1½′ writings; try to complete the ¶

All letters are used.

1.5 SI
5.6 AWL
80% HFW

Just a few years ago, a zone number was included in most envelope addresses for the purpose of expediting the sorting of mail by hand. As the years went by, however, post offices experienced such an increase in work load that a change in the methods of sorting mail was required. As a result, ZIP Code and the optical scanning system were devised. Now, all envelopes can be fed through a machine that "reads" the final two lines of each address and automatically sorts the mail.

76C Communication Aid: APOSTROPHE [15] full sheet; 1½″ top margin; 70-space line; SS; DS between items

1. For the heading, type APOSTROPHE.
2. Type the rules and examples given below (with figures); underline the side headings.
3. Type the application paragraph, inserting the proper punctuation as you type.

Words

Rules 4

(1) The singular possessive is usually formed by adding 's; but for words 20
having more than one syllable and ending in s, only the apostrophe 33
is added. 35

(2) When plural nouns do not end in s, add 's to form the possessive. 50

(3) Add only the apostrophe to form the possessive of plural nouns ending 64
in s. 66

(4) The possessive of initials, abbreviations, etc., is formed with 's. 81

Examples 84

(1) The Countess' son (my boss's uncle) financed his brother's trips. 99

(2) Children's shoes and women's robes are on sale at the local shop. 113

(3) The girls' shoes and boys' coats will be shipped by fast express. 127

(4) William Wright, Jr.'s signature must appear on the YMCA's checks. 141

Application Paragraph 150

Janets problem: She cannot locate her hostess address. It is in 163
her purse, which she left lying with several girls coats in the ladies 178
lounge in one of Miamis larger hotels. Her initials are on the purse. 193
If it is not found, she will stay at Jills house until next Wednesday. 207

SECTION 13 Production Measurement

LESSONS 73-74

In Section 13 you will be asked to type problems similar to those typed in prior lessons. Follow directions and make any necessary decisions. Proofread before taking problems from the typewriter. If you finish before time is called, begin Problem 1 again. Use the current date and your reference initials. Make a carbon copy; type an appropriate envelope; erase and correct errors.

Paragraph Copy: Full sheet; 70-space line; DS; 5-space ¶ indention.

Materials Needed: Letterheads in regular and executive sizes (or appropriate substitutes); interoffice communication forms; carbon paper; file copy sheets; and envelopes.

$$\text{N-PRAM} = \frac{\text{Gross (total) words} - \text{Penalties}}{\text{Length (in minutes) of writing}}$$

Penalties for Errors: Deduct 10 words for each error not erased on an original copy; deduct 5 words for each error not erased on a carbon copy.

LESSON 73

73A Preparatory Practice (5) each line at least 3 times

Alphabet	Frank eloquently extemporized on his subject, "Letting a Vision Grow."
Figure/symbol	Invoice #46-891 lists credit terms of $2\frac{1}{2}$/15, n/30. We can save $7.49.
Adjacent keys	Three tired wrens stopped on their return trip to the old poplar tree.
Fluency	It is fine to be a "good sport" if one doesn't lose his individuality.
	| 1 | 2 | 3 | 4 | 5 | 6 | 7 | 8 | 9 | 10 | 11 | 12 | 13 | 14 |

73B Speed/Control Building: STATISTICAL COPY (10) one 3′ exploratory writing; then two 3′ control-level writings

All letters are used.

		GWAM 1′	GWAM 3′	
¶ 1	When you begin organizing to type a letter, judge what you perceive	14	5	64
1.5 SI	to be the approximate length of the letter; as, short, average, long, or	28	9	69
5.6 AWL	2-page, for example. Making such a decision assists you to identify (1)	43	14	74
80% HFW	where a date ought to be typed and (2) an appropriate width for lateral	57	19	79
	margins. For any business letters you type in the next few lessons, the	72	24	84
	first line of the letter address should be typed 4 lines below the date.	86	29	89
¶ 2	A few reminders about the guidelines for letter placement may be	13	33	93
1.5 SI	helpful. You probably recall that for a short letter, 2-inch lateral	27	38	98
5.6 AWL	margins are appropriate and that the date can be typed on about Line 20.	42	43	103
80% HFW	For an average letter, $1\frac{1}{2}$-inch margins are more suitable; and the date	56	47	107
	can be typed higher, on about Line 15. For a long letter or one that	70	52	112
	will require 2 pages, use 1-inch margins with the date typed on about	84	57	117
	Line 12. Refer to page 106 for additional review.	94	60	120
1′ GWAM	| 1 | 2 | 3 | 4 | 5 | 6 | 7 | 8 | 9 | 10 | 11 | 12 | 13 | 14 |			
3′ GWAM	| 1 | 2 | 3 | 4 | 5 |			

75C Technique Improvement: TABULATING (10) 3 times; DS between groups

Full sheet; 3″ top margin; SS; decide spaces between columns

21,232	34,313	41,454
56,515	61,676	78,717
81,898	90,919	10,090
42,325	23,057	87,906
32,464	70,658	78,998

75D Communication Pretest: APOSTROPHE (10) Full sheet; 2″ top margin; 50-space line; DS; 10 spaces between columns

Type a 2-column report using the words at the right for the first column. For the second column, type each of the words to show plural possession; for example, type *mouse's* as *mice's*. Check your results with 76E, page 156.

mouse's	month's	child's
gentleman's	lady's	bird's
girl's	deer's	my
rose's	boss's	foreman's

75E Technique Improvement: STROKING (10) each line 3 times on the control level

Hold your arms and hands quiet. Center the stroking action in your fingers.

1	i, o	Clio and Leroi avoided joining a trio of soil biologists going to Rio.
2	m, n	Name some of the men from Miami who minimized the importance of money.
3	r, e	Rex retired a red retriever, who never erred in her three-year career.
4	s, a	Sara Aster has the last essay that asserts Sam Caster was no assassin.
5	s, d	Sandy strode to the dais and delivered the saddest address of the day.
6	t, r	Ruth rented a hall for a party prior to Trent's departure for Toronto.
7	v, b	The very brave boys have driven visibly vibrating vehicles to Batavia.
8	er, re	Letters I received there were more errorfree but were delivered later.

| 1 | 2 | 3 | 4 | 5 | 6 | 7 | 8 | 9 | 10 | 11 | 12 | 13 | 14 |

LESSON 76

76A Preparatory Practice (5) each line at least 3 times

Alphabet	His five calm blue oxen, wearing antique yokes, won the judges' prize.
Figure/symbol	King & Wynn collected $6,582, plus 4½% interest, less $137.90 in fees.
Home row	Daylight was fading; Hal adjusted the waning little spark of gaslight.
Fluency	They can spend eight days with the formal chairman of the civic corps.

| 1 | 2 | 3 | 4 | 5 | 6 | 7 | 8 | 9 | 10 | 11 | 12 | 13 | 14 |

73C Production Measurement ㉟ 25′ timing; compute N-PRAM

Problem 1: Modified Block Letter with Centered Subject Line; Postscript (WB p. 151)

	Words

Mixed punctuation; begin letter 2 lines higher than usual

Professor John S. Scranton Southern Nevada University Las Vegas NV 89109 Dear Professor Scranton Subject: INTRODUCTORY MARKETING (¶ 1) I have some good news and some bad news for you. (¶ 2) Let me give you the bad news first. The last printing of the textbook you use in your principles of marketing class, INTRODUCTORY MARKETING, will come off the press February 1. When our supply has been exhausted, no more will be available. (¶ 3) Now the good news! Before the start of your fall session, the second edition of INTRODUCTORY MARKETING will be ready for your use. This exciting book is one that you and your students will enjoy using. It brings the marketplace to you as a laboratory and makes marketing the alive and fascinating subject that it ought to be. (¶ 4) One of the first copies of this new edition will be sent to you for examination. Let me know what you think of it. A card for your comments will be enclosed with the book; and because we sincerely believe that your reaction will be favorable, we shall also enclose an order blank for your use. Very truly yours WILLIAMSON PRESS T. C. Redwing Senior Editor xx PRINCIPLES OF ADVERTISING, by Schless and Gray, is being revised also. A copy of this fine revision will be sent to you in May.

Words: 16, 29, 41, 55, 69, 83, 96, 110, 124, 138, 153, 166, 181, 196, 211, 225, 238, 252/267

Problem 2: AMS Simplified Letter (WB p. 153)

Make the appropriate changes in Problem 1 to convert the letter to the AMS simplified style. (Use the word count shown for Problem 1, but deduct 13 words for omitted parts. Begin the letter in the usual position.)

Problem 3: Chain-Feeding Envelopes

Type an envelope for each of the addresses shown at the right. Provide an appropriate title for each addressee. If time permits, type a second set of envelopes to the same addresses. For each envelope typed, add 10 words for your gross word count.

Ivan Metaxa 389 Hillside Street Syracuse, NY 13208

Helen Blass 288 Carroll Avenue Asheville, NC 28801

Victoria J. Brown 15 Swift Drive Raleigh, NC 27606

Anne Low 369 Clifton Avenue Mansfield, OH 44907

Joseph E. Sparrow 202 Mary Street Peoria, IL 61603

Marie Strong 5 Lloyd Street Scranton, PA 18510

Rick S. Brooks 504 Secoffee Street Miami, FL 33133

E. F. Maz 1723 Oxford Avenue Green Bay, WI 54303

Sue O'Harra 3111 Yacht Street Bridgeport, CT 06605

Roy Quick 757 Duke Street Newport News, VA 23607

Problem 4: Interoffice Memorandum with Enclosure Notation (WB p. 155)

	Words

Provide punctuation as needed; correct it where wrong

TO: Richard Toivenen, Branch Manager FROM: P. J. Lopez, General Sales Manager DATE: (current) SUBJECT: Marketing Information (¶ 1) I am enclosing a two page questionnaire asking for the following data. Where should our new line of adhesive products initially be introduced? (¶ 2) This new line will be shown at our annual sales meeting, but before it can be introduced onto the market, the information requested in the questionnaire must be obtained and analyzed. (¶ 3) Until I receive replies from all branch managers our plans for promotion must wait. Will you please therefore, rush your reply to me. xx Enclosure

Words: 14, 29, 42, 55, 68, 82, 95, 109, 122

SECTION 14 Tables with Special Features

LESSONS 75-80

Machine Adjustments. Unless otherwise directed, proceed as follows: SS drill copy on a 70-space line. Indent ¶ copy 5 spaces, DS, 70-space line. Letterhead or plain paper for production copy. Follow directions for each problem. You need not make cc's of the problems in this section.

LESSON 75

75A Preparatory Practice (5) each line at least 3 times

Alphabet	Happily, Monique believed George's zany joke was excruciatingly funny.
Figure/symbol	Ken's stock, bought at $135\frac{1}{2}$, sold for $248\frac{1}{4}$ in the 1969-70 bull market.
Shift keys	Karen, Lee, Jo Anne, and Bill attend North Madison Junior High School.
Fluency	The worker who takes pride in his work seldom has to do any job twice.
	| 1 | 2 | 3 | 4 | 5 | 6 | 7 | 8 | 9 | 10 | 11 | 12 | 13 | 14 |

75B Speed Building: STATISTICAL (15) two 2′ writings; then two 3′ writings. Try to maintain or improve GWAM on each writing.

All letters are used.

1.5 SI
5.6 AWL
80% HFW

	GWAM 2′	3′	
If we study money just as a tool used to facilitate business, only	7	4	57
a medium that will be accepted in exchange for goods, services, and	14	9	61
other assets needs to be emphasized. Many things have served as money	21	14	66
through the ages, but today two kinds of money are used in significant	28	18	71
amounts––currency (paper money and coins) and demand deposits (checking	35	23	75
accounts). As $1 in currency and $1 in demand deposits can be freely	42	28	80
converted into each other at the option of a bank's customers, both are	49	33	85
money to an equal degree. While currency is used for a great variety	56	37	90
of small transactions, most of the money payments in our economy are	63	42	94
made by check. In fact, nearly 80 percent, or $170 billion, of the $220	70	47	99
billion total money stock at the end of 1970 was in the form of demand	77	51	103
deposits.	78	52	104

2′ GWAM | 1 | 2 | 3 | 4 | 5 | 6 | 7 |
3′ GWAM | 1 | 2 | 3 | 4 | 5 |

LESSON 74

74A Preparatory Practice [5] each line at least 3 times

Alphabet	Fred Zwik gave an excellent speech by quoting many famous journalists.
Figure/symbol	Its weight is 36#; height, 2′8″; length, 27′9″; code number, 14-5809*.
Left hand	Fred Carteret traced garden addresses for several crates of red beets.
Fluency	Take what I own that is valuable, but do not deprive me of my dignity.
	| 1 | 2 | 3 | 4 | 5 | 6 | 7 | 8 | 9 | 10 | 11 | 12 | 13 | 14 |

74B Growth Index [15] two 5′ control-level writings; compute GWAM

All letters are used.

		GWAM 1′	GWAM 5′	
¶ 1	The importance of education has increased and is increasing. Three	14	3	56
1.5 SI	basic reasons account for our need of more education. First of all, we	28	6	59
5.6 AWL	are living in a changing, complex society that comes to us as a direct	42	8	62
80% HFW	result of learning. Living for us is easier; improved education is	56	11	65
	needed, though, if we are to continue to make our lives easier and at	70	14	68
	the same time to cope successfully with the kind of problems that arise	84	17	71
	when life does become easier.	90	18	72
¶ 2	The need for knowledge is basic to our form of government, too.	13	21	74
1.5 SI	Each citizen in a democracy is asked to pass judgment on proposals that	27	23	77
5.6 AWL	will affect him, his family, his country. Even when he buys an article	42	26	80
80% HFW	in a store, he casts an economic vote in a free enterprise system. When	56	29	83
	a person expresses political or economic preferences, he votes; and he	71	32	86
	must be aware of what he is doing. Our form of government will not	84	35	89
	flourish in ignorance.	89	36	90
¶ 3	Finally, it might be said that the need for education is basic to	13	38	92
1.5 SI	humanity. Knowledge is practical; it works for us. But beyond the func-	28	41	95
5.6 AWL	tional side of learning is the fact that the acquisition of knowledge is	42	44	98
80% HFW	an enriching experience. Simply to know, to get at truth, can be reward	57	47	101
	enough, whether or not the information gained is useful. An active mind	72	50	104
	looks for answers; and the time it takes to find them, hours or years,	86	53	107
	is usually worth it.	90	54	108
1′ GWAM	| 1 | 2 | 3 | 4 | 5 | 6 | 7 | 8 | 9 | 10 | 11 | 12 | 13 | 14 |			
5′ GWAM	| 1 | 2 | 3 |			

74C Production Measurement [30] 25′ timing; figure N-PRAM

Problem 1: Letter on Executive-Size Paper *(WB p. 157)*

Block style; open punctuation; 2 cc's; retain 1 cc

	Words
Chippewa Lumber Supply Company 799 Wisconsin Avenue Des Moines,	16
IA 50316 Gentlemen (¶ 1) Effective immediately, we are announcing	28
a price increase of one cent per board foot on all plywood sheeting,	42
regardless of size, strength, or finish. (¶ 2) Informing customers of a rise	56
in prices is not a pleasant matter, but we know you will understand that	71

the recent increase in freight rates has made our present price list | 84
inoperative. Despite intense pressure, we have delayed a price change | 99
for some time; now it is unavoidable. (¶ 3) We appreciate the orders you | 112
have given us in the past; we assure you of the same cheerful, prompt | 126
service in the future. Very truly yours S. K. Johnson President xx | 140
Enclosure

142/157

Problem 2: Letter with Special Features (WB p. 159)

Modified block style; mixed punctuation

Retype the letter in Problem 1 on a full sheet. Add in their proper positions the special business-letter features shown below. Use the extra cc from Problem 1 as a planning sheet.

SUBJECT: Price Increase

Postscript:

This price change involves plywood ONLY. Our other prices remain unchanged.

SOUTH CAROLINA PINE COMPANY

Attention Purchasing Officer

AIRMAIL

(Add 33 words to the count in Problem 1 to accommodate the added features in this problem.)

Problem 3: Modified Block Letter with Attention Line (WB p. 161)

Mixed punctuation

Words

October 20, 19-- Atlas Wheel Company | 7
5000 Pitt Street New Orleans, LA 70115 | 15
Attention Accounts Payable Gentlemen (¶ 1) | 23
This letter is a friendly reminder that your | 32
account with us is overdue. We should have | 41
received your check for $174 before the first | 50
of the month. (¶ 2) We know that occasion- | 57
ally an account will be overlooked in the end- | 67
of-the-month rush and that, in fact, your check | 76
may already be in the mail to us. (¶ 3) If you | 85
have mailed your check, please accept this | 93
letter as a thank you; if not, won't you just | 102
accept it as a very gentle nudge in our direc- | 111
tion? Sincerely yours Clifton E. DuLong | 119
Credit Manager xx | 123/135

Problem 4: Interoffice Memorandum (WB p. 163)

Do not type envelopes

Words

TO: Carl Bledsoe, T. Laurens Green, Marvin Shay FROM: E. T. Sancho, | 12
Regional Manager DATE: *Current* SUBJECT: Sale of Overstocked Mate- | 23
rials (¶ 1) It has come to my attention that with the current high levels | 37
of inventories, some of our divisional offices are disposing of overstocked | 52
materials to local customers at greatly reduced prices. Perhaps it would | 67
be well for one divisional office to circularize the others before dis- | 81
posing of usable stock. In this way we could take care of our own needs | 95
before disposing of stock. (¶ 2) I am eager to balance our inventories as | 109
rapidly as possible and do not wish to slow down the sale or disposal of | 124
surplus materials. I shall, however, appreciate your notifying other | 138
divisions before selling surplus materials. xx | 147

REFERENCE GUIDE

Typewriter Operative Parts

Typewriters have similar operative parts, the names of which vary somewhat from typewriter to typewriter even when the function is the same. These similar operative parts are identified in the four segments of a typewriter given below and on page ii. Each segment is a composite and not an exact segment of any one typewriter. For this reason, the exact location of a part identified in the segment may be slightly different from that on your typewriter; but the differences are, for the most part, few and slight.

Extra parts that are peculiar to your typewriter can be identified by reference to the instructional booklet distributed by the manufacturer of the typewriter. This booklet can be very helpful to you because its content is directed to the operation of one specific make of machine.

In using the illustrations, follow the line from the number to the part location. Know the function of each part, as explained in the textbook, and learn to operate it with maximum efficiency.

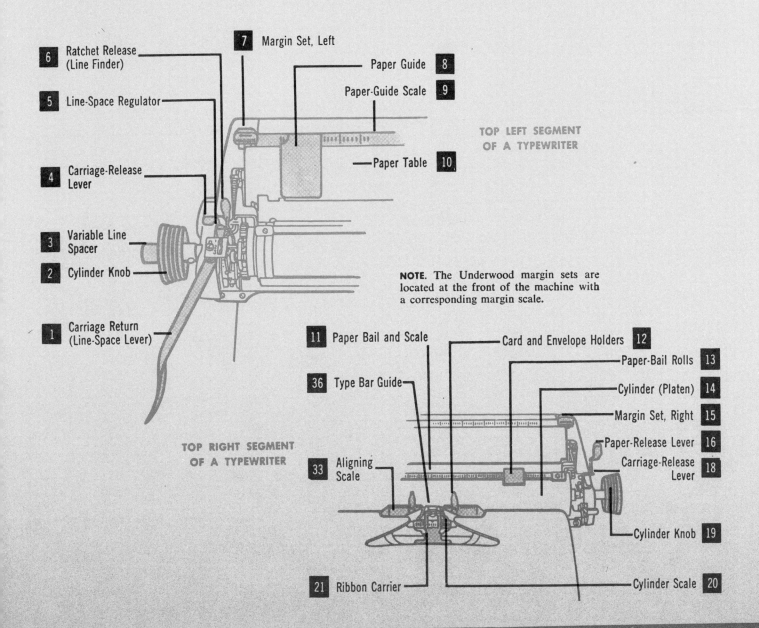

6 Ratchet Release (Line Finder)

7 Margin Set, Left

5 Line-Space Regulator

8 Paper Guide

9 Paper-Guide Scale

TOP LEFT SEGMENT OF A TYPEWRITER

4 Carriage-Release Lever

10 Paper Table

3 Variable Line Spacer

2 Cylinder Knob

NOTE. The Underwood margin sets are located at the front of the machine with a corresponding margin scale.

1 Carriage Return (Line-Space Lever)

11 Paper Bail and Scale

12 Card and Envelope Holders

13 Paper-Bail Rolls

36 Type Bar Guide

14 Cylinder (Platen)

15 Margin Set, Right

16 Paper-Release Lever

TOP RIGHT SEGMENT OF A TYPEWRITER

33 Aligning Scale

18 Carriage-Release Lever

19 Cylinder Knob

21 Ribbon Carrier

20 Cylinder Scale

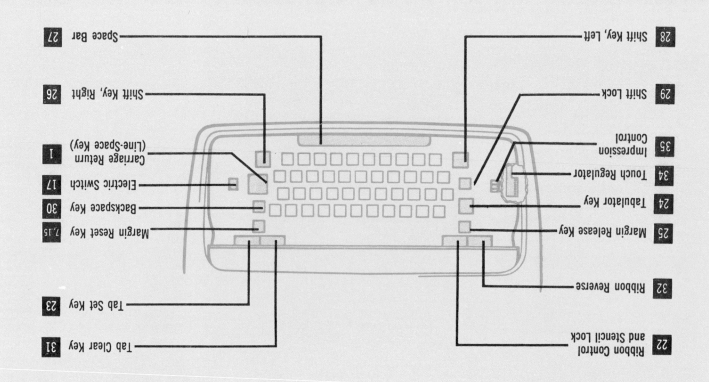

27	Space Bar
28	Shift Key, Left
26	Shift Key, Right
29	Shift Lock
1	Carriage Return (Line-Space Key)
35	Impression Control
17	Electric Switch
34	Touch Regulator
30	Backspace Key
24	Tabulator Key
7,15	Margin Reset Key
25	Margin Release Key
23	Tab Set Key
32	Ribbon Reverse
31	Tab Clear Key
22	Ribbon Control and Stencil Lock

LOWER SEGMENT OF AN ELECTRIC TYPEWRITER

CHECK YOUR TYPEWRITER TO SEE IF:
1. The position is different for: ¢ @ * ___ (underline)
2. These keys have "repeat" action: *backspace, space bar, carriage return, hyphen-underline*
3. Extra keys are used: + = ! 1

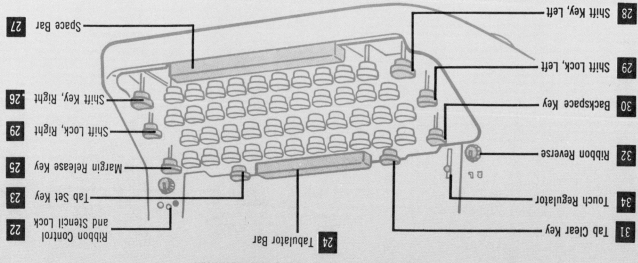

27	Space Bar
28	Shift Key, Left
29	Shift Lock, Left
26	Shift Key, Right
30	Backspace Key
29	Shift Lock, Right
32	Ribbon Reverse
25	Margin Release Key
34	Touch Regulator
23	Tab Set Key
31	Tab Clear Key
22	Ribbon Control and Stencil Lock
24	Tabulator Bar

LOWER SEGMENT OF A MANUAL TYPEWRITER

Paper Guide and Centering Point

Typewriters are of 3 types in regard to setting the paper guide and arriving at the center point.

Type 1: Royal, Olympia, Smith-Corona

Set the paper guide on 0 on the paper-guide scale. On 8½″ by 11″ paper inserted with the left edge against the guide, the centering point is 42 for pica and 51 for elite machines.

Type 2: IBM Model D, Remington

The fixed centering point is 0 for both pica and elite machines. Marks on the paper-guide scale aid the typist in setting the paper guide to center copy correctly.

Type 3: Smith-Corona Nonelectric, IBM Selectric, Olivetti

A variety of marks appear on the paper table or copy-guide scale to aid the typist in setting the paper-guide scale to center 8½″ by 11″ paper. Marks on the paper-bail scale indicate the center point of the paper.

In the absence of such marks, set the paper guide and insert the paper. Add the carriage scale reading on the left edge of the paper to the reading at the right edge. Divide this sum by 2 for the center point.

Standard Centering Directions

All typewriters have at least 1 scale, usually the cylinder scale **(20)**, that reads from 0 at the left to 85 or more at the right. The spaces on this scale match the spacing mechanism of the machine (pica or elite).

To simplify direction giving, your instructor may ask you to insert paper into your machine so that the left edge corresponds to 0 on the carriage scale. The center point on the carriage scale for 8½″ by 11″ paper will then be 42 for pica and 51 (or, for convenience, 50) for elite.

Setting the Margin Stops (7, 15)

Center typed material horizontally by setting stops for the left and right margins. Typewriters differ in mechanical adjustments, and the bell rings at different points on different machines; but the carriage locks at the point where the right margin stop is set. After the bell rings, there will be from 6 to 11 or more strokes before the carriage locks, some machines allowing more but none fewer than 6 spaces.

Test your typewriter to determine the number of spaces at which the bell rings before the carriage locks. Take this into consideration when setting the right margin stop. Because the ringing of the bell is a cue to return the carriage, set the right stop 3 to 7 spaces beyond the desired line ending. Then the bell cue will come approximately 3 strokes before the point at which you want the line to end.

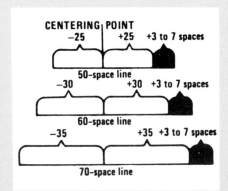

Mechanics of Setting Margin Stops

IBM Model D and Olivetti Electric

To set the left margin stop, depress the return key to return the carriage to the present margin stop. Hold down the margin set key as you move the carriage to the desired new margin point; then release the margin set key.

To set the right margin stop, move the carriage against the present right margin stop. Depress and hold down the margin set key as you move the carriage to the desired new margin position; then release the margin set key.

IBM Selectric

To set left and right margin stops, push in on the appropriate stop and slide it to the desired position on the margin scale; release the stop. Use the space bar to move the carriage out of the way when setting a margin stop to the right of the carrier's present position.

Olympia and Olivetti Nonelectric

To set left and right margin stops, move the left and right margin stops to the desired position on the margin scale.

Remington Electric and Nonelectric

Move the left margin stop to the desired left margin setting. Move the right margin stop to the desired right margin setting.

Smith-Corona Electric and Nonelectric

Depress the left carriage-release button and the left margin button and move the carriage to the desired margin setting. Release the 2 buttons simultaneously. Set the right margin similarly.

Know your typewriter

Your machine may have timesaving features not included in the foregoing discussion of operating parts. Learn these features from a study of the manufacturer's pamphlet that describes and illustrates the operating parts of the typewriter you are using. It will have many ideas for improving your operating manipulations.

You can get such pamphlets without cost from the manufacturer of your typewriter.

Changing Typewriter Ribbons

Techniques for changing ribbons vary from machine to machine. The steps that follow are basic to all machines.

1. Wind the ribbon on 1 spool—usually the right one.

2. Raise and lock the ribbon carrier as follows:
Depress the shift lock. Set the ribbon control for typing on the lower portion of the ribbon. Depress and lock any 2 central keys, such as y and t.

3. Remove the ribbon from the carrier. Remove both spools from the machine.

4. Hook the new ribbon on the empty spool and wind several inches of new ribbon on it. Be sure that the ribbon winds and unwinds in the correct direction.

5. Place both spools on their holders. Thread the ribbon indicator through the ribbon carrier.

6. Release the shift lock. Return the ribbon indicator to type on the upper portion of the ribbon. Unlock the 2 keys.

7. Clean the keys often to make your work sharp and clear.

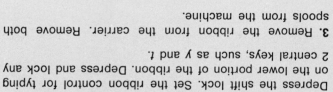
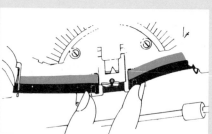

Ribbon threaded through the ribbon-carrier mechanism

Electric

Nonelectric

Path of the ribbon as it winds and unwinds on the 2 spools

Drawing Lines (Rules)

Horizontal Rules. Position the cardholder of the type bar guide at the point at which you want to start the rule. Place the pencil point through the cardholder or on the type-bar guide, depress the carriage-release lever, and draw the carriage across for a line of the desired length.

Vertical Rules. Position the carriage at the starting point desired. Release the line finder. Place the pencil point through the cardholder or on the type-bar guide above the ribbon. Roll the platen up the page until you have a line of the desired length. Reset the line finder.

Communications Design Associates

801 JACKSON STREET, WEST   CABLE: COMDA
CHICAGO, ILLINOIS   60607   TELEPHONE: (312) 342-9753

November 21, 19--

Higgins and Ransom, Inc.
7260 Queen City Avenue
Cincinnati, OH 45238

Attention Mr. Frank Nunn

Gentlemen:

The modified block style has some distinctive features,
as shown in this letter and in the enclosed pamphlet.

The date, the complimentary close, and the name and official title of the dictator begin at the horizontal center
of the paper; thus, one tabulator setting works for all
these lines.

Special lines (reference, enclosure, and carbon copy notations) begin at the left margin, a double space below the
last closing line. When the dictator's name is used in
the closing lines, the reference notation consists of the
typist's initials only. The dictator's initials, if used,
precede those of the typist.

The modified block style is widely used by the clients
for whom we prepare letters. We think you will like it.

                    Sincerely yours,

                    Charles Harley Chambers

                    Charles Harley Chambers
                    Public Service Director

mew

Enclosure: Styling Business Letters

cc Ms. Alicia LeClair

Modified block. mixed

Communications Design Associates

801 JACKSON STREET, WEST   CABLE: COMDA
CHICAGO, ILLINOIS   60607   TELEPHONE: (312) 342-9753

                    March 15, 19--
AIRMAIL

Miss Terry Mahle, Office Manager
Standard Steel Equipment Company
270 - 53d Street
Brooklyn, NY 11232

Dear Miss Mahle

    The pamphlet about letter formats that you requested
is enclosed. One of the styles described in the pamphlet
is the modified block style with indented paragraphs.
This letter illustrates that style.

    A mailing notation is typed at the left margin, a
double space below the date; however, the date and the
closing lines are begun at midpoint of the paper. The
first line of each paragraph is indented five spaces.

    We are using open punctuation, which omits punctu-
ation after the salutation and complimentary close.

    Although we do not usually use the company name in
the closing lines, we do so here to illustrate the correct
style. We are also omitting the dictator's name in the
closing lines to illustrate the reference notation style
that is then used.

    After you have examined your copy of Styling Business
Letters, will you please send us your impressions of it?

                    Sincerely yours

                    COMMUNICATIONS DESIGN ASSOCIATES

                    Charles Harley Chambers

                    Public Service Director

CHChambers:mew

Enclosure

Modified block, indented ¶, open

Communications Design Associates

801 JACKSON STREET, WEST   CABLE: COMDA
CHICAGO, ILLINOIS   60607   TELEPHONE: (312) 342-9753

February 12, 19--

Miss Doris Marshall
62200 Beacon Hill Road
Waterbury, CT 06716

Dear Miss Marshall

Subject: Styling Business Letters

Thank you for your request of a copy of our letter writing manual. This manual is not yet in print, but I hope
that the mimeographed copies currently available will
meet your needs.

We have adopted the block style of letter, of which this
letter is an example. All lines begin at the left margin, including enumerations. The machine adjustments,
therefore, are simple and save the typist's time.

We hope you will find this little pamphlet helpful. If
you want extra copies when they come off the press, just
let us know.

Sincerely yours

Charles Harley Chambers

Charles Harley Chambers
Public Service Director

mew

Enclosure

The block style may also be used for personal business
letters.

Block, open

Communications Design Associates

801 JACKSON STREET, WEST   CABLE: COMDA
CHICAGO, ILLINOIS   60607   TELEPHONE: (312) 342-9753

October 15, 19--

Mr. Salvadore Palucci
Manager, Apex Company
39501 Bartlett Avenue
Boston, MA 02129

AMS SIMPLIFIED STYLE

This letter is typed in the timesaving simplified style
recommended by the Administrative Management Society.
To type a letter in the AMS style, follow these steps:

1. Use block style.

2. Omit the salutation and complimentary close.

3. Provide a subject line and type it in ALL CAPS a
    triple space below the address. Type the first line
    of the body a triple space below the subject line.

4. Start enumerated items at the left margin, but indent
    unnumbered listed items five spaces.

5. Type the writer's name and title in ALL CAPS on one
    line at least four line spaces below the body of the
    letter.

6. Type only the typist's initials a double space below
    the writer's name.

Correspondents in your company will like the AMS simplified style for the eye appeal it gives letters, as well
as the reduction in letter writing costs it offers.

Klaus Vander Geer

KLAUS VANDER GEER, VICE PRESIDENT

ath

AMS Simplified

LETTER STYLES

Addressing Envelopes

Address Placement and Spacing. Single-space and block the address lines. The bottom line must include the city and state names and the ZIP Code, in that sequence. Leave 2 spaces between the state name or abbreviation and the ZIP Code.

When the ZIP Code is known, use the 2-letter abbreviation (page viii) in all caps without punctuation. If the ZIP Code is unavailable, type the state name in full or use the standard abbreviation.

For a small envelope, start the address lines 2″ from the top and 2½″ from the left edge.

For a large envelope, start the address lines 2½″ from the top and 4″ from the left edge.

Return Address. Start the return address on the second line from the top and 3 spaces from the left edge.

Postal Notations. Type postal notations such as AIRMAIL and SPECIAL DELIVERY, below the space required for the stamp.

Addressee Notations. Type HOLD FOR ARRIVAL, PERSONAL, PLEASE FORWARD, and the like, a triple space below the return address and 3 spaces from the left edge.

Joseph P. McDaniel ◄ *Line 2*
5003 Columbia Street
Seattle, Washington 98104
└ *3 spaces*

Line 11 or 12

2½″

Mr. Clark Greenwood, Manager
National Stores, Incorporated
2349 North Mayfair Street
Spokane, Washington 99207

Small envelope

Communications Design Associates
801 JACKSON STREET WEST   CABLE   COMDA
CHICAGO, ILLINOIS   60607   TELEPHONE (312) 342-9753

DS

Personal

2½″(Line 15 or 16)

AIRMAIL

4″

Miss Elizabeth M. Bradford
Cascade Engineering Company
218 Jefferson Street, West
Springfield, IL 62702

Large envelope

Folding-and-Inserting Procedure

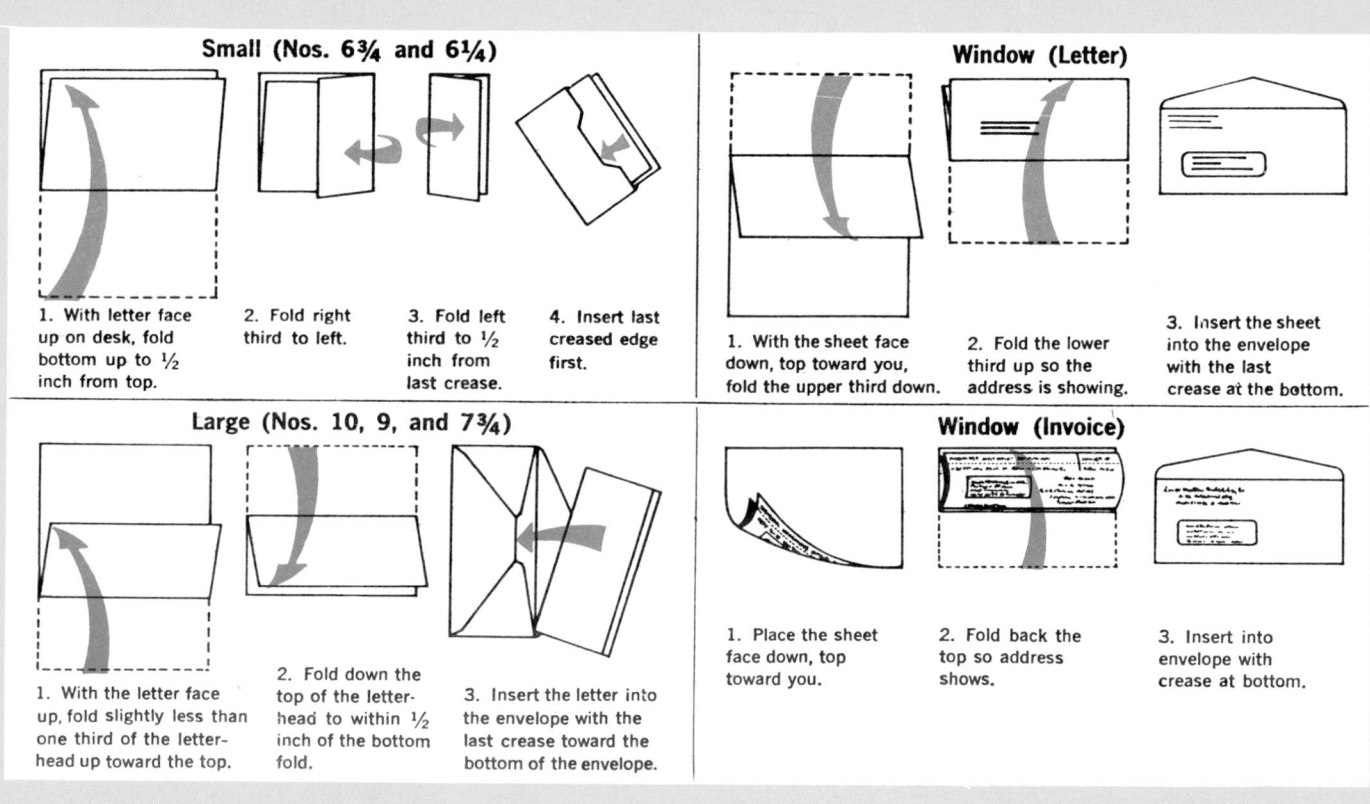

Small (Nos. 6¾ and 6¼)

1. With letter face up on desk, fold bottom up to ½ inch from top.
2. Fold right third to left.
3. Fold left third to ½ inch from last crease.
4. Insert last creased edge first.

Window (Letter)

1. With the sheet face down, top toward you, fold the upper third down.
2. Fold the lower third up so the address is showing.
3. Insert the sheet into the envelope with the last crease at the bottom.

Large (Nos. 10, 9, and 7¾)

1. With the letter face up, fold slightly less than one third of the letterhead up toward the top.
2. Fold down the top of the letterhead to within ½ inch of the bottom fold.
3. Insert the letter into the envelope with the last crease toward the bottom of the envelope.

Window (Invoice)

1. Place the sheet face down, top toward you.
2. Fold back the top so address shows.
3. Insert into envelope with crease at bottom.

Letter-Placement Pointers

LETTER PLACEMENT TABLE

Body of Letter	Letter Length	Side Margins	Dateline on	PUNCTUATION STYLES
Up to 100 words	Short	2″	Line 20	**Mixed punctuation:** Use a colon after the salutation and a comma after the complimentary close.
101 to 300 words	{ Short-average	1½″	Line 17	
	Average	1½″	Line 15	
	Long-average	1½″	Line 13	
301 to 350 words	Long	1″	Line 12	**Open punctuation:** Omit these marks.
Over 350 words	2-page	1″	Line 12	

The letter-placement table shown above is a *guide*—to be used only until experience has taught the typist to make quick mental judgments regarding the width of the margins and the placement of the dateline.

Dateline. The horizontal placement of the date depends upon the letter style, the design of the letterhead, or a combination of these factors.

In the block and AMS simplified styles, type the date at the left margin.

In the modified block styles, begin the date at the center point or type it to end at the right margin.

Letter Address. Type the first line of the address on the fourth line space below the date. Type an official title, when used, on either the first or the second line—whichever gives better balance.

Attention Line. Type an attention line, when used, at the left margin on the second line below the letter address and a double space above the salutation.

Subject Line. Type a subject line on the second line below the salutation. In block and AMS simplified styles, type the subject line at the left margin. In other styles, type it at the left margin, at paragraph point, or centered. Type the word *Subject* in all caps or with only the first letter capitalized; or omit it.

Company Name in Closing. When the company name is used in the closing lines, type it in all caps on the second line below the complimentary close.

Typewritten Name and Official Title. Type the name and official title of the writer of a letter on the fourth line space below the complimentary close or on the fourth line space below the company name when it is used. Except in the AMS simplified style, the writer's title may go on the same line as his name or on the line below his name—whichever gives better balance.

Enclosure Notation. Type the enclosure notation (*Enclosure*, *Enclosures: 2*, or the like) a double space below the reference notation.

Multipage Letters. Leave at least 2 lines of a paragraph at the foot of a page and at least 2 lines at the top of the next page of a multipage letter. Start the heading on the second and subsequent pages on Line 7, and leave 2 blank lines below the heading. Use the same side margins on all pages of a letter.

SECOND-PAGE HEADINGS

```
Mr. A. C. Dowling
Page 2
November 4, 19--
```

Block style

```
Mr. A. C. Dowling      2       November 4, 19--
```

Horizontal style

Guides for Word and Sentence-Part Division

Divide—

1. Words at the ends of lines to keep the right margin as even as possible, but avoid excessive division

2. Words between syllables only, using a dictionary or word-division manual as a guide

3. Hyphenated words at hyphens only

4. A word in which the final consonant is doubled when adding a suffix: between the double letters, as *control-ling*

5. A word that ends in double letters: after the double letters when adding a suffix, as *will-ing*

6. The parts of a date, if necessary, between the day of the month and the year

Do not—

7. Divide a word of 5 or fewer letters

8. Separate a 1-letter syllable at the beginning or end of a word

9. Separate a 2-letter syllable at the end of a word

10. Divide the last word on a page or the last word of a paragraph

11. Separate from the rest of a word a syllable without a vowel, as *would-n't*, or numbers typed in figures, as 1,897,-458

Avoid—

12. Dividing names except to separate the initials or given name from the surname

Assembling a Carbon Pack

Method 1 (desk assembly)

1. Place the second or file copy sheet (on which the carbon copy is to be made) flat on the desk; then place a carbon sheet, carbon (glossy) side down, on top of the sheet. Add the original sheet (letterhead or plain sheet) on top of the carbon sheet.

NOTE: For each carbon copy desired, add one "set" (the copy sheet and a carbon sheet).

2. Pick up the carbon pack and turn it so that the second sheets and the glossy sides of the carbon sheets face you.

3. To straighten the pack, tap the top of the sheets gently on the desk.

4. Insert the pack by holding it firmly in one hand while turning the cylinder slowly with the other.

Method 2 (machine assembly)

1. Assemble stationery for insertion into the typewriter (original on top; copy sheets beneath).

2. Insert stationery, turning the cylinder until the sheets are gripped slightly by the feed rolls; then lay all but the last sheet over the top of the machine.

Desk assembly of a carbon pack

Guides for inserting a carbon pack

1. *To keep sheets straight when feeding,* place pack under an envelope flap or in the fold of a plain sheet of paper.

2. *To "start" the carbon pack:*
  a. Release the paper-release lever.
  b. Feed the pack around the cylinder until sheets appear at the front; then
  c. Reset the paper-release lever.
  d. After the pack is inserted, remove the envelope or paper fold.

3. *To avoid wrinkling,* release and reset the paper-release lever after the pack has been partially inserted.

Removing the stationery sheets

After typing the page, roll the platen up to the point at which the stationery is releasable but the feed rolls still grip the carbon sheets. Grasp the top of the stationery pack and remove it; then remove the carbon sheets.

3. Place a carbon sheet (glossy side *toward you*) between the last two sheets of stationery; then flip back each sheet of stationery as you add another carbon sheet.

Machine assembly of a carbon pack

Two-Letter Abbreviations for State, District, and Territory Names

These 2-letter abbreviations, recommended by the U.S. Postal Service, should be used in business addresses for which ZIP Codes are known and used.

Alabama	AL	Illinois	IL	North Carolina	NC
Alaska	AK	Indiana	IN	North Dakota	ND
Arizona	AZ	Iowa	IA	Ohio	OH
Arkansas	AR	Kansas	KS	Oklahoma	OK
California	CA	Kentucky	KY	Oregon	OR
Canal Zone	CZ	Louisiana	LA	Pennsylvania	PA
Colorado	CO	Maine	ME	Puerto Rico	PR
Connecticut	CT	Maryland	MD	Rhode Island	RI
Delaware	DE	Massachusetts	MA	South Carolina	SC
District of Columbia	DC	Michigan	MI	South Dakota	SD
Florida	FL	Minnesota	MN	Tennessee	TN
Georgia	GA	Mississippi	MS	Texas	TX
Guam	GU	Missouri	MO	Utah	UT
Hawaii	HI	Montana	MT	Vermont	VT
Idaho	ID	Nebraska	NE	Virgin Islands	VI
		Nevada	NV	Virginia	VA
		New Hampshire	NH	Washington	WA
		New Jersey	NJ	West Virginia	WV
		New Mexico	NM	Wisconsin	WI
		New York	NY	Wyoming	WY

MANUSCRIPT DOCUMENTATION

When, within a manuscript, a writer cites material that did not originate with him, he must acknowledge the source of the information. This obligation is usually satisfied with footnotes, a process of documentation. Footnotes serve other purposes as well.

Footnotes provide the most versatile method for referring the reader to information outside the text material. They may be used for these purposes: (1) acknowledge the source of information, (2) support arguments, (3) provide additional material for the reader, (4) identify quoted material, (5) elaborate on the meaning within the text, or (6) refer the reader to other parts of the text.[1]

Placement of Footnote Reference Figures

Footnotes are indicated by typing a reference figure as a superior figure following the material being documented, placed where a minimum interruption of thought results. Four placements of footnote reference figures in common use are described below.

After the quotation. The preferred position of the reference figures is at the end of material that is directly or indirectly quoted or paraphrased.

After the introductory statement. An almost equally accepted placement is at the end of the statement that introduces directly quoted material.

[1]Erwin M. Keithley and Philip J. Schreiner, A Manual of Style for the Preparation of Papers & Reports (2d ed.; Cincinnati: South-Western Publishing Co., 1971), p. 38.

At least 1"   1

First page, topbound

MANUSCRIPT DOCUMENTATION

When, within a manuscript, a writer cites material that did not originate with him, he must acknowledge the source of the information. This obligation is usually satisfied with footnotes, a process of documentation. Footnotes serve other purposes as well.

Footnotes provide the most versatile method for referring the reader to information outside the text material. They may be used for these purposes: (1) acknowledge the source of information, (2) support arguments, (3) provide additional material for the reader, (4) identify quoted material, (5) elaborate on the meaning within the text, or (6) refer the reader to other parts of the text.[1]

Placement of Footnote Reference Figures

Footnotes are indicated by typing a reference figure as a superior figure following the material being documented, placed where a minimum interruption of thought results. Four placements of footnote reference figures in common use are described below.

After the quotation. The preferred position of the reference figures is at the end of material that is directly or indirectly quoted or paraphrased.

After the introductory statement. An almost equally accepted placement is at the end of the statement that introduces directly quoted material.

After the name of the author. A less accepted practice, but one enjoying considerable use, is to place the reference figure

[1]Erwin M. Keithley and Philip J. Schreiner, A Manual of Style for the Preparation of Papers & Reports (2d ed.; Cincinnati: South-Western Publishing Co., 1971), p. 38.

At least 1"   1

First page, unbound

MANUSCRIPT DOCUMENTATION

When, within a manuscript, a writer cites material that did not originate with him, he must acknowledge the source of the information. This obligation is usually satisfied with footnotes, a process of documentation. Footnotes serve other purposes as well.

Footnotes provide the most versatile method for referring the reader to information outside the text material. They may be used for these purposes: (1) acknowledge the source of information, (2) support arguments, (3) provide additional material for the reader, (4) identify quoted material, (5) elaborate on the meaning within the text, or (6) refer the reader to other parts of the text.[1]

Placement of Footnote Reference Figures

Footnotes are indicated by typing a reference figure as a superior figure following the material being documented, placed where a minimum interruption of thought results. Four placements of footnote reference figures in common use are described below.

After the quotation. The preferred position of reference figures is at the end of material that is directly or indirectly quoted or paraphrased.

After the introductory statement. An almost equally accepted placement is at the end of the statement that introduces directly quoted material.

[1]Erwin M. Keithley and Philip J. Schreiner, A Manual of Style for the Preparation of Papers & Reports (2d ed.; Cincinnati: South-Western Publishing Co., 1971), p. 38.

At least 1"   1

First page, leftbound

1½" top margin   2

After the name of the author. A less accepted practice, but one enjoying considerable use, is to place the reference figure after the name of the author of the cited work. A major disadvantage of this practice is the inconsistency that results if references are made to materials without mentioning the author's name in the body of the manuscript or when reference is made to materials without a named author.

After a side or a paragraph heading. If most or all of the material following the heading is based on source material, it is acceptable to place the reference figure following the side or paragraph heading. The side heading that introduces the next paragraph illustrates this procedure.

Placement of Footnotes[2]

Although footnotes may be typed in the body of a manuscript directly below the line in which the reference occurs, the preferred placement is in numerical order to end approximately one inch from the foot of the page (even on a page not completely full, such as the last page of a chapter). A single space and an inch-and-a-half divider line separate the footnotes from the body of the report.

Numbering and Spacing Footnotes

Each footnote should be preceded without spacing by a reference figure raised one-half line space. Footnotes should be single-spaced

[2]Kate L. Turabian, A Manual for Writers of Term Papers, Theses, and Dissertations (3d ed., Rev.; Chicago: The University of Chicago Press, 1967), p. 27.

At least 1"   2

Second page, topbound

1" top margin   2

after the name of the author of the cited work. A major disadvantage of this practice is the inconsistency that results if references are made to materials without mentioning the author's name in the body of the manuscript or when reference is made to materials without a named author.

After a side or a paragraph heading. If most or all of the material following the heading is based on source material, it is acceptable to place the reference figure following the side or paragraph heading. The side heading that introduces the next paragraph illustrates this procedure.

Placement of Footnotes[2]

Although footnotes may be typed in the body of a manuscript directly below the line in which the reference occurs, the preferred placement is in numerical order to end approximately one inch from the foot of the page (even on a page not completely full, such as the last page of a chapter). A single space and an inch-and-a-half divider line separate the footnotes from the body of the report.

Numbering and Spacing Footnotes

Each footnote should be preceded without spacing by a reference figure raised one-half line space. Footnotes should be single-spaced with a double space between them. The first line of a footnote should be indented to paragraph point. Footnotes should preferably be numbered consecutively throughout a short manuscript. If a report is divided into chapters, numbering can be consecutive

[2]Kate L. Turabian, A Manual for Writers of Term Papers, Theses, and Dissertations (3d ed., Rev.; Chicago: The University of Chicago Press, 1967), p. 27.

At least 1"   2

Second page, unbound

1" top margin   2

After the name of the author. A less accepted practice, but one enjoying considerable use, is to place the reference figure after the name of the author of the cited work. A major disadvantage of this practice is the inconsistency that results if references are made to materials without mentioning the author's name in the body of the manuscript or when reference is made to materials without a named author.

After a side or a paragraph heading. If most or all of the material following the heading is based on source material, it is acceptable to place the reference figure following the side or paragraph heading. The side heading that introduces the next paragraph illustrates this procedure.

Placement of Footnotes[2]

Although footnotes may be typed in the body of a manuscript directly below the line in which the reference occurs, the preferred placement is in numerical order to end approximately one inch from the foot of the page (even on a page not completely full). A single space and an inch-and-a-half divider line separate the footnotes from the body of the report.

Numbering and Spacing Footnotes

Each footnote should be preceded without spacing by a reference figure raised one-half line space. Footnotes should be single-spaced with a double space between them. The first line of a footnote should be indented to paragraph point.

[2]Kate L. Turabian, A Manual for Writers of Term Papers, Theses, and Dissertations (3d ed., Rev.; Chicago: The University of Chicago Press, 1967), p. 27.

At least 1"   2

Second page, leftbound

2½"

MANUSCRIPT DOCUMENTATION

2½"

Name of Student

Class or Section

2½"

Date

Title page

Same margin as on page 1

TABLE OF CONTENTS

Table of contents

Same margin as on page 1

BIBLIOGRAPHY

"Commentary." A daily analysis of news broadcast on Radio Station KDKA, Pittsburgh, Pennsylvania, January 11, 1974.

"Don't Drink the Water." Newsweek (July 23, 1973), p. 48.

Grant, Patricia S. "The Lot of a Latter-Day Edison." Money, Vol. 2, No. 8 (August, 1973), p. 40.

Keithley, Erwin M., and Philip J. Schreiner. A Manual of Style for the Preparation of Papers & Reports, 2d ed. Cincinnati: South-Western Publishing Co., 1971.

Kerwin, E. R. "Will the Real Office Expert Please Stand Up." From a talk given before the Portland, Maine, Chamber of Commerce, September 15, 1974.

Lawrence, T. E. Seven Pillars of Wisdom. Garden City: Doubleday & Company, Inc., 1935.

A Manual of Style, 12th ed. Chicago: The University of Chicago Press, 1969.

Perrin, Porter G. Writer's Guide and Index to English, 4th ed., prepared and edited by Karl W. Dykema and Wilma R. Ebbitt. Chicago: Scott, Foresman and Company, 1965.

Savings and Loan Fact Book. Chicago: United States Savings and Loan League, 1971.

Turabian, Kate L. A Manual for Writers of Term Papers, Theses, and Dissertations, 3d ed., Rev. Chicago: The University of Chicago Press, 1967.

U.S. Department of Commerce, Bureau of the Census, Statistical Abstract of the United States, 1972, 93d ed. Washington: U.S. Government Printing Office, 1972.

Bibliography

Reference Guide   Summary of Manuscript Styles   ix

Correction Symbols (Proofreaders' Marks)

Typed or printed copy can be corrected with proof-readers' marks. The typist must be able to interpret these marks in retyping the corrected copy or *rough draft*. Some commonly used proofreaders' marks are shown below.

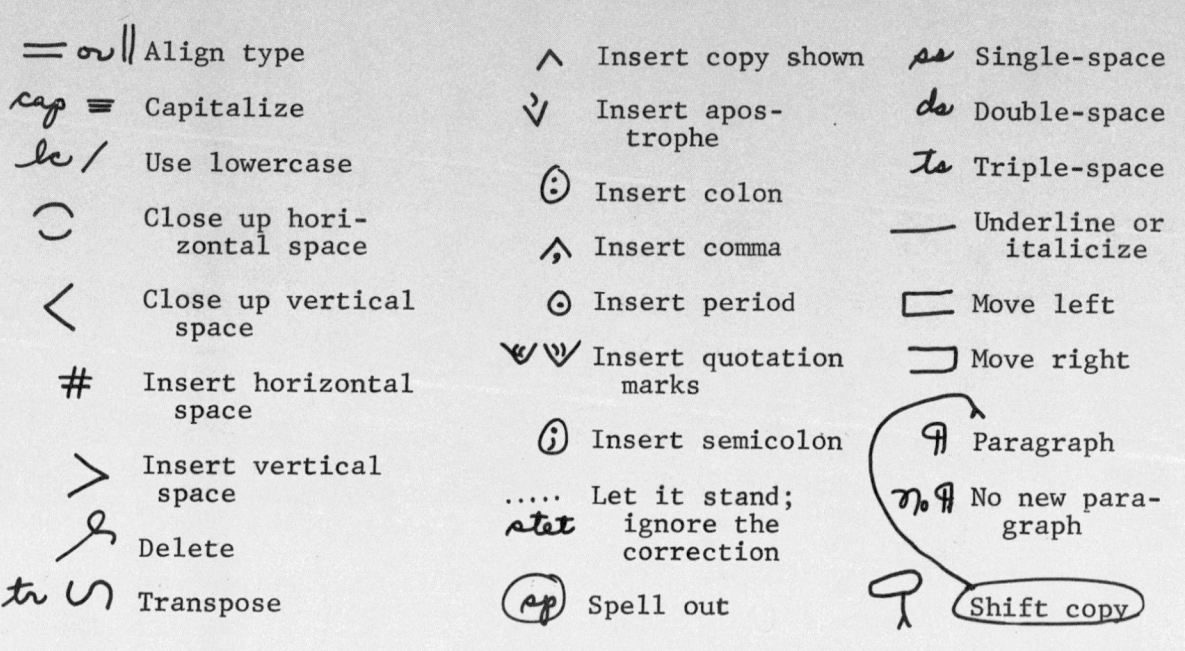

Align type	
Capitalize	
Use lowercase	
Close up horizontal space	
Close up vertical space	
Insert horizontal space	
Insert vertical space	
Delete	
Transpose	

Insert copy shown	Single-space
Insert apostrophe	Double-space
Insert colon	Triple-space
Insert comma	Underline or italicize
Insert period	Move left
Insert quotation marks	Move right
Insert semicolon	Paragraph
Let it stand; ignore the correction	No new paragraph
Spell out	Shift copy

Centering Summary

Horizontal centering (backspace-from-center method)

Regular headings

1. From the center, backspace once for each 2 strokes in the heading or line to be centered, disregarding an odd or leftover stroke.

2. Start typing where the backspacing ends.

Spread headings

1. From the center, backspace once for each stroke in the heading.

2. From this point, type the heading, spacing once between the letters and 3 times between the words.

Vertical centering

Backspace-from-center method

1. Position the paper at the vertical center:
   8½″ by 11″: Line 34
   8½″ by 5½″: Line 17
   5½″ by 8½″: Line 26

2. Roll the platen back once for each 2 lines (including any blank lines). Disregard an odd or leftover line.

3. Start typing where the roll-back ends.

(For reading position on a full sheet, roll the platen back 2 additional line spaces.)

Mathematical method

1. Count the lines and blank line spaces in the problem.

2. Subtract that number of lines from the number of lines available on the sheet.

3. Divide the result by 2 to get the number of blank lines in the top margin. Disregard a fraction.

4. Space down from the top edge the number of line spaces for the top margin, plus 1 to reach the first typing line.

Tabulation Summary

Vertical placement of tables

Exact. Count total lines to be used, including any blank lines; subtract total from lines available; divide remainder by 2 (disregarding a fraction). Leave this number of blank lines in the top margin.

Reading Position. Start the material 2 lines above the computed exact center.

Roll-Back Method. Insert the paper; roll it to the vertical center. Roll the cylinder back (toward you) once for every 2 lines in the table. This will place the copy in exact vertical center. For reading position, roll the cylinder back 2 additional lines.

Spacing After Headings. Leave 1 blank line between a main and a secondary heading and between a column heading and its column. Leave 2 blank lines below a main heading, if a secondary heading is not used, or after a secondary heading when both a main and a secondary heading are used.

Horizontal placement of tables

Centered Headings. After determining the top margin and spacing down to the starting line, center the main heading; DS and center a secondary heading, if used; then TS--as noted above.

Columns (Backspace-from-Center Method). Note the longest item in each column. If a column heading is the longest item, count it as such unless judgment indicates otherwise. Decide the number of spaces to leave between columns (preferably an even number).

Backspace from the center of the paper once for every 2 strokes in the longest line of each column and once for every 2 spaces between the columns (the *intercolumns*). Count any odd or leftover stroke with the next column or intercolumn. At the point where you complete the backspacing, set the left *margin* stop for the first column.

From the left margin, space forward once for each stroke in the first column and once for each space between the first and second columns. Set the first *tab* stop. Follow this procedure to set tab stops for the remaining columns.

Column Headings. Center column headings over the columns. When you have counted a column heading as the longest item in a column, you may need to reset the tab stop to center the *column* below the *heading.*

There are several methods of centering a column heading over a column, but probably the easiest is to add the cyclinder-scale figures for the first and last strokes in the column. Dividing this sum by 2 will result in the center point of the column.

Column headings are usually underlined.

Horizontal rulings

Horizontal lines or *rulings* are often used in tables to set off the column headings. Usually, a full-width double ruling is typed above the column headings and a single ruling below them. A single ruling is also typed below the last line of the table.

These rulings can be the exact width of the table, or they can extend several spaces on each side of it. To type rulings the exact width of the table, first determine the placement of the columns. After setting the tab stop for the last column, continue spacing forward once for each stroke in the last column. Immediately after stroking for the last stroke, set the right margin stop to lock the carriage at that point. You can then type rulings across the page until the carriage locks.

Double Rulings. DS from the last line of the centered heading; type the first of the double rulings; then operate the variable line spacer and move the cylinder forward slightly; type the second ruling. DS between this double ruling and the column headings.

Single Rulings. SS from the column headings; type a single ruling; DS and type the first items in the columns. After typing the last items in the columns, SS and type a single ruling.

Source Note (If Used). DS from the last single ruling; type the source note at the left margin or indent 3 to 5 spaces.

Tab stops for columns of figures

Uneven Columns. When a column contains items uneven in length, set the tab stop at a point that will suit the greatest number of entries. After tabulating, backspace for longer items or space forward for shorter ones.

Dollar Signs. In a money column, type a dollar sign before the first amount in the column and before the total, if one is shown. Type the dollar sign before the first amount aligned 1 space to the left of the longest amount in the column, which might be the total.

Totals. Totals are treated as a part of the column. For easier reading, totals are usually separated by a blank line from the last item in the column.

Erasing and Correcting Errors

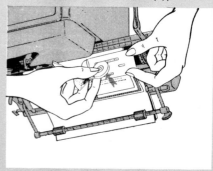
Using an eraser shield

1. Depress the margin-release key and move the carriage to the extreme left or right.

2. To avoid disturbing the type alignment, turn the cylinder forward if the error is in the upper 2/3 of the paper; backward, on the lower 1/3 of the paper.

3. To erase on the original sheet, lift the paper bail and place a 5" by 3" card in front of the first carbon sheet.

Use a hard (typewriter) eraser and an eraser shield. Brush away eraser crumbs.

4. Move the protective card in front of the second carbon, if more than 1 copy is being made. Use a soft (pencil) eraser.

5. When the error has been erased on all copies, remove the protective card, position the carriage at the proper point, and type the correction.

Squeezing and Expanding Words

Conventional typewriters

In correcting errors, it is often possible to "squeeze" or "expand" words.

1. An omitted letter at the beginning or end of a word:
Erase the entire word and retype it according to the procedure given in No. 2, below.

2. An omitted letter within a word:

Error: a leter within
Correction: a letter within

Corrective steps with a nonrepetitive space bar:
a. Erase the incorrect word.
b. Position the carriage at the space after the letter a.
c. Press down and hold the space bar; strike the / key.
d. Release the space bar and repeat the process for each remaining letter.

Corrective steps with a repetitive space bar:

Error: a letter within
Correction: a letter within

Follow the same procedure as in Step 2, except start the correction 1 space to the right.

3. An extra letter within a word:

Error: a letter within
Correction: a letter within

Follow the same steps by manually centering the carriage between the guides on the cylinder or paper-bail scale.

IBM Selectric typewriter

When making corrections, locate the horizontal position of the typing element by using either the black line on the clear-view card holder (circled below) or the red arrow on the margin scale. If you use the card holder as your indicator, position the

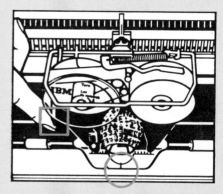

black line at the point on the paper at which you want to insert the new character. Then return to the line of type and insert the correction.

Squeezing Words

Error: the ordr today
Correction: the order today

To crowd the "e" into "ordr," erase the final "r." Backspace until the black line on the card holder is over the space formerly occupied by the final "r." Place the palm of the right hand on the top of the front cover. Reach under the cover and press LEFT against the carrier position post with your finger until the black line is moved back one-half space (as indicated in the illustration). Hold the carrier in this position

and type the "e." Repeat the procedure for the "r."

Expanding Words

Error: He will send
Correction: He can send

To replace "will" with "can," first erase "will." Type "c" in place of "w" and type "n" in the place of final "l."

Position the black line on the card holder over the position occupied by the first "l." Place the palm of the right hand on the top of the front cover. Reach under the cover and press left against the carrier position post with your finger until the black line of the card holder is directly between the "i" and "l." Type "a." Release the carrier and continue to type.

INDEX